The
Carolina Reader

Second Edition

Edited by Lee Bauknight with Kevin Trumpeter

FOUNTAINHEAD
PRESS

As a textbook publisher, we are faced with enormous environmental issues due the large amount of paper contained in our print products. Since our inception in 2002, we have worked diligently to be as eco-friendly as possible.

Our "green" initiatives include:

Electronic Products
We deliver products in non-paper form whenever possible. This includes pdf downloadables, flash drives, & CD's.

Electronic Samples
We use a new electronic sampling system, called Xample. Instructor samples are sent via a personalized web page that links to pdf downloads.

FSC Certified Printers
All of our Printers are certified by the Forest Service Council which promotes environmentally and socially responsible management of the world's forests. This program allows consumer groups, individual consumers and businesses to work together hand in hand to promote responsible use of the world's forests as a renewable and sustainable resource.

Recycled Paper
Almost all of our products are printed on a minimum of 10-30% post consumer waste recycled paper.

Support of Green Causes
When we do print, we donate a portion of our revenue to Green causes. Listed below are a few of the organizations that have received donations from Fountainhead Press. We welcome your feedback and suggestions for contributions, as we are always searching for worthy initiatives.
Rainforest 2 Reef
Environmental Working Group

Cover design: Doris Bruey
Cover image: Erin Schell
Book designer: Ellie Moore

For information, please call or write:
1-800-586-0330
Fountainhead Press
Southlake, TX 76092

Web site: www.fountainheadpress.com
E-mail: customerservice@fountainheadpress.com

Second Edition

ISBN: 978-1-59871-371-8

Printed in the United States of America

Contents

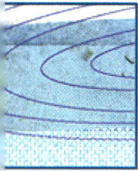

CHAPTER 1

Stimulus and Response

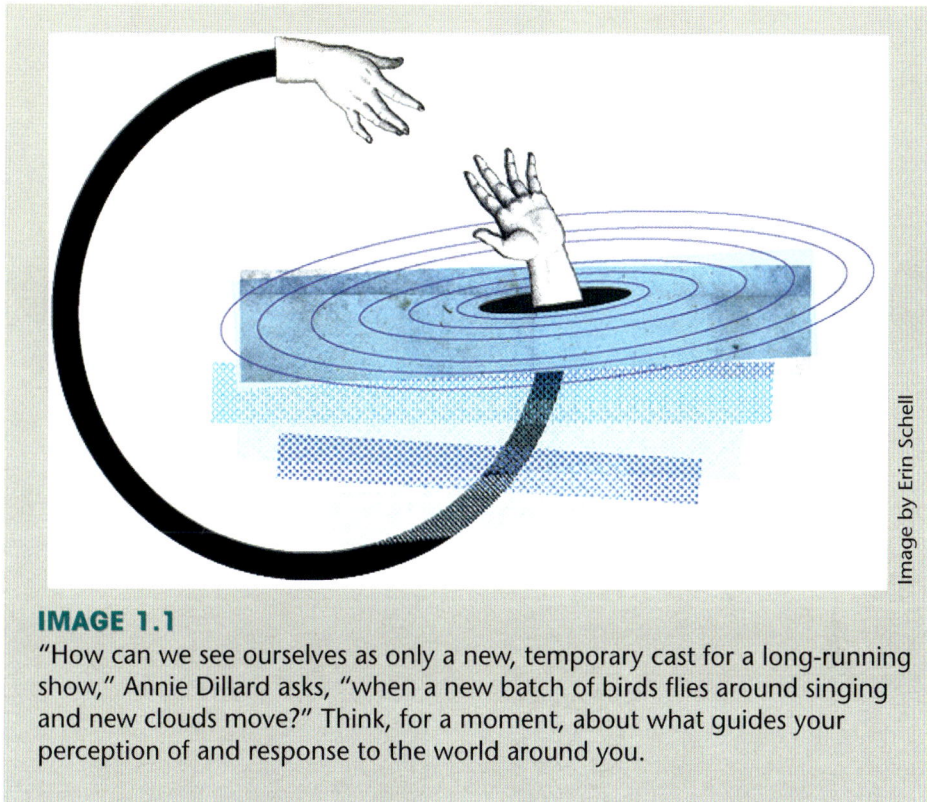

IMAGE 1.1

"How can we see ourselves as only a new, temporary cast for a long-running show," Annie Dillard asks, "when a new batch of birds flies around singing and new clouds move?" Think, for a moment, about what guides your perception of and response to the world around you.

Image by Erin Schell

Are you ready for the intelligence-augmented 'You+' that futurist Jamais Cascio argues is already in the works? Or are you more comfortable with 'Classic You,' the You born of Plato's cave and nurtured on education and knowledge, creativity and imagination? The readings in this chapter challenge you to think in new ways about how you perceive, experience, and respond to (and in) the world.

Plato, one of the monumental figures in Western thought and philosophy, lived and taught in ancient Greece from about 427–428 B.C. to 347 B.C. In "The Allegory of the Cave" from Book VII of The Republic, *Plato uses an imaginary dialogue between Socrates (the teacher) and Glaucon (the student) to expound on the nature of perception and reality; on knowledge and truth; on teaching and learning; and on the philosopher's place in society.*

THE ALLEGORY OF THE CAVE   Plato

And now, I said, let me show in a figure how far our nature is enlightened or unenlightened:— Behold! human beings living in an underground den, which has a mouth open towards the light and reaching all along the den; here they have been from their childhood, and have their legs and necks chained so that they cannot move, and can only see before them, being prevented by the chains from turning round their heads. Above and behind them a fire is blazing at a distance, and between the fire and the prisoners there is a raised way; and you will see, if you look, a low wall built along the way, like the screen which marionette players have in front of them, over which they show the puppets.

I see.

And do you see, I said, men passing along the wall carrying all sorts of vessels, and statues and figures of animals made of wood and stone and various materials, which appear over the wall? Some of them are talking, others silent.

You have shown me a strange image, and they are strange prisoners.

Like ourselves, I replied; and they see only their own shadows, or the shadows of one another, which the fire throws on the opposite wall of the cave?

True, he said; how could they see anything but the shadows if they were never allowed to move their heads?

And of the objects which are being carried in like manner they would only see the shadows?

Yes, he said.

And if they were able to converse with one another, would they not suppose that they were naming what was actually before them?

Very true.

And suppose further that the prison had an echo which came from the other side, would they not be sure to fancy when one of the passers-by spoke that the voice which they heard came from the passing shadow?

No question, he replied.

To them, I said, the truth would be literally nothing but the shadows of the images.

That is certain.

And now look again, and see what will naturally follow if the prisoners are released and disabused of their error. At first, when any of them is liberated and compelled suddenly to stand up and turn his neck round and walk and look towards the light, he will suffer sharp pains; the glare will distress him, and he will be unable to see the realities of which in his former state he had seen the shadows; and then conceive some one saying to him, that what he saw before was an illusion, but that now, when he is approaching nearer to being and his eye is turned towards more real existence, he has a clearer vision,—what will be his reply? And you may further imagine that his instructor is pointing to the objects as they pass and requiring him to name them,—will he not be perplexed? Will he not fancy that the shadows which he formerly saw are truer than the objects which are now shown to him?

Far truer.

And if he is compelled to look straight at the light, will he not have a pain in his eyes which will make him turn away and take in the objects of vision which he can see, and which he will conceive to be in reality clearer than the things which are now being shown to him?

True, he said.

And suppose once more, that he is reluctantly dragged up a steep and rugged ascent, and held fast until he's forced into the presence of the sun himself, is he not likely to be pained and irritated? When he approaches the light his eyes will be dazzled, and he will not be able to see anything at all of what are now called realities.

Not all in a moment, he said.

He will require to grow accustomed to the sight of the upper world. And first he will see the shadows best, next the reflections of men and other objects in the water, and then the objects themselves; then he will gaze upon the light of the moon and the stars and the spangled heaven; and he will see the sky and the stars by night better than the sun or the light of the sun by day?

Certainly.

Last of all he will be able to see the sun, and not mere reflections of him in the water, but he will see him in his own proper place, and not in another; and he will contemplate him as he is.

Certainly.

He will then proceed to argue that this is he who gives the seasons and the years, and is the guardian of all that is in the visible world, and in a certain way the cause of all things which he and his fellows have been accustomed to behold?

Clearly, he said, he would first see the sun and then reason about him.

And when he remembered his old habitation, and the wisdom of the den and his fellow-prisoners, do you not suppose that he would felicitate himself on the change, and pity them?

Certainly, he would.

And if they were in the habit of conferring honours among themselves on those who were quickest to observe the passing shadows and to remark which of them went before, and which followed after, and which were together; and who were therefore best able to draw conclusions as to the future, do you think that he would care for such honours and glories, or envy the possessors of them? Would he not say with Homer,

'Better to be the poor servant of a poor master,'
and to endure anything, rather than think as they do and live after their manner?

Yes, he said, I think that he would rather suffer anything than entertain these false notions and live in this miserable manner.

Imagine once more, I said, such a one coming suddenly out of the sun to be replaced in his old situation; would he not be certain to have his eyes full of darkness?

To be sure, he said.

And if there were a contest, and he had to compete in measuring the shadows with the prisoners who had never moved out of the den, while his sight was still weak, and before his eyes had become steady (and the time which would be needed to acquire this new habit of sight might be very considerable) would he not be ridiculous? Men would say of him that up he went and down he came without his eyes; and that it was better not even to think of ascending; and if any one tried to loose another and lead him up to the light, let them only catch the offender, and they would put him to death.

No question, he said.

This entire allegory, I said, you may now append, dear Glaucon, to the previous argument; the prison-house is the world of sight, the light of the fire is the sun, and you will not misapprehend me if you interpret the journey upwards to be the ascent of the soul into the intellectual world according to my poor belief, which, at your desire, I have expressed—whether rightly or wrongly God knows. But, whether true or false, my opinion is that in the world of knowledge the idea of good appears last of all, and is seen only with an effort; and, when seen, is also inferred to be the universal author of all things beautiful and right, parent of light and of the lord of light in this visible world, and the immediate source of reason and truth in the intellectual; and that this is the power upon which he who would act rationally, either in public or private life, must have his eye fixed.

I agree, he said, as far as I am able to understand you.

Moreover, I said, you must not wonder that those who attain to this beatific vision are unwilling to descend to human affairs; for their souls are ever hastening into the upper world where they desire to dwell; which desire of theirs is very natural, if our allegory may be trusted.

Yes, very natural.

And is there anything surprising in one who passes from divine contemplations to the evil state of man, misbehaving himself in a ridiculous manner; if, while his eyes are blinking and before he has become accustomed to the surrounding darkness, he is compelled to fight in courts of law, or in other places, about the images or the shadows of images of justice, and is endeavouring to meet the conceptions of those who have never yet seen absolute justice?

Anything but surprising, he replied.

Any one who has common sense will remember that the bewilderments of the eyes are of two kinds, and arise from two causes, either from coming out of the light or from going into the light, which is true of the mind's eye, quite as much as of the bodily eye; and he who remembers this when he sees any one whose vision is perplexed and weak, will not be too ready to laugh; he will first ask whether that soul of man has come out of the brighter light, and is unable to see because unaccustomed to the dark, or having turned from darkness to the day is dazzled by excess of light. And he will count the one happy in his condition and state of being, and he will pity the other; or, if he have a mind to laugh at the soul which comes from below into the light, there will be more reason in this than in the laugh which greets him who returns from above out of the light into the den.

That, he said, is a very just distinction.

But then, if I am right, certain professors of education must be wrong when they say that they can put a knowledge into the soul which was not there before, like sight into blind eyes.

They undoubtedly say this, he replied.

Whereas, our argument shows that the power and capacity of learning exists in the soul already; and that just as the eye was unable to turn from darkness to light without the whole body, so too the instrument of knowledge can only by the movement of the whole soul be turned from the world of becoming into that of being, and learn by degrees to endure the sight of being, and of the brightest and best of being, or in other words, of the good.

Very true.

And must there not be some art which will effect conversion in the easiest and quickest manner; not implanting the faculty of sight, for that exists already, but has been turned in the wrong direction, and is looking away from the truth?

Yes, he said, such an art may be presumed.

And whereas the other so-called virtues of the soul seem to be akin to bodily qualities, for even when they are not originally innate they can be implanted later by habit and exercise, the virtue of wisdom more than anything else contains a divine element which always remains, and by this conversion is rendered useful and profitable; or, on the other hand, hurtful and useless. Did you never observe the narrow intelligence flashing from the keen eye of a clever rogue—how eager he is, how clearly his paltry soul sees the way to his end; he is the reverse of blind, but his keen eyesight is forced into the service of evil, and he is mischievous in proportion to his cleverness.

Very true, he said.

But what if there had been a circumcision of such natures in the days of their youth; and they had been severed from those sensual pleasures, such as eating and drinking, which, like leaden weights, were attached to them at their birth, and which drag them down and turn the vision of their souls upon the things that are below—if, I say, they had been released from these impediments and turned in the opposite direction, the very same faculty in them would have seen the truth as keenly as they see what their eyes are turned to now.

Very likely.

Yes, I said; and there is another thing which is likely, or rather a necessary inference from what has preceded, that neither the uneducated and uninformed of the truth, nor yet those who never make an end of their education, will be able ministers of State; not the former, because they have no single aim of duty which is the rule of all their actions, private as well as public; nor the latter, because they will not act at all except upon compulsion, fancying that they are already dwelling apart in the islands of the blest.

Very true, he replied.

Then, I said, the business of us who are the founders of the State will be to compel the best minds to attain that knowledge which we have already shown to be the greatest of all—they must continue to ascend until they arrive at the good; but when they have ascended and seen enough we must not allow them to do as they do now.

What do you mean?

I mean that they remain in the upper world: but this must not be allowed; they must be made to descend again among the prisoners in the den, and partake of their labours and honours, whether they are worth having or not.

But is not this unjust? he said; ought we to give them a worse life, when they might have a better?

You have again forgotten, my friend, I said, the intention of the legislator, who did not aim at making any one class in the State happy above the rest; the happiness was to be in the whole State, and he held the citizens together by persuasion and necessity, making them benefactors of the State, and therefore benefactors of one another; to this end he created them, not to please themselves, but to be his instruments in binding up the State.

True, he said, I had forgotten.

Observe, Glaucon, that there will be no injustice in compelling our philosophers to have a care and providence of others; we shall explain to them that in other States, men of their class are not obliged to share in the toils of politics: and this is reasonable, for they grow up at their own sweet will, and the government would rather not have them. Being self-taught, they cannot be expected to show any gratitude for a culture which they have never received. But we have brought you into the world to be rulers of the hive, kings of yourselves and of the other citizens, and have educated you far better and more perfectly than they have been educated, and you are better able to share in the double duty. Wherefore each of you, when his turn comes, must go down to the general underground abode, and get the habit of seeing in the dark. When you have acquired the habit, you will see ten thousand times better than the inhabitants of the den, and you will know what the several images are, and what they represent, because you have seen the beautiful and just and good in their truth. And thus our State which is also yours will be a reality, and not a dream only, and will be administered in a spirit unlike that of other States, in which men fight with one another about shadows only and are distracted in the struggle for power, which in their eyes is a great good. Whereas the truth is that the State in which the rulers are most reluctant to govern is always the best and most quietly governed, and the State in which they are most eager, the worst.

Quite true, he replied.

And will our pupils, when they hear this, refuse to take their turn at the toils of State, when they are allowed to spend the greater part of their time with one another in the heavenly light?

Impossible, he answered; for they are just men, and the commands which we impose upon them are just; there can be no doubt that every one of them will take office as a stern necessity, and not after the fashion of our present rulers of State.

Yes, my friend, I said; and there lies the point. You must contrive for your future rulers another and a better life than that of a ruler, and then you may have a well-ordered State; for only in the State which offers this, will they rule who are truly rich, not in silver and gold, but in virtue and wisdom, which are the true blessings of life. Whereas if they go to the administration of public affairs, poor and hungering after their own private advantage, thinking that hence they are to snatch the chief good, order there can never be; for they will be fighting about office, and the civil and domestic broils which thus arise will be the ruin of the rulers themselves and of the whole State.

Most true, he replied.

And the only life which looks down upon the life of political ambition is that of true philosophy. Do you know of any other?

Indeed, I do not, he said.

■ READING AND WRITING

1. Draw the den that Plato describes, its inhabitants, and light source. What does this help you understand about "The Allegory of the Cave"?
2. What are the central points that Plato makes about perception, knowledge, and learning in the "Allegory"?
3. The speaker in this piece is Socrates, and he argues that a liberated prisoner must return to the den after becoming enlightened. Why, according to Socrates, is this difficult? Why is it important?
4. Plato seems to think that only a few individuals can ever leave the cave and become enlightened by understanding the Beautiful, Just, and Good. Has our thinking about this changed since the 4th century B.C.?

■ DEVELOPING LONGER RESPONSES

5. Pretend you are a lawyer tasked with defending Plato's argument that most of us experience life as series of shadows cast on a cave wall. How would you go about making your case? What evidence might you use to prove it?

> *"A single death is a tragedy, a million is a statistic," poet, essayist, and novelist Annie Dillard writes in "The Wreck of Time," quoting Josef Stalin. Later, she asks, "How can an individual count?" a question she uses to challenge readers on multiple levels. This essay, first published in* Harper's *in 1998, was adapted for her book* For the Time Being *(2000).*

THE WRECK OF TIME: TAKING OUR CENTURY'S MEASURE   Annie Dillard

I

Ted Bundy, the serial killer, after his arrest, could not fathom the fuss. What was the big deal? David Von Drehle quotes an exasperated Bundy in *Among the Lowest of the Dead*: "I mean, there are *so* many people."

One R. Houwink, of Amsterdam, uncovered this unnerving fact: The human population of earth, arranged tidily, would just fit into Lake Windermere, in England's Lake District.

Recently in the Peruvian Amazon a man asked the writer Alex Shoumatoff, "Isn't it true that the whole population of the United States can be fitted into their cars?"

How are we doing in numbers, we who have been alive for this most recent installment of human life? How many people have lived and died?

"The dead outnumber the living, in a ratio that could be as high as 20 to 1," a demographer, Nathan Keyfitz, wrote in a 1991 letter to the historian Justin Kaplan. "Credible estimates of the number of people who have ever lived on the earth run from 70 billion to over 100 billion." Averaging those figures puts the total persons ever born at about 85 billion. We living people now number 5.8 billion. By these moderate figures, the dead outnumber us about fourteen to one. The dead will always outnumber the living.

Dead Americans, however, if all proceeds, will not outnumber living Americans until the year 2030, because the nation is young. Some of us will be among the dead then. Will we know or care, we who once owned the still bones under the quick ones, we who spin inside the planet with our heels in the air? The living might well seem foolishly self-important to us, and overexcited.

We who are here now make up about 6.8 percent of all people who have appeared to date. This is not a meaningful figure. These times are, one might say, ordinary times, a slice of time like any other. Who can bear to hear this, or who will consider it? Are we not especially significant because our century is—our century and its nuclear bombs, its unique and unprecedented Holocaust, its serial exterminations and refugee populations, our century and its warming, its silicon chips, men on the moon, and spliced genes? No, we are not and it is not.

Since about half of all the dead are babies and children, we will be among the longest-boned dead and among the dead who grew the most teeth—for what those distinctions might be worth among beings notoriously indifferent to appearance and all else.

In Juan Rolfo's novel *Pedro Páramo*, a dead woman says to her dead son, "Just think about pleasant things, because we're going to be buried for a long time."

II

On April 30, 1991—on that one day—138,000 people drowned in Bangladesh. At dinner I mentioned to my daughter, who was then seven years old, that it was hard to imagine 138,000 people drowning.

"No, it's easy," she said. "Lots and lots of dots, in blue water."

The paleontologist Pierre Teilhard de Chardin, now dead, sent a dispatch from a dig. "In the middle of the tamarisk bush you find a red-brick town, partially exposed. … More than 3,000 years before our era, people were living there who played with dice like our own, fished with hooks like ours, and wrote in characters we can't yet read."

Who were these individuals who lived under the tamarisk bush? Who were the people Ted Bundy killed? Who was the statistician who reckoned that everybody would fit into Lake Windermere? The Trojans likely thought well of themselves, one by one; their last settlement died out by 1,100 $_{B.C.E.}$ Who were the people Stalin killed, or any of the 79.2 billion of us now dead, and who are the 5.8 billion of us now alive?

"God speaks succinctly," said the rabbis.

Is it important if you have yet died your death, or I? Your father? Your child? It is only a matter of time, after all. Why do we find it supremely pertinent, during any moment of any century on earth, which among us is topsides? Why do we concern ourselves over which side of the membrane of topsoil our feet poke?

"A single death is a tragedy, a million deaths is a statistic," Joseph Stalin, that connoisseur, gave words to this disquieting and possibly universal sentiment.

How can an individual count? Do we individuals count only to us other suckers, who love and grieve like elephants, bless their hearts? Of Allah, the Koran says, "Not so much as the weight of an ant in earth or heaven escapes from the Lord." That is touching, that Allah, God, and their ilk care when one ant dismembers another, or note when a sparrow falls, but I strain to see the use of it.

Ten years ago we thought there were two galaxies for each of us alive. Lately, since we loosed the Hubble Space Telescope, we have revised our figures. There are nine galaxies for each of us. Each galaxy harbors an average of 100 billion suns. In our galaxy, the Milky Way, there are sixty-nine suns for each person alive. The Hubble shows, says a report, that the universe "is at least 15 billion years old." Two galaxies, nine galaxies … sixty-nine suns, 100 billions suns—

These astronomers are nickel-and-diming us to death.

III

What were you doing on April 30, 1991, when a series of waves drowned 138,000 people? Where were you when you first heard the astounding, heartbreaking news? Who told you? What, seriatim, were your sensations? Who did you tell? Did you weep? Did your anguish last days or weeks?

All my life I have loved this sight: a standing wave in a boat's wake, shaped like a thorn. I have seen it rise from many oceans, and I saw it rise from the Sea of Galilee. It was a peak about a foot high. The standing wave broke at its peak, and foam slid down its glossy hollow. I watched the foaming wave on the port side. At every instant we were bringing this boat's motor, this motion, into new water. The stir, as if of life, impelled each patch of water to pinch and inhabit this same crest. Each crest tumbled upon itself and released a slide of white foam. The foam's bubbles popped and dropped into the general sea while they were still sliding down the dark wave. They trailed away always, and always new waters peaked, broke, foamed, and replenished.

What I saw was the constant intersection of two wave systems. Lord Kelvin first described them. Transverse waves rise abaft the stern and stream away perpendicular to the boat's direction of travel. Diverging waves course out in a V shape behind the boat. Where the waves converge, two lines of standing crests persist at an unchanging angle to the direction of the boat's motion. We think of these as the boat's wake. I was studying the highest standing wave, the one nearest the boat. It rose from the trough behind the stern and spilled foam. The curled wave crested over clear water and tumbled down. All its bubbles broke, thousands a second, unendingly. I could watch the present; I could see time and how it works.

On a shore, 8,000 waves break a day. James Trefil, a professor of physics, provides these facts. At any one time, the foam from breaking waves covers between 3 and 4 percent of the earth's surface. This acreage of foam is equal to the entire continent of North America. By coincidence, the U.S. population, in other words, although it is the third largest population among nations, is as small a portion of the earth's people as breaking waves' white foam is of the sea.

"God rises up out of the sea like a treasure in the waves," wrote Thomas Merton.

We see generations of waves rise from the sea that made them, billions of individuals at a time; we see them dwindle and vanish. If this does not astound you, what will? Or what will move you to pity?

IV

One tenth of the land on earth is tundra. At any time, it is raining on only 5 percent of the planet's surface. Lightning strikes the planet about a hundred times every second. The insects outweigh us. Our chickens outnumber us four to one. One fifth of us are Muslims. One fifth of us live in China. And every seventh person is a Chinese peasant. Almost one tenth of us live within range of an active volcano. More than 2 percent of us are mentally retarded. We humans drink tea—over a billion cups a day. Among us we speak 10,000 languages.

We are civilized generation number 500 or so, counting from 10,000 years ago, when we settled down. We are *Homo sapiens* generation number 7,500, counting from 150,000 years ago, when our species presumably arose; and we are human generation number 125,000 counting from the earliest forms of *Homo.*

Every 110 hours a million more humans arrive on the planet than die into the planet. A hundred million of us are children who live on the streets. Over a hundred million of us live in countries where we hold no citizenship. Twenty-three million of us are refugees. Sixteen million of us live in Cairo. Twelve million fish for a living from small boats. Seven and a half million of us are Uygurs. One million of us crew on freezer trawlers. Nearly a thousand of us a day commit suicide.

Head-spinning numbers cause the mind to go slack, the *Hartford Courant* says. But our minds must not go slack. How can we think straight if our minds go slack? We agree that we want to think straight.

Anyone's close world of family and friends composes a group smaller than almost all sampling errors, smaller than almost all rounding errors, a group invisible, at whose loss the world will not blink. Two million children die a year from diarrhea, and 800,000 from measles. Do we blink? Stalin starved 7 million Ukrainians in one year, Pol Pot killed 1 million Cambodians, the flu epidemic of 1918 killed 21 or 22 million people … shall this go on? Or do you suffer, as Teilhard de Chardin did, the sense of being "an atom lost in the universe"? Or do you not suffer this sense? How about what journalists call "compassion fatigue"? Reality fatigue? At what limit for you do other individuals blur? Vanish? How old are you?

V

Los Angeles airport has 25,000 parking spaces. This is about one space for every person who died in 1985 in Colombia when a volcano erupted. This is one space for each of the corpses of more than two years' worth of accidental killings from leftover land mines of recent wars. At five to a car, almost all the Inuit in the world could park at LAX. Similarly, if you propped up or stacked four bodies to a car, you could fit into the airport parking lot all the corpses from the firestream bombing of Tokyo in March 1945, or the corpses of Londoners who died in the plague, or the corpses of Burundians killed in civil war since 1993. But you could not fit America's homeless there, not even at twenty to a car.

Since sand and dirt pile up on everything, why does the world look fresh for each new crowd? As natural and human debris raises the continents, vegetation grows on the piles. It is all a stage—we know this—a temporary stage on top of many layers of stages, but every year a new crop of sand, grass, and tree leaves freshens the set and perfects the illusion that ours is the new and urgent world now. When Keats was in Rome, I read once, he saw pomegranate trees overhead; they bloomed in dirt blown onto the Coliseum's broken walls. How can we doubt our own time, in which each bright instant probes the future? In every arable soil in the world we grow grain over tombs—sure, we know this. But do not the dead generations seem to us dark and still as mummies, and their times always faded like scenes painted on walls at Pompeii?

How can we see ourselves as only a new, temporary cast for a long-running show when a new batch of birds flies around singing and new clouds move? Living things from hyenas to bacteria whisk the dead away like stagehands hustling between scenes. To help a living space last while we live on it, we brush or haul away the blowing sand and hack or burn the greenery. We are mowing the grass at the cutting edge.

VI

In northeast Japan, a seismic sea wave killed 27,000 people on June 15, 1896. Do not fail to distinguish this infamous wave from the April 30, 1991, waves that drowned 138,000 Bangladeshi. You were not tempted to confuse, conflate, forget, or ignore these deaths, were you?

On the dry Laetoli plain of northern Tanzania, Mary Leakey found a trail of hominid footprints. The three barefoot people—likely a short man and woman and child *Australopithecus afarensis*—walked closely together. They walked on moist volcanic tuff and ash. We have a record of those few seconds from a day about 3.6 million years ago—before hominids even chipped stone tools. More ash covered their footprints and hardened. Ash also preserved the pockmarks of the raindrops that fell beside the three who walked; it was a rainy day. We have almost ninety feet of the three's steady footprints intact. We do not know where they were going or why. We do not know why the woman paused and turned left, briefly, before continuing. "A remote ancestor," Leakey said, "experienced a moment of doubt." Possibly they watched the Sadiman volcano erupt, or they took a last look back before they left. We do know we cannot make anything so lasting as these three barefoot ones did.

After archeologists studied this long strip of record for several years, they buried it again to save it. Along one preserved portion, however, new tree roots are already cracking the footprints, and in another place winds threaten to sand them flat; the preservers did not cover them deeply enough. Now they are burying them again.

Jeremiah, walking toward Jerusalem, saw the smoke from the Temple's blaze. He wept; he saw the blood of the slain. "He put his face close to the ground and saw the footprints of sucklings and infants who were walking into captivity: in Babylon. He kissed the footprints.

Who were these individuals? Who were the three who walked together and left footprints in the rain? Who was that eighteenth-century Ukrainian peasant the Baal Shem Tov, the founder of modern Hasidism, who taught, danced, and dug clay? He was among the generations of children of Babylonian exiles whose footprints on the bare earth Jeremiah kissed. Centuries later the Emperor Hadrian destroyed another such son of exile in Rome, Rabbi Akiba. Russian Christians and European Christians tried, and Hitler tried, to wipe all those survivors of children of exile from the ground of the earth as a man wipes a plate— survivors of exiles whose footprints on the ground I kiss, and whose feet.

Who and of what import were the men whose bones bulk the Great Wall, the 30 million Mao starved, or the 11 million children under five who die each year now? Why, they are the insignificant others, of course; living or dead, they are just some of the plentiful others. And you?

Is it not late? A late time to be living? Are not our current generations the important ones? We have changed the world. Are not our heightened times the important ones, the ones since Hiroshima? Perhaps we are the last generation—there is a comfort. Take the bomb threat away and what are we? We are ordinary beads on a never-ending string. Our time is a routine twist of an improbable yarn.

We have no chance of being here when the sun burns out. There must be something ultimately heroic about our time, something that sets it above all those other times. Hitler, Stalin, Mao, and Pol Pot made strides in obliterating whole peoples, but this has been the human effort all along, and we have only enlarged the means, as have people in every century in history. (That genocides recur does not mean that they are similar. Each instance of human evil and each victim's death possesses its unique history and form. To generalize, as Cynthia Ozick points out, is to "befog" evil's specificity.)

Dire things are happening. Plague? Funny weather? Why are we watching the news, reading the news, keeping up with the news? Only to enforce our fancy—probably a necessary lie—that these are crucial times, and we are in on them. Newly revealed, and I am in the know: crazy people, bunches of them! New diseases, sways in power, floods! Can the news from dynastic Egypt have been any different?

As I write this, I am still alive, but of course I might well have died before you read it. Most of the archeologists who reburied hominid footprints have likely not yet died their deaths; the paleontologist Teilhard is pushing up daisies.

Chinese soldiers who breathed air posing for 7,000 individual day portraits—twenty-two centuries ago—must have thought it a wonderful difference that workers buried only their simulacra then so that their sons could bury their flesh a bit later. One wonders what they did in the months or years they gained. One wonders what one is, oneself, up to these days.

VII

Was it wisdom Mao Tse-tung attained when—like Ted Bundy—he awakened to the long view?

"The atom bomb is nothing to be afraid of," Mao told Nehru. "China has many people. … The deaths of ten or twenty million people is nothing to be afraid of." A witness said Nehru showed shock. Later, speaking in Moscow, Mao displayed yet more generosity: he boasted that he was willing to lose 300 million people, half of China's population.

Does Mao's reckoning shock me really? If sanctioning the death of strangers could save my daughter's life, would I do it? Probably. How many others' lives would I be willing to sacrifice? Three? Three hundred million?

An English journalist, observing the Sisters of Charity in Calcutta, reasoned: "Either life is always and in all circumstances sacred, or intrinsically of no account; it is inconceivable that it should be in some cases the one, and in some the other."

One small town's soup kitchen, St. Mary's, serves 115 men a night. Why feed 115 individuals? Surely so few people elude most demographics and achieve statistical insignificance. After all, there are 265 million Americans, 15 million people who live in Mexico City, 16 million in greater New York, 26 million in greater Tokyo. Every day 1.5 million people walk through Times Square in New York; every day almost as many people—1.4 million—board a U.S. passenger plane. And so forth. We who breathe air now will join the already dead layers of us who breathed air once. We arise from dirt and dwindle to dirt, and the might of the universe is arrayed against us.

■ READING AND WRITING

1. What is Dillard's main point in this essay? What is she trying to persuade her audience to think or do?

2. What is the effect of Dillard's quoting so many people? Do all of these voices strengthen her claims? What do these voices say about Dillard's relationship to the topic of death and the randomness of violence?

3. Explain Dillard's critique of the use of numbers and statistics to represent human beings and to quantify human suffering. Do you think there is a better way to talk about human tragedies—and to make distant tragedies seem significant—than by using statistics?

4. Dillard poses a number of questions throughout her essay. How would you respond to this one, from the end of the piece: "One small town's soup kitchen, St. Mary's, serves 115 men a night. *Why feed 115 individuals?*"

■ DEVELOPING LONGER RESPONSES

5. Throughout the essay, Dillard meditates on one central issue (the significance or sacredness of life in a world of random death) mostly by juxtaposing various quotations, anecdotes, and reported conversation. Use a similar quotation/collage method to ponder another issue (some possibilities: happiness, success, commitment, loyalty, virtue, evil, love).

■ USING RESEARCH

6. Like many great writers, Dillard offers a new way of talking about a very old issue: What can we say about the value of life in light of the certainty, and ubiquity, of death? Many philosophers, theologians, and scientists have pondered this issue at length. Your research task is twofold: First, make a list of at least four academic disciplines, other than English or literature, that deal with this question. And, second, find one primary source from one of these disciplines and compare the source's treatment of the issue with Dillard's.

Matt Richtel, who writes about technology for The New York Times, won the 2010 Pulitzer Prize for National Reporting for "Driven to Distraction," a series about driving and multitasking that spurred legislative efforts across the nation to deal with the problem. He wrote this piece for the June 6, 2010, edition of The Times.

HOOKED ON TECHNOLOGY, AND PAYING A PRICE Matt Richtel

When one of the most important e-mail messages of his life landed in his in-box a few years ago, Kord Campbell overlooked it. Not just for a day or two, but 12 days. He finally saw it while sifting through old messages: a big company wanted to buy his Internet start-up. "I stood up from my desk and said, 'Oh my God, oh my God, oh my God,' " Mr. Campbell said. "It's kind of hard to miss an e-mail like that, but I did."

The message had slipped by him amid an electronic flood: two computer screens alive with e-mail, instant messages, online chats, a Web browser and the computer code he was writing.

While he managed to salvage the $1.3 million deal after apologizing to his suitor, Mr. Campbell continues to struggle with the effects of the deluge of data. Even after he unplugs, he craves the stimulation he gets from his electronic gadgets. He forgets things like dinner plans, and he has trouble focusing on his family.

His wife, Brenda, complains, "It seems like he can no longer be fully in the moment."

This is your brain on computers.

Scientists say juggling e-mail, phone calls and other incoming information can change how people think and behave. They say our ability to focus is being undermined by bursts of information. These play to a primitive impulse to respond to immediate opportunities and threats. The stimulation provokes excitement—a dopamine squirt—that researchers say can be addictive. In its absence, people feel bored.

The resulting distractions can have deadly consequences, as when cellphone-wielding drivers and train engineers cause wrecks. And for millions of people like Mr. Campbell, these urges can inflict nicks and cuts on creativity and deep thought, interrupting work and family life.

While many people say multitasking makes them more productive, research shows otherwise. Heavy multitaskers actually have more trouble focusing and shutting out irrelevant information, scientists say, and they experience more stress. And scientists are discovering that even after the multitasking ends, fractured thinking and lack of focus persist. In other words, this is also your brain off computers.

"The technology is rewiring our brains," said Nora Volkow, director of the National Institute of Drug Abuse and one of the world's leading brain scientists. She and other researchers compare the lure of digital stimulation less to that of drugs and alcohol than to food and sex, which are essential but counterproductive in excess.

Technology use can benefit the brain in some ways, researchers say. Imaging studies show the brains of Internet users become more efficient at finding information. And players of some video games develop better visual acuity.

More broadly, cellphones and computers have transformed life. They let people escape their cubicles and work anywhere. They shrink distances and handle countless mundane tasks, freeing up time for more exciting pursuits.

For better or worse, the consumption of media, as varied as e-mail and TV, has exploded. In 2008, people consumed three times as much information each day as they did in 1960. And they are constantly shifting their attention. Computer users at work change windows or check e-mail or other programs nearly 37 times an hour, new research shows.

The nonstop interactivity is one of the most significant shifts ever in the human environment, said Adam Gazzaley, a neuroscientist at the University of California, San Francisco. "We are exposing our brains to an environment and asking them to do things we weren't necessarily evolved to do," he said. "We know already there are consequences."

Mr. Campbell, 43, came of age with the personal computer, and he is a heavier user of technology than most. But researchers say the habits and struggles of Mr. Campbell and his family typify what many experience—and what many more will, if trends continue.

For him, the tensions feel increasingly acute, and the effects harder to shake.

The Campbells recently moved to California from Oklahoma to start a software venture. Mr. Campbell's life revolves around computers. He goes to sleep with a laptop or iPhone on his chest, and when he wakes, he goes online. He and Mrs. Campbell, 39, head to the tidy kitchen in their four-bedroom hillside rental in Orinda, an affluent suburb of San Francisco, where she makes breakfast and watches a TV news feed in the corner of the computer screen while he uses the rest of the monitor to check his e-mail.

Major spats have arisen because Mr. Campbell escapes into video games during tough emotional stretches. On family vacations, he has trouble putting down his devices. When he rides the subway to San Francisco, he knows he will be offline 221 seconds as the train goes through a tunnel.

Their 16-year-old son, Connor, tall and polite like his father, recently received his first C's, which his family blames on distraction from his gadgets. Their 8-year-old daughter, Lily, like her mother, playfully tells her father that he favors technology over family.

"I would love for him to totally unplug, to be totally engaged," says Mrs. Campbell, who adds that he becomes "crotchety until he gets his fix." But she would not try to force a change. "He loves it. Technology is part of the fabric of who he is," she says. "If I hated technology, I'd be hating him, and a part of who my son is too."

■ Always On

Mr. Campbell, whose given name is Thomas, had an early start with technology in Oklahoma City. When he was in third grade, his parents bought him Pong, a video game. Then came a

string of game consoles and PCs, which he learned to program. In high school, he balanced computers, basketball and a romance with Brenda, a cheerleader with a gorgeous singing voice. He studied too, with focus, uninterrupted by e-mail. "I did my homework because I needed to get it done," he said. "I didn't have anything else to do."

He left college to help with a family business, then set up a lawn mowing service. At night he would read, play video games, hang out with Brenda and, as she remembers it, "talk a lot more." In 1996, he started a successful Internet provider. Then he built the start-up that he sold for $1.3 million in 2003 to LookSmart, a search engine.

Mr. Campbell loves the rush of modern life and keeping up with the latest information. "I want to be the first to hear when the aliens land," he said, laughing. But other times, he fantasizes about living in pioneer days when things moved more slowly: "I can't keep everything in my head."

No wonder. As he came of age, so did a new era of data and communication.

At home, people consume 12 hours of media a day on average, when an hour spent with, say, the Internet and TV simultaneously counts as two hours. That compares with five hours in 1960, say researchers at the University of California, San Diego. Computer users visit an average of 40 Web sites a day, according to research by RescueTime, which offers time-management tools.

As computers have changed, so has the understanding of the human brain. Until 15 years ago, scientists thought the brain stopped developing after childhood. Now they understand that its neural networks continue to develop, influenced by things like learning skills.

So not long after Eyal Ophir arrived at Stanford in 2004, he wondered whether heavy multitasking might be leading to changes in a characteristic of the brain long thought immutable: that humans can process only a single stream of information at a time.

Going back a half-century, tests had shown that the brain could barely process two streams, and could not simultaneously make decisions about them. But Mr. Ophir, a student-turned-researcher, thought multitaskers might be rewiring themselves to handle the load.

His passion was personal. He had spent seven years in Israeli intelligence after being weeded out of the air force—partly, he felt, because he was not a good multitasker. Could his brain be retrained? Mr. Ophir, like others around the country studying how technology bent the brain, was startled by what he discovered.

■ The Myth of Multitasking

The test subjects were divided into two groups: those classified as heavy multitaskers based on their answers to questions about how they used technology, and those who were not.

In a test created by Mr. Ophir and his colleagues, subjects at a computer were briefly shown an image of red rectangles. Then they saw a similar image and were asked whether any of the rectangles had moved. It was a simple task until the addition of a twist: blue rectangles were added, and the subjects were told to ignore them.

The multitaskers then did a significantly worse job than the non-multitaskers at recognizing whether red rectangles had changed position. In other words, they had trouble filtering out the blue ones—the irrelevant information. So, too, the multitaskers took longer than non-multitaskers to switch among tasks, like differentiating vowels from consonants and then odd from even numbers. The multitaskers were shown to be less efficient at juggling problems.

Other tests at Stanford, an important center for research in this fast-growing field, showed multitaskers tended to search for new information rather than accept a reward for putting older, more valuable information to work. Researchers say these findings point to an interesting dynamic: multitaskers seem more sensitive than non-multitaskers to incoming information.

The results also illustrate an age-old conflict in the brain, one that technology may be intensifying. A portion of the brain acts as a control tower, helping a person focus and set priorities. More primitive parts of the brain, like those that process sight and sound, demand that it pay attention to new information, bombarding the control tower when they are stimulated.

Researchers say there is an evolutionary rationale for the pressure this barrage puts on the brain. The lower-brain functions alert humans to danger, like a nearby lion, overriding goals like building a hut. In the modern world, the chime of incoming e-mail can override the goal of writing a business plan or playing catch with the children.

"Throughout evolutionary history, a big surprise would get everyone's brain thinking," said Clifford Nass, a communications professor at Stanford. "But we've got a large and growing group of people who think the slightest hint that something interesting might be going on is like catnip. They can't ignore it." Mr. Nass says the Stanford studies are important because they show multitasking's lingering effects: "The scary part for guys like Kord is, they can't shut off their multitasking tendencies when they're not multitasking."

Melina Uncapher, a neurobiologist on the Stanford team, said she and other researchers were unsure whether the muddied multitaskers were simply prone to distraction and would have had trouble focusing in any era. But she added that the idea that information overload causes distraction was supported by more and more research.

A study at the University of California, Irvine, found that people interrupted by e-mail reported significantly increased stress compared with those left to focus. Stress hormones have been shown to reduce short-term memory, said Gary Small, a psychiatrist at the University of California, Los Angeles.

Preliminary research shows some people can more easily juggle multiple information streams. These "supertaskers" represent less than 3 percent of the population, according to scientists at the University of Utah.

Other research shows computer use has neurological advantages. In imaging studies, Dr. Small observed that Internet users showed greater brain activity than nonusers, suggesting they were growing their neural circuitry. At the University of Rochester, researchers found that players of some fast-paced video games can track the movement of a third more objects on a screen than nonplayers. They say the games can improve reaction and the ability to pick out details amid clutter.

"In a sense, those games have a very strong both rehabilitative and educational power," said the lead researcher, Daphne Bavelier, who is working with others in the field to channel these changes into real-world benefits like safer driving.

There is a vibrant debate among scientists over whether technology's influence on behavior and the brain is good or bad, and how significant it is.

"The bottom line is, the brain is wired to adapt," said Steven Yantis, a professor of brain sciences at Johns Hopkins University. "There's no question that rewiring goes on all the time," he added. But he said it was too early to say whether the changes caused by technology were materially different from others in the past.

Mr. Ophir is loath to call the cognitive changes bad or good, though the impact on analysis and creativity worries him. He is not just worried about other people. Shortly after he came to Stanford, a professor thanked him for being the one student in class paying full attention and not using a computer or phone. But he recently began using an iPhone and noticed a change; he felt its pull, even when playing with his daughter. "The media is changing me," he said. "I hear this internal ping that says: check e-mail and voice mail."

"I have to work to suppress it."

Kord Campbell does not bother to suppress it, or no longer can.

■ Interrupted by a Corpse

It is a Wednesday in April, and in 10 minutes, Mr. Campbell has an online conference call that could determine the fate of his new venture, called Loggly. It makes software that helps companies understand the clicking and buying patterns of their online customers.

Mr. Campbell and his colleagues, each working from a home office, are frantically trying to set up a program that will let them share images with executives at their prospective partner. But at the moment when Mr. Campbell most needs to focus on that urgent task, something else competes for his attention: "Man Found Dead Inside His Business."

That is the tweet that appears on the left-most of Mr. Campbell's array of monitors, which he has expanded to three screens, at times adding a laptop and an iPad. On the left screen, Mr. Campbell follows the tweets of 1,100 people, along with instant messages and group chats. The middle monitor displays a dark field filled with computer code, along with Skype, a service that allows Mr. Campbell to talk to his colleagues, sometimes using video. The monitor on the right keeps e-mail, a calendar, a Web browser and a music player.

Even with the meeting fast approaching, Mr. Campbell cannot resist the tweet about the corpse. He clicks on the link in it, glances at the article and dismisses it. "It's some article about something somewhere," he says, annoyed by the ads for jeans popping up.

The program gets fixed, and the meeting turns out to be fruitful: the partners are ready to do business. A colleague says via instant message: "YES."

Other times, Mr. Campbell's information juggling has taken a more serious toll. A few weeks earlier, he once again overlooked an e-mail message from a prospective investor. Another time, Mr. Campbell signed the company up for the wrong type of business account on Amazon.com, costing $300 a month for six months before he got around to correcting it. He has burned hamburgers on the grill, forgotten to pick up the children and lingered in the bathroom playing video games on an iPhone.

Mr. Campbell can be unaware of his own habits. In a two-and-a-half hour stretch one recent morning, he switched rapidly between e-mail and several other programs, according to data from RescueTime, which monitored his computer use with his permission. But when asked later what he was doing in that period, Mr. Campbell said he had been on a long Skype call, and "may have pulled up an e-mail or two."

The kind of disconnection Mr. Campbell experiences is not an entirely new problem, of course. As they did in earlier eras, people can become so lost in work, hobbies or TV that they fail to pay attention to family.

Mr. Campbell concedes that, even without technology, he may work or play obsessively, just as his father immersed himself in crossword puzzles. But he says this era is different because he can multitask anyplace, anytime. "It's a mixed blessing," he said. "If you're not careful, your marriage can fall apart or your kids can be ready to play and you'll get distracted."

■ The Toll on Children

Father and son sit in armchairs. Controllers in hand, they engage in a fierce video game battle, displayed on the nearby flat-panel TV, as Lily watches. They are playing Super Smash Bros. Brawl, a cartoonish animated fight between characters that battle using anvils, explosives and other weapons.

"Kill him, Dad," Lily screams. To no avail. Connor regularly beats his father, prompting expletives and, once, a thrown pillow. But there is bonding and mutual respect. "He's a lot more tactical," says Connor. "But I'm really good at quick reflexes."

Screens big and small are central to the Campbell family's leisure time. Connor and his mother relax while watching TV shows like "Heroes." Lily has an iPod Touch, a portable DVD player and her own laptop, which she uses to watch videos, listen to music and play games.

Lily, a second-grader, is allowed only an hour a day of unstructured time, which she often spends with her devices. The laptop can consume her. "When she's on it, you can holler her name all day and she won't hear," Mrs. Campbell said.

Researchers worry that constant digital stimulation like this creates attention problems for children with brains that are still developing, who already struggle to set priorities and resist impulses.

Connor's troubles started late last year. He could not focus on homework. No wonder, perhaps. On his bedroom desk sit two monitors, one with his music collection, one with Facebook and Reddit, a social site with news links that he and his father love. His iPhone availed him to relentless texting with his girlfriend.

When he studied, "a little voice would be saying, 'Look up' at the computer, and I'd look up," Connor said. "Normally, I'd say I want to only read for a few minutes, but I'd search every corner of Reddit and then check Facebook."

His Web browsing informs him. "He's a fact hound," Mr. Campbell brags. "Connor is, other than programming, extremely technical. He's 100 percent Internet savvy." But the parents worry too. "Connor is obsessed," his mother said. "Kord says we have to teach him balance."

So in January, they held a family meeting. Study time now takes place in a group setting at the dinner table after everyone has finished eating. It feels, Mr. Campbell says, like togetherness.

■ No Vacations   *Lauren Creel* ★

For spring break, the family rented a cottage in Carmel, Calif. Mrs. Campbell hoped everyone would unplug. But the day before they left, the iPad from Apple came out, and Mr. Campbell snapped one up. The next night, their first on vacation, "We didn't go out to dinner," Mrs. Campbell mourned. "We just sat there on our devices."

She rallied the troops the next day to the aquarium. Her husband joined them for a bit but then begged out to do e-mail on his phone. Later she found him playing video games.

The trip came as Mr. Campbell was trying to raise several million dollars for his new venture, a goal that he achieved. Brenda said she understood that his pursuit required intensity but was less understanding of the accompanying surge in video game.

His behavior brought about a discussion between them. Mrs. Campbell said he told her that he was capable of logging off, citing a trip to Hawaii several years ago that they called their second honeymoon. "What trip are you thinking about?" she said she asked him. She recalled that he had spent two hours a day online in the hotel's business center.

On Thursday, their fourth day in Carmel, Mr. Campbell spent the day at the beach with his family. They flew a kite and played whiffle ball. Connor unplugged too. "It changes the mood of everything when everybody is present," Mrs. Campbell said.

The next day, the family drove home, and Mr. Campbell disappeared into his office.

Technology use is growing for Mrs. Campbell as well. She divides her time between keeping the books of her husband's company, homemaking and working at the school library. She checks e-mail 25 times a day, sends texts and uses Facebook.

Recently, she was baking peanut butter cookies for Teacher Appreciation Day when her phone chimed in the living room. She answered a text, then became lost in Facebook, forgot about the cookies and burned them. She started a new batch, but heard the phone again, got lost in messaging, and burned those too. Out of ingredients and shamed, she bought cookies at the store.

She feels less focused and has trouble completing projects. Some days, she promises herself she will ignore her device. "It's like a diet—you have good intentions in the morning and then you're like, 'There went that,'" she said.

Mr. Nass at Stanford thinks the ultimate risk of heavy technology use is that it diminishes empathy by limiting how much people engage with one another, even in the same room.

"The way we become more human is by paying attention to each other," he said. "It shows how much you care." That empathy, Mr. Nass said, is essential to the human condition. "We are at an inflection point," he said. "A significant fraction of people's experiences are now fragmented."

READING AND WRITING

1. Richtel quotes one researcher as saying that "technology is rewiring our brains." Explain what this means, in the context of Richtel's article, and summarize the evidence that Richtel uses to support this contention.
2. How does Richtel use the Campbell family to help connect with his readers and to drive home the importance of this issue?
3. Explain what Richtel calls the "myth of multitasking." Does he change your thinking about multitasking? Explain your response.

USING RESEARCH

4. Go online and find Richtel's Pulitzer Prize-winning series "Driven to Distraction" (the entire report is available at www.nytimes.com). Spend some time sorting through and reading the stories and other elements of the series, and then write a brief essay in which you do the following:

   ■ explain the rhetorical exigency of the issue (or the argument the author makes about why his readers should care about the topic);

   ■ summarize the main findings of the series;

   ■ and describe the public and legislative response to the series.

Nicholas Carr, whose most recent book is The Big Switch: Rewiring the World, From Edison to Google *(2008), writes on the social, intellectual, and business implications of technology. He uses his own experience as a starting point in this examination of how digital technologies such as Google's search engines affect intelligence. He wrote this essay for the July/August 2008 issue of* Atlantic Monthly.

IS GOOGLE MAKING US STUPID? Nicholas Carr

"Dave, stop. Stop, will you? Stop, Dave. Will you stop, Dave?" So the supercomputer HAL pleads with the implacable astronaut Dave Bowman in a famous and weirdly poignant scene toward the end of Stanley Kubrick's *2001: A Space Odyssey*. Bowman, having nearly been sent to a deep-space death by the malfunctioning machine, is calmly, coldly disconnecting the memory circuits that control its artificial "brain." "Dave, my mind is going," HAL says, forlornly. "I can feel it. I can feel it."

I can feel it, too. Over the past few years I've had an uncomfortable sense that someone, or something, has been tinkering with my brain, remapping the neural circuitry, reprogramming the memory. My mind isn't going—so far as I can tell—but it's changing. I'm not thinking the way I used to think. I can feel it most strongly when I'm reading. Immersing myself in a book or a lengthy article used to be easy. My mind would get caught up in the narrative or the turns of the argument, and I'd spend hours strolling through long stretches of prose. That's rarely the case anymore. Now my concentration often starts to drift after two or three pages. I get fidgety, lose the thread, begin looking for something else to do. I feel as if I'm always dragging my wayward brain back to the text. The deep reading that used to come naturally has become a struggle.

I think I know what's going on. For more than a decade now, I've been spending a lot of time online, searching and surfing and sometimes adding to the great databases of the Internet. The Web has been a godsend to me as a writer. Research that once required days in the stacks or periodical rooms of libraries can now be done in minutes. A few Google searches, some quick clicks on hyperlinks, and I've got the telltale fact or pithy quote I was after. Even when I'm not working, I'm as likely as not to be foraging in the Web's info-thickets reading and writing emails, scanning headlines and blog posts, watching videos and listening to podcasts, or just tripping from link to link to link. (Unlike footnotes, to which they're sometimes likened, hyperlinks don't merely point to related works; they propel you toward them.)

For me, as for others, the Net is becoming a universal medium, the conduit for most of the information that flows through my eyes and ears and into my mind. The advantages of having immediate access to such an incredibly rich store of information are many, and they've been widely described and duly applauded. "The perfect recall of silicon memory," *Wired*'s Clive Thompson has written, "can be an enormous boon to thinking." But that boon comes at a price. As the media theorist Marshall McLuhan pointed out in the 1960s, media are not just passive channels of information. They supply the stuff of thought, but they also shape the process of thought. And what the Net seems to be doing is chipping away my capacity for concentration and contemplation. My mind now expects to take in information the way the Net distributes it: in a swiftly moving stream of particles. Once I was a scuba diver in the sea of words. Now I zip along the surface like a guy on a Jet Ski.

I'm not the only one. When I mention my troubles with reading to friends and acquaintances—literary types, most of them—many say they're having similar experiences. The more they use the Web, the more they have to fight to stay focused on long pieces of writing. Some of the bloggers I follow have also begun mentioning the phenomenon. Scott Karp, who writes a blog about online media, recently confessed that he has stopped reading books altogether. "I was a lit major in college, and used to be [a] voracious book reader," he wrote. "What happened?" He speculates on the answer: "What if I do all my reading on the web not so much because the way I read has changed, i.e. I'm just seeking convenience, but because the way I THINK has changed?"

Bruce Friedman, who blogs regularly about the use of computers in medicine, also has described how the Internet has altered his mental habits. "I now have almost totally lost the ability to read and absorb a longish article on the web or in print," he wrote earlier this year. A pathologist who has long been on the faculty of the University of Michigan Medical School, Friedman elaborated on his comment in a telephone conversation with me. His thinking, he said, has taken on a "staccato" quality, reflecting the way he quickly scans short passages of text from many sources online. "I can't read *War and Peace* anymore," he admitted. "I've lost the ability to do that. Even a blog post of more than three or four paragraphs is too much to absorb. I skim it."

Anecdotes alone don't prove much. And we still await the long-term neurological and psychological experiments that will provide a definitive picture of how Internet use affects cognition. But a recently published study of online research habits, conducted by scholars from University College London, suggests that we may well be in the midst of a sea change in the way we read and think. As part of the five-year research program, the scholars examined computer logs documenting the behavior of visitors to two popular research sites, one operated by the British Library and one by a U.K. educational consortium, that provide access to journal articles, e-books, and other sources of written information. They found that people using the sites exhibited "a form of skimming activity," hopping from one source to another and rarely returning to any source they'd already visited. They typically read no more than one or two pages of an article or book before they would "bounce" out to another site. Sometimes they'd save a long article, but there's no evidence that they ever went back and actually read it. The authors of the study report:

> It is clear that users are not reading online in the traditional sense; indeed there are signs that new forms of "reading" are emerging as users "power browse" horizontally through titles, contents pages and abstracts going for quick wins. It almost seems that they go online to avoid reading in the traditional sense.

   Thanks to the ubiquity of text on the Internet, not to mention messaging on cell phones, we may well be reading more today tha. or 1980s, when television was our medium of choice. But it's a diffe and behind it lies a different kind of thinking—perhaps even a new so are not only what we read," says Maryanne Wolf, a developmental p. University and the author of *Proust and the Squid: The Story and Scie. Brain.* "We are how we read." Wolf worries that the style of reading Net, a style that puts "efficiency" and "immediacy" above all else, may l capacity for the kind of deep reading that emerged when an earlier technol _y, the printing press, made long and complex works of prose commonplace. When we read online, she says, we tend to become "mere decoders of information." Our ability to interpret text, to make the rich mental connections that form when we read deeply and without distraction, remains largely disengaged.

   Reading, explains Wolf, is not an instinctive skill for human beings. It's not etched into our genes the way speech is. We have to teach our minds how to translate the symbolic characters we see into the language we understand. And the media or other technologies we use in learning and practicing the craft of reading play an important part in shaping the neural circuits inside our brains. Experiments demonstrate that readers of ideograms, such as the Chinese, develop a mental circuitry for reading that is very different from the circuitry found in those of us whose written language employs an alphabet. The variations extend across many regions of the brain, including those that govern such essential cognitive functions as memory and the interpretation of visual and auditory stimuli. We can expect as well that the circuits woven by our use of the Net will be different from those woven by our reading of books and other printed works.

Sometime in 1882, Friedrich Nietzsche bought a typewriter—a Malling-Hansen Writing Ball, to be precise. His vision was failing, and keeping his eyes focused on a page had become exhausting and painful, often bringing on crushing headaches. He had been forced to curtail his writing, and he feared that he would soon have to give it up. The typewriter rescued him, at least for a time. Once he had mastered touch-typing, he was able to write with his eyes closed, using only the tips of his fingers. Words could once again flow from his mind to the page.

   But the machine had a subtler effect on his work. One of Nietzsche's friends, a composer, noticed a change in the style of his writing. His already terse prose had become even tighter, more telegraphic. "Perhaps you will through this instrument even take to a new idiom," the friend wrote in a letter, noting that, in his own work, his "'thoughts' in music and language often depend on the quality of pen and paper."

   "You are right," Nietzsche replied, "our writing equipment takes part in the forming of our thoughts." Under the sway of the machine, writes the German media scholar Friedrich A. Kittler, Nietzsche's prose "changed from arguments to aphorisms, from thoughts to puns, from rhetoric to telegram style."

   The human brain is almost infinitely malleable. People used to think that our mental meshwork, the dense connections formed among the 100 billion or so neurons inside our skulls, argely fixed by the time we reached adulthood. But brain researchers have discovered that that's not the case. James Olds, a professor of neuroscience who directs the Krasnow Institute for Advanced Study at George Mason University, says that even the adult mind "is very plastic." Nerve cells routinely break old connections and form new ones. "The brain," according to Olds, "has the ability to reprogram itself on the fly, altering the way it functions."

As we use what the sociologist Daniel Bell has called our "intellectual technologies"— the tools that extend our mental rather than our physical capacities—we inevitably begin to take on the qualities of those technologies. The mechanical clock, which came into common use in the 14th century, provides a compelling example. In *Technics and Civilization*, the historian and cultural critic Lewis Mumford described how the clock "disassociated time from human events and helped create the belief in an independent world of mathematically measurable sequences." The "abstract framework of divided time" became "the point of reference for both action and thought."

The clock's methodical ticking helped bring into being the scientific mind and the scientific man. But it also took something away. As the late MIT computer scientist Joseph Weizenbaum observed in his 1976 book, *Computer Power and Human Reason: From Judgment to Calculation*, the conception of the world that emerged from the widespread use of timekeeping instruments "remains an impoverished version of the older one, for it rests on a rejection of those direct experiences that formed the basis for, and indeed constituted, the old reality." In deciding when to eat, to work, to sleep, to rise, we stopped listening to our senses and started obeying the clock.

The process of adapting to new intellectual technologies is reflected in the changing metaphors we use to explain ourselves to ourselves. When the mechanical clock arrived, people began thinking of their brains as operating "like clockwork." Today, in the age of software, we have come to think of them as operating "like computers." But the changes, neuroscience tells us, go much deeper than metaphor. Thanks to our brain's plasticity, the adaptation occurs also at a biological level.

The Internet promises to have particularly far-reaching effects on cognition. In a paper published in 1936, the British mathematician Alan Turing proved that a digital computer, which at the time existed only as a theoretical machine, could be programmed to perform the function of any other information-processing device. And that's what we're seeing today. The Internet, an immeasurably powerful computing system, is subsuming most of our other intellectual technologies. It's becoming our map and our clock, our printing press and our typewriter, our calculator and our telephone, and our radio and TV.

When the Net absorbs a medium, that medium is re-created in the Net's image. It injects the medium's content with hyperlinks, blinking ads, and other digital gewgaws, and it surrounds the content with the content of all the other media it has absorbed. A new e-mail message, for instance, may announce its arrival as we're glancing over the latest headlines at a newspaper's site. The result is to scatter our attention and diffuse our concentration.

The Net's influence doesn't end at the edges of a computer screen, either. As people's minds become attuned to the crazy quilt of Internet media, traditional media have to adapt to the audience's new expectations. Television programs add text crawls and pop-up ads, and magazines and newspapers shorten their articles, introduce capsule summaries, and crowd their pages with easy-to-browse info-snippets. When, in March of this year, *The

New York Times decided to devote the second and third pages of every edition to article abstracts, its design director, Tom Bodkin, explained that the "shortcuts" would give harried readers a quick "taste" of the day's news, sparing them the "less efficient" method of actually turning the pages and reading the articles. Old media have little choice but to play by the new-media rules.

Never has a communications system played so many roles in our lives—or exerted such broad influence over our thoughts—as the Internet does today. Yet, for all that's been written about the Net, there's been little consideration of how, exactly, it's reprogramming us. The Net's intellectual ethic remains obscure.

About the same time that Nietzsche started using his typewriter, an earnest young man named Frederick Winslow Taylor carried a stopwatch into the Midvale Steel plant in Philadelphia and began a historic series of experiments aimed at improving the efficiency of the plant's machinists. With the approval of Midvale's owners, he recruited a group of factory hands, set them to work on various metalworking machines, and recorded and timed their every movement as well as the operations of the machines. By breaking down every job into a sequence of small, discrete steps and then testing different ways of performing each one, Taylor created a set of precise instructions—an "algorithm," we might say today—for how each worker should work. Midvale's employees grumbled about the strict new regime, claiming that it turned them into little more than automatons, but the factory's productivity soared.

More than a hundred years after the invention of the steam engine, the Industrial Revolution had at last found its philosophy and its philosopher. Taylor's tight industrial choreography—his "system," as he liked to call it—was embraced by manufacturers throughout the country and, in time, around the world. Seeking maximum speed, maximum efficiency, and maximum output, factory owners used time-and-motion studies to organize their work and configure the jobs of their workers. The goal, as Taylor defined it in his celebrated 1911 treatise, *The Principles of Scientific Management*, was to identify and adopt, for every job, the "one best method" of work and thereby to effect "the gradual substitution of science for rule of thumb throughout the mechanic arts." Once his system was applied to all acts of manual labor, Taylor assured his followers, it would bring about a restructuring not only of industry but of society, creating a utopia of perfect efficiency. "In the past the man has been first," he declared; "in the future the system must be first."

Taylor's system is still very much with us; it remains the ethic of industrial manufacturing. And now, thanks to the growing power that computer engineers and software coders wield over our intellectual lives, Taylor's ethic is beginning to govern the realm of the mind as well. The Internet is a machine designed for the efficient and automated collection, transmission, and manipulation of information, and its legions of programmers are intent on finding the "one best method"—the perfect algorithm—to carry out every mental movement of what we've come to describe as "knowledge work." Google's headquarters, in Mountain View, California—the Googleplex—is the Internet's high church, and the religion practiced inside its walls is Taylorism. Google, says its chief executive, Eric Schmidt, is "a company that's founded around the science of measurement," and it is striving to "systematize everything" it does. Drawing on the terabytes of behavioral data it collects through its search engine and other sites, it carries out thousands of experiments a day, according to the *Harvard Business Review*, and it uses the results to refine the algorithms that increasingly control how people find information and extract meaning from it. What Taylor did for the work of the hand, Google is doing for the work of the mind.

The company has declared that its mission is "to organize the world's information and make it universally accessible and useful." It seeks to develop "the perfect search engine," which it defines as something that "understands exactly what you mean and gives you back exactly what you want." In Google's view, information is a kind of commodity, a utilitarian resource that can be mined and processed with industrial efficiency. The more pieces of information we can "access" and the faster we can extract their gist, the more productive we become as thinkers.

Where does it end? Sergey Brin and Larry Page, the gifted young men who founded Google while pursuing doctoral degrees in computer science at Stanford, speak frequently of their desire to turn their search engine into an artificial intelligence, a HAL-like machine that might be connected directly to our brains. "The ultimate search engine is something as smart as people—or smarter," Page said in a speech a few years back. "For us, working on search is a way to work on artificial intelligence." In a 2004 interview with *Newsweek*, Brin said, "Certainly if you had all the world's information directly attached to your brain, or an artificial brain that was smarter than your brain, you'd be better off." Last year, Page told a convention of scientists that Google is "really trying to build artificial intelligence and to do it on a large scale."

Such an ambition is a natural one, even an admirable one, for a pair of math whizzes with vast quantities of cash at their disposal and a small army of computer scientists in their employ. A fundamentally scientific enterprise, Google is motivated by a desire to use technology, in Eric Schmidt's words, "to solve problems that have never been solved before," and artificial intelligence is the hardest problem out there. Why wouldn't Brin and Page want to be the ones to crack it?

Still, their easy assumption that we'd all "be better off" if our brains were supplemented, or even replaced, by an artificial intelligence is unsettling. It suggests a belief that intelligence is the output of a mechanical process, a series of discrete steps that can be isolated, measured, and optimized. In Google's world, the world we enter when we go online, there's little place for the fuzziness of contemplation. Ambiguity is not an opening for insight but a bug to be fixed. The human brain is just an outdated computer that needs a faster processor and a bigger hard drive.

The idea that our minds should operate as high-speed data-processing machines is not only built into the workings of the Internet, it is the network's reigning business model as well. The faster we surf across the Web—the more links we click and pages we view—the more opportunities Google and other companies gain to collect information about us and to feed us advertisements. Most of the proprietors of the commercial Internet have a financial stake in collecting the crumbs of data we leave behind as we flit from link to link—the more crumbs, the better. The last thing these companies want is to encourage leisurely reading or slow, concentrated thought. It's in their economic interest to drive us to distraction.

Maybe I'm just a worrywart. Just as there's a tendency to glorify technological progress, there's a countertendency to expect the worst of every new tool or machine. In Plato's *Phaedrus*, Socrates bemoaned the development of writing. He feared that, as people came to rely on the written word as a substitute for the knowledge they used to carry inside their heads, they would, in the words of one of the dialogue's characters, "cease to exercise their memory and become forgetful." And because they would be able to "receive a quantity of information without proper instruction," they would "be thought very knowledgeable when they are for the most part quite ignorant." They would be "filled with the conceit of wisdom instead of real wisdom." Socrates wasn't wrong—the new technology did often have the effects he feared—but he was shortsighted. He couldn't foresee the many ways that writing and reading would serve to spread information, spur fresh ideas, and expand human knowledge (if not wisdom).

The arrival of Gutenberg's printing press, in the 15th century, set off another round of teeth gnashing. The Italian humanist Hieronimo Squarciafico worried that the easy availability of books would lead to intellectual laziness, making men "less studious" and weakening their minds. Others argued that cheaply printed books and broadsheets would undermine religious authority, demean the work of scholars and scribes, and spread sedition and debauchery. As New York University professor Clay Shirky notes, "Most of the arguments made against the printing press were correct, even prescient." But, again, the doomsayers were unable to imagine the myriad blessings that the printed word would deliver.

So, yes, you should be skeptical of my skepticism. Perhaps those who dismiss critics of the Internet as Luddites or nostalgists will be proved correct, and from our hyperactive, data-stoked minds will spring a golden age of intellectual discovery and universal wisdom. Then again, the Net isn't the alphabet, and although it may replace the printing press, it produces something altogether different. The kind of deep reading that a sequence of printed pages promotes is valuable not just for the knowledge we acquire from the author's words but for the intellectual vibrations those words set off within our own minds. In the quiet spaces opened up by the sustained, undistracted reading of a book, or by any other act of contemplation, for that matter, we make our own associations, draw our own inferences and analogies, foster our own ideas. Deep reading, as Maryanne Wolf argues, is indistinguishable from deep thinking.

If we lose those quiet spaces, or fill them up with "content," we will sacrifice something important not only in our selves but in our culture. In a recent essay, the playwright Richard Foreman eloquently described what's at stake:

> I come from a tradition of Western culture, in which the ideal (my ideal) was the complex, dense and "cathedral-like" structure of the highly educated and articulate personality—a man or woman who carried inside themselves a personally constructed and unique version of the entire heritage of the West. [But now] I see within us all (myself included) the replacement of complex inner density with a new kind of self—evolving under the pressure of information overload and the technology of the "instantly available."

As we are drained of our "inner repertory of dense cultural inheritance," Foreman concluded, we risk turning into "'pancake people'—spread wide and thin as we connect with that vast network of information accessed by the mere touch of a button."

I'm haunted by that scene in *2001*. What makes it so poignant, and so weird, is the computer's emotional response to the disassembly of its mind: its despair as one circuit after another goes dark, its childlike pleading with the astronaut—"I can feel it. I can feel it. I'm afraid"—and its final reversion to what can only be called a state of innocence. HAL's outpouring of feeling contrasts with the emotionlessness that characterizes the human figures in the film, who go about their business with an almost robotic efficiency. Their thoughts and actions feel scripted, as if they're following the steps of an algorithm. In the world of *2001*, people have become so machinelike that the most human character turns out to be a machine. That's the essence of Kubrick's dark prophecy: as we come to rely on computers to mediate our understanding of the world, it is our own intelligence that flattens into artificial intelligence.

■ READING AND WRITING

1. What, according to Carr, is the difference between assimilating information and learning?
2. Carr writes that the "Web has been a godsend to me as a writer" but also that this "boon comes at a price." Summarize the advantages that Carr says the Internet offers as well as the drawbacks that he worries might accompany long-term use.
3. Carr uses Google's desire to develop the "perfect search engine" to discuss two kinds of intelligence. How would you describe these? Do you see any reason for concern about the influence technology might be having on intelligence?
4. Do you think Carr presents an effective argument? Why or why not? Does he address possible counterarguments? What are they?

■ DEVELOPING LONGER RESPONSES

5. Write a brief essay in which you answer the following question: Does using the Internet encourage or discourage individuality? Support your response with specific examples based on your experience and on Carr's conclusions.

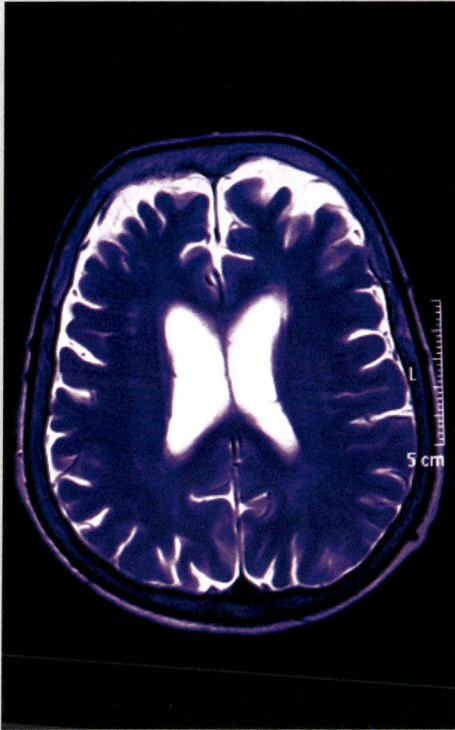

IMAGE 1.2

Matt Richtel, Nicholas Carr, and Jamais Cascio all write about the effects that technology is (or might be) having on our cognitive abilities. "'We are exposing our brains to an environment and asking them to do things we weren't necessarily evolved to do,'" one neuroscientist says in Richtel's article. "'We know already there are consequences.'" Do you feel the effects of technologically driven overstimulation in your life?

According to his biography at TED.com, Jamais Cascio rejects the "nightmare scenarios of global catastrophe and social meltdown" we so often hear from other futurists in favor of "a different, often surprising alternative: What if human beings, and all of our technology, could actually manage to change things for the better?" In this article, first published in the July/August issue of Atlantic Monthly, *Cascio argues that humans have the means, right now, to overcome just about anything by harnessing technology and pharmacology to boost intelligence.*

GET SMARTER   Jamais Cascio

Seventy-four thousand years ago, humanity nearly went extinct. A super-volcano at what's now Lake Toba, in Sumatra, erupted with a strength more than a thousand times that of Mount St. Helens in 1980. Some 800 cubic kilometers of ash filled the skies of the Northern Hemisphere, lowering global temperatures and pushing a climate already on the verge of an ice age over the edge. Some scientists speculate that as the Earth went into a deep freeze, the population of *Homo sapiens* may have dropped to as low as a few thousand families.

The Mount Toba incident, although unprecedented in magnitude, was part of a broad pattern. For a period of 2 million years, ending with the last ice age around 10,000 B.C., the Earth experienced a series of convulsive glacial events. This rapid-fire climate change meant that humans couldn't rely on consistent patterns to know which animals to hunt, which plants to gather, or even which predators might be waiting around the corner.

How did we cope? By getting smarter. The neurophysiologist William Calvin argues persuasively that modern human cognition—including sophisticated language and the capacity to plan ahead—evolved in response to the demands of this long age of turbulence. According to Calvin, the reason we survived is that our brains changed to meet the challenge: we transformed the ability to target a moving animal with a thrown rock into a capability for foresight and long-term planning. In the process, we may have developed syntax and formal structure from our simple language.

Our present century may not be quite as perilous for the human race as an ice age in the aftermath of a super-volcano eruption, but the next few decades will pose enormous hurdles that go beyond the climate crisis. The end of the fossil-fuel era, the fragility of the global food web, growing population density, and the spread of pandemics, as well as the emergence of radically transformative bio- and nanotechnologies—each of these threatens us with broad disruption or even devastation. And as good as our brains have become at planning ahead, we're still biased toward looking for near-term, simple threats. Subtle, long-term risks, particularly those involving complex, global processes, remain devilishly hard for us to manage.

But here's an optimistic scenario for you: if the next several decades are as bad as some of us fear they could be, we can respond, and survive, the way our species has done time and again: by getting smarter. But this time, we don't have to rely solely on natural evolutionary processes to boost our intelligence. We can do it ourselves.

Most people don't realize that this process is already under way. In fact, it's happening all around us, across the full spectrum of how we understand intelligence. It's visible in the hive mind of the Internet, in the powerful tools for simulation and visualization that are jump-starting new scientific disciplines, and in the development of drugs that some people (myself included) have discovered let them study harder, focus better, and stay awake longer with full clarity. So far, these augmentations have largely been outside of our bodies, but they're very much part of who we are today: they're physically separate from us, but we and they are becoming cognitively inseparable. And advances over the next few decades, driven by breakthroughs in genetic engineering and artificial intelligence, will make today's technologies seem primitive. The nascent jargon of the field describes this as "intelligence augmentation." I prefer to think of it as "You+."

Scientists refer to the 12,000 years or so since the last ice age as the Holocene epoch. It encompasses the rise of human civilization and our co-evolution with tools and technologies that allow us to grapple with our physical environment. But if intelligence augmentation has the kind of impact I expect, we may soon have to start thinking of ourselves as living in an entirely new era. The focus of our technological evolution would be less on how we manage and adapt to our physical world, and more on how we manage and adapt to the immense amount of knowledge we've created. We can call it the Nöocene epoch, from Pierre Teilhard de Chardin's concept of the Nöosphere, a collective consciousness created by the deepening interaction of human minds. As that epoch draws closer, the world is becoming a very different place.

Of course we've been augmenting our ability to think for millennia. When we developed written language, we significantly increased our functional memory and our ability to share insights and knowledge across time and space. The same thing happened with the invention of the printing press, the telegraph, and the radio. The rise of urbanization allowed a fraction of the populace to focus on more-cerebral tasks—a fraction that grew inexorably as more complex economic and social practices demanded more knowledge work, and industrial technology reduced the demand for manual labor. And caffeine and nicotine, of course, are both classic cognitive-enhancement drugs, primitive though they may be.

With every technological step forward, though, has come anxiety about the possibility that technology harms our natural ability to think. These anxieties were given eloquent expression in these pages by Nicholas Carr, whose essay "Is Google Making Us Stupid?" (July/August 2008 *Atlantic*) argued that the information-dense, hyperlink-rich, spastically churning Internet medium is effectively rewiring our brains, making it harder for us to engage in deep, relaxed contemplation.

Carr's fears about the impact of wall-to-wall connectivity on the human intellect echo cyber-theorist Linda Stone's description of "continuous partial attention," the modern phenomenon of having multiple activities and connections under way simultaneously.

We're becoming so accustomed to interruption that we're starting to find focusing difficult, even when we've achieved a bit of quiet. It's an induced form of ADD—a "continuous partial attention-deficit disorder," if you will.

There's also just more information out there—because unlike with previous information media, with the Internet, creating material is nearly as easy as consuming it. And it's easy to mistake more voices for more noise. In reality, though, the proliferation of diverse voices may actually improve our overall ability to think. In *Everything Bad Is Good for You*, Steven Johnson argues that the increasing complexity and range of media we engage with have, over the past century, made us smarter, rather than dumber, by providing a form of cognitive calisthenics. Even pulp-television shows and video games have become extraordinarily dense with detail, filled with subtle references to broader subjects, and more open to interactive engagement. They reward the capacity to make connections and to see patterns—precisely the kinds of skills we need for managing an information glut.

Scientists describe these skills as our "fluid intelligence"—the ability to find meaning in confusion and to solve new problems, independent of acquired knowledge. Fluid intelligence doesn't look much like the capacity to memorize and recite facts, the skills that people have traditionally associated with brainpower. But building it up may improve the capacity to think deeply that Carr and others fear we're losing for good. And we shouldn't let the stresses associated with a transition to a new era blind us to that era's astonishing potential. We swim in an ocean of data, accessible from nearly anywhere, generated by billions of devices. We're only beginning to explore what we can do with this knowledge-at-a-touch.

Moreover, the technology-induced ADD that's associated with this new world may be a short-term problem. The trouble isn't that we have too much information at our fingertips, but that our tools for managing it are still in their infancy. Worries about "information overload" predate the rise of the Web (Alvin Toffler coined the phrase in 1970), and many of the technologies that Carr worries about were developed precisely to help us get some control over a flood of data and ideas. Google isn't the problem; it's the beginning of a solution.

In any case, there's no going back. The information sea isn't going to dry up, and relying on cognitive habits evolved and perfected in an era of limited information flow—and limited information access—is futile. Strengthening our fluid intelligence is the only viable approach to navigating the age of constant connectivity.

When people hear the phrase *intelligence augmentation*, they tend to envision people with computer chips plugged into their brains, or a genetically engineered race of post-human super-geniuses. Neither of these visions is likely to be realized, for reasons familiar to any Best Buy shopper. In a world of ongoing technological acceleration, today's cutting-edge brain implant would be tomorrow's obsolete junk—and good luck if the protocols change or you're on the wrong side of a "format war" (anyone want a Betamax implant?). And then there's the question of stability: Would you want a chip in your head made by the same folks that made your cell phone, or your PC?

Likewise, the safe modification of human genetics is still years away. And even after genetic modification of adult neurobiology becomes possible, the science will remain in flux; our understanding of how augmentation works, and what kinds of genetic modifications are possible, would still change rapidly. As with digital implants, the brain modification you might undergo one week could become obsolete the next. Who would want a 2025-vintage brain when you're competing against hotshots with Model 2026?

Yet in one sense, the age of the cyborg and the super-genius has already arrived. It just involves external information and communication devices instead of implants and genetic modification. The bioethicist James Hughes of Trinity College refers to all of this as "exocortical technology," but you can just think of it as "stuff you already own." Increasingly, we buttress our cognitive functions with our computing systems, no matter that the connections are mediated by simple typing and pointing. These tools enable our brains to do things that would once have been almost unimaginable:

■ powerful simulations and massive data sets allow physicists to visualize, understand, and debate models of an 11-dimension universe;

■ real-time data from satellites, global environmental databases, and high-resolution models allow geophysicists to recognize the subtle signs of long-term changes to the planet;

■ cross-connected scheduling systems allow anyone to assemble, with a few clicks, a complex, multimodal travel itinerary that would have taken a human travel agent days to create.

If that last example sounds prosaic, it simply reflects how embedded these kinds of augmentation have become. Not much more than a decade ago, such a tool was outrageously impressive—and it destroyed the travel-agent industry.

That industry won't be the last one to go. Any occupation requiring pattern-matching and the ability to find obscure connections will quickly morph from the domain of experts to that of ordinary people whose intelligence has been augmented by cheap digital tools. Humans won't be taken out of the loop—in fact, many, many *more* humans will have the capacity to do something that was once limited to a hermetic priesthood. Intelligence augmentation decreases the need for specialization and increases participatory complexity.

As the digital systems we rely upon become faster, more sophisticated, and (with the usual hiccups) more capable, we're becoming more sophisticated and capable too. It's a form of co-evolution: we learn to adapt our thinking and expectations to these digital systems, even as the system designs become more complex and powerful to meet more of our needs—and eventually come to adapt to *us*.

Consider the Twitter phenomenon, which went from nearly invisible to nearly ubiquitous (at least among the online crowd) in early 2007. During busy periods, the user can easily be overwhelmed by the volume of incoming messages, most of which are of only passing interest. But there is a tiny minority of truly valuable posts. (Sometimes they have extreme value, as they did during the October 2007 wildfires in California and the November 2008 terrorist attacks in Mumbai.) At present, however, finding the most-useful bits requires wading through messages like "My kitty sneezed!" and "I hate this taco!"

But imagine if social tools like Twitter had a way to learn what kinds of messages you pay attention to, and which ones you discard. Over time, the messages that you don't really care about might start to fade in the display, while the ones that you do want to see could get brighter. Such attention filters—or focus assistants—are likely to become important parts of how we handle our daily lives. We'll move from a world of "continuous partial attention" to one we might call "continuous augmented awareness."

As processor power increases, tools like Twitter may be able to draw on the complex simulations and massive data sets that have unleashed a revolution in science. They could become individualized systems that augment our capacity for planning and foresight, letting us play "what-if" with our life choices: where to live, what to study, maybe even where to go for dinner. Initially crude and clumsy, such a system would get better with more data and more experience; just as important, we'd get better at asking questions. These systems, perhaps linked to the cameras and microphones in our mobile devices, would eventually be able to pay attention to what we're doing, and to our habits and language quirks, and learn to interpret our sometimes ambiguous desires. With enough time and complexity, they would be able to make useful suggestions without explicit prompting.

And such systems won't be working for us alone. Intelligence has a strong social component; for example, we already provide crude cooperative information-filtering for each other. In time, our interactions through the use of such intimate technologies could dovetail with our use of collaborative knowledge systems (such as Wikipedia), to help us not just to build better data sets, but to filter them with greater precision. As our capacity to provide that filter gets faster and richer, it increasingly becomes something akin to collaborative intuition—in which everyone is effectively augmenting everyone else.

In pharmacology, too, the future is already here. One of the most prominent examples is a drug called modafinil. Developed in the 1970s, modafinil—sold in the U.S. under the brand name Provigil—appeared on the cultural radar in the late 1990s, when the American military began to test it for long-haul pilots. Extended use of modafinil can keep a person awake and alert for well over 32 hours on end, with only a full night's sleep required to get back to a normal schedule.

While it is FDA-approved only for a few sleep disorders, like narcolepsy and sleep apnea, doctors increasingly prescribe it to those suffering from depression, to "shift workers" fighting fatigue, and to frequent business travelers dealing with time-zone shifts. I'm part of the latter group: like more and more professionals, I have a prescription for modafinil in order to help me overcome jet lag when I travel internationally. When I started taking the drug, I expected it to keep me awake; I didn't expect it to make me feel smarter, but that's exactly what happened. The change was subtle but clear, once I recognized it: within an hour of taking a standard 200-mg tablet, I was much more alert, and thinking with considerably more clarity and focus than usual. This isn't just a subjective conclusion. A University of Cambridge study, published in 2003, concluded that modafinil confers a measurable cognitive-enhancement effect across a variety of mental tasks, including pattern recognition and spatial planning, and sharpens focus and alertness.

I'm not the only one who has taken advantage of this effect. The Silicon Valley insider webzine *Tech Crunch* reported in July 2008 that some entrepreneurs now see modafinil as an important competitive tool. The tone of the piece was judgmental, but the implication was clear: everybody's doing it, and if you're not, you're probably falling behind.

This is one way a world of intelligence augmentation emerges. Little by little, people who don't know about drugs like modafinil or don't want to use them will face stiffer competition from the people who do. From the perspective of a culture immersed in athletic doping wars, the use of such drugs may seem like cheating. From the perspective of those who find that they're much more productive using this form of enhancement, it's no more cheating than getting a faster computer or a better education.

Modafinil isn't the only example; on college campuses, the use of ADD drugs (such as Ritalin and Adderall) as study aids has become almost ubiquitous. But these enhancements are primitive. As the science improves, we could see other kinds of cognitive-modification drugs that boost recall, brain plasticity, even empathy and emotional intelligence. They would start as therapeutic treatments, but end up being used to make us "better than normal." Eventually, some of these may become over-the-counter products at your local pharmacy, or in the juice and snack aisles at the supermarket. Spam e-mail would be full of offers to make your brain bigger, and your idea production more powerful.

Such a future would bear little resemblance to *Brave New World* or similar narcomantic nightmares; we may fear the idea of a population kept doped and placated, but we're more likely to see a populace stuck in overdrive, searching out the last bits of competitive advantage, business insight, and radical innovation. No small amount of that innovation would be directed toward inventing the next, more powerful cognitive-enhancement technology.

This would be a different kind of nightmare, perhaps, and cause waves of moral panic and legislative restriction. Safety would be a huge issue. But as we've found with athletic doping, if there's a technique for beating out rivals (no matter how risky), shutting it down is nearly impossible. This would be yet another pharmacological arms race—and in this case, the competitors on one side would just keep getting smarter.

The most radical form of superhuman intelligence, of course, wouldn't be a mind augmented by drugs or exocortical technology; it would be a mind that isn't human at all. Here we move from the realm of extrapolation to the realm of speculation, since solid predictions about artificial intelligence are notoriously hard: our understanding of how the brain creates the mind remains far from good enough to tell us how to construct a mind in a machine.

But while the concept remains controversial, I see no good argument for why a mind running on a machine platform instead of a biological platform will forever be impossible; whether one might appear in five years or 50 or 500, however, is uncertain. I lean toward 50, myself. That's enough time to develop computing hardware able to run a high-speed neural network as sophisticated as that of a human brain, and enough time for the kids who will have grown up surrounded by virtual-world software and household robots—that is, the people who see this stuff not as "Technology," but as everyday tools—to come to dominate the field.

Many proponents of developing an artificial mind are sure that such a breakthrough will be the biggest change in human history. They believe that a machine mind would soon modify itself to get smarter—and with its new intelligence, then figure out how to make itself smarter still. They refer to this intelligence explosion as "the Singularity," a term applied by the computer scientist and science-fiction author Vernor Vinge. "Within thirty years, we will have the technological means to create superhuman intelligence," Vinge wrote in 1993. "Shortly after, the human era will be ended." The Singularity concept is a secular echo of Teilhard de Chardin's "Omega Point," the culmination of the Nöosphere at the end of history. Many believers in Singularity—which one wag has dubbed "the Rapture for nerds"—think that building the first real AI will be the last thing humans do. Some imagine this moment with terror, others with a bit of glee.

My own suspicion is that a stand-alone artificial mind will be more a tool of narrow utility than something especially apocalyptic. I don't think the theory of an explosively self-improving AI is convincing—it's based on too many assumptions about behavior and the nature of the mind. Moreover, AI researchers, after years of talking about this prospect, are already ultra-conscious of the risk of runaway systems.

More important, though, is that the same advances in processor and process that would produce a machine mind would also increase the power of our own cognitive-enhancement technologies. As intelligence augmentation allows us to make *ourselves* smarter, and then smarter still, AI may turn out to be just a sideshow: we could always be a step ahead.

So what's life like in a world of brain doping, intuition networks, and the occasional artificial mind?

Banal.

Not from our present perspective, of course. For us, now, looking a generation ahead might seem surreal and dizzying. But remember: people living in, say, 2030 will have lived every moment from now until then—we won't jump into the future. For someone going from 2009 to 2030 day by day, most of these changes wouldn't be jarring; instead, they'd be incremental, almost overdetermined, and the occasional surprises would quickly blend into the flow of inevitability.

By 2030, then, we'll likely have grown accustomed to (and perhaps even complacent about) a world where sophisticated foresight, detailed analysis and insight, and augmented awareness are commonplace. We'll have developed a better capacity to manage both partial attention and laser-like focus, and be able to slip between the two with ease—perhaps by popping the right pill, or eating the right snack. Sometimes, our augmentation assistants will handle basic interactions on our behalf; that's okay, though, because we'll increasingly see those assistants as extensions of ourselves.

The amount of data we'll have at our fingertips will be staggering, but we'll finally have gotten over the notion that accumulated information alone is a hallmark of intelligence. The power of all of this knowledge will come from its ability to inform difficult decisions, and to support complex analysis. Most professions will likely use simulation and modeling in their day-to-day work, from political decisions to hairstyle options. In a world of augmented intelligence, we will have a far greater appreciation of the consequences of our actions.

This doesn't mean we'll all come to the same conclusions. We'll still clash with each other's emotions, desires, and beliefs. If anything, our arguments will be more intense, buttressed not just by strongly held opinions but by intricate reasoning. People in 2030 will look back aghast at how ridiculously unsubtle the political and cultural disputes of our present were, just as we might today snicker at simplistic advertising from a generation ago.

Conversely, the debates of the 2030s would be remarkable for us to behold. Nuance and multiple layers will characterize even casual disputes; our digital assistants will be there to catch any references we might miss. And all of this will be everyday, banal reality. Today, it sounds mind-boggling; by then, it won't even merit comment.

What happens if such a complex system collapses? Disaster, of course. But don't forget that we already depend upon enormously complex systems that we no longer even think of as technological. Urbanization, agriculture, and trade were at one time huge innovations. Their collapse (and all of them are now at risk, in different ways, as we have seen in recent months) would be an even greater catastrophe than the collapse of our growing webs of interconnected intelligence.

A less apocalyptic but more likely danger derives from the observation made by the science-fiction author William Gibson: "The future is already here, it's just unevenly distributed." The rich, whether nations or individuals, will inevitably gain access to many augmentations before anyone else. We know from history, though, that a world of limited access wouldn't last forever, even as the technology improved: those who sought to impose limits would eventually face angry opponents with newer, better systems.

Even as competition provides access to these kinds of technologies, though, development paths won't be identical. Some societies may be especially welcoming to biotech boosts; others may prefer to use digital tools. Some may readily adopt collaborative approaches; others may focus on individual enhancement. And around the world, many societies will reject the use of intelligence-enhancement technology entirely, or adopt a cautious wait-and-see posture.

The bad news is that these divergent paths may exacerbate cultural divides created by already divergent languages and beliefs. National rivalries often emphasize cultural differences, but for now we're all still standard human beings. What happens when different groups quite literally think in very, very different ways?

The good news, though, is that this diversity of thought can also be a strength. Coping with the various world-historical dangers we face will require the greatest possible insight, creativity, and innovation. Our ability to build the future that we want—not just a future we can survive—depends on our capacity to understand the complex relationships of the world's systems, to take advantage of the diversity of knowledge and experience our civilization embodies, and to fully appreciate the implications of our choices. Such an ability is increasingly within our grasp. The Nöocene awaits.

■ READING AND WRITING

1. According to Cascio, how have we been "augmenting our ability to think for millennia"?
2. How do you feel about evolving into what Cascio calls "You+"?
3. In explaining the use of drugs to augment intelligence, Cascio writes: "From the perspective of a culture immersed in athletic doping wars, the use of such drugs may seem like cheating. From the perspective of those who find that they're much more productive using this form of enhancement, it's no more cheating than getting a faster computer or a better education." Do you agree with Cascio's point? Explain your response.
4. In "The Allegory of the Cave," Plato writes that "in the world of knowledge the idea of good appears last of all, and is seen only with an effort…" How might Cascio respond to this concept of knowledge and "the idea of good"?

■ DEVELOPING LONGER RESPONSES

5. "Get Smart" is, in part, a response to Nicholas Carr's "Is Google Making Us Stupid?" Write a brief essay in which you analyze how Cascio addresses Carr's concerns about technology's ill effects on learning and concentration. Do you find Cascio's counterarguments persuasive? Why or why not?

IMAGE 1.3
"I cannot see an outstretched hand and not put something there," Elie Wiesel says in "Am I My Brother's Keeper." How do you respond when you see others in need?

■ **USING RESEARCH**

Using the internet, the library, and/or primary sources (such as interviews with service providers), compile an annotated bibliography of six sources that help you understand the problem of homelessness in Columbia and nearby areas. Open your annotated bibliography with an introduction that summarizes your findings.

Holocaust survivor and Nobel laureate Elie Wiesel is a teacher, a writer, and one of the world's most persistent and eloquent voices for peace and moral responsibility. His best-known book is Night, *a memoir about his time in a Nazi death camp as a child, though he has written scores of other books, speeches, and essays. Richard D. Heffner is a professor of communications and public policy at Rutgers University and the producer and longtime host of the radio program* The Open Mind. *The text that follows is from the 2001 book* Conversations with Elie Wiesel.

AM I MY BROTHER'S KEEPER?
Elie Wiesel and Richard D. Heffner

Elie, this is a question that perhaps is not understood too well by a good many people in our time. What does it mean to you?

It is a question that Cain asked of God, having killed Abel: "Am I my brother's keeper?" And the answer, of course, is, we are all our brothers' keepers. Why? Either we see in each other brothers, or we live in a world of strangers. I believe that there are no strangers in God's creation. There are no strangers in a world that becomes smaller and smaller. Today I know right away when something happens, whatever happens, anywhere in the world. So there is no excuse for us not to be involved in these problems. A century ago, by the time the news of a war reached another place, the war was over. Now people die and the pictures of their dying are offered to you and to me while we are having dinner. Since I know, how can I not transform that knowledge into responsibility? So the key word is "responsibility." That means I must keep my brother.

Yet it seems that despite the fact that we live in an age of rapid, immediate communications, we know so little about what is happening to our brothers.

We are careless. Somehow life has been cheapened in our own eyes. The sanctity of life, the sacred dimension of every minute of human existence, is gone. The main problem is that there are so many situations that demand our attention. There are so many tragedies that need our involvement. Where do you begin? We know *too* much. No, let me correct myself. We are *informed* about too many things. Whether information is transformed into knowledge is a different story, a different question.

But we are in the world of communication. Nothing has caught the fantasy, the imagination, of the world these last years as communication has. So many radio stations, so many television stations, so many publications, so many talk shows. It's always more and more information that is being fed. And I'm glad that these things are happening, because I think people should be informed.

However, let us say that on a given day a tragedy has taken place. For a day we are all glued to the television. Three days later, we are still glued. A week later, another tragedy occurs and then the first tragedy is overshadowed by the next one. I remember when I saw the hungry children of Biafra for the first time. I didn't sleep. I tried everything I could to address the problem—to write articles and call up people and organize activities to send food to those children. But if you had shown those pictures for a whole month, by the second month people would not have been moved by them. What happened to the information there? It is still stored, but yet we don't act upon it, because we are summoned by the current event.

There seems to be almost an inevitability about what you are describing, because extending and perfecting the means of communication is certainly a major thrust of our times.

I would like to be able to say to my students that there are so many things in the world that solicit your attention and your involvement that you can choose any one. I really don't mind where that particular event is taking place. But I would like my students to be fully involved in *some* event. Today, for instance, they will say, "I go to zone A, and then I go to zone B." But as long as zone A has not been covered fully, as long as it is a human problem, I don't think we can abandon it. All the areas must be covered. I would not want to live in a world today in which a person or a community, because of color, because of religion, because of ethnic origin, or because of social conditions, would feel totally neglected or abandoned. There must be someone who speaks to and for that group, every group.

Is there any question but that we have seen the faces of those who suffer and yet we are not moved sufficiently?

I plead your case: In 1945, all the newspapers and magazines in the United States showed the pictures of the concentration camps. And yet for another five years, displaced persons remained in those camps. How many were allowed to come to America? They were told, "Those who want to go to Palestine, good. All the others, come and we shall give you what you really need most—human warmth?" Furthermore, look at what happened in South Africa. Apartheid was a blasphemy. We saw these white racists killing. I remember images that moved me to anger— images of funeral processions. Whites had killed blacks because they were black. And then the whites disrupted the funerals, killing more black people. That is the limit of endurance, the limit of any tolerance. We should have protested louder. And yet we didn't.

We talk about a world that is, perhaps, too much with us, so much so that there is no time to focus. How do you help your students deal with that?

I mentioned Cain and Abel. Why did Cain kill Abel? It is not because he was jealous. According to the text that we read and comment upon, it was because Cain spoke to Abel, his younger brother, and he told him of his pain, of his abandonment, of his solitude—that God didn't want to accept his offering. In the Bible it's said, "And Cain spoke to Abel." And we don't even know whether Abel listened. There was no dialogue. So the first act, really, among brothers, was a lack of communication.

So what I would teach my students is communication. I believe in dialogue. I believe if people talk, and they talk sincerely, with the same respect that one owes to a close friend or to God, something will come out of that, something good. I would call it presence. I would like my students to be present whenever people need a human presence. I urge very little upon my students, but that is one thing I do. To people I love, I wish I could say, "I will suffer in your place." But I cannot. Nobody can. Nobody should. I can be present, though. And when you suffer, you need a presence.

When you say "communicate," you mean to accept communication, don't you?

To be able to give and to receive at the same time.

Does it seem to you that we're not listening to the world around us, that we're so much involved in our individual pursuits?

Absolutely. I think the noise around us has become deafening. People talk but nobody listens. People aren't afraid of that silence. Have you seen those youngsters and not-so-young people go around in the street with a Walkman on their ears? They don't want to hear anything. They want to hear only their own music. Which is the same music, by the way, that they heard yesterday. It's a kind of repetition which is deafening. People don't want to hear the world. The world is, I think, in need of being heard.

Elie, I find that as I get older and older still, I so often find that I want to shut things out, because I can't focus on what needs to be focused on if I'm listening to everything. That seems to me to be where we began, in a sense.

To me too, of course. So often I want to turn off everything and say, "Look, it's easier to talk about *Romeo and Juliet* than to talk about what's happening today anywhere in the world." Naturally. Because in that play, there is a text and there is a story. It's a story I can turn in any direction I want, really. You think that *Romeo and Juliet* is a story of love. It's a story of hate. So whatever subject I discuss, I can always turn it one way or another. It's familiar, graspable. I prefer to discuss Plato, naturally. But we must open our eyes, and—

I don't want to be a devil's advocate here. I understand the subjective need not to feel that I am my brother's keeper, the subjective need to shut out the pain—

Sure. You couldn't take it. There is a need to remember, and it may last only a day or a week at a time. We cannot remember all the time. That would be impossible; we would be numb. If I were to remember all the time, I wouldn't be able to function. A person who is sensitive, always responding, always listening, always ready to receive someone else's pain … how can one live? One must forget that we die; if not, we wouldn't live.

So what do we do? Can we both attend to our own needs and to the various needs of our family and friends and still extend the notion of "Am I my brother's keeper?" way beyond Abel to the far points of the world?

Perhaps we cannot, but we must try. Because we cannot, we must, even though Kant used to say, "We can, therefore we must." There is so much forgetfulness, so much indifference today, that we must **fight** it. We must fight for the sake of our own future. Is this the nature of human beings? Yes, it's part of our nature.

I know it all seems like too much—even in our own city, New York. There is so much hate and so much mistrust and distrust that you wonder what can reach these people who live together, who can live together, who after all must live together. Where do you begin? Now, I always feel very strongly about the person who needs me. I don't know who that person is, but if the person needs me, I somehow must think of that person more than about myself. Why? Because I see my own life in him or her. I remember there were times when I needed people, and they were not there. If there is a governing precept in my life, it is that: If somebody needs me, I must be there.

When I ask the question that we began with—"Am I my brother's keeper?"—I most often receive a blank stare. Obviously that stare comes from people for whom the concept is, if not anathema, at least terribly foreign. More so now, don't you think?

More so, because it involves us more deeply, because it goes further. If I say yes, then I have to do something about it. Then it really goes further than that: What does it mean? Who is my brother? It's a definition. Who is my brother? Is any person in the street my brother? Is a person in Somalia my brother? Is a person in Armenia my brother? Come on. If I say, "My brother," what do I mean? Have I seen them? Have I met them? So of course it could be a poetic expression, which means very little. But if you say that there are people in the world who need a brother, I will say, "Then I would like to be that brother." I don't always succeed, of course. I cannot. I am only an individual. I am alone, as you are alone. What can we do? We can be the brother to one person and then another person, to ten people, a hundred people in our whole life. Does it mean that we are brothers to everybody in the world? No, we cannot be. So even if we say that at least we can tell a story about a brother who is looking for a brother and finds one, I think that's quite enough.

Yes, but aren't we experiencing a new kind of isolationism today? "Please, I can't solve these problems. Don't burden me with them. I'm not my brother's keeper!"

> Today brothers become strangers. How do you expect strangers to become brothers? People who live in the same country today are strangers to one another. Take what's happened in Eastern Europe when the reactionary, exclusionary forces rule. They are neighbors, close to one another, but they see in each other a threat, a source of suspicion, a conqueror, not a brother. I think it's an historical phenomenon, which is worrisome.

Elie, what's the scriptural response to the question "Am I my brother's keeper?"

> It is actually written as a dialogue, a scenario. Cain kills Abel. And God says to him, "Hi, good morning, how are you?" "All right," says Cain. Then God says, "By the way, where is your brother?" "I don't know," is the answer. "What do you mean, you don't know?" asks God. The answer: "I don't know. Am I my brother's keeper?" And then God says, "Come on, you know. I hear the voice of your brother's blood coming from the bowels of the earth. And you want to cheat me." The whole thing is a little bit silly. Does it mean that God didn't know where Abel was? God is playing a game. It's simply a story which I like to interpret as meaning that it is possible, unfortunately, throughout history, for two brothers to be brothers and yet to become the victim and/or the assassin of the other. However, I go one step further and I try to teach my students that we learn another lesson: Whoever kills, kills his brother.

Kills his brother or kills some part of himself?

> It's possible, as I interpret it, that Cain and Abel were only one person. Cain killed Abel in Cain.

The Darwinian response to "Am I my brother's keeper?" is: "Of course not. If you pretend to be, you are interfering with natural selection." How do we build again upon the more ancient notion that indeed we are our brothers' keepers in many, many, ways?

> But remember again, Cain was *not* his brother's keeper. He killed him.

But the question asked by God—

> The question is good.

I know that's your specialty—questions.

> I love questions, true. Because there is "quest" in "question." I love that. But today, I would like to put a face on words. When I see words, I see a face. When

you speak about, let's say, "my brother's keeper," I see faces of people I knew or know, or people I've just seen this morning. Crossing the street, there is an old man with his hand outstretched. Now, am I his keeper?

Are you?

I must tell you that when I see that, I always feel strange. Because on the one hand, reason tells me that if I give him a dollar, he will go and buy alcohol. But then I say to myself, So what? Who am I to decide what he will do with the money that I give him? I cannot see an outstretched hand and not put something there. It's impossible. I know sometimes it's a weakness. I want to feel better, not to feel bad about it. But in fact I cannot.

You talked about communications before. If we don't "listen" by providing, presumably our brother will rise up and strike us down.

Or we would strike him down. Who are we? Children of Cain or children of Abel?

What's your answer?

You know, in my tradition, there is a marvelous way out. We are neither the children of Cain nor the children of Abel. There was a third son that Adam and Eve had afterward called Seth. And we are children of Seth. Which means you can be both.

Is that a cop-out?

No, not really. I think we are always oscillating between the temptation for evil and an attraction to goodness. It's enough for me to close my eyes and remember what men are capable of doing, to become terribly, profoundly, totally pessimistic, because they haven't changed. But then again, I open my eyes and close them again and say, "It would be absurd not to absorb some images and turn them into good consciousness." And it's up to us to choose. We are free to choose.

Don't you think that in our country at this time we're less concerned with, have less compassion for, those who suffer?

Absolutely. But it's really about what you are doing all your life. Can we really help more than the people around us? I go around the world, I travel, and whenever I hear about someone suffering, I try to go there and bear witness. That's my role, at least to bear witness. To say, "I've seen, I was there." Sometimes it inspires others to do what I am doing. More often than not, it doesn't.

If the moral imperative that you pose is one that seemingly is rejected in our time, why do you maintain this posture: "We must be caring, rather than careless?"

> Because I don't have a position of power. Maybe that's the reason. You and I can afford to speak on moral issues. We don't have to make a decision on them. I am sure that if you had someone facing you here who had power, a senator or a member of the Cabinet, he or she would say, "We cannot do this or that." Why? "Because so much money would be needed. We don't have the money. Housing would be required. We don't have the housing." So I can afford, really, only to pose questions, and I know that.

Yes, but I'm convinced that you raise questions because you know what the right moral answers are.

> That's true.

And you believe that by raising those questions, we will come to those answers.

> I would like to think that. But even if I knew that I would not succeed, I would still raise those questions.

Why?

> Otherwise, why am I here? I have the feeling, honestly, that my life is an offering. I could have died every minute between '44 and '45. So once I have received this gift, I must justify it. And the only way to justify life is by affirming the right to life of anyone who needs such affirmation.

Aren't you affirming, too, a conviction that something will be done in response to your question?

> Here and there one person might listen and do something. Another person might listen and not do something. But I prefer to think, that here and there, there are small miracles. And there are: a good student, a good reader, a friend. I think we spoke about it years ago: Once upon a time, I was convinced I could change the whole world. Now I'm satisfied with small measures of grace. If we could open the door of one jail and free one innocent person … if I could save one child from starvation, believe me, to me it would be worth as much as, if not more than, all the work that I am doing and all the recognition that I may get for it.

You've spoken about those who put people in the death camps and brought about their deaths directly. You also speak about others who stood around indifferently. Do you feel that that is increasingly a theme in our own times?

Oh, more and more. I have the feeling that everything I do is a variation on the same theme. I'm simply trying to pull the alarm and say, "Don't be indifferent." Simply because I feel that indifference now is equal to evil. Evil, we know more or less what it is. But indifference to disease, indifference to famine, indifference to dictators, somehow it's here and we accept it. And I have always felt that the opposite of culture is not ignorance; it is indifference. And the opposite of morality is not immorality; it's again indifference. And we don't realize how indifferent we are simply because we cannot *not* be a little indifferent. We cannot think all the time of all the people who die. If, while I sit with you, I could see the children who are dying now while we talk, we wouldn't be able to talk, you and I. We would have to take a plane, go there and do something. We wouldn't be able to continue to try to be logical and rational.

You've said that if we ignore suffering, we become accomplices, as so many did during the Holocaust. Where is it written that we are not moral accomplices?

But we are.

But what can you expect of us?

Learning. After all, I don't compare situations. I don't compare any period to the period of the Second World War. But we have learned something. I have the feeling that sometimes it takes a generation for an event to awaken our awareness. But if now, so many years after that event, we are still behaving as though it did not occur, then what is the purpose of our work as teachers, as writers, as men and women who are concerned with one another's lives?

We have a tradition in this country of extending ourselves through our wealth, our material well-being. That tradition was set aside somewhat for some time. Do you think we will recapture it more fully?

I hope so. I hope that there will be enough students and teachers and writers and poets and communicators to bring back certain values. If a father cannot feed his children, then his human rights are violated. We are such a wealthy society. I think of the United States and am overtaken by gratitude. This nation has gone to war twice in its history to fight for other people's freedoms. Then, after the wars, consider the economic help, the billions of dollars that we have given to those poor countries ravaged, destroyed by the enemy. And even now, what would the free world do without us? We have always been ready to help.

So why not? It would show that we still have compassion. Now, those are nice words, I know. But what else do we have? We have words, and sometimes we try to act upon them.

■ READING AND WRITING

1. Definitions play an important role in Wiesel's comments. What does he mean when he distinguishes between information and knowledge? How does he define responsibility? How does he link knowledge and responsibility? How does he define presence?
2. What role does listening play in Wiesel's world view?
3. How does Wiesel use references to God, religion, and religious texts in his argument? Think especially about his audience and his ethos.
4. Weisel's comments about our responsibilities, and our desensitization to those responsibilities, implicate technology and the media. Technology allows us to know more than ever before about the sufferings of our "brothers and sisters" throughout the world, he argues, but it also can overwhelm us to the point that a kind of numbness sets in. How, according to Wiesel, can we deal with this conundrum?

■ DEVELOPING LONGER RESPONSES

5. Wiesel argues that we should show hands-on, practical compassion to victims of misfortune and oppression—the more concrete, the better. Yet the language in which he makes this argument is unremittingly abstract. Find five places in the text where Wiesel uses abstract language or concepts to make his points. Does this detract from his overall meaning? Why or why not?

Judith Lichtenberg, a professor of philosophy at Georgetown University, is working on a book on the idea of charity. She wrote this piece in October 2010 for the New York Times *blog called The Stone, described by the newspaper as "a forum for contemporary philosophers on issues both timely and timeless."*

IS PURE ALTRUISM POSSIBLE?
Judith Lichtenberg

Who could doubt the existence of altruism?

True, news stories of malice and greed abound. But all around us we see evidence of human beings sacrificing themselves and doing good for others. Remember Wesley Autrey? On Jan. 2, 2007, Mr. Autrey jumped down onto the tracks of a New York City subway platform as a train was approaching to save a man who had suffered a seizure and fallen. A few months later the Virginia Tech professor Liviu Librescu blocked the door to his classroom so his students could escape the bullets of Seung-Hui Cho, who was on a rampage that would leave 32 students and faculty members dead. In so doing, Mr. Librescu gave his life.

Still, doubting altruism is easy, even when it seems at first glance to be apparent. It's undeniable that people sometimes act in a way that benefits others, but it may seem that they always get something in return—at the very least, the satisfaction of having their desire to help fulfilled. Students in introductory philosophy courses torture their professors with this reasoning. And its logic can seem inexorable.

Contemporary discussions of altruism quickly turn to evolutionary explanations. Reciprocal altruism and kin selection are the two main theories. According to reciprocal altruism, evolution favors organisms that sacrifice their good for others in order to gain a favor in return. Kin selection—the famous "selfish gene" theory popularized by Richard Dawkins—says that an individual who behaves altruistically towards others who share its genes will tend to reproduce those genes. Organisms may be altruistic; genes are selfish. The feeling that loving your children more than yourself is hard-wired lends plausibility to the theory of kin selection.

These evolutionary theories explain a puzzle: how organisms that sacrifice their own "reproductive fitness"—their ability to survive and reproduce—could possibly have evolved. But neither theory fully accounts for our ordinary understanding of altruism.

The defect of reciprocal altruism is clear. If a person acts to benefit another in the expectation that the favor will be returned, the natural response is: "That's not altruism!" Pure altruism, we think, requires a person to sacrifice for another without consideration of personal gain. Doing good for another person because something's in it for the do-er is the very opposite of what we have in mind. Kin selection does better by allowing that organisms may genuinely sacrifice their interests for another, but it fails to explain why they sometimes do so for those with whom they share no genes, as Professor Librescu and Mr. Autrey did.

When we ask whether human beings are altruistic, we want to know about their motives or intentions. Biological altruism explains how unselfish behavior might have evolved but, as Frans de Waal has suggested, it implies nothing about the motives or intentions of the agent: after all, birds and bats and bees can act altruistically. This fact helps to explain why, despite these evolutionary theories, the view that people never intentionally act to benefit others except to obtain some good for themselves still possesses a powerful lure over our thinking.

The lure of this view—egoism—has two sources, one psychological, the other logical. Consider first the psychological. One reason people deny that altruism exists is that, looking inward, they doubt the purity of their own motives. We know that even when we appear to act unselfishly, other reasons for our behavior often rear their heads: the prospect of a future favor, the boost to reputation, or simply the good feeling that comes from appearing to act unselfishly. As Kant and Freud observed, people's true motives may be hidden, even (or perhaps especially) from themselves. Even if we think we're acting solely to further another person's good, that might not be the real reason. (There might be no single "real reason"—actions can have multiple motives.)

So the psychological lure of egoism as a theory of human action is partly explained by a certain humility or skepticism people have about their own or others' motives. There's also a less flattering reason: denying the possibility of pure altruism provides a convenient excuse for selfish behavior. If "everybody is like that"—if everybody must be like that— we need not feel guilty about our own self-interested behavior or try to change it.

The logical lure of egoism is different: the view seems impossible to disprove. No matter how altruistic a person appears to be, it's possible to conceive of her motive in egoistic terms. On this way of looking at it, the guilt Mr. Autrey would have suffered had he ignored the man on the tracks made risking his life worth the gamble. The doctor who gives up a comfortable life to care for AIDS patients in a remote place does what she wants to do, and therefore gets satisfaction from what only appears to be self-sacrifice. So, it seems, altruism is simply self-interest of a subtle kind.

The impossibility of disproving egoism may sound like a virtue of the theory, but, as philosophers of science know, it's really a fatal drawback. A theory that purports to tell us something about the world, as egoism does, should be falsifiable. Not false, of course, but capable of being tested and thus proved false. If every state of affairs is compatible with egoism, then egoism doesn't tell us anything distinctive about how things are.

A related reason for the lure of egoism, noted by Bishop Joseph Butler in the 18th century, concerns ambiguity in the concepts of desire and the satisfaction of desire. If people possess altruistic motives, then they sometimes act to benefit others without the prospect of gain to themselves. In other words, they desire the good of others for its own sake, not simply as a means to their own satisfaction. It's obvious that Professor Librescu desired that his students not die, and acted accordingly to save their lives. He succeeded, so his desire was satisfied. But he was not satisfied—since he died in the attempt to save the students. From the fact that a person's desire is satisfied we can draw no conclusions about effects on his mental state or well-being.

Still, when our desires are satisfied we normally experience satisfaction; we feel good when we do good. But that doesn't mean we do good only in order to get that "warm glow"—that our true incentives are self-interested (as economists tend to claim). Indeed, as de Waal argues, if we didn't desire the good of others for its own sake, then attaining it wouldn't produce the warm glow.

Common sense tells us that some people are more altruistic than others. Egoism's claim that these differences are illusory—that deep down, everybody acts only to further their own interests—contradicts our observations and deep-seated human practices of moral evaluation.

At the same time, we may notice that generous people don't necessarily suffer more or flourish less than those who are more self-interested. Altruists may be more content or fulfilled than selfish people. Nice guys don't always finish last.

But nor do they always finish first. The point is rather that the kind of altruism we ought to encourage, and probably the only kind with staying power, is satisfying to those who practice it. Studies of rescuers show that they don't believe their behavior is extraordinary; they feel they must do what they do, because it's just part of who they are. The same holds for more common, less newsworthy acts—working in soup kitchens, taking pets to people in nursing homes, helping strangers find their way, being neighborly. People who act in these ways believe that they ought to help others, but they also want to help, because doing so affirms who they are and want to be and the kind of world they want to exist. As Prof. Neera Badhwar has argued, their identity is tied up with their values, thus tying self-interest and altruism together. The correlation between doing good and feeling good is not inevitable—inevitability lands us again with that empty, unfalsifiable egoism—but it is more than incidental.

Altruists should not be confused with people who automatically sacrifice their own interests for others. We admire Paul Rusesabagina, the hotel manager who saved over 1,000 Tutsis and Hutus during the 1994 Rwandan genocide; we admire health workers who give up comfortable lives to treat sick people in hard places. But we don't admire people who let others walk all over them; that amounts to lack of self-respect, not altruism.

Altruism is possible and altruism is real, although in healthy people it intertwines subtly with the well-being of the agent who does good. And this is crucial for seeing how to increase the amount of altruism in the world. Aristotle had it right in his "Nicomachean Ethics": we have to raise people from their "very youth" and educate them "so as both to delight in and to be pained by the things that we ought."

■ READING AND WRITING

1. Explain how Lichtenberg answers the question she poses in the title of her essay: "Is True Altruism Possible?"
2. Lichtenberg writes that "doubting altruism is easy, even when it seems at first glance to be apparent." Why is this so? Do you agree with Lichtenberg's assertion?

■ DEVELOPING LONGER RESPONSES

3. Based on Lichtenberg's essay and Elie Wiesel's discussion with Richard D. Heffner in "Am I My Brother's Keeper?" write a brief essay in which you define the concept of "altruism." Make sure you present clear criteria for your definition, as well as examples of acts that are altruistic and those that are not.

■ USING RESEARCH

4. In her essay, Lichtenberg mentions "the famous 'selfish gene' theory popularized by Richard Dawkins." Use whatever online resources you have at your disposal to compile an annotated bibliography of four to five sources that help you understand what the "selfish gene" theory is and how it relates to Lichtenberg's claims about altruism.

Jeremy Kahn is an independent journalist who writes about international affairs, politics, business, the environment and the arts. His work has appeared in many media outlets, including Newsweek International, The New York Times, The New Republic, Slate, *and* The Atlantic, *where this article was published in April 2007.*

THE STORY OF A SNITCH   Jeremy Kahn

John Dowery Jr. was happy to be working again. He had recently spent 11 months cooped up, a prisoner in his own home. In November 2003, two officers investigating the sound of gunfire in East Baltimore had arrested him after a car and foot chase. They said that Dowery, who had been riding in the back of a blue Mitsubishi, had jumped out of the car, placed a loaded .38-caliber handgun on the ground, and tried to flee. A 36-year-old heroin addict with a felony drug conviction, Dowery was facing federal prosecution and the prospect of up to eight years without parole. While he awaited trial, he had been "put on the box"—confined to his house, his whereabouts monitored by a transmitter locked around his ankle.

Staring down almost a decade behind bars can change a man, make him long for a second chance. And now it seemed Dowery had been given one. In October 2004, he had cut a deal, agreeing to become a witness in a murder trial. In exchange for his testimony, and as a result of good behavior, the feds had eased the terms of his pretrial detention. He had entered a drug-treatment program and landed a job working the graveyard shift at a condiment factory in the suburbs. For the first time in years, he was clean and sober, and life was looking up.

Each night, Dowery rode the commuter rail from the city to the plant; each morning, he rode it home again. He didn't mind the odd hours; having worked as a baker, he was accustomed to being nocturnal. Shortly after dawn on October 19, 2005, he got off the train as usual. It was a brisk morning, with clouds dappling the sky but no hint of rain. He decided to skip the bus and walk the mile to his house on Bartlett Avenue.

He ambled past the massive Board of Education building, with its columns, and headed down North Avenue to Greenmount Cemetery. There he turned left, passing the abandoned row houses where the "corner boys" were already opening for business, hoping to find a junkie in need of a morning fix. Farther on, past still-shuttered hair salons and check-cashing outfits, he turned down East 24th toward Bartlett. Just after seven o'clock, he reached his front porch and called out for his girlfriend, Yolanda, to let him in. Then he sensed something behind him.

He spun around to find two men dressed in black standing in his small front yard. One held a gun. As Dowery scrambled for his neighbor's porch, the man pulled the trigger. Dowery leaped from the porch and raced around the side of his house, the two men close behind him, the gunman firing the whole way. He managed to stagger through his back door before his legs gave out. The attackers, believing their work accomplished, took off. A neighbor would later tell police that she heard one of them say, "We busted his motherfucking ass."

Dowery had been shot in the back and in both arms and legs—six times in all. Only the skilled hands of the surgeons at Johns Hopkins spared his life. And yet, in the eyes of many people in the blocks around Bartlett, John Dowery had gotten what was coming to him.

*****

In many Baltimore neighborhoods, talking to the law has become a mortal sin, a dishonorable act punishable by social banishment—or worse. Prosecutors in the city can rattle off a litany of brutal retaliations: houses firebombed, witnesses and their relatives shot, contract hits on 10-year-olds. Witness intimidation, they say, badly hampers their ability to fight crime, and it affects nearly every murder case they try.

Prosecutors in most major U.S. cities tell similar stories. Two years ago in Philadelphia, a drug kingpin was convicted of witness intimidation after he was taped threatening to kill those who testified against him. Five relatives of one witness in the case had already died, in a house fire that prosecutors believe was the drug lord's doing. Last year in San Francisco, two gang members beat a murder rap after the state's star witness turned up dead. Several years ago in Denver, a key homicide witness was sexually assaulted in what prosecutors believe was a "contract" attack designed to frighten him out of testifying.

Police and prosecutors have been contending with reluctant witnesses for decades. But according to law-enforcement experts, the problem is getting dramatically worse, and is reflected in falling arrest and conviction rates for violent crimes. In cities with populations between half a million (for example, Tucson) and a million (Detroit), the proportion of violent crimes cleared by an arrest dropped from about 45 percent in the late 1990s to less than 35 percent in 2005, according to the FBI. Conviction rates have similarly dropped. At the same time, crime has spiked. Murder rates have risen more or less steadily since 2000. Last December, the FBI voiced concern over a jump in violent crime, which in 2005 showed its biggest increase in more than a decade.

The reasons for witnesses' reluctance appear to be changing and becoming more complex, with the police confronting a new cultural phenomenon: the spread of the gangland code of silence, or omertá, from organized crime to the population at large. Those who cooperate with the police are labeled "snitches" or "rats"—terms once applied only to jailhouse informants or criminals who turned state's evidence, but now used for "civilian" witnesses as well. This is particularly true in the inner cities, where gangsta culture has been romanticized through rap music and other forms of entertainment, and where the motto "Stop snitching," expounded in hip-hop lyrics and emblazoned on caps and T-shirts, has become a creed.

The metastasis of this culture of silence in minority communities has been facilitated by a gradual breakdown of trust in the police and the government. The erosion began during the civil-rights era, when informants were a favorite law-enforcement tool against groups like the Black Panthers. But it accelerated because of the war on drugs. David Kennedy, the director of the Center for Crime Prevention and Control at the John Jay

College of Criminal Justice, in New York, told me: "This is the reward we have reaped for 20 years of profligate drug enforcement in these communities." When half the young black men in a neighborhood are locked up, on bail, or on parole, the police become the enemy. Add to this the spread of racialized myths—that crack was created by the CIA to keep blacks in their place, for example—and you get a toxic mix. Kennedy thinks the silence of many witnesses doesn't come from fear, but from anger.

The growing culture of silence helps to legitimize witness intimidation. At the same time, criminals have become more adept at enforcing the code, using increasingly sophisticated methods to bribe, intimidate, and harm witnesses. Defendants and their surrogates have obtained witnesses' supposedly confidential grand-jury testimony and tacked it to their doors, along with threatening notes. They have adopted new technology like cell-phone cameras and text-messaging to spread the word about who is snitching; threats have even been text-messaged to the phones of sequestered witnesses. And every incident in which a witness is assaulted or murdered heightens the climate of fear and mistrust—the sense that the law either can't or won't protect ordinary people.

*****

On October 13, 2004, a year before he was shot while returning home from work, John Dowery was still electronically shackled to his house. Sometime after 3 p.m. that day, he looked out his front window and saw his friend James Wise coming up the street. Dowery and Wise, whom everyone called Jay, shared a love of basketball—and of heroin. Today Jay was with a younger man Dowery didn't recognize. They stopped outside the chain-link fence around Dowery's front yard. Jay called to Dowery, then came up to the door. He seemed nervous. He wanted Dowery's advice.

Jay said the other man had a gun. They were planning to rob an old drug dealer named Reds, who operated from a vacant lot a few doors down. Dowery told him it was a bad idea. At 40, Jay was no innocent, but neither was he an experienced stickup artist. Even if the two men could pull off the robbery, stickup boys in East Baltimore don't usually live long: On the street, robbing a dealer is a capital offense. "I told him basically not to do it," Dowery would later say. "But he ain't listen."

Dowery looked on from his front door as the two men walked down the street and entered the "cut" where Reds worked. He watched a flock of dope fiends suddenly flee the alley, like ducks flushed from the reeds. Seconds later, Reds darted out too. Then Jay and his partner emerged and raced down the street.

The two had timed their escape poorly. Sauntering up the street just then was Tracy Love, an athletic 20-year-old with cornrows and a meticulously trimmed beard and mustache, whom everyone knew as "Boo-Boo." Prosecutors later alleged that Boo-Boo oversaw the Bartlett Avenue drug operation. Jay and his accomplice brushed right past him. As Dowery watched, Boo-Boo pivoted and began to follow them down the hill.

Fifteen minutes later, Dowery heard the wail of police sirens and the thump-thump of a helicopter overhead. Boo-Boo strode back up Bartlett with his younger half-brother, Tamall Parker, who went by "Moo-Moo." "I got that motherfucker, six times in the chest," Dowery later recalled Boo-Boo shouting—ostensibly to his crew down the street, but loudly enough that anyone out on the block could hear. "Next time, one of y'all gonna do it. I'm tired of doing this shit."

According to police and prosecutors, this is what happened after Jay and his partner, a man police would identify as Joseph Bassett, robbed Reds and left Bartlett Avenue: Boo-Boo went to find Moo-Moo. They got into a white Lexus with sparkling chrome hubcaps and began cruising the neighborhood, hunting for Jay and Bassett. Unaware they were being pursued, Jay and Bassett met up with a couple of prostitutes a few blocks away. Jay knew one of them, Doris Dickerson. He told her about the robbery and offered her drugs. She said she would catch up with him in a minute, and walked into an alley. Bassett also left for a few minutes. Just as Doris and Jay were about to meet back up, at the corner of Bonaparte and Robb, Boo-Boo and Moo-Moo spotted Jay. Boo-Boo let Moo-Moo out of the car, then drove around the corner and waited. Moo-Moo tugged the hood of his sweatshirt up around his face, approached Jay, and pulled out a 9-mm handgun. He opened up, firing at least 13 times. The bullets punched holes in Jay's chest and abdomen; at least one smashed into his skull.

James Sylvester Wise Jr. was dead—the 229th murder of the year in a city that would rack up 278 by the end of December. Although 10 people called 911 to report the shooting, many refused to give their names. Six told the emergency operators that they did not want to talk to the police when they arrived. One caller, John Craddock, said he had seen a man running down the street and jumping into a white Lexus. He could not see the man's face, but he thought he could make out part of the license plate—a blue-and-white temporary tag with the numbers 3, 4, and 9. Police dispatchers put out a description of the car, but to no avail. Officers canvassed the block but turned up no additional witnesses or information. None of the three who knew the most about the killing—Dowery, Bassett, or Dickerson—came forward.

*****

A man gunned down on a busy street. No identifying witnesses; no suspects. In this, James Wise's murder was typical. Colonel Frederick Bealefeld III, Baltimore's chief of detectives, says the police used to be able to rely on people's consciences and sense of civic duty to generate leads in murder investigations. But today, few witnesses are willing to offer information, even anonymously. "How hard is it for someone to get on the phone and say … 'The guy who shot up this block—it is wrong, here's who that person is'?" Bealefeld asks. "Yet we don't get a ton of those kinds of calls. And if we graphed it out, if we tracked it over the years, you would see a very clear decline."

A 26-year veteran of the force and the grandson of a cop, Bealefeld has seen these changes firsthand. His grandfather walked a beat on Greenmount Avenue, not far from Bartlett. In 30 years with the department, he fired his gun exactly once in the line of duty. "No way he could walk that beat and do that now," Bealefeld says. "He took it for granted that the community respected him. Today's police can't take that for granted." By the time Bealefeld joined the force, in 1980, things had become much more dangerous for both the police and the citizens of Baltimore. But during the '80s, working narcotics, he could still find confidential informants with relative ease. Over time, that too started to change.

Bealefeld says he does not want to underestimate the fear people feel on the streets, or their lack of trust in the law. But he thinks witness intimidation has also become a cover for indifference. "How do I separate your intransigence to take part in a civic responsibility, and a moral responsibility, from your alleged fear?" he asks, the anger rising in his voice. "'I am not doing it, because I am afraid'—that is easy to say. You may not be doing it because you are a jerk and don't care about anybody but yourself and have no love for your fellow man."

Bealefeld is right that disentangling fear from other factors is not easy. But when I spoke with people in the blocks near where James Wise was murdered, it was the fear that was most palpable. "Round here it's not a good idea to talk to the police," Jacob Smith, a thoughtful 13-year-old walking home from school in East Baltimore, told me. "People, they like, if they know you talk to the police, they don't be around you. And if people talk on them and they get locked up, their friends come up on you and hurt you or something." (The ostracism and retaliation he spoke of got wide airing as a plotline last season in HBO's *The Wire*, set in Baltimore and created by David Simon, a former crime reporter, and Ed Burns, a former police officer: A teenager thought by his peers to have snitched was beaten, and eventually his house was firebombed.)

All over Baltimore, whenever I asked people about cooperating with the law, I got the same response. "Why would you talk to the police? All you are doing is putting a label on yourself," said Barry Nelson, a 42-year-old part-time handyman who was waiting for a meal from a charity the day I met him. "They ain't going to be back to protect you after you done told on some cats." Randolph Jones, a retiree who was sweeping leaves from the sidewalk in front of his house in Northwest Baltimore, said he would call the police if something happened on his block. But the drug dealing and shootings on the next block over? He won't pick up the phone. Jones said the police try, but as soon as they arrest one corner boy, another moves in. "You got to live here, and the police can't do much," he said. "You don't want to end up like that family in East Baltimore, the Dawsons."

The Dawsons come up in almost every conversation about reluctant witnesses in Baltimore. Angela Dawson had tried to shoo drug dealers away from the sidewalk outside the East Baltimore row house where she lived with her husband, Carnell, and their five children. She had frequently called the police. The dealers decided to strike back. In October 2002, the Dawsons' house was firebombed. Angela Dawson and all her children were killed in the blaze; Carnell Dawson died in the hospital a week later. A drug dealer named Darrell Brooks was convicted of the crime and is serving life without parole. But the sentence has done little to reassure potential witnesses. More than four years later, the Dawsons still haunt the city.

*****

John Dowery knew Boo-Boo and Moo-Moo had shot someone; he prayed that it wasn't Jay, that it was the other guy. But the next day's newspaper confirmed his fear about his friend. Jay's death shook Dowery. But it also made him more determined to get his life back on track. And in the tragedy of his friend's murder, Dowery sensed opportunity. If he told the police what he knew about the killing, perhaps he could get a lighter sentence on his gun charge. On the other hand, talking was dangerous: If Boo-Boo and Moo-Moo found out, they might come after him or his family. So Dowery struggled with the decision. A day went by, then a week. Then he picked up the phone and called his public defender.

On October 27, Dowery, along with his lawyer and the prosecutor handling his gun charge, met with Michael Baier, the Baltimore homicide detective assigned to Jay's murder. Dowery told Baier what he knew about the killing. He also said that Boo-Boo and Moo-Moo, who were still hanging around Bartlett, had ditched their distinctive white Lexus. His statement provided a crucial break in the case.

Another break came the following week, when Joseph Bassett, Jay's accomplice, was busted selling heroin to undercover cops. With his long rap sheet, Bassett knew he was in trouble. He tried offering up an illegal .32 he kept at home, in the hope that the officers would let him go in exchange for getting the gun off the street. When that failed, he said he might know something about a murder on Bonaparte. The officers brought Bassett downtown to homicide, where he told Baier about robbing Reds. He also said he had seen two men in a white Lexus circling the block, and that he saw the car stop and a man get out and shoot Jay. Baier showed him a photo lineup. Bassett identified Tracy Love as the driver of the car and Tamall Parker as the shooter.

Parker and Love were picked up two days later. Baier had several other pieces of evidence: The two suspects' mother had recently returned to the dealership a white Lexus with the temporary license tag 38491L. Video from a warehouse surveillance camera near the murder scene had captured what appeared to be a white Lexus circling the block in the minutes before Jay was killed. An analysis of Love's cell phone records determined that the phone had not left East Baltimore that day, a finding that directly contradicted Love and Parker's alibi: They said they had spent the day in their mother's hair salon, in West Baltimore.

Baier did not have a confession or a murder weapon, however. So at trial, a lot would depend on the testimony of Dowery and Bassett—convicted felons who had come forward at least in part because they were facing charges themselves. Eventually they would be joined by a third witness, also in trouble with the law: Doris Dickerson, picked up for prostitution, told police that she was heading toward Jay when she heard shots. She saw Jay fall to the ground and Moo-Moo run away. She too identified Parker as the killer from a photo lineup.

Witnesses of this sort would once have made a prosecutor blanch. Now, they are usually all prosecutors have. One problem with such witnesses is that defense attorneys can use their records to attack their credibility. The fewer witnesses the state has and the more a defense attorney expects to be able to discredit them, the more likely she is to advise her client against a plea bargain. This means more cases go to trial, at significant expense to the state. And at trial, there is a decent chance—in Baltimore, about 50 percent in a nonfatal shooting, and 38 percent in a murder—that the defendant will walk.

Witnesses in the drug trade are also highly susceptible to being coerced into changing their stories or not showing up in court. If a witness goes missing, his prior statements generally aren't admissible. And a witness who "backs up"—legal slang for recanting— can create doubt, including reasonable doubt, in the minds of jurors.

Not surprisingly, defense attorneys have a different take. Elizabeth Julian, Baltimore's chief public defender, believes the problems of witness intimidation are overstated. She told me that the real issue is police tactics that encourage suspects to lie about their knowledge of other crimes, and she pointed out that it is perfectly legal for police to mislead potential witnesses into thinking they won't have to testify in court. "If you are being asked, and you are getting a 'Get Out of Jail Free' card tonight, people take it. That's human nature," she says. In her view, many witnesses who back up are telling the truth on the stand. It's their initial statements that were false—either outright fabrications or some mixture of fact and rumor. Julian jokes that the word on the street, rather than "Stop snitching," ought to be "Stop lying."

*****

As it happened, Dowery decided to become a witness—just as witness intimidation in the city was about to explode into a national story. The spark was an underground DVD titled *Stop Fucking Snitching* that began circulating in Baltimore in November 2004. In it Rodney Thomas, a rapper known locally as Skinny Suge, talks about what he thinks should happen to informants: "To all you snitches and rats ... I hope you catch AIDS in your mouth, and your lips the first thing to die, yo bitch." The DVD also includes numerous segments in which young men on the street rail against snitches.

In its subject matter, the DVD was more evolution than revolution. The slogan "Stop snitching" had been around since at least 1999, when it was popularized by the Boston rapper Tangg da Juice. The video would have remained a local curiosity except for one thing: It includes a cameo by Carmelo Anthony, a Baltimore native who became an NBA star with the Denver Nuggets. Anthony appears in only six of the film's 108 minutes, and spends most of that time poking fun at a former coach and a rival player. As he later told *The Baltimore Sun*, "I was back on my block, chillin'. I was going back to show love to everybody, thinking it was just going to be on the little local DVD, that it was just one of my homeboys recording." But his celebrity, combined with the DVD's charged subject matter, created a sensation.

For Baltimore's police, prosecutors, and judges, eager to raise awareness about witness intimidation, *Stop Fucking Snitching* was a gift. "Think how bold criminals must be to make a DVD," Baltimore Circuit Judge John M. Glynn told the local press. "It shows that threatening snitches has become mainstream." Patricia Jessamy, the state's attorney for Baltimore, had hundreds of copies made and distributed them to politicians and the national media. The publicity helped her win passage of a tougher witness-intimidation law, one the Maryland legislature had voted down the year before. The police department made a show of arresting the DVD's stars, including a man accused of carrying out contract killings, and created its own video, *Keep Talking*, to encourage future witnesses to come forward.

Stop Fucking Snitching was produced by Rodney Bethea, a 33-year-old barber and entrepreneur. I met him in his small West Baltimore store, One Love Underground, which pulls double duty as a barbershop and a boutique from which he sells his own line of urban fashions. Bethea told me the authorities and media had misinterpreted the DVD. It was not intended to encourage violence against witnesses, he said; he had simply set out to make a freestyle documentary, and snitching happened to emerge as a major theme. He also said that the term snitch has a very specific meaning on the streets and in the video. "They are referring to people that are engaged in illegal activities, making a profit from it, and then when it comes time for the curtains to close—you do the crime, you do the time—now no one wants to go to jail," he told me, pulling on his goatee. "That is considered a snitch. The old lady that lives on the block that call the police because guys are selling drugs in front of her house, she's not a snitch, because she is what would be considered a civilian."

Bethea believes there is a double standard—and perhaps a tinge of racism—in law enforcement's criticism of the "Stop snitching" culture. "When you think about it, I mean, who likes a snitch?" he said. "The government don't like a snitch. Their word for it is treason. What is the penalty for treason?" He pointed out that the police have their own code of silence, and that officers who break it by reporting police misconduct are stigmatized in much the same way as those who break the code of silence on the street.

Bethea's argument has a certain elegance. But the distinction he draws between the drug dealer who flips and the civilian who is just trying to get dealers off her stoop has ceased to mean much. Just ask the Dawsons. Or Edna McAbier, a community activist who tried to clean up drugs in her North Baltimore neighborhood. The local chapter of the Bloods considered blowing her head off with a shotgun but settled for firebombing her house, in January 2005—not long after *Stop Fucking Snitching* made news. McAbier escaped with her life, and her house was not badly damaged; those responsible received long prison sentences. But though the gang members didn't succeed in killing her, they did silence her: She left Baltimore out of fear for her safety. And the city got the message: If you break the code, you are in danger—even if you are a "civilian."

*****

By the time of the McAbier firebombing, John Dowery was starting to reap the rewards of his decision to testify in the state's prosecution of Tracy Love and Tamall Parker. His own trial had been postponed indefinitely. He had been released from home confinement, his drug-treatment program was going well, and he had started working.

So far, Baier had kept Dowery's name out of the investigative records, referring to him simply as "a Federal Suspect" and "the Source" so the state would not have to disclose him as a witness until closer to the trial date. He had also deferred taking a taped statement from Dowery, out of concern for his safety. These were sound precautions: On several occasions, prosecutors have intercepted "kites"—letters from a defendant, smuggled out of jail—detailing the prosecution's witness list and instructing friends or relatives to "talk" to those on it. But Baier could not keep Dowery's name a secret forever. Sooner or later, the government would have to tell defense lawyers that he was going to testify. In the meantime, suspicions about Dowery had already begun to circulate in the neighborhood. "Somebody approached me saying 'Yeah, you snitching on us,'" he told Baier.

The case against Love and Parker languished. A trial was set for early April 2005 and then postponed until May, and then postponed again, and then again—seven times in all. In Baltimore, as in most major U.S. cities, the large number of cases and the shortage of judges, courtrooms, and lawyers make such delays common. Some cases have been postponed more than 30 times and have dragged on for more than five years. And each postponement increases the risk that witnesses who were cooperative will cease to be so— that they will move and leave no forwarding address, change their stories, genuinely forget facts, or turn up dead. "The defense attorneys play this game," says Brian Matulonis, the lieutenant in charge of Baltimore's Homicide Operations Squad. "If the witness is not there, they are ready to go. If the witness is there, they ask for a postponement."

On May 20, 2005, Baier finally took a taped statement from Dowery. It was delivered to defense lawyers in June. Soon afterward, Dowery got a phone call from Love.

"That's fucked, man. Why you gonna do me like that?" the defendant seethed.

"I said I didn't know what he was talking about," Dowery would tell the jurors during the trial. "I was testifying the whole time. But I just act like I didn't know what he was talking about."

A few weeks later, Love called Dowery again. "He like, 'Man, other guy, he say he ain't gonna testify. What about you?'"

Dowery again played dumb. "I say, 'Man, he lied. I don't know whatcha talking about. You cool.'" Love seemed satisfied. "It was, like, a friendlier conversation the second time," Dowery would testify.

Dowery was nervous about the calls and about becoming known in the neighborhood as a snitch. But he didn't believe he was in immediate danger. The trial kept getting pushed back. Summer gave way to fall. Then came the morning when two men met him at his front door with a gun.

*****

One of Jessamy's primary weapons against witness intimidation is her office's witness-assistance program. Unlike the federal witness-protection program—the one most people know about from the movies—Baltimore's program can't provide marshals to guard witnesses around the clock for years. It can't offer witnesses a new identity in some distant city. Instead, the Baltimore program—run by a staff of two, with an annual budget of $500,000—tries to get witnesses out of harm's way by putting them in low-budget hotels that serve as temporary safe houses. The average stay is 90 days. The program also helps witnesses relocate permanently, generally within Maryland, providing a security deposit or first month's rent, moving costs, and vouchers for food and transportation. If necessary, it helps with job placement and drug treatment.

In most cases, this is enough to keep witnesses safe. Few Baltimore drug gangs have much reach beyond a couple of blocks, let alone outside the city. Still, many witnesses refuse the help. Almost a third of the 255 witnesses whom prosecutors referred to the program last year did not even come to an initial meeting. Of the 176 who did, only 36 entered safe housing. "Many of these people have never left their neighborhood," says Heather Courtney, a witness-assistance coordinator. "A lot of people can't handle it. They just can't be out of that neighborhood. That is all they know."

Even after the shooting, Dowery did not want to leave East Baltimore. He had spent his whole life there. His entire family—aunts, uncles, cousins—lived nearby, most on or near Bartlett. This included many of his nine children. In a neighborhood of absentee fathers, Dowery doted on his kids. Two of them lived with him and Yolanda. And he tried to stay involved in the lives of the others.

Eventually the witness coordinators prevailed upon Yolanda, who in turn convinced Dowery that they should leave. After less than two weeks in a hotel, Dowery, Yolanda, and their five-year-old daughter moved to a house outside the city. Most of his relatives remained in the old neighborhood.

*****

The trial of Tracy Love and Tamall Parker for the murder of James Wise began on January 26, 2006, in the cramped courtroom of Baltimore Circuit Judge Sylvester Cox. During opening arguments, Christopher Nosher, the boyish assistant state's attorney prosecuting the case, appeared confident. Although Judge Cox had barred any reference to the shooting attack on Dowery, ruling that the defendants had not been definitively linked to the incident, Dowery would be allowed to testify about the phone calls from Love. For Nosher, this was a coup: jurors can be instructed to interpret a threat against a witness as "consciousness of guilt." Evidence of intimidation can also help juries understand why witnesses may back up on the stand.

Nosher had another reason to be confident: He knew that all of his witnesses would show. John Craddock, the man who had caught three numbers of the Lexus's license plate, had never wavered during the long pretrial process. Bassett, Jay's accomplice, had been convicted of his drug charges and was serving a seven-year sentence, so he wasn't going anywhere. And both Dowery and Doris Dickerson had remained cooperative.

In this respect, the trial was unusual. Witnesses so commonly miss court dates in Baltimore, whether from fear or irresponsibility, that Jessamy's office has resorted to arresting them just to compel their appearance. Jessamy acknowledges that arresting witnesses is hardly ideal—it tends to make them hostile to the prosecution and more likely to back up, and it further sours police-community relations. "But if you've done everything you can to get them to come voluntarily, then you do what you have to do," she says.

That afternoon, Dowery took the stand. He had always been skinny, but in the witness box he looked gaunt. His long, loose-fitting black shirt covered a colostomy bag, a result of the October 2005 shooting. Dowery spoke in a deep, soft voice as Nosher walked him through the events he witnessed on the day James Wise was murdered.

As he began his testimony, a commotion electrified the hallway outside. Several friends of Boo-Boo and Moo-Moo tried to rush into the courtroom carrying cell phones, which they held near their thighs, fingers resting on the camera buttons. Detective Baier was also in the hall, awaiting his turn to testify. He spotted the cell phones and stepped in front of the men, barring their path to the door. "Whoa, you can't come in here," he told them. "It's a closed courtroom." This was not true, but it kept the men from entering. Then, for laughs, Baier took out his own cell phone and took pictures of them.

Incidents of intimidation at the courthouse are no longer aberrations. Gang members sometimes line the courthouse steps, forming a gantlet that witnesses and jurors must walk through. Family members of defendants have come to court wearing Stop Snitching

T-shirts and hats. In a Pittsburgh case last year, a key (though hostile) prosecution witness came to court in Stop Snitching gear. He was ejected because his garb was considered intimidating to other witnesses, and without his testimony, the district attorney dropped the charges. At the close of a Baltimore trial two years ago, jurors were so frightened of the defendants and of gang members in the gallery that the forewoman refused to read the guilty verdict aloud; so did another juror asked to do so by the judge. The judge eventually read the verdict herself and, as a precaution, had sheriff's deputies accompany the jurors out of the building.

*****

Dowery endured a withering cross-examination, but he escaped the stand largely undamaged. Nosher's two other eyewitnesses did not. Dickerson developed sudden memory loss, claiming not to recall key details of what she had seen. Then Love's lawyer got her to admit she was probably high on heroin when the shooting took place. As for Bassett, he backed up right away. "First, I would like to say I don't appreciate being here against my will," he said in a high, squeaky voice that seemed incongruous coming from a man of his bulk. He went on to say that he never saw Jay after the robbery, never saw anyone shoot Jay, never saw a white Lexus at the end of Bonaparte, and never told Baier that he had seen any of these things. When Nosher showed him the photo lineup he had signed, in which he had identified Parker as the shooter, Bassett said that Baier "basically picked the dude out for me." What about his taped statement? He had been forced to make it, he said. "I gave them the plot of the story; they put their own characters with it."

The jury heard from other prosecution witnesses: Craddock talked about seeing the Lexus and part of the license tag. Baier testified about the investigation, stating that he had not coerced Bassett or helped him pick photos from the lineup. A telecommunications expert testified about the location of Love's cell phone. Video from the warehouse surveillance camera was shown to the jury. The defense put on no witnesses of its own. But after two days of deliberation, the jury announced that it could not reach a unanimous verdict. Judge Cox was forced to declare a mistrial.

*****

At first, the prosecutors planned to retry the case. But over the summer, the federal government decided to take over. (With Dowery's cooperation, it had already been working on a case against Love, Parker, and James Dinkins, a man police believe was involved in Dowery's shooting.) In late August, Parker, Love, and Dinkins were indicted on federal charges of conspiracy to distribute heroin. As of this writing, the trial is scheduled to begin in late March.

Federal prosecutions are one method cities are using to combat witness intimidation. A law passed by Congress last December explicitly makes witness intimidation in a state case grounds for federal prosecution. Rod Rosenstein, the U.S. attorney for Maryland, says the federal government has a big advantage over the states in breaking through the code of silence: leverage. Federal sentencing guidelines provide for long prison terms and, unlike the state system, do not allow for probation or parole. "We don't appeal to their sense of civility and morality," Rosenstein says. "We get a hammer over their heads. They realize that cooperating is the only way they can get out from under these hefty federal sentences."

Some states are looking to bring their laws into line with federal practices. The Maryland law Jessamy helped pass elevates witness intimidation from a misdemeanor to a felony punishable by a minimum of five years. It also allows prosecutors to introduce a witness's prior statements even if the witness isn't at the trial, if they can provide "clear and convincing evidence" that the defendant was responsible for the witness's absence. Still, Jessamy isn't satisfied. The new law excludes child-abuse and domestic-violence cases. And rarely can prosecutors obtain the kind of evidence of intimidation it requires. Even when they can, Jessamy says, trying to persuade judges to apply the law "is like pouring water on a stone."

Cities are also pushing to increase funding for witness assistance. The federal law passed in December allows the U.S. attorney general to dispense grants to states for witness protection. But Congress appropriated only $20 million annually for these grants through 2010. By contrast, a bill that Representative Elijah Cummings of Maryland introduced two years ago would have provided $90 million annually to support state witness-assistance programs; that bill died in committee. Since the start of the new congressional session, in January, several bills to strengthen the protection of witnesses in state cases have been introduced; as of this writing, they are all still in committee.

Federal prosecutions, new laws, more money—these are the blunt instruments of policy-makers. They might chip away at the edges of the problem. But to really reduce witnesses' reluctance to participate in the judicial process will require something beyond the abilities of cops and courts: a cultural transformation in America's inner cities. In Philadelphia, Boston, and Washington, D.C., authorities have tried to prohibit the sale of Stop Snitching clothing (they succeeded in Washington). But there is no indication that criminalizing a fashion and political statement will alter the underlying sentiment. Leonard Hamm, a long-serving Baltimore police officer who returned to head the city's department in 2004 after an eight-year absence, sees the problem this way: "I think that the community is going to have to get sick and tired of the shootings and the killings and the memorial services. And all we can do as police is be there when they say they are ready." But what if the community is never ready? Many inner-city neighborhoods have no community. The institutions that once held them together—the churches, the associations, the businesses—are shells of what they were, if they exist at all.

*****

For Dowery, the mistrial was unnerving. Yet in some ways it was better than a guilty verdict. He was still planning to testify for the federal government against Love, Parker, and Dinkins. This would further postpone his gun case. In addition, as a federal witness, he began receiving some token financial assistance from the FBI.

Dowery's family would visit him in the suburbs. Still, he missed them, and he missed his friends. So he occasionally sneaked back to the old neighborhood for a day or two, usually staying with his mother and trying to keep a low profile. In the spring, he proudly watched his two eldest sons graduate from high school. And he didn't want to skip Thanksgiving at his aunt's house, on Bartlett Avenue. "He was tired of hiding out," his aunt, Joyce Garner, told me.

On Thanksgiving night, more than 20 members of Dowery's family gathered for a feast. Dowery was in a good mood, reminiscing about old times. Garner remembers that he came to talk to her as she was cooking. She asked if he was worried about being back in the neighborhood. "He just talked about the Lord to us and gave us a big hug and said, 'God's got it,'" she recalled. Toward the end of dinner, Dowery excused himself. He wanted to run across the street to buy a pack of cigarettes and have a beer.

The sign over its beige stucco facade calls the Kozy Korner a "Cut-Rate & Lounge." Two doors separate the bar from the street. The first opens onto a grungy vestibule where a cashier sells beer and liquor from behind a bulletproof window. The second is locked; customers must be buzzed through. Once inside, they are greeted by a dark, narrow room. A Baltimore Ravens poster is affixed to one wall. A rendering of the Last Supper, with a black Jesus and black disciples, decorates the other. Three video gambling machines flash and hum.

When Dowery arrived, a dozen other patrons were packed into the space. He recognized one of them: a former girlfriend called Toot. They chatted inside the doorway while he smoked and sipped a beer. Just after 10 o'clock, the door opened, and two men entered. This time Dowery's sixth sense—the feeling that had told him to turn around on his porch that morning a year earlier—failed him. One of the men drew a gun, pointed it at Dowery's head, and fired. Then the other did the same. This time, the doctors couldn't save him.

And although the bar was crowded, no one has come forward to say they saw a thing. It's just another homicide in inner-city America, with no suspects, and no witnesses.

■ READING AND WRITING

1. Kahn's article offers different perspectives on what "snitching" means. How do the various groups represented in Kahn's piece—police and prosecutors, the public, suspects and witnesses—view the term differently? How do you define "snitching"?
2. Kahn explores the "Stop Snitching" subculture among poor, mostly black residents of Baltimore. What, according to the article, led to the development of this subculture? What other kinds of communities or groups impose codes of silence on their members? How do these groups justify their codes?
3. The dilemma of whether to report a crime and cooperate with police relates directly to the question of what we, as citizens and neighbors, owe our communities. But it is complicated by other issues—including personal safety and family obligations—as the stories of John Dowery, Jr., Edna McAbier, and the Dawson family clearly show. At what point do our obligations to the health of society cancel out what we owe to those closest to us? Does Kahn suggest an answer to this question?

■ DEVELOPING LONGER RESPONSES

4. Although he doesn't present a clear claim, Kahn does imply an argument. Write a brief essay in which you summarize Kahn's position and explain how he develops and presents his argument implicitly.

■ RESEARCH AND WRITING PROJECTS

1. Aristotle, Descartes, Hume, Spinoza, Hegel, and Coleridge (to name a few in the Western tradition) each developed theories of imagination as part of their philosophical projects. Create an annotated bibliography of primary texts that focus on theories of imagination. Your bibliography should consist of at least six texts from six different authors (only two of whom should come from the list above) and should include an introduction that summarizes and contextualizes your research.

2. Using the essays by Richtel, Carr, and Cascio as starting points, further research the questions they raise about the effects that developing technologies are having on abilities to think and learn. Find at least four other reliable sources that explore these issues and use them to develop an argument about the consequences of the further integration of various technologies into our intellectual and imaginative lives.

3. Consider how "snitching"—breaking some cultural code of silence to inform on those who commit criminal acts—relates to the larger ideas of witnessing, altruism, and response discussed in "Am I My Brother's Keeper?" and "Is Altruism Possible?" Using the library, find at least three sources (*not* dictionaries or encyclopedias) that define "witnessing" and "altruism." Based on your research and on the Wiesel, Lichtenberg, and Kahn essays, think about the ways that snitching relates to or contradicts these concepts and compose a definitional argument in which you address the following question: Is snitching—even with its negative connotations of betrayal—a form of altruism? Your paper should make use of at least three sources in addition to the readings in this chapter.

4. Jeremy Kahn's "The Story of a Snitch" inspired lively discussion in the mainstream press and the blogosphere. This response was part of an even larger debate about relationship between law enforcement and African Americans that goes back to this country's founding. Kahn makes small references to this history to explain why some black communities are reluctant to work with police. What is the source of this suspicion, mistrust, and fear of law enforcement? Do these feelings seem justified? How can law enforcement agencies overcome this problem? Use the

library's resources to explore these questions. One course of inquiry you may wish to consider is the government's use of questionable practices and false eyewitness testimony to infiltrate and break up activist groups during the civil rights movement.

5. Using Elie Wiesel's claim that we are morally obligated to turn knowledge of injustice into responsibility and, sometimes, into action, develop an argument that proposes a response to an issue raised by one of the other readings in this textbook. Your instructor may require that you conduct further research to complete your essay.

2 Food for Thought

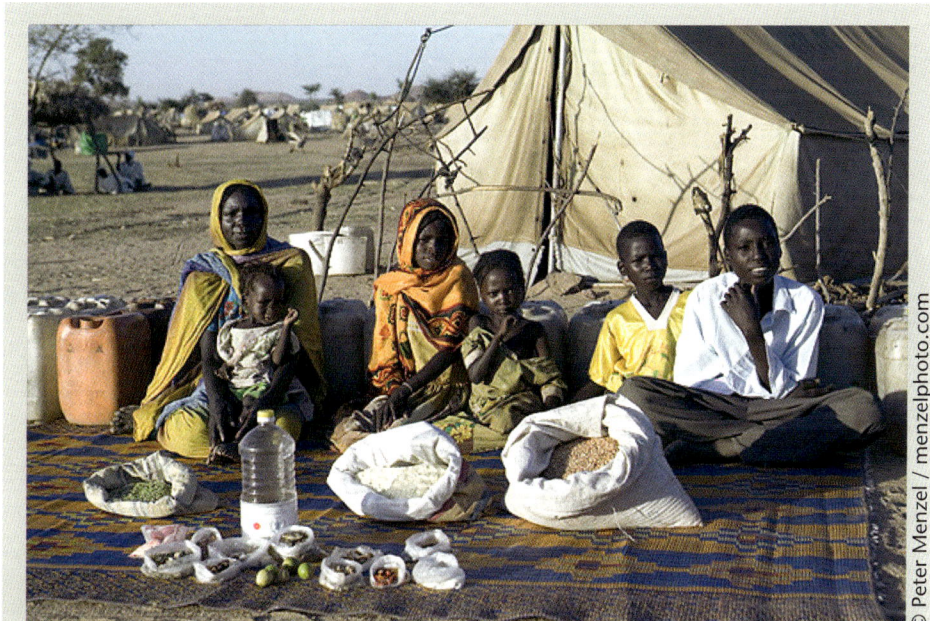

IMAGE 2.1 shows one of the families featured in *Hungry Planet: What the World Eats* by Peter Menzel and Faith D'Aluisio. This 2005 book presents a photographic study of families from around the world, revealing what they eat during the course of one week. The Aboubakar family, pictured here, of the Breidjing Camp in Chad spent 685 CFA Francs, or $1.23, for a week's worth of food. Think about the rhetorical effects of this photograph. How does it make you feel? What does it make you think? What arguments does it make? Compare this image with those on pages 88 and 143.

While it may be true that we are *what* we eat, the writers in this chapter present compelling evidence that we are *how* we eat, too. These academics, poets, journalists, and activists argue that the food choices we make—individually, as communities, and as a nation—can affect everything from our health to the health of the planet, from the livelihood and culture of billions of people to economic and political stability around the world. Chew on that for a while.

Elisabeth Townsend writes about food, wine, and travel for The Boston Globe *and other newspapers and magazines. She conducted the following interview with primatologist Richard Wrangham in 2005 for* Gastronomica: The Journal of Food and Culture. *Wrangham's book* Catching Fire: How Cooking Made Us Human—The Cooking Ape *was a working title—was published in 2009.*

excerpts from
THE COOKING APE Elisabeth Townsend

Primatologist Richard Wrangham might be best known for the 1996 book he coauthored with writer Dale Peterson, *Demonic Males: Apes and the Origins of Human Violence,* where he used his research on intergroup aggression in chimpanzees to reflect on combative male behavior. Wrangham's twenty-five years of research have always been based on a deep interest in human evolution and behavior, and recently he's shifted his focus to the evolution of cooking in humans.

An anthropology professor at Harvard University, Wrangham, fifty-six, was first mesmerized by Africa when he spent a year working in Kafue National Park in western Zambia before going to college. There, he assisted a research biologist in studying the behavior and ecology of the waterbuck, falling "in love with the excitement of finding out about African habitats and species." He's been back to Africa every year since then, with only one exception—the year his first son was born.

Though Wrangham has made his reputation explaining the similarities and differences across species in primate social organizations, he expects that his work on cooking will have the broadest impact because cooking affects many human behaviors—such as those associated with food choice, familial relationships, and food production that can satisfy a huge world population. His favorite part of the day is when he can steal an hour from teaching to analyze chimp data or to work on his new book, *The Cooking Ape.* But Wrangham is happiest at his Ugandan research site, enjoying those quiet moments alone with the chimps, watching their relationships and catching up on the social gossip. He hasn't eaten a mammal since 1976 because of his profound empathy for the ones he has enjoyed and spent so much time with in the wild. Occasionally, his vegetarianism makes life a bit harder, as when a host offers him meat, but

Richard Wrangham
Photo by Jim Harrison

he'll never turn down seconds on a chocolate roulade. Wrangham spoke from his home in Weston, Massachusettes.

ET: *What prompted your research into how cooking affected human evolution?*
RW: As a Primatologist, I am often asked to think about human evolution. I sat one evening in my living room preparing a lecture for the next day, thinking about the standard story that involved hunting being important around two million years ago. As I was staring at the fire, I had an almost ghostly experience where I just allowed my eyes to be drawn deep into the fire. I could feel around me the presence of hominids, from up to one million years ago, sitting in the African bush.

I started thinking about the fact that fire is something that has been on the Earth ever since there's been plant vegetation and how when I'm in the bush there is no way that I'm going to spend a night without sitting next to a fire. I was thinking about the impact of fire on the "cookability" of food.

Then I thought, "Well, would there really have been a fire for our early ancestors—a million years ago, say?"

I realized I didn't know the answer to the question. But I also realized that it was extremely difficult to imagine that they did not have cooking, because even as long as 1,500,000 years ago humans looked incredibly similar from the neck down to humans living today. Even our heads are very similar—though we have larger brains and we don't have quite as big a mouth or teeth as they did. So surely, if those million-year-old ancestors were generally like us in the size and shape of their bodies, they should have been eating cooked food. After all, cooking has this huge impact. It changes so much about how we relate to the natural environment: it changes the ease with which we digest the food; it changes the availability of calories; and it changes the distribution of food.

If cooking has such a big evolutionary impact, in other words, and we haven't changed much, then there are only two possibilities. Either we somehow managed to adopt cooking without it affecting us very much, which would be very mysterious, or it happened so early that cooking had already been adopted by a million years ago.

ET: *What's an example of how changes in the food supply affected primates and how that led you to think cooking had a significant impact on humans?*
RW: If you compare chimpanzees to gorillas, they eat very similar things. They both like to eat fruits when fruits are available. They both eat more leaves and stems when there aren't many fruits available. But there's one relatively small difference when there's a shortage of fruit, gorillas will switch entirely to eating leaves and stems, whereas chimpanzees absolutely insist on finding their daily ration of fruits before they go bulk up on leaves and stems. That's why gorillas can live entirely without fruit—in the mountains of Uganda, for instance—whereas we don't know of any place where chimpanzees can live entirely without access to fruit.

The small difference in food supply between chimps and gorillas can account for the fact that the gorillas are three to four times the body size of chimpanzees and that they live in more-stable groups. Therefore, gorillas have an entirely different set of sexual relationships, with males being enormously bigger than females, and so on. This is just one example where a relatively small difference in the food supply creates a big difference in the way that two species look and behave. And to shift from eating raw food to eating cooked food is a much bigger change!

ET: *How did cooking change calorie intake and thus the human species?*
RW: Amazingly, we still don't have a good picture of the most important ways in which cooking changes food. There are different effects on plant foods and meat, though. One impact on plant foods is probably to increase digestibility. That means that our food has a relatively low proportion of indigestible materials; in modern surveys you see the 10 percent or less of what we eat is indigestible plant material (fiber, in other words). Whereas in chimpanzees, for instance, fiber is over 30 percent, which therefore seems a reasonable guess for what it might have been like in our raw-food-eating ancestors. Well, if we ate 30 percent fiber, compared with 10 percent now, that 20 percent of the food our ancestors were eating was just bulk material passing through the gut. So, they simply absorbed less energy.

That 20 percent figure is a lot. When we compare the actual rate of energy expenditure in human foragers, which is between 1.5 and 2.2 times the basal metabolic rate, as compared with 1.4 times for chimpanzees, we're getting a lot of extra energy from somewhere compared to the chimpanzees. Where are we getting it from? I think it's because the food that humans are eating is more digestible. Instead of spending all day with our guts holding a high proportion of indigestible material, we're able to have a higher continuous stream of calories going through our guts.

What's the result? Maybe, it explains why humans used so much energy, starting around 1.9 million years ago. First, that's when we got our bigger body, made by the greater amount of energy. Second, it means that we can have a relatively large proportion of expensive organs, such as brains (they're expensive in the sense of using calories at a particularly high rate). For a long time people have been interested in the notion that, since the brain is unusually expensive, our ancestors needed to have some way of getting more energy in order to afford having a bigger brain. At 1.9 million years ago, you have arguably the largest increase in brain size in evolution. Third, there's the opportunity for longer travel distance per day because you just got more energy to put into traveling. Chimpanzees are quite long-distance travelers at 2.5, 3, 4.5 kilometers a day, but humans, males in particular, are traveling 9, 10, 15, 20 kilometers a day—a lot more than chimps.

This extra energy probably comes from the fact that, as a result of cooking, we're able to eat a relatively compact food that is full of calories. And then at the same time, of course, the food has become softer, and that enables us to have smaller teeth and smaller jaws, a flatter face, and less prognathous jaws. At the same time we, in fact, have smaller guts and a shift in the arrangement of our guts that reflects the fact that we're eating food that is relatively highly digestible. So we have long small intestines, the part of the gut that absorbs the products of digestion, and we have short large intestines where fermentation goes on when you retain food that takes twenty-four hours or more to be fermented under the action of bacteria. We have relatively little food that comes in that needs to be fermented. All of these changes are easily explained by the adoption of cooking.

ET: *How much did our brains and bodies change as a result of eating cooked food?*
RW: The standard estimate is that female bodies increased in weight by about 60 percent around the 1.9-million-year mark. So, if you compare the body size of about 125 pounds for an average woman with the average range of 70 to 80 pounds for a chimp, it's really quite a big increase. And the brain size is going up…it might be 60 percent.

ET: *You've said that cooking and meat eating are the only two proposals for what transformed the ape into a human. Why couldn't the changes just be from eating more raw meat rather than cooking?*
RW: We don't know too much about what it's like to chew raw meat because people don't do it. But chimpanzees are a good model because they have teeth that are just about the same size in relation to their bodies as those of our early ancestors 1.9 million years ago. When we look at chimpanzees eating raw meat, it turns out that they're eating it so slowly that it would just take a tremendous amount of time to rely on eating nothing but raw meat. And that would be a problem.

Think about how many calories our early ancestors would have needed at that stage, estimated at somewhere in the low 2000s. This would take five to six hours a day of simply chewing *without* going out and finding more meat, cutting it up, and looking after your babies and so on. And they would have had to develop some kind of tooth arrangement that was sharp and enabled them to chop it up quickly and swallow it in the manner of a carnivore.

It just seems very unlikely that, at any time since 1.9 million years ago, our ancestors were chewing for half the day, because animals that chew a lot have got deep jaws and robust bones in the mouth to accommodate the stresses of the chewing. That's not what you see—our ancestors' jaws have been built relatively lightly ever since 1.9 million years ago. So, it's not that I think that meat is unimportant; it probably was eaten a lot. It's just that to become important it had to be tenderized to allow it to be eaten easily. The tenderizing could have begun in a physical way by hammering it with stones, maybe, but cooking would have solved the problem much more efficiently.

ET: *When did humans learn how to master fire and then use it for cooking?*
RW: No one knows for sure. But there is such good evidence from caves in southern Europe that humans controlled fire by 400,000 years ago that essentially everyone accepts that fire was controlled by then. So the conservative view is that we started our control of fire then. The 800,000-year date recently published by Goren-Inbar and colleagues in *Science* (April, 2004) is perhaps the best evidence yet for an earlier date for fire. It's particularly nice support for the notion that control of fire must have started before we can see it, because around 800,000 years ago even less happened in human evolution than at 500,000 years ago. People rarely lived in caves before 400,000 years ago, so the remains of earlier campfires can't easily be found. But the more radical view, which seems right to me, is that bits and pieces of archaeological evidence for control of fire at earlier dates, all the way back to 1.9 million years ago, are right. In other words, I believe our species started to control fire at 1.9 million years ago.

Then, the question is, what's the relationship between control of fire and cooking? Some people imagine a period when our ancestors had fire but ate raw food. But, once we had control of fire, I think that we would have started cooking very soon, maybe within a week, maybe within ten generations—but waiting 1,000 or 10,000 or 100,000 years? It's unthinkable. Modern primates, such as monkeys in captivity, allow foods to cook in fires before they take them out. It's obviously just not a big cognitive step from controlling fire to cooking.

So, if humans were cooking by 800,000 years ago, it seems likely that they had been cooking since 1.9 million years ago, because that's when our modern frame evolved. Basically nothing happened in human evolution between 1.9 million years and 800,000 years ago to suggest any improvement in the diet—certainly nothing as radical as being able to shift from raw to cooked food.

ET: *Who was the first cook?*
RW: It was not fully human. It was one of these prehuman hominids around the 2-million-years-ago mark, living somewhere in Africa, perhaps an australopithecine or a species like Homo ergaster [an early form of Homo erectus].

Whenever cooking evolved, we've got this problem of how on earth did the first cook manage to solve the problem of getting to use fire and controlling it rather than running away from it.

One fantasy that I enjoy is the notion that there was something like the chimera that we now see in western Turkey. In western Turkey you've got a mountain, Mount Olympus, where there were several holes in the ground, quite small, just a foot or two across, with fire coming out of them. This fire has been going for at least 2,700 years, judging by the fact that Homer recorded its presence.

To call it permanent fire is too exaggerated, perhaps, but it's said that an earthquake was a cause of some release of gas that's been seeping out ever since then and which has been burning all that time. There are several places around the world where you get little patches of permanent fire burning like this. So it doesn't seem unreasonable to imagine that there was some permanent fire in Africa somewhere.

We know that chimpanzees can learn to be happy with fire. Kanzi is a captive Bonobo (pygmy chimpanzee) who goes for walks with Sue Savage-Rumbaugh in the forests of Georgia (United States). When she asks him to go get firewood and to use matches to light a fire and then to cook up some sausages, he does so. These things are not that difficult for a species as big-brained as a chimpanzee.

So, it's relatively easy to imagine an australopithecine who keeps coming back, sees these flames roaring out of the ground, and starts playing with them. Then it wouldn't be long before they see what happens to one of the roots they have been eating when it is heated by the fire. That may not be the way it happened, but at least it gives a sense of the possibility of the transition. You don't have to be fully human, I think, to imagine that you could tame fire. So, if indeed you were prehuman and started being able to use fire, then that knowledge could be passed on from generation to generation in the many, many years before these species would have actually been able to make fire.

Photo courtesy of shutterstock

ET: *How do you imagine they were cooking?*

RW: The cooking would have been very, very simple. Once you've got a campfire, then it's the way that people cook nowadays. In the bush the main plant food would be roots— African versions of carrots or potatoes often dug from the edge of swamps or lakes. Many would be tough and leathery, pretty nasty in the best of times, but improved enormously by being heated. You'd just rest these on the coals next to the dying flames. After twenty minutes and occasionally turning them, the roots change from something that is extremely fibrous into something that is a lot softer and easier to eat.

Very often the way that people eat meat is they throw a small animal on the flames and that singes the hair off. Then they cut it up. We know that at 1.9 million years they were capable of cutting meat up because there are cut marks [made by stone knives] on fossil animal bones that go back 2.5 million years. So they could have laid strips of meat onto sticks above the fire. Well, maybe it would have taken a little time before that happened. But it doesn't seem very difficult if they had already been cutting up meat for 500,000 years to imagine that they could put small chunks on the embers next to the fire or next to the flames themselves. And all you need to do is heat meat to 170° Fahrenheit, and it reduces enormously the problems that make meat so difficult to eat when it's raw, which is the toughness. Heat coagulates the collagen fibers that make meat tough and turns them brittle. Suddenly, you've got something that you can eat pretty quickly.

ET: *How did humans make the transition from cooking over an outdoor fire to hearths and then to earth ovens?*

RW: No one knows. I imagine that the way things started is that the first kind of controlled fire would be simply sticks on the flat earth. Then at some point you'd start digging a little pit and you might surround it with some stones that would protect it against the wind a little bit further, and maybe other ways I don't know about making the fire more efficient.

An earth oven is a little hole that has been dug in the ground. Hot stones are put into the hole, and the food that you want to cook is put in with those hot stones. Then you stop the hole with earth, and the heat from the stones combined with the moisture of the earth leads to a sort of steaming effect, and you get a rather nice, gentle, slow cooking. That's practiced nowadays in various parts of the world, such as New Guinea and India.

There are other complicated kinds of hearth arrangements in sites in southern Europe, for instance in France in Pech de l'Azé II, that go back 250,000 to 300,000 years. At the entrance you have one kind of hearth arrangement, rings of stones where probably there was some kind of lighting arrangement to scare off predators from coming into the cave. And then inside the cave, in addition to something like an earth oven, there was apparently a cooking area more than a yard across, indicated by flat stones whose red and black colors indicate repeated burning.

But to assume that earth ovens start very quickly seems to me to be an unnecessarily optimistic assumption. Earth ovens look like a pretty complicated kind of technical achievement. I had assumed that this was just a signal that cooking had been going on so long at the point that they had been able to devise various rather ingenious ways of making cooked food even nicer.

ET: *How did cooking affect the social structure?*
RW: I think the social structure is a really interesting question because this is in many ways the biggest gap in the way anybody has thought about cooking so far. Everyone's aware that cooking would have improved the quality of food, so it's not that big a deal to think about it affecting our energy and our teeth and so on. But there's been amazingly little thought given to this question of what cooking did to social structure.

My colleagues and I made the following argument in a paper that we wrote in 1999 that cooking lay at the base of human evolution: The huge problem that cooking presents is that it changes a species from feeding as it picks the food to forcing a species to keep its food for some time, which will be at least twenty minutes to probably several hours during the period when it is gathering it and going to cook it. That means for a period of time there is individual ownership, and once you have ownership, then there is the possibility of competition over those owned goods.

In other words, just as with any other animal where somebody gets a piece of food that is relatively valuable, others will try to pinch it. Female lions bring down the antelope; the male lion comes and takes it away. The low-ranking male chimp kills a monkey; the high-ranking chimp comes and takes it away. The female baboon digs for some roots; the male baboon watches, and just as she reaches to get the results of her labor, he says, "I'll take over, thank you." And in a similar way it seems impossible to imagine that when our ancestors first started cooking there wasn't pressure by which the hungry high-ranking individuals would not have taken advantage of the low-ranking individuals who had done all the hard work to get some meat or dig up the roots and get it cooked. And that problem seems to me to be really severe. We need to think about how we solved it.

ET: *How do you suppose humans solved this problem?*

RW: The human species is the only one, in all of the animals we know, in which there is a thing we call "sexual division of labor." I think it is a slight misnomer because it underestimates the extent to which there is a bias in favor of the male. It implies that the male and female are equal, doing equally well under the sexual division of labor. But women are always the ones that get to do the least favorite tasks, and women are the ones who predictably have to take responsibility for producing a meal in the evening.

Men are free to do what they want. A man can go off every day and hunt for three weeks and never get anything, and still he's going to get food, given to him by his wife in the form of a cooked meal when he returns in the evening. But if a woman goes off and tries to dig for food and never gets anything, she's in big trouble. A man knows that he can rely on a woman to produce food for him; a woman has nobody to rely on, she has to do it for herself.

So a woman is more like a chimpanzee, as it were: she is producing for herself, and then she has the problem of somebody who's taking some food away from her. A man is an entirely new species of animal, because a man is relying on others to feed him every evening. Now it's true that he will often produce foods that he will give to his wife, and the relationship can be beneficial. But some men don't. Some men are lousy producers, and they are still able to take advantage of the system. The problem is not so much why did men and women divide and then cooperate. We should be asking this question instead: "Why it is that men are able to get away without having to be responsible for their own food supply?"

ET: *Why aren't men responsible for their own food supply?*

RW: I put these two observations together: On the one hand, there's the fact that you know that there's going to be pressure to steal the food of low-ranking individuals. On the other hand, there's the fact that only in our species is there a sex that doesn't have to collect their own food every day. Among hunters and gatherers, men are able to get away with not feeding themselves. The solution is that males have developed a relationship with females in which they protect a female's food supply from everybody else in the community. And in exchange, she feeds him.

The way I imagine it working in the past was something like this. Around the ancient campfire you have females getting their own food. Then you find males who are coming back in the evening, having been unsuccessful in hunting or getting any other food. Maybe they were off chasing other women instead of trying to find honey. So now they've got nothing to eat, and they bully a female into giving them some of her food.

And that kind of social pressure creates a situation in which it pays every female to develop a friendly relationship with a male who will protect her from being bullied by a whole herd of males. Better to have one male to protect your food supply and predictably feed him, if he can keep everybody else off, than be a lone female who is exposed to the possibility of theft from many other individuals. The male is an effective protector of her food supply because he's part of a system of respect among males. In a sense, he pays other males to stay away because he's part of a food-getting system in which whenever he does get food, he shares it on a predictably culturally agreed equal basis with other males. So, all the males are in an arrangement whereby they agree not to interfere with each other, and the female is in a relationship with the male whereby he agrees to keep all the other males off. It seems to make sense.

ET: *How has cooking affected human life history—how fast we grow, for instance?*
RW: These are areas that still haven't been well explored. But of course one of the most dramatic things about human life history is the fact that we have children that are dependent. This is different from chimpanzees, for instance, where the infants are weaned at about the three- to five-year stage and then they're independent. The only way chimpanzees feed each other is through nursing.

Whereas with humans, the child is being fed until it's an early adolescent. Children make some contribution to the domestic work and food gathering and so on, but nevertheless, the net flow of energy is definitely from the parent to the child, not just until weaning but all the time until at least 10 to 12 years old. So, childhood (a period of economic dependency beyond weaning) is normally regarded as a special human feature.

And childhood is made possible by cooking, because a species that cooks can easily overproduce. A chimpanzee that spends six hours collecting and chewing her own food doesn't have time to collect extra food to give to her children. But a foraging woman can collect and cook enough food to feed her family. Instead of spending six hours a day eating, she spends only about one hour eating. That leaves enough time to gather and cook for others.

Then, earlier in the life span, for at least 20,000 years, babies have been given cooked mush so they can abandon nursing very early. The result is that the mother has less energetic strain on her body, so she's able to have a relatively quick interbirth interval of three to four years, whereas in chimpanzees it's more like five to six years. That is presumably because even though the women still have children with them, they're able to feed them by cooking and still get enough food themselves to return to a high rate of ovulation.

So, cooking gives us big families—dependent children, produced relatively quickly.

ET: *What effect does cooking have on the human mortality rate?*
RW: Well, it's very interesting that humans have a very low rate of mortality. If you compare humans and chimps, at every age humans are dying more slowly than chimpanzees. This is not because of predation, because most of the chimp populations have not been subject to predation. It's just something inherent about their bodies. The implication is that the immune system or other systems of defense are less effective in chimps than they are in humans. I don't want to suggest that this is well known, but I think it's an interesting speculation. Part of what's happening as humans are able to acquire more energy as a result of cooking and eating superior food may be that they're able to divert a proportion of that energy into the kinds of defenses that enable us to live a long time.

ET: *Are there problems with humans today eating too much or only meat?*
RW: Nowadays, people can eat a tremendous amount of meat because there's a lot of fat to go with it. But if you're eating meat from the wild, which has very little fat and is mostly

protein, then there is a problem with getting rid of the urea that is produced by digestion of excess protein. Urea poisoning can result. So too much meat can definitely be bad for you.

Of course, people in rich countries eat too much of everything. Indeed, the irony is that although cooked food has been so important for human evolution, raw food might be one of the healthiest diets for today. A raw-food diet is possible in rich countries today because of our low level of physical activity, the high agricultural quality of foods that go into a modern raw-food diet, and the extensive processing that makes raw foods palatable and easily digested. Even so, it takes a tremendous amount of determination to stick to a raw-food diet, because you'll feel hungry so much of the time. If you can do it, however, you'll bring your caloric intake nicely down, and maybe you'll have the philosophical satisfaction of imagining what the lives of our prehuman ancestors were like in those distant days before cooking was invented.

■ READING AND WRITING

1. Summarize the causal links that Wrangham lays out in his argument that mastering fire and using it to cook are what made humans who we are.
2. Wrangham uses a range of evidence—primary and secondary studies, empirical analysis, deductive and inductive reasoning—to convince his audiences of the radical change in the human species with the advent of cooking. Find examples of the different kinds of evidence Wrangham presents to support his claims and evaluate the strengths and weaknesses of his case.

■ USING RESEARCH

3. In his interview, Wrangham locates our evolution from ape to human in cooking and meat eating. Search online—either the internet or the databases available through the library—for responses to Wrangham's ideas and to his book *Catching Fire: How Cooking Made Us Human*. What kind of reaction has Wrangham's book generated? Do any readers find his claims controversial? Explain your response.

Poet, novelist, and essayist Wendell Berry has spent much of his life thinking, writing, and teaching about American life in general and agricultural life in particular. Berry wrote the following essay in 1989, and as it makes clear, he is an eloquent and determined critic of farm and food policies that continue to move Americans further away from the land—literally and figuratively.

THE PLEASURES OF EATING Wendell Berry

Many times, after I have finished a lecture on the decline of American farming and rural life, someone in the audience has asked, "What can city people do?"

"Eat responsibly," I have usually answered. Of course, I have tried to explain what I mean by that, but afterwards I have invariably felt there was more to be said than I had been able to say. Now I would like to attempt a better explanation.

I begin with the proposition that eating is an agricultural act. Eating ends the annual drama of the food economy that begins with planting and birth. Most eaters, however, are no longer aware that this is true. They think of food as an agricultural product, perhaps, but they do not think of themselves as participants in agriculture. They think of themselves as "consumers." If they think beyond that, they recognize that they are passive consumers. They buy what they want—or what they have been persuaded to want—within the limits of what they can get. They pay, mostly without protest, what they are charged. And they mostly ignore certain critical questions about the quality and the cost of what they are sold: How fresh is it? How pure or clean is it, how free of dangerous chemicals? How far was it transported, and what did transportation add to the cost? How much did manufacturing or packaging or advertising add to the cost? When the food product has been manufactured or "processed" or "precooked," how has that affected its quality or price or nutritional value?

Most urban shoppers would tell you that food is produced on farms. But most of them do not know what farms, or what kinds of farms, or where the farms are, or what knowledge of skills are involved in farming. They apparently have little doubt that farms will continue to produce, but they do not know how or over what obstacles. For them, then, food is pretty much an abstract idea—something they do not know or imagine—until it appears on the grocery shelf or on the table.

The specialization of production induces specialization of consumption. Patrons of the entertainment industry, for example, entertain themselves less and less and have become more and more passively dependent on commercial suppliers. This is certainly true also of patrons of the food industry, who have tended more and more to be mere consumers—passive, uncritical, and dependent. Indeed, this sort of consumption may be said to be one of the chief goals of industrial production. The food industrialists have by now persuaded millions of consumers to prefer food that is already prepared. They will grow, deliver, and cook your food for you and (just like your mother) beg you to eat it. That they do not yet offer to insert it, prechewed, into our mouth is only because they have found no profitable way to do so. We may rest assured that they would be glad to find such a way. The ideal industrial food consumer would be strapped to a table with a tube running from the food factory directly into his or her stomach.

Perhaps I exaggerate, but not by much. The industrial eater is, in fact, one who does not know that eating is an agricultural act, who no longer knows or imagines the connections between eating and the land, and who is therefore necessarily passive and uncritical—in short, a victim. When food, in the minds of eaters, is no longer associated with farming and with the land, then the eaters are suffering a kind of cultural amnesia that is misleading and dangerous. The current version of the "dream home" of the future involves "effortless" shopping from a list of available goods on a television monitor and heating precooked food by remote control. Of course, this implies and depends on, a perfect ignorance of the history of the food that is consumed. It requires that the citizenry should give up their hereditary and sensible aversion to buying a pig in a poke. It wishes to make the selling of pigs in pokes an honorable and glamorous activity. The dreams in this dream home will perforce know nothing about the kind or quality of this food, or where it came from, or how it was produced and prepared, or what ingredients, additives, and residues it contains—unless, that is, the dreamer undertakes a close and constant study of the food industry, in which case he or she might as well wake up and play an active an responsible part in the economy of food.

There is, then, a politics of food that, like any politics, involves our freedom. We still (sometimes) remember that we cannot be free if our minds and voices are controlled by someone else. But we have neglected to understand that we cannot be free if our food and its sources are controlled by someone else. The condition of the passive consumer of food is not a democratic condition. One reason to eat responsibly is to live free.

But if there is a food politics, there are also a food esthetics and a food ethics, neither of which is dissociated from politics. Like industrial sex, industrial eating has become a degraded, poor, and paltry thing. Our kitchens and other eating places more and more resemble filling stations, as our homes more and more resemble motels. "Life is not very interesting," we seem to have decided. "Let its satisfactions be minimal, perfunctory, and fast." We hurry through our meals to go to work and hurry through our work in order to "recreate" ourselves in the evenings and on weekends and vacations. And then we hurry, with the greatest possible speed and noise and violence, through our recreation—for what? To eat the billionth hamburger at some fast-food joint hellbent on increasing the "quality" of our life? And all this is carried out in a remarkable obliviousness to the causes and effects, the possibilities and the purposes, of the life of the body in this world.

One will find this obliviousness represented in virgin purity in the advertisements of the food industry, in which food wears as much makeup as the actors. If one gained one's whole knowledge of food from these advertisements (as some presumably do), one would not know that the various edibles were ever living creatures, or that they all come from the soil, or that they were produced by work. The passive American consumer, sitting down to a meal of pre-prepared or fast food, confronts a platter covered with inert, anonymous substances that have been processed, dyed, breaded, sauced, gravied, ground, pulped, strained, blended, prettified, and sanitized beyond resemblance to any part of any creature that ever lived. The products of nature and agriculture have been made, to all appearances, the products of industry. Both eater and eaten are thus in exile from biological reality. And the result is a kind of solitude, unprecedented in human experience, in which the eater may think of eating as, first, a purely commercial transaction between him and a supplier and then as a purely appetitive transaction between him and his food.

And this peculiar specialization of the act of eating is, again, of obvious benefit to the food industry, which has good reasons to obscure the connection between food and farming. It would not do for the consumer to know that the hamburger she is eating came from a steer who spent much of his life standing deep in his own excrement in a feedlot, helping to pollute the local streams, or that the calf that yielded the veal cutlet on her plate spent its life in a box in which it did not have room to turn around. And, though her sympathy for the slaw might be less tender, she should not be encouraged to meditate on the hygienic and biological implications of mile-square fields of cabbage, for vegetables grown in huge monocultures are dependent on toxic chemicals—just as animals in close confinements are dependent on antibiotics and other drugs.

The consumer, that is to say, must be kept from discovering that, in the food industry—as in any other industry—the overriding concerns are not quality and health, but volume and price. For decades now the entire industrial food economy, from the large farms and feedlots to the chains of supermarkets and fast-food restaurants has been obsessed with volume. It has relentlessly increased scale in order to increase volume in order (probably) to reduce costs. But as scale increases, diversity declines; as diversity declines, so does health; as health declines, the dependence on drugs and chemicals necessarily increases. As capital replaces labor, it does so by substituting machines, drugs, and chemicals for human workers and for the natural health and fertility of the soil. The food is produced by any means or any shortcuts that will increase profits. And the business of the cosmeticians of advertising is to persuade the consumer that food so produced is good, tasty, healthful, and a guarantee of marital fidelity and long life.

It is possible, then, to be liberated from the husbandry and wifery of the old household food economy. But one can be thus liberated only by entering a trap (unless one sees ignorance and helplessness as the signs of privilege, as many people apparently do). The trap is the ideal of industrialism: a walled city surrounded by valves that let merchandise in but no consciousness out. How does one escape this trap? Only voluntarily, the same way that one went in: by restoring one's consciousness of what is involved in eating; by reclaiming responsibility for one's own part in the food economy. One might begin with the illuminating principle of Sir Albert Howard's *The Soil and Health*, that we should understand "the whole problem of health in soil, plant, animal, and man as one great subject." Eaters, that is, must understand that eating takes place inescapably in the world, that it is inescapably an agricultural act, and how we eat determines, to a considerable extent, how the world is used. This is a simple way of describing a relationship that is inexpressibly complex. To eat responsibly is to understand and enact, so far as we can, this complex relationship. What can one do? Here is a list, probably not definitive:

1. Participate in food production to the extent that you can. If you have a yard or even just a porch box or a pot in a sunny window, grow something to eat in it. Make a

little compost of your kitchen scraps and use it for fertilizer. Only by growing some food for yourself can you become acquainted with the beautiful energy cycle that revolves from soil to seed to flower to fruit to food to offal to decay, and around again. You will be fully responsible for any food that you grow for yourself, and you will know all about it. You will appreciate it fully, having known it all its life.

2. Prepare your own food. This means reviving in your own mind and life the arts of kitchen and household. This should enable you to eat more cheaply, and it will give you a measure of "quality control": you will have some reliable knowledge of what has been added to the food you eat.

3. Learn the origins of the food you buy, and buy the food that is produced closest to your home. The idea that every locality should be, as much as possible, the source of its own food makes several kinds of sense. The locally produced food supply is the most secure, freshest, and the easiest for local consumers to know about and to influence.

4. Whenever possible, deal directly with a local farmer, gardener, or orchardist. All the reasons listed for the previous suggestion apply here. In addition, by such dealing you eliminate the whole pack of merchants, transporters, processors, packagers, and advertisers who thrive at the expense of both producers and consumers.

5. Learn, in self-defense, as much as you can of the economy and technology of industrial food production. What is added to the food that is not food, and what do you pay for those additions?

6. Learn what is involved in the best farming and gardening.

7. Learn as much as you can, by direct observation and experience if possible, of the life histories of the food species.

The last suggestion seems particularly important to me. Many people are now as much estranged from the lives of domestic plants and animals (except for flowers and dogs and cats) as they are from the lives of the wild ones. This is regrettable, for these domestic creatures are in diverse ways attractive; there is such pleasure in knowing them. And farming, animal husbandry, horticulture, and gardening, at their best, are complex and comely arts; there is much pleasure in knowing them, too.

It follows that there is great displeasure in knowing about a food economy that degrades and abuses those arts and those plants and animals and the soil from which they come. For anyone who does know something of the modern history of food, eating away from home can be a chore. My own inclination is to eat seafood instead of red meat or poultry when I am traveling. Though I am by no means a vegetarian, I dislike the thought that some animal has been made miserable in order to feed me. If I am going to eat meat, I want it to be from an animal that has lived a pleasant, uncrowded life outdoors, on bountiful pasture, with good water nearby and trees for shade. And I am getting almost as fussy about food plants. I like to eat vegetables and fruits that I know have lived happily and healthily in good soil, not the products of the huge, bechemicaled factory-fields that I have seen, for example, in the Central Valley of California. The industrial farm is said to have been patterned on the factory production line. In practice, it looks more like a concentration camp.

The pleasure of eating should be an extensive pleasure, not that of the mere gourmet. People who know the garden in which their vegetables have grown and know that the garden is healthy and remember the beauty of the growing plants, perhaps in the dewy first light of morning when gardens are at their best. Such a memory involves itself with the food and is one of the pleasures of eating. The knowledge of the good health of the garden relieves and frees and comforts the eater. The same goes for eating meat. The thought of the good pasture and of the calf contentedly grazing flavors the steak. Some, I know, will think of it as bloodthirsty or worse to eat a fellow creature you have known all its life. On the contrary, I think it means that you eat with understanding and with gratitude. A significant part of the pleasure of eating is in one's accurate consciousness of the lives and the world from which food comes. The pleasure of eating, then, may be the best available standard of our health. And this pleasure, I think, is pretty fully available to the urban consumer who will make the necessary effort.

I mentioned earlier the politics, esthetics, and ethics of food. But to speak of the pleasure of eating is to go beyond those categories. Eating with the fullest pleasure—pleasure, that is, that does not depend on ignorance—is perhaps the profoundest enactment of our connection with the world. In this pleasure we experience and celebrate our dependence and our gratitude, for we are living from mystery, from creatures we did not make and powers we cannot comprehend. When I think of the meaning of food, I always remember these lines by the poet William Carlos Williams, which seem to me merely honest:

> There is nothing to eat,
> seek it where you will,
> but the body of the Lord.
> The blessed plants
> and the sea, yield it
> to the imagination
> intact.

■ READING AND WRITING

1. What does Berry mean when he encourages people to "eat responsibly"?
2. Berry's famous line "eating is an agricultural act" has become a battle cry for farmers and food activists around the world. How do you define "eating"? How else might the term be defined to reflect the politics of food?
3. Berry concludes his piece with a list of seven concrete actions readers can take to become more responsible eaters. Revise this list to target a dorm-dwelling, college-aged audience. Think about, for instance, how you might make these suggestions more realistic for a person living in a dorm with little to no kitchen or garden spaces.

■ USING RESEARCH

4. Berry describes "patrons of the food industry" as "passive, uncritical, and dependent" for their lack of active questioning and involvement in food production. Do you know where your food comes from? Interview one of your food providers—your school's food contractor, the manager or chef at a restaurant that you frequently visit, your grocery's produce or meat manager, or a farmer at a farmers' market—and trace the steps a particular food item goes through to make it to you. Where was the item grown, processed, handled? How was it grown? By whom? How and how far was it transported? What route did your food travel to get to you? When necessary, conduct online research to fill in any gaps.

© Peter Menzel / menzelphoto.com

IMAGE 2.2 shows the Revis family of North Carolina, one of many families featured in *Hungry Planet: What the World Eats* by Peter Menzel and Faith D'Aluisio, a 2005 book that presents a photographic study of what people around the world eat during the course of one week. The Revises spent $341.98 on their week's worth of food, compared with the $1.23 spent by the Aboubakar family of the Breidjing Camp in Chad (see page 71) and the $68.53 spent by the Ahmed family of Cairo, Egypt (see page 143). What are the rhetorical effects of viewing these images as a group? What arguments might the authors have been trying to make by collecting photographs like these from around the world?

Robert Paarlberg is B.F. Johnson professor of political science at Wellesley College, an associate at Harvard University's Weatherhead Center for International Affairs, and author of Food Politics: What Everyone Needs to Know. *He wrote this essay for the May/June 2010 edition of* Foreign Policy *magazine.*

ATTENTION WHOLE FOOD SHOPPERS
Robert Paarlberg

From Whole Foods recyclable cloth bags to Michelle Obama's organic White House garden, modern eco-foodies are full of good intentions. We want to save the planet. Help local farmers. Fight climate change—and childhood obesity, too. But though it's certainly a good thing to be thinking about global welfare while chopping our certified organic onions, the hope that we can help others by changing our shopping and eating habits is being wildly oversold to Western consumers. Food has become an elite preoccupation in the West, ironically, just as the most effective ways to address hunger in poor countries have fallen out of fashion.

Helping the world's poor feed themselves is no longer the rallying cry it once was. Food may be today's cause célèbre, but in the pampered West, that means trendy causes like making food "sustainable"—in other words, organic, local, and slow. Appealing as that might sound, it is the wrong recipe for helping those who need it the most. Even our understanding of the global food problem is wrong these days, driven too much by the single issue of international prices. In April 2008, when the cost of rice for export had tripled in just six months and wheat reached its highest price in 28 years, a *New York Times* editorial branded this a "World Food Crisis." World Bank President Robert Zoellick warned that high food prices would be particularly damaging in poor countries, where "there is no margin for survival." Now that international rice prices are down 40 percent from their peak and wheat prices have fallen by more than half, we too quickly conclude that the crisis is over. Yet 850 million people in poor countries were chronically undernourished before the 2008 price spike, and the number is even larger now, thanks in part to last year's global recession. This is the real food crisis we face.

It turns out that food prices on the world market tell us very little about global hunger. International markets for food, like most other international markets, are used most heavily by the well-to-do, who are far from hungry. The majority of truly undernourished people—62 percent, according to the U.N. Food and Agriculture Organization—live in either Africa or South Asia, and most are small farmers or rural landless laborers living in the countryside of Africa and South Asia. They are significantly shielded from global price fluctuations both by the trade policies of their own governments and by poor roads and infrastructure. In Africa, more than 70 percent of rural households are cut off from the closest urban markets because, for instance, they live more than a 30-minute walk from the nearest all-weather road.

Poverty—caused by the low income productivity of farmers' labor—is the primary source of hunger in Africa, and the problem is only getting worse. The number of "food insecure" people in Africa (those consuming less than 2,100 calories a day) will increase 30 percent over the next decade without significant reforms, to 645 million, the U.S. Agriculture Department projects.

What's so tragic about this is that we know from experience how to fix the problem. Wherever the rural poor have gained access to improved roads, modern seeds, less expensive fertilizer, electrical power, and better schools and clinics, their productivity and their income have increased. But recent efforts to deliver such essentials have been undercut by deeply misguided (if sometimes well-meaning) advocacy against agricultural modernization and foreign aid.

In Europe and the United States, a new line of thinking has emerged in elite circles that opposes bringing improved seeds and fertilizers to traditional farmers and opposes linking those farmers more closely to international markets. Influential food writers, advocates, and celebrity restaurant owners are repeating the mantra that "sustainable food" in the future must be organic, local, and slow. But guess what: rural Africa already has such a system, and it doesn't work. Few smallholder farmers in Africa use any synthetic chemicals, so their food is *de facto* organic. High transportation costs force them to purchase and sell almost all of their food locally. And food preparation is painfully slow. The result is nothing to celebrate: average income levels of only $1 a day and a one-in-three chance of being malnourished.

If we are going to get serious about solving global hunger, we need to de-romanticize our view of pre-industrial food and farming. And that means learning to appreciate the modern, science-intensive, and highly capitalized agricultural system we've developed in the West. Without it, our food would be more expensive and less safe. In other words, a lot like the hunger-plagued rest of the world.

■ Original Sins

Thirty years ago, had someone asserted in a prominent journal or newspaper that the Green Revolution was a failure, he or she would have been quickly dismissed. Today the charge is surprisingly common. Celebrity author and eco-activist Vandana Shiva claims the Green Revolution has brought nothing to India except "indebted and discontented farmers." A 2002 meeting in Rome of 500 prominent international NGOs, including Friends of the Earth and Greenpeace, even blamed the Green Revolution for the rise in world hunger. Let's set the record straight.

The development and introduction of high-yielding wheat and rice seeds into poor countries, led by American scientist Norman Borlaug and others in the 1960s and '70s, paid huge dividends. In Asia these new seeds lifted tens of millions of small farmers out of desperate poverty and finally ended the threat of periodic famine. India, for instance, doubled its wheat production between 1964 and 1970 and was able to terminate all dependence on international food aid by 1975. As for indebted and discontented farmers, India's rural poverty rate fell from 60 percent to just 27 percent today. Dismissing these great achievements as a "myth" (the official view of Food First, a California-based organization that campaigns globally against agricultural modernization) is just silly.

It's true that the story of the Green Revolution is not everywhere a happy one. When powerful new farming technologies are introduced into deeply unjust rural social systems, the poor tend to lose out. In Latin America, where access to good agricultural land and credit has been narrowly controlled by traditional elites, the improved seeds made available by the Green Revolution increased income gaps. Absentee landlords in Central America, who previously allowed peasants to plant subsistence crops on underutilized land, pushed them off to sell or rent the land to commercial growers who could turn a profit using the new seeds. Many of the displaced rural poor became slum dwellers. Yet even in Latin America, the prevalence of hunger declined more than 50 percent between 1980 and 2005.

In Asia, the Green Revolution seeds performed just as well on small non-mechanized farms as on larger farms. Wherever small farmers had sufficient access to credit, they took up the new technology just as quickly as big farmers, which led to dramatic income gains and no increase in inequality or social friction. Even poor landless laborers gained, because more abundant crops meant more work at harvest time, increasing rural wages. In Asia, the Green Revolution was good for both agriculture and social justice.

And Africa? Africa has a relatively equitable and secure distribution of land, making it more like Asia than Latin America and increasing the chances that improvements in farm technology will help the poor. If Africa were to put greater resources into farm technology, irrigation, and rural roads, small farmers would benefit.

■ Organic Myths

There are other common objections to doing what is necessary to solve the real hunger crisis. Most revolve around caveats that purist critics raise regarding food systems in the United States and Western Europe. Yet such concerns, though well-intentioned, are often misinformed and counterproductive—especially when applied to the developing world.

Take industrial food systems, the current bugaboo of American food writers. Yes, they have many unappealing aspects, but without them food would be not only less abundant but also less safe. Traditional food systems lacking in reliable refrigeration and sanitary packaging are dangerous vectors for diseases. Surveys over the past several decades by the Centers for Disease Control and Prevention have found that the U.S. food supply became steadily safer over time, thanks in part to the introduction of industrial-scale technical improvements. Since 2000, the incidence of E. coli contamination in beef has fallen 45 percent. Today in the United States, most hospitalizations and fatalities from unsafe food come not from sales of contaminated products at supermarkets, but from the mishandling or improper preparation of food inside the home. Illness outbreaks from contaminated foods sold in stores still occur, but the fatalities are typically quite limited. A nationwide scare over unsafe spinach in 2006 triggered the virtual suspension of all fresh and bagged spinach sales, but only three known deaths were recorded. Incidents such as these command attention in part because they are now so rare. Food Inc. should be criticized for filling our plates with too many foods that are unhealthy, but not foods that are unsafe.

Where industrial-scale food technologies have not yet reached into the developing world, contaminated food remains a major risk. In Africa, where many foods are still purchased in open-air markets (often uninspected, unpackaged, unlabeled, unrefrigerated, unpasteurized, and unwashed), an estimated 700,000 people die every year from food- and water-borne diseases, compared with an estimated 5,000 in the United States.

Food grown organically—that is, without any synthetic nitrogen fertilizers or pesticides—is not an answer to the health and safety issues. *The American Journal of Clinical Nutrition* last year published a study of 162 scientific papers from the past 50 years on the health benefits of organically grown foods and found no nutritional advantage over conventionally grown foods. According to the Mayo Clinic, "No conclusive evidence shows that organic food is more nutritious than is conventionally grown food."

Health professionals also reject the claim that organic food is safer to eat due to lower pesticide residues. Food and Drug Administration surveys have revealed that the highest dietary exposures to pesticide residues on foods in the United States are so trivial (less than one one-thousandth of a level that would cause toxicity) that the safety gains from buying organic are insignificant. Pesticide exposures remain a serious problem in the developing world, where farm chemical use is not as well regulated, yet even there they are more an occupational risk for unprotected farmworkers than a residue risk for food consumers.

When it comes to protecting the environment, assessments of organic farming become more complex. Excess nitrogen fertilizer use on conventional farms in the United States has polluted rivers and created a "dead zone" in the Gulf of Mexico, but halting synthetic nitrogen fertilizer use entirely (as farmers must do in the United States to get organic certification from the Agriculture Department) would cause environmental problems far worse.

Here's why: Less than 1 percent of American cropland is under certified organic production. If the other 99 percent were to switch to organic and had to fertilize crops without any synthetic nitrogen fertilizer, that would require a lot more composted animal manure. To supply enough organic fertilizer, the U.S. cattle population would have to increase roughly fivefold. And because those animals would have to be raised organically on forage crops, much of the land in the lower 48 states would need to be converted to pasture. Organic field crops also have lower yields per hectare. If Europe tried to feed itself organically, it would need an additional 28 million hectares of cropland, equal to all of the remaining forest cover in France, Germany, Britain, and Denmark combined.

Mass deforestation probably isn't what organic advocates intend. The smart way to protect against nitrogen runoff is to reduce synthetic fertilizer applications with taxes, regulations, and cuts in farm subsidies, but not try to go all the way to zero as required by the official organic standard. Scaling up registered organic farming would be on balance harmful, not helpful, to the natural environment.

Not only is organic farming less friendly to the environment than assumed, but modern conventional farming is becoming significantly more sustainable. High-tech farming in rich countries today is far safer for the environment, per bushel of production, than it was in the 1960s, when Rachel Carson criticized the indiscriminate farm use of DDT in her environmental classic, *Silent Spring*. Thanks in part to Carson's devastating critique, that era's most damaging insecticides were banned and replaced by chemicals that could be applied in lower volume and were less persistent in the environment. Chemical use in American agriculture peaked soon thereafter, in 1973. This was a major victory for environmental advocacy.

And it was just the beginning of what has continued as a significant greening of modern farming in the United States. Soil erosion on farms dropped sharply in the 1970s with the introduction of "no-till" seed planting, an innovation that also reduced dependence on diesel fuel because fields no longer had to be plowed every spring. Farmers then began conserving water by moving to drip irrigation and by leveling their fields with lasers to minimize wasteful runoff. In the 1990s, GPS equipment was added to tractors, autosteering the machines in straighter paths and telling farmers exactly where they were in the field to within one square meter, allowing precise adjustments in chemical use. Infrared sensors were brought in to detect the greenness of the crop, telling a farmer exactly how much more (or less) nitrogen might be needed as the growing season went forward. To reduce wasteful nitrogen use, equipment was developed that can insert fertilizers into the ground at exactly the depth needed and in perfect rows, only where it will be taken up by the plant roots.

These "precision farming" techniques have significantly reduced the environmental footprint of modern agriculture relative to the quantity of food being produced. In 2008, the Organization for Economic Cooperation and Development published a review of the "environmental performance of agriculture" in the world's 30 most advanced industrial countries—those with the most highly capitalized and science-intensive farming systems. The results showed that between 1990 and 2004, food production in these countries continued to increase (by 5 percent in volume), yet adverse environmental impacts were reduced in every category. The land area taken up by farming declined 4 percent, soil erosion from both wind and water fell, gross greenhouse gas emissions from farming declined 3 percent, and excessive nitrogen fertilizer use fell 17 percent. Biodiversity also improved, as increased numbers of crop varieties and livestock breeds came into use.

■ Seeding the Future

Africa faces a food crisis, but it's not because the continent's population is growing faster than its potential to produce food, as vintage Malthusians such as environmental advocate Lester Brown and advocacy organizations such as Population Action International would have it. Food production in Africa is vastly less than the region's known potential, and that is why so many millions are going hungry there. African farmers still use almost no fertilizer; only 4 percent of cropland has been improved with irrigation; and most of the continent's cropped area is not planted with seeds improved through scientific plant breeding, so cereal yields are only a fraction of what they could be. Africa is failing to keep up with population growth not because it has exhausted its potential, but instead because too little has been invested in reaching that potential.

One reason for this failure has been sharply diminished assistance from international donors. When agricultural modernization went out of fashion among elites in the developed world beginning in the 1980s, development assistance to farming in poor countries collapsed. Per capita food production in Africa was declining during the 1980s and 1990s and the number of hungry people on the continent was doubling, but the U.S. response was to withdraw development assistance and simply ship more food aid to Africa. Food aid doesn't help farmers become more productive—and it can create long-term dependency. But in recent years, the dollar value of U.S. food aid to Africa has reached 20 times the dollar value of agricultural development assistance.

The alternative is right in front of us. Foreign assistance to support agricultural improvements has a strong record of success, when undertaken with purpose. In the 1960s, international assistance from the Rockefeller Foundation, the Ford Foundation, and donor governments led by the United States made Asia's original Green Revolution possible. U.S. assistance to India provided critical help in improving agricultural education, launching a successful agricultural extension service, and funding advanced degrees for Indian agricultural specialists at universities in the United States. The U.S. Agency for International Development, with the World Bank, helped finance fertilizer plants and infrastructure projects, including rural roads and irrigation. India could not have done this on its own—the country was on the brink of famine at the time and dangerously dependent on food aid. But instead of suffering a famine in 1975, as some naysayers had predicted, India that year celebrated a final and permanent end to its need for food aid.

Foreign assistance to farming has been a high-payoff investment everywhere, including Africa. The World Bank has documented average rates of return on investments in agricultural research in Africa of 35 percent a year, accompanied by significant reductions in poverty. Some research investments in African agriculture have brought rates of return estimated at 68 percent. Blind to these realities, the United States cut its assistance to agricultural research in Africa 77 percent between 1980 and 2006.

When it comes to Africa's growing hunger, governments in rich countries face a stark choice: They can decide to support a steady new infusion of financial and technical assistance to help local governments and farmers become more productive, or they can take a "worry later" approach and be forced to address hunger problems with increasingly expensive shipments of food aid. Development skeptics and farm modernization critics keep pushing us toward this unappealing second path. It's time for leaders with vision and political courage to push back.

READING AND WRITING

1. Read "Declare Your Independence" by Joel Salatin (at the end of this chapter). After considering the arguments Paarlberg and Salatin make, develop a list of points that each author might use to respond to the other's central claims.

2. Look at the images from the book *Hungry Planet: What the World Eats* on pages 71 and 88 (others can be found at www.time.com/time/ photogallery/0,29307,1626519,00.html or you can do a Google search for the terms *hungry planet time*). Of these families pictured, who do you think eats local? Who eats organic? Which of the diets do you think is most nutritious? Which is the most environmentally sustainable? How do these images affect your reading of Paarlberg's essay?

USING RESEARCH

3. In contrast to most of the readings in this collection, Paarlberg throws his support behind industrial food production: "If we are going to get serious about solving global hunger, we need to de-romanticize our view of preindustrial food and farming. And that means learning to appreciate the modern, science-intensive, and highly capitalized agricultural system we've developed in the West. Without it, our food would be more expensive and less safe." Conduct research to examine public discussion about the best farming practices to address world hunger. Then, write a brief essay in which you explain the issue to an audience that might not be familiar with it. To do this well, you will have to pay attention to the credibility of the sources you find and to the arguments these sources make.

Jessica B. Harris, a professor at the City University of New York, is the author of 10 cookbooks that document the culture and food of the African diaspora. This memoir was published in Gastropolis: Food and New York City, *a 2009 collection about New Yorkers' relationships with food.*

THE CULINARY SEASONS OF MY CHILDHOOD Jessica B. Harris

Few culinary traditions are as undocumented as those of middle-class African Americans. Scroll back to the 1950s, when segregation was still rampant in the South, and the foodways are even less well known. Although they are briefly mentioned in a few autobiographical narratives and in some fiction, the concern of most African Americans was more than throwing off the shackles of southern segregations that our forebears had come north to escape. This is reflected in our life tales more than in our recollections of meals eaten and foods purchased. The result is that most outsiders believe that ham hocks and hard times are the only remnants of our culinary past. Certainly there were plenty of ham hocks and no shortage of hard times. In fact, my New Jersey-born and-raised mother always claimed that that state could best Mississippi in the racist sweepstakes and that she had the stories to prove it! In North and South alike, middle-class African Americans ate the same cornbread and fried chicken and chitterlings and foods from the traditions of the African diaspora as did our less well-off counterparts, but we also ate differently, foods that expressed our middle classness and reflected our social and political aspirations.

Even though chitterlings might be on the menu, they could equally likely be accompanied by a mason jar of corn liquor or a crystal goblet of champagne. Southern specialties like fried porgies and collard greens show up for dinner, but they might be served along with dishes becoming common in an increasingly omnivorous United States that was just beginning its love affair with food. Nowhere is this more evident than in my own life and in the culinary season of my childhood.

A descendant of the enslaved and free Africans who made their way north in the Great Migration, I grew up in a transplanted southern culture that still remains a vibrant region of the African American culinary world. My family, like many others long separated from the South, raised me in ways that continued their eating traditions, so now I can head south and sop biscuits in gravy, suck chewy bits of fat from a pig's foot spattered with hot sauce, and yes'm and no'm with the best of 'em.

But that's not all of me. I also am a postwar baby who was the only child of striving middle-class parents who were old enough to have been young African American adults in the poverty of the Great Depression. They showered me with love and childhood coddling that makes my childhood seem like an African American version of *The Little Princess*. I also am a child at the confluence of two major African American culinary traditions. My mother's family could claim a smidge of black southern aristocracy, as they were descended from free people of color who migrated to Roanoke, Virginia. My father's family was from Tennessee and had upcountry Georgia roots that extended down the Natchez Trace. Both families showed their backgrounds at the table.

My maternal grandmother, Bertha Philpot Jones, was the quintessential African American matriarch presiding over a groaning board filled with savory goods. The role has become a visual cliché in movies like *The Nutty Professor Part II: The Klumps, Soul Food*, and *Dear Departed*, which revel in the dysfunction of African American life. No such dysfunction, however, was tolerated at Grandma Jones's table; she would not allow it. She was the matriarch and absolute sovereign of the Jones family; she ruled with a delicate but steel-boned hand, and the family marched to her tune. Watermelon-rind pickles spiced with fragrant cinnamon and whole cloves and the reassuring warmth of a full oven wafting smells of roasted joints and freshly baked bread are the aromas I most associate with her. She was a Baptist minister's wife and could put a hurtin' on some food. She had to, for as the minister's wife, she had not only her own brood of twelve children plus husband to feed, but the church folks who dropped in to take care of as well. She pickled fruits like Seckel pears, which had a curiously tart-sweet taste that comes back to me even today. The smell of Parker House rolls, the warmth of the kitchen, and the closeness of a large family all were part of the thrill of Grandma Jones's house. I didn't see her often—only on holidays and special occasions when we'd take the Holland Tunnel to head off to Plainfield, New Jersey, to visit and sit around the table.

Ida Irene Harris, my paternal grandmother, was at the other end of the culinary spectrum. I saw her much more often, at least once a week. When I travel in the South, folks are astounded to hear that as a child I had no southern roots, no grandmother to visit by segregated train or bus under the tutelage of kindly porters and with a tag pinned to my coat. Instead, my South was in the North, for Grandma Harris, in her day-to-day existence, re-created the preserved-in-amber South of her nineteenth-century rural youth in the precincts of her small apartment in the South Jamaica projects. I remember her apartment well, particularly the kitchen, with the four-burner stove on which she made lye soap, the refrigerator that always contained a pitcher of grape Kool-Aid with lemons cut up in it, and the sink in which she washed clothes, punching them with a broomstick to make sure they would get clean. Most of all, I remember the taste of the collard greens that she prepared: verdant, lush with just enough smoked pig tarts and fat for seasoning; they were the culinary embodiment of her love and, along with her silky beaten biscuits, one of the few dishes that she made well.

Grandma Harris lived in a self-created southern world. For years, she maintained a small garden plot at the back of the South Jamaica projects. This was just after the victory gardens of World War II when tenants could plant a small plot of land if they wished. Grandma Harris grew southern staples: collard and mustard greens, peanuts, snap beans, and more. I remember her weeding the peanuts and breaking off a leaf of the greens to test for ripening as the Long Island Rail Road train roared by on the tracks above. She taught me to love the slip of boiled peanuts, to sop biscuits in Alaga syrup with butter cut up in it, and to savor the tart sourness of buttermilk long before there was any romance to things southern.

I didn't understand the education she'd given me until years later, in Senegal's Theatre Daniel Sorano, I heard a griot sing. It was as though Grandma Harris had leaned down from the clouds and touched me. The timbre, the tone, the almost keening wail of the Mandinka singer captured the tuneless songs that Grandma sang as she went about her daily tasks, as much as the tastes of the Senegalese food recalled flavors from my childhood. It was then that I realized that unknown to both of us, Grandma Harris had taught me the ways of the past in her demeanor, her stalwartness, her faith, and her food. Those ways would help me survive. She also taught me to behave. I will never forget the summer day when she administered the only childhood whipping I can recall.

"Whipping" was not a word that was used in my house as I was growing up. I was a Dr. Spock baby through and through, and discipline was more about firm conversation than about Daddy's belt. At Grandma Harris's apartment, though, the rules changed and that one time, I knew I was going to get a whipping for sure.

Grandma Harris was another kind of old-line southern matriarch. It didn't matter that she lived on the third floor of the South Jamaica projects in Queens; her world was deeply rooted in the traditions of her South. She would brook no contradiction about manners. In her home, New Year's was celebrated with a mix of collard, mustard, and turnip greens that she had stewed down to a low gravy to accompany the obligatory hoppin' John and chitterlings. I always passed on the chitterlings and ate the hoppin' John, but the greens were my favorite. I had even more respect for them after they caused my downfall and earned me my only childhood whipping.

It happened on a summer's day when I was about six or seven. My mother worked, so I was sent to Grandma's apartment to spend the day in the traditional, extended-family day-care arrangement. I spent most of those urban summer days of my early childhood in her small one-bedroom apartment reading in a chair and staying out from under her feet in order to avoid going outside to play with the other kids, who invariably made fun of my private-school vowels and bookish ways. She, on the other side, spent her days insisting that I go out and play with the "nice children" who all called her Mother Harris.

On the day in question, when I had managed to avoid the dreaded piss-smelling barrels and rough boys and girls of the playground, she looked up from her sewing and said, "Jessica, come here." I was in for it. I was pleasantly surprised when, instead of ordering me downstairs, she instead went for her purse and gave me some money wrapped in a hankie with instructions to go to Miranda's, the Italian-owned corner market, and get a piece of "streak-a-lean-streak-a-fat" for the greens that she was going to cook.

Thrilled at being sent on an errand and overjoyed at escaping the barrel torture, I headed off. The walk was short, only a scant block through the maze of red-brick buildings that had not yet deteriorated into the breeding ground of hopelessness they were to become. A few small trees were in leaf, and the sounds of other children playing reminded me how grown up I was. I was on an errand. Arriving at Miranda's, I went directly to the meat counter, where, as in most African American neighborhoods, there was a vast array of pig parts both identifiable and unknown. Having not a clue about streak-a-lean-streak-a-fat but feeling exceptionally sophisticated in my seven-year-old head, I pointed to the slab bacon that my mother used to season things and asked for the requisite amount. It was brought out for my examination, and I grandly pronounced it fine. Cut off to the desired thickness and wrapped in slick brown paper, it was presented to me with solemnity. I tucked it into the net shopping bag that Grandma had provided and headed back home, proud and pleased.

I pushed open the heavy downstairs door and ran up the concrete steps, heels clanking on the metal treads that lined them. When I got to 3B, I pushed through the door that Grandma always kept open in those kinder times and headed in to present my parcel. To my amazement, when she opened it, she began to mutter and ask me what I had gotten.

"Steak-a-lean-streak-a-fat," I replied.

"Did you ask for it?" she questioned.

"No, I pointed it out to the man," I ventured with increasing timidity.

"Well, this isn't it! I wanted what I asked for, streak-a-lean-streak-a-fat," she countered. "This is slab bacon!"

"It's the same thing, isn't it?" I queried.

"NO! Now you march right back there and get me what I asked for, streak-a-lean-streak-a-fat. Take this back!"

"But?"

"No Buts!" Just march back there, young lady! Right Now!"

I trudged back to Miranda's, each step made heavier with the thought of having to tell the butcher that I'd made an error and hoping that he'd take back the offending bacon. The joy of escape of the prior hour had soured into a longing for the nasty boys and the stinky barrels. Luckily, the man took pity on bourgie old me and took back the bacon, replacing it with a fattier piece of streaky pork that was a fraction of the price.

When I got back to the building, Grandma was sitting on the benches out front and waiting for me. She uttered the five words that I'd never heard her say: "Go cut me a switch."

Terrified, I set off and hunted for the smallest branch that I could find in this virtually treeless urban landscape, knowing what was coming next. I returned with a smallish green switch that I had unearthed lord knows where. She took a few halfhearted passes at my legs, solemnly repeating with each one, "Don't think you're smarter than your elders." Tears flowed on both sides: mine because I'd certainly learned my lesson through the humiliation of returning the bacon followed by the public whipping, Grandma's because she adored me and wanted a respectful granddaughter. Despite that childhood trauma, I still love collard greens and never eat my New Year's mess of them without remembering Grandma Harris. I always season them with what I have come to think of as streak-a-lean-streak-a-fat-cut-me-a-switch; savor their smoky, oily splendor; and think of the southern lessons she taught me with every bite.

The other days of my early summers were spent with my working parents. We left New York City for family vacations, and I can remember the ice man delivering big blocks of ice wrapped in burlap to chill the icebox of the small cabin that we rented on Three Mile Harbor Road in East Hampton long before the area attained its current vogue. The year after my whipping, when I was eight, we visited Oak Bluffs, Massachusetts, the African American summer community on Martha's Vineyard that has become much touted these days. It was love at first sight, and my parents bought a summer house there that winter.

From the time I was nine until the present, this house has been a part of every summer. Then we made long trips on the Boston Post Road and the Merritt Parkway up to the

Wood's Hole ferry dock. Old habits die hard, and my parents in the 1950s would no more think of hitting the road without a shoebox full of fried chicken, deviled eggs, pound cake, oranges, and raisins and a thermos full of lemonade or some other cool drink that they would leave home without maps and a tank full of gas.

Oak Bluffs was just beginning to grow in popularity among New Yorkers; Bostonians knew about its glories long before we did. Middle-class African Americans from New York and New Jersey summered in Sag Harbor near the Hamptons, but my prescient father did not want to be so close to the city that friends could drop in unannounced on the weekends, so it was Martha's Vineyard for us. We joked that if we lost our way to the Vineyard, we could simply follow the trail of chicken bones left by fellow black New Yorkers and find the ferry pier with no problem. Like us, they were marked by segregated back doors and the lack of on-the-road facilities and also stuck to the old ways. We brought our chicken along for years until the Connecticut Turnpike was completed, and then we gradually left the chicken and deviled eggs at home and settled for the mediocre fare of the rest stops. I was thrilled several years ago when a friend, Alexander Smalls, opened a restaurant in Grand Central Terminal celebrating our traveling ways; it was called the Shoebox Café. While the menu was his own inventive interpretation of the black food of the South, I knew he was also honoring the past that many black Americans share.

My Vineyard summers were where I caught my first fish, a porgy of respectable size, and learned to strip the skin off an eel and find out just how delicious the sweet meat was, once you got over the snake look, and to pick mussels off the docks at Menemsha. The days were punctuated by sharing meals with family and friends, waiting for my father to appear on the Friday night "daddy boat" to spend the weekends, and savoring rainy days because my mother treated us with one of her fantastic blueberry cobblers prepared with berries we had picked before the storm came, from the bushes that grew wild along the roadside. July folded into August marked by county fairs, cotton candy, Illumination Night, Darling's molasses puff, swordfish at Giordano's restaurant, and movies at the Strand or Islander movie houses, accompanied by hot buttered popcorn served from a copper kettle. Soon it was time to pack the car again and head back to our house in Queens. I never really minded because autumn brought the return to school, and my world expanded one hundredfold. My school saw to that.

The United Nations International School was and is a special place. As the first non-UN-connected child to attend the school and one of very few Americans enrolled in the early years, my playmates were the world. UNIS, as the school is called by the cognoscenti, was small, then so small that it added a grade each year until it finally stretched from prekindergarten through high school. Inside Queens's Parkway Village apartments that had been transformed into classrooms, I made lifelong friends and learned how to function in a world that extended to the globe's four corners. A trip to Vasu's or Shikha's house brought smells of the Indian subcontinent, and on occasions when I was fortunate enough to be invited to birthday parties, there were tastes of rich spices and heady unknown flavors that would never have turned up on the table of my garlic-free household. The rich stews of central Europe were featured at Danuta's, and steak and kidney pie might turn up on the table at Eluned's. I can still feel the rasp of the embossed silver spoon-backs that were used on the table at Jennifer and Susan's house in Great Neck and remember their mother's wonderful way with shortbread with nostalgia that can still make my mouth water more than forty-five years later. The annual round of birthday parties was interrupted by school events like international potluck suppers. Parents brought dishes from around the globe, and students began culinary competitions like eating spaghetti with chopsticks in the days before Asian noodle bowls and the vast array of Italian pastas became common culinary currency.

As more Americans joined the school community, even they displayed amazing culinary inventiveness, and I remember being invited to a formal Coke-tail party at Anne's house, where we were served all manner of multihued nonalcoholic cocktails in delicate stemmed glassware complete with swizzle sticks, umbrella garnishes, and lots of maraschino cherries at a birthday fete that was every young girl's dream. All the class events seemed to center on international households of like-acting folk who proved to me at an early age that no matter what turned up on the table, it was to be savored and eaten with gusto.

During the twelve or so years that I attended UNIS, I grew to understand something about the world's food. My core group of friends spent many of those years together, and we became familiar with one another's households and foods and, with that growing knowledge, came to realize that the table was not only where we held our parties and our class fetes but also where we worked out our problems and got answers to questions about one another. With hindsight, I now realize that we achieved at our birthday tables and communal suppers the same détente and understanding that the parents of many of my friends worked so hard to attain at the tables at which they tried to bring peace to the world.

If my grandmothers' tables gave me a grounding in the African American past that is so much the bedrock of all that I do, and UNIS gave me an understanding of the food of the world, a palate that is open to tasting just about anything, and the knowledge that more friends are made around the table than just about anywhere else, my parents and our daily life completed the picture with the finishing touches.

I have saved my household for last, for it, more than any of the other outside influences, marked the season of my childhood eating. While I grew up at the confluence of two African American culinary traditions and lived in an international world at school, at home on Anderson Road in St. Albans, Queens, my surroundings were a wondrous combination of my parents' dueling culinary wills.

Very few African Americans are to the manor born; most of us have a past of want or need, if not for love, than for cash and the opportunities it can bring. My father, Jesse Brown Harris, was such a person. He was a black man and a striking one at that, aubergine-hued with the carriage of an emperor of Songhai. Early photos show him tall and slender, looking very proprietary about his little family of three. Daddy was not a numbers runner. Daddy was not a welfare ducker or an absentee father. Daddy was just Daddy, and the constancy of that statement and my lack of awareness that this was not the norm for all black children made me different.

As a teenager, Daddy had lived over the stables and worked as a Shabbas goy in Williamsburg, Brooklyn. Until the day he died, he was marked by a childhood of grinding poverty during which he had worn flour-bag suits to school and church, cadged coal at the railroad yard for heat, and picked dandelion leaves on the Fisk College campus for dinner. He was torn between the desire to overcome his past and provide differently for his family and the need to remember it with honor.

My father ate southern food whenever he could cajole my mother into preparing the hog maws or chitterlings that he adored. We even put a stove into the basement of our house so that the smell would not taint our living quarters. He would occasionally bring home cartons of buttermilk, which he would savor with squares of the flaky and hot cornbread that my mother baked at the drop of a hat. Sunday breakfast was his special time, and he would proudly sit at the head of the table and sop up his preferred mix of Karo dark with butter cut up in it with the hoecake that was off-limits to anyone else in the household.

He was the only one in his family of man children who did not and could not cook. My Uncle Bill, his older brother, gave me my first taste of rabbit stew, and my Uncle Jim's spaghetti sauce was the stuff of family legend. Actually, my father cared little for food, but he loved restaurants and, with his increasing affluence, dined out with the best of them. In the early years, dining out meant heading to the local silver bullet diner near our house for specials like mashed potatoes with gravy and Salisbury steak or sauerbraten (the neighborhood was German before we moved in). The bakery on Linden Boulevard, the main shopping street, sold flaky butter cookies and gingerbread at Christmas. Later, when St. Albans became blacker, we would head to Sister's Southern Diner after church on Sundays, still dressed in our Sabbath finery, for down-home feasts of smothered pork chops and greens or stewed okra and fried fish in an orgy of southern feasting that Mommy did not have to cook. In later years, restaurants like the Brasserie, La Fonda del Sol, and the Four Seasons were where we celebrated birthdays and anniversaries. There, my father's duality surfaced, and he would order wine for the bucket or "spittoon," as we had baptized it in our family jargon, and crepes suzette or Caesar salad for the flamboyant tableside service, but we three secretly knew that all the while what he really wanted was a ham hock and some butterbeans to satisfy the tastes of his youth.

My mother, though, truly loved food and had amazing taste buds that could analyze the components of a dish with startling accuracy. She would then reproduce her version of it at home, to the delight of all. Trained as a dietician, my mother reveled in entertaining and entranced her friends with her culinary inventiveness. Decades later, she revealed that at school, she had been required to sit through classes on how to keep black people out of restaurants and was discouraged from doing anything with food demonstrations that would put her in public view. After a brief stint as a dietitian at Bennett College in North Carolina and an even briefer stay in domestic service as a private dietitian, she found that she did not enjoy the field. Instead, she put her talents to use at the supper table, and I grew up eating homemade applesauce and tea sandwiches of olives and cream cheese when my friends were chowing down Gerber's finest and processed cheese spread. Weeknights featured balanced meals like breaded veal cutlets with carrots and peas and a salad, alternating with sublime fried chicken and mashed potatoes or rice and always a green vegetable and salad, or string beans, potatoes, and ham ends slow cooked into what we called a New England boiled dinner.

Parties were the occasion for pulling out all the stops. My mother would prepare ribbon and pinwheel sandwiches from whole wheat bread, cream cheese, white bread, and strips of red and green bell pepper, long before the spectrum opened up to admit such hues as orange, purple, white, and even yellow! She created cabarets in the basement—persuading her friends to come as babies or in nightclothes, hiring calypso singers, serving drinks with small umbrellas, and devising smoking centerpieces with dry ice and punch bowls—and, each Sunday, presided over table overflowing with roasts and a multiplicity of vegetables.

My mother created magic in the kitchen and made cooking exciting and fun, with a trick for every dish and a sense of adventure at the stove. As her only child, I got the benefit of this knowledge and accompanied her in the kitchen almost from my birth. In later years, she began to tire of the kitchen, but eventually, she renewed her interest in things culinary and discovered the wonder of ingredients like confit of duck, fresh garlic, pimentos, and arugula. Ever curious, her life was a constant adventure. I did not learn to cook; I simply absorbed it in her kitchen, moving from high chair to small tasks to whole dishes and entire meals.

I am very much the product of all of this, and these seasons of my personal and yet very New York childhood gave me the foods of the world on my plate. For the first years of my life, my fork ranged throughout the world from the simple country food of Grandma Harris to the more elegant Virginia repasts of Grandma Jones and the dishes of the 1950s and 1960s that were, for me, the tastes of home. I also sampled fare from the globe's four corners at the homes of my international classmates and learned that no matter where our origins or our regionalisms, when we eat together and share the commensalisms of the table, we make ourselves and our worlds better. It has been said that we are what we eat. I certainly am, and in the many seasons of my New York youth, that included an amazing amount of mighty good food.

■ READING AND WRITING

1. Though Harris has written a memoir essay, she does present an implicit argument about food. What is her claim? What kinds of support does she provide to persuade her audience?
2. How does Harris use her family history to reject and correct common stereotypes about foods that African Americans eat? How does she use food to weave together the various threads of her family background?
3. Compare Harris's essay with one of the more explicit arguments in this chapter (Paarlberg's, for example, or Berry's or Salatin's). Which do you think is more effective as an argument? Why?

■ DEVELOPING LONGER RESPONSES

4. Late in her essay, Harris writes: "My core group of friends … became familiar with one another's households and foods and, with that growing knowledge, came to realize that the table was not only where we

held our parties and our class fetes but also where we worked out our problems and got answers to questions about one another." Develop a brief personal essay in which you explore how food and the experience of preparing or sharing a meal provided more to you than simple sustenance.

Alice Waters, owner and founder of Chez Panisse Restaurant and Foundation in Berkeley, California, has championed local, organic food for more than thirty-eight years. She is introducing her ideas into public schools through Edible Education, a model garden and kitchen program. This essay was first published in the September 21, 2009 edition of The Nation.

A HEALTHY CONSTITUTION   Alice Waters

I was moved by the way Morgan Spurlock framed a narrow long-distance shot down the corridor of a Beckley, West Virginia, middle school in his outstanding 2004 film, *Super Size Me*. The film is about the toll that fast and processed food takes on all of us. Clearly visible in the background of this particular shot were dozens of students, many of whom were overweight.

Perhaps it should come as no surprise that Beckley's cafeteria offers only processed food, which is high in fat, sodium and sugar and of very little nutritional value.

Contrast this with the Central Alternative High School in Appleton, Wisconsin. The school serves troubled youth, but teachers, parents and administrators found a way to turn things around; and when they did, discipline problems dropped sharply. Their secret? Instead of the usual processed meals, the school cafeteria offers fresh, locally grown, low-fat, low-sugar alternatives. The healthier meals are delicious. The students love them. They perform better in class and don't get sick as often.

We are learning that when schools serve healthier meals, they solve serious educational and health-related problems. But what's missing from the national conversation about school lunch reform is the opportunity to use food to teach values that are central to democracy. Better food isn't just about test scores, health and discipline. It is about preparing students for the responsibilities of citizenship.

That's why we need to talk about edible education, not just school lunch reform. Edible education is a radical yet common-sense approach to teaching that integrates classroom instruction, school lunch, cooking and gardening into the studies of math, science, history and reading.

Edible education involves not only teaching children about where food comes from and how it is produced but giving them responsibilities in the school garden and kitchen. Students literally enjoy the fruits of their labor when the food they grow is served in healthy, delicious lunches that they can help prepare.

I learned this firsthand through the Chez Panisse Foundation—the organization I helped create to inspire a network of food activists around the world with edible education programs in their own communities. Here in Berkeley, I see children in our edible education program learn about responsibility, sharing and stewardship and become more connected to themselves and their peers. In the process, they come to embody the most important values of citizenship.

Listen to what one student named Charlotte has to say: "Next we went from the blue corn to the sweet corn and each picked an ear to grill. I must say it tasted really good, even without butter." Or Mati: "I think cleaning up is as important as eating. Cleaning up is sort of fun. And we can't just leave it for the teachers, because we made the mess." Or Jose: "I remember the first time I came to the kitchen. I was afraid to do anything. But then I realized, this is my kitchen. So then I started to enjoy it."

Charlotte, Mati and Jose are learning about so much more than lunch. They're learning that farmers depend on the land; we depend on farmers; and our nation depends on all of us. That cooperation with one another is necessary to nurture the community. And that, by setting the table for one another, we also take care of ourselves. School should be the place where we build democracy, not just by teaching about the Constitution but by becoming connected to our communities and the land in more meaningful ways.

In 1785, Thomas Jefferson declared that "Cultivators of the earth are the most valuable citizens. They are the most vigorous, the most independent, the most virtuous, and they are tied to their country and wedded to its liberty and interests by the most lasting bonds."

I believe he was right. The school cafeteria, kitchen and garden, like the town square, can and should be the place where we plant and nourish the values that guide our democracy. We need to join a delicious revolution that can reconnect our children to the table and to what it means to be a steward. This is the picture of a caring society, and this is the promise of edible education.

■ READING AND WRITING

1. How, according to Waters, can food be used "to teach values that are central to democracy?"
2. Explain the link that Waters makes between healthy meals and learning. What kind of evidence does she offer to support these links? Do you think more evidence would have strengthened her argument?

■ USING RESEARCH

3. Are any schools in South Carolina serving what Waters would call "fresh, locally grown, low-fat, low-sugar" meals? Are any schools in the state involved in anything like the "edible education" program she describes?

Matthew Scully served as special assistant and deputy director of speechwriting to President George W. Bush and also wrote for vice presidents Dick Cheney and Dan Quayle. The author of Dominion: The Power of Man, the Suffering of Animals, and the Call to Mercy, *Scully wrote this essay for the May 23, 2005, issue of* The American Conservative *magazine.*

FEAR FACTORIES: THE CASE FOR COMPASSIONATE CONSERVATISM— FOR ANIMALS   Matthew Scully

A few years ago I began a book about cruelty to animals and about factory farming in particular, problems that had been in the back of my mind for a long while. At the time I viewed factory farming as one of the lesser problems facing humanity—a small wrong on the grand scale of good and evil but too casually overlooked and too glibly excused.

This view changed as I acquainted myself with the details and saw a few typical farms up close. By the time I finished the book, I had come to view the abuses of industrial farming as a serious moral problem, a truly rotten business for good reason passed over in polite conversation. Little wrongs, when left unattended, can grow and spread to become grave wrongs, and precisely this had happened on our factory farms.

The result of these ruminations was *Dominion: The Power of Man, the Suffering of Animals, and the Call to Mercy.* And though my tome never quite hit the bestseller lists, there ought to be some special literary prize for a work highly recommended in both the *Wall Street Journal* and *Vegetarian Teen.* When you enjoy the accolades of PETA and *Policy Review*, Deepak Chopra and Gordon Liddy, Peter Singer and Charles Colson, you can at least take comfort in the diversity of your readership.

The book also provided an occasion for fellow conservatives to get beyond their dislike for particular animal-rights groups and to examine cruelty issues on the merits. Conservatives have a way of dismissing the subject, as if where animals are concerned nothing very serious could ever be at stake. And though it is not exactly true that liberals care more about these issues—you are no more likely to find reflections or exposés concerning cruelty in *The Nation* or *The New Republic* than in any journal of the Right— it is assumed that animal-protection causes are a project of the Left, and that the proper conservative position is to stand warily and firmly against them.

I had a hunch that the problem was largely one of presentation and that by applying their own principles to animal-welfare issues conservatives would find plenty of reasons to be appalled. More to the point, having acknowledged the problems of cruelty, we could then support reasonable remedies. Conservatives, after all, aren't shy about discoursing on moral standards or reluctant to translate the most basic of those standards into law. Setting aside the distracting rhetoric of animal rights, that's usually what these questions come down to: what moral standards should guide us in our treatment of animals, and when must those standards be applied in law?

Industrial livestock farming is among a whole range of animal-welfare concerns that extends from canned trophy-hunting to whaling to product testing on animals to all sorts of more obscure enterprises like the exotic-animal trade and the factory farming of bears in China for bile believed to hold medicinal and aphrodisiac powers. Surveying the various uses to which animals are put, some might be defensible, others abusive and unwarranted, and it's the job of any conservative who attends to the subject to figure out which are which. We don't need novel theories of rights to do this. The usual distinctions that conservatives draw between moderation and excess, freedom and license, moral goods and material goods, rightful power and the abuse of power, will all do just fine.

As it is, the subject hardly comes up at all among conservatives, and what commentary we do hear usually takes the form of ridicule directed at animal-rights groups. Often conservatives side instinctively with any animal-related industry and those involved, as if a thing is right just because someone can make money off it or as if our sympathies belong always with the men just because they are men.

I had an exchange once with an eminent conservative columnist on this subject. Conversation turned to my book and to factory farming. Holding his hands out in the "stop" gesture, he said, "I don't want to know." Granted, life on the factory farm is no one's favorite subject, but conservative writers often have to think about things that are disturbing or sad. In this case, we have an intellectually formidable fellow known to millions for his stern judgments on every matter of private morality and public policy. Yet nowhere in all his writings do I find any treatment of any cruelty issue, never mind that if you asked him he would surely agree that cruelty to animals is a cowardly and disgraceful sin.

And when the subject is cruelty to farmed animals—the moral standards being applied in a fundamental human enterprise—suddenly we're in forbidden territory and "I don't want to know" is the best he can do. But don't we have a responsibility to know? Maybe the whole subject could use his fine mind and his good heart.

As for the rights of animals, rights in general are best viewed in tangible terms, with a view to actual events and consequences. Take the case of a hunter in Texas named John Lockwood, who has just pioneered the online safari. At his canned-hunting ranch outside San Antonio, he's got a rifle attached to a camera and the camera wired up to the Internet, so that sportsmen going to Live-shot.com will actually be able to fire at baited animals by remote control from their computers. "If the customer were to wound the animal," explains the *San Antonio Express-News*, "a staff person on site could finish it off." The "trophy mounts" taken in these heroics will then be prepared and shipped to the client's door, and if it catches on Lockwood will be a rich man.

Very much like animal farming today, the hunting "industry" has seen a collapse in ethical standards, and only in such an atmosphere could Lockwood have found inspiration for this latest innovation—denying wild animals the last shred of respect. Under the laws of Texas and other states, Lockwood and others in his business use all sorts of methods once viewed as shameful: baits, blinds, fences to trap hunted animals in ranches that advertise a "100-percent-guaranteed kill." Affluent hunters like to unwind by shooting cage-reared pheasants, ducks, and other birds, firing away as the fowl of the air are released before them like skeet, with no limit on the day's kill. Hunting supply stores are filled with lures, infrared lights, high-tech scopes, and other gadgetry to make every man a marksman.

Lockwood doesn't hear anyone protesting those methods, except for a few of those nutty activist types. Why shouldn't he be able to offer paying customers this new hunting experience as well? It is like asking a smut-peddler to please have the decency to keep children out of it. Lockwood is just one step ahead of the rest, and there is no standard of honor left to stop him.

First impressions are usually correct in questions of cruelty to animals, and here most of us would agree that Live-shot.com does not show our fellow man at his best. We would say that the whole thing is a little tawdry and even depraved, that the creatures Lockwood has "in stock" are not just commodities. We would say that these animals deserve better than the fate he has in store for them.

As is invariably the case in animal-rights issues, what we're really looking for are safeguards against cruel and presumptuous people. We are trying to hold people to their obligations, people who could spare us the trouble if only they would recognize a few limits on their own conduct.

Conservatives like the sound of "obligation" here, and those who reviewed *Dominion* were relieved to find me arguing more from this angle than from any notion of rights. "What the PETA crowd doesn't understand," Jonah Goldberg wrote, "or what it deliberately confuses, is that human compassion toward animals is an obligation of humans, not an entitlement for animals." Another commentator put the point in religious terms: "[W]e have a moral duty to respect the animal world as God's handiwork, treating animals with 'the mercy of our Maker' ... But mercy and respect for animals are completely different from rights for animals—and we should never confuse the two." Both writers confessed they were troubled by factory farming and concluded with the uplifting thought that we could all profit from further reflection on our obligation of kindness to farm animals.

The only problem with this insistence on obligation is that after a while it begins to sounds like a hedge against actually being held to that obligation. It leaves us with a high-minded attitude but no accountability, free to act on our obligations or to ignore them without consequences, personally opposed to cruelty but unwilling to impose that view on others.

Treating animals decently is like most obligations we face, somewhere between the most and the least important, a modest but essential requirement to living with integrity. And it's not a good sign when arguments are constantly turned to precisely how much is mandatory and how much, therefore, we can manage to avoid.

If one is using the word "obligation" seriously, moreover, then there is no practical difference between an obligation on our end not to mistreat animals and an entitlement on their end not to be mistreated by us. Either way, we are required to do and not do the same things. And either way, somewhere down the logical line, the entitlement would have to arise from a recognition of the inherent dignity of a living creature. The moral standing of our fellow creatures may be humble, but it is absolute and not something within our power to confer or withhold. All creatures sing their Creator's praises, as this truth is variously expressed in the Bible, and are dear to Him for their own sakes.

A certain moral relativism runs through the arguments of those hostile or indifferent to animal welfare—as if animals can be of value only for our sake, as utility or preference decrees. In practice, this outlook leaves each person to decide for himself when animals rate moral concern. It even allows us to accept or reject such knowable facts about animals as their cognitive and emotional capacities, their conscious experience of pain and happiness.

Elsewhere in contemporary debates, conservatives meet the foe of moral relativism by pointing out that, like it or not, we are all dealing with the same set of physiological realities and moral truths. We don't each get to decide the facts of science on a situational basis. We do not each go about bestowing moral value upon things as it pleases us at the moment. Of course, we do not decide moral truth at all: we discern it. Human beings in their moral progress learn to appraise things correctly, using reasoned moral judgment to perceive a prior order not of our devising.

C.S. Lewis in *The Abolition of Man* calls this "the doctrine of objective value, the belief that certain attitudes are really true, and others really false, to the kind of thing the universe is and the kind of things we are." Such words as honor, piety, esteem, and empathy do not merely describe subjective states of mind, Lewis reminds us, but speak to objective qualities in the world beyond that merit those attitudes in us. "[T]o call children delightful or old men venerable," he writes, "is not simply to record a psychological fact about our own parental or filial emotions at the moment, but to recognize a quality which demands a certain response from us whether we make it or not."

This applies to questions of cruelty as well. A kindly attitude toward animals is not a subjective sentiment; it is the correct moral response to the objective value of a fellow creature. Here, too, rational and virtuous conduct consists in giving things their due and in doing so consistently. If one animal's pain—say, that of one's pet—is real and deserving of sympathy, then the pain of essentially identical animals is also meaningful, no matter what conventional distinctions we have made to narrow the scope of our sympathy. If it is wrong to whip a dog or starve a horse or bait bears for sport or grossly abuse farm animals, it is wrong for all people in every place.

The problem with moral relativism is that it leads to capriciousness and the despotic use of power. And the critical distinction here is not between human obligations and animal rights, but rather between obligations of charity and obligations of justice.

Active kindness to animals falls into the former category. If you take in strays or help injured wildlife or donate to animal charities, those are fine things to do, but no one says you should be compelled to do them. Refraining from cruelty to animals is a different matter, an obligation of justice not for us each to weigh for ourselves. It is not simply unkind behavior, it is unjust behavior, and the prohibition against it is non-negotiable. Proverbs reminds us of this—"a righteous man regardeth the life of his beast, but the tender mercies of the wicked are cruel"—and the laws of America and of every other advanced nation now recognize the wrongfulness of such conduct with our cruelty statutes. Often applying felony-level penalties to protect certain domestic animals, these state and federal statutes declare that even though your animal may elsewhere in the law be defined as your property, there are certain things you may not do to that creature, and if you are found harming or neglecting the animal, you will answer for your conduct in a court of justice.

There are various reasons the state has an interest in forbidding cruelty, one of which is that cruelty is degrading to human beings. The problem is that many thinkers on this subject have strained to find indirect reasons to explain why cruelty is wrong and thereby to force animal cruelty into the category of the victimless crime. The most common of these explanations asks us to believe that acts of cruelty matter only because the cruel person does moral injury to himself or sullies his character—as if the man is our sole concern and the cruelly treated animal is entirely incidental.

Once again, the best test of theory is a real-life example. In 2002, Judge Alan Glenn of Tennessee's Court of Criminal Appeals heard the case of a married couple named Johnson, who had been found guilty of cruelty to 350 dogs lying sick, starving, or dead in their puppy-mill kennel—a scene videotaped by police. Here is Judge Glenn's response to their supplications for mercy:

> The victims of this crime were animals that could not speak up to the unbelievable conduct of Judy Fay Johnson and Stanley Paul Johnson that they suffered. Several of the dogs have died and most had physical problems such as intestinal worms, mange, eye problems, dental problems and emotional problems and socialization problems … . Watching this video of the conditions that these dogs were subjected to was one of the most deplorable things this Court has observed. …
>
> [T]his Court finds that probation would not serve the ends of justice, nor be in the best interest of the public, nor would this have a deterrent effect for such gross behavior. … The victims were particularly vulnerable. You treated the victims with exceptional cruelty. …
>
> There are those who would argue that you should be confined in a house trailer with no ventilation or in a cell three-by-seven with eight or ten other inmates with no plumbing, no exercise and no opportunity to feel the sun or smell fresh air. However, the courts of this land have held that such treatment is cruel and inhuman, and it is. You will not be treated in the same way that you treated these helpless animals that you abused to make a dollar.

Only in abstract debates of moral or legal theory would anyone quarrel with Judge Glenn's description of the animals as "victims" or deny that they were entitled to be treated better. Whether we call this a "right" matters little, least of all to the dogs, since the only right that any animal could possibly exercise is the right to be free from human abuse, neglect, or, in a fine old term of law, other "malicious mischief." What matters most is that prohibitions against human cruelty be hard and binding. The sullied souls of the Johnsons are for the Johnsons to worry about. The business of justice is to punish their offense and to protect the creatures from human wrongdoing. And in the end, just as in other matters of morality and justice, the interests of man are served by doing the right thing for its own sake.

There is only one reason for condemning cruelty that doesn't beg the question of exactly why cruelty is a wrong, a vice, or bad for our character: that the act of cruelty is an intrinsic evil. Animals cruelly dealt with are not just things, not just an irrelevant detail in some self-centered moral drama of our own. They matter in their own right, as they matter to their Creator, and the wrongs of cruelty are wrongs done to them. As *The Catholic Encyclopedia* puts this point, there is a "direct and essential sinfulness of cruelty to the animal world, irrespective of the results of such conduct on the character of those who practice it."

Our cruelty statutes are a good and natural development in Western law, codifying the claims of animals against human wrongdoing, and, with the wisdom of men like Judge Glenn, asserting those claims on their behalf. Such statutes, however, address mostly random or wanton acts of cruelty. And the persistent animal-welfare questions of our day center on institutional cruelties—on the vast and systematic mistreatment of animals that most of us never see.

Having conceded the crucial point that some animals rate our moral concern and legal protection, informed conscience turns naturally to other animals—creatures entirely comparable in their awareness, feeling, and capacity for suffering. A dog is not the moral equal of a human being, but a dog is definitely the moral equal of a pig, and it's only human caprice and economic convenience that say otherwise. We have the problem that these essentially similar creatures are treated in dramatically different ways, unjustified even by the very different purposes we have assigned to them. Our pets are accorded certain protections from cruelty, while the nameless creatures in our factory farms are hardly treated like animals at all. The challenge is one of consistency, of treating moral equals equally, and living according to fair and rational standards of conduct.

Whatever terminology we settle on, after all the finer philosophical points have been hashed over, the aim of the exercise is to prohibit wrongdoing. All rights, in practice, are protections against human wrongdoing, and here too the point is to arrive at clear and consistent legal boundaries on the things that one may or may not do to animals, so that every man is not left to be the judge in his own case.

More than obligation, moderation, ordered liberty, or any of the other lofty ideals we hold, what should attune conservatives to all the problems of animal cruelty—and especially to the modern factory farm—is our worldly side. The great virtue of conservatism is that it begins with a realistic assessment of human motivations. We know man as he is, not only the rational creature but also, as Socrates told us, the rationalizing creature, with a knack for finding an angle, an excuse, and a euphemism. Whether it's the pornographer who thinks himself a free-speech champion or the abortionist who looks in the mirror and sees a reproductive health-care services provider, conservatives are familiar with the type.

So we should not be all that surprised when told that these very same capacities are often at work in the things that people do to animals—and all the more so in our $125 billion a year livestock industry. The human mind, especially when there is money to be had, can manufacture grand excuses for the exploitation of other human beings. How much easier it is for people to excuse the wrongs done to lowly animals.

Where animals are concerned, there is no practice or industry so low that someone, somewhere, cannot produce a high-sounding reason for it. The sorriest little miscreant who shoots an elephant, lying in wait by the water hole in some canned-hunting operation, is just "harvesting resources," doing his bit for "conservation." The swarms of government-subsidized Canadian seal hunters slaughtering tens of thousands of newborn pups—hacking to death these unoffending creatures, even in sight of their mothers—offer themselves as the brave and independent bearers of tradition. With the same sanctimony and deep dishonesty, factory-farm corporations like Smithfield Foods, ConAgra, and Tyson Foods still cling to countrified brand names for their labels—Clear Run Farms, Murphy Family

Farms, Happy Valley—to convince us and no doubt themselves, too, that they are engaged in something essential, wholesome, and honorable.

Yet when corporate farmers need barbed wire around their Family Farms and Happy Valleys and laws to prohibit outsiders from taking photographs (as is the case in two states) and still other laws to exempt farm animals from the definition of "animals" as covered in federal and state cruelty statutes, something is amiss. And if conservatives do nothing else about any other animal issue, we should attend at least to the factory farms, where the suffering is immense and we are all asked to be complicit.

If we are going to have our meats and other animal products, there are natural costs to obtaining them, defined by the duties of animal husbandry and of veterinary ethics. Factory farming came about when resourceful men figured out ways of getting around those natural costs, applying new technologies to raise animals in conditions that would otherwise kill them by deprivation and disease. With no laws to stop it, moral concern surrendered entirely to economic calculation, leaving no limit to the punishments that factory farmers could inflict to keep costs down and profits up. Corporate farmers hardly speak anymore of "raising" animals, with the modicum of personal care that word implies. Animals are "grown" now, like so many crops. Barns somewhere along the way became "intensive confinement facilities" and the inhabitants mere "production units."

The result is a world in which billions of birds, cows, pigs, and other creatures are locked away, enduring miseries they do not deserve, for our convenience and pleasure. We belittle the activists with their radical agenda, scarcely noticing the radical cruelty they seek to redress.

At the Smithfield mass-confinement hog farms I toured in North Carolina, the visitor is greeted by a bedlam of squealing, chain rattling, and horrible roaring. To maximize the use of space and minimize the need for care, the creatures are encased row after row, 400 to 500 pound mammals trapped without relief inside iron crates seven feet long and 22 inches wide. They chew maniacally on bars and chains, as foraging animals will do when denied straw, or engage in stereotypical nest-building with the straw that isn't there, or else just lie there like broken beings. The spirit of the place would be familiar to police who raided that Tennessee puppy-mill run by Stanley and Judy Johnson, only instead of 350 tortured animals, millions—and the law prohibits none of it.

Efforts to outlaw the gestation crate have been dismissed by various conservative critics as "silly," "comical," "ridiculous." It doesn't seem that way up close. The smallest scraps of human charity—a bit of maternal care, room to roam outdoors, straw to lie on— have long since been taken away as costly luxuries, and so the pigs know the feel only of concrete and metal. They lie covered in their own urine and excrement, with broken legs from trying to escape or just to turn, covered with festering sores, tumors, ulcers, lesions, or what my guide shrugged off as the routine "pus pockets."

C.S. Lewis's description of animal pain—"begun by Satan's malice and perpetrated by man's desertion of his post"—has literal truth in our factory farms because they basically run themselves through the wonders of automation, and the owners are off in spacious corporate offices reviewing their spreadsheets. Rarely are the creatures' afflictions examined by a vet or even noticed by the migrant laborers charged with their care, unless of course some ailment threatens production—meaning who cares about a lousy ulcer or broken leg, as long as we're still getting the piglets?

Kept alive in these conditions only by antibiotics, hormones, laxatives, and other additives mixed into their machine-fed swill, the sows leave their crates only to be driven or dragged into other crates, just as small, to bring forth their piglets. Then it's back to the gestation crate for another four months, and so on back and forth until after seven or eight pregnancies they finally expire from the punishment of it or else are culled with a club or bolt-gun.

As you can see at www.factoryfarming.com/gallery.htm, industrial livestock farming operates on an economy of scale, presupposing a steady attrition rate. The usual comforting rejoinder we hear—that it's in the interest of farmers to take good care of their animals—is false. Each day, in every confinement farm in America, you will find cull pens littered with dead or dying creatures discarded like trash.

For the piglets, it's a regimen of teeth cutting, tail docking (performed with pliers, to heighten the pain of tail chewing and so deter this natural response to mass confinement), and other mutilations. After five or six months trapped in one of the grim warehouses that now pass for barns, they're trucked off, 355,000 pigs every day in the life of America, for processing at a furious pace of thousands per hour by migrants who use earplugs to muffle the screams. All of these creatures, and billions more across the earth, go to their deaths knowing nothing of life, and nothing of man, except the foul, tortured existence of the factory farm, having never even been outdoors.

But not to worry, as a Smithfield Foods executive assured me, "They love it." It's all "for their own good." It is a voice conservatives should instantly recognize, as we do when it tells us that the fetus feels nothing. Everything about the picture shows bad faith, moral sloth, and endless excuse-making, all readily answered by conservative arguments.

We are told "they're just pigs" or cows or chickens or whatever and that only urbanites worry about such things, estranged as they are from the realities of rural life. Actually, all of factory farming proceeds by a massive denial of reality—the reality that pigs and other animals are not just production units to be endlessly exploited but living creatures with natures and needs. The very modesty of those needs—their humble desires for straw, soil, sunshine—is the gravest indictment of the men who deny them.

Conservatives are supposed to revere tradition. Factory farming has no traditions, no rules, no codes of honor, no little decencies to spare for a fellow creature. The whole thing is an abandonment of rural values and a betrayal of honorable animal husbandry—to say nothing of veterinary medicine, with its sworn oath to "protect animal health" and to "relieve animal suffering."

Likewise, we are told to look away and think about more serious things. Human beings simply have far bigger problems to worry about than the well being of farm animals, and surely all of this zeal would be better directed at causes of human welfare.

You wouldn't think that men who are unwilling to grant even a few extra inches in cage space, so that a pig can turn around, would be in any position to fault others for pettiness. Why are small acts of kindness beneath us, but not small acts of cruelty? The larger problem with this appeal to moral priority, however, is that we are dealing with suffering that occurs through human agency. Whether it's miserliness here, carelessness there, or greed throughout, the result is rank cruelty for which particular people must answer.

Since refraining from cruelty is an obligation of justice, moreover, there is no avoiding the implications. All the goods invoked in defense of factory farming, from the efficiency and higher profits of the system to the lower costs of the products, are false goods unjustly derived. No matter what right and praiseworthy things we are doing elsewhere in life, when we live off a cruel and disgraceful thing like factory farming, we are to that extent living unjustly, and that is hardly a trivial problem.

For the religious-minded, and Catholics in particular, no less an authority than Pope Benedict XVI has explained the spiritual stakes. Asked recently to weigh in on these very questions, Cardinal Ratzinger told German journalist Peter Seewald that animals must be respected as our "companions in creation." While it is licit to use them for food, "we cannot just do whatever we want with them. ... Certainly, a sort of industrial use of creatures, so that geese are fed in such a way as to produce as large a liver as possible, or hens live so packed together that they become just caricatures of birds, this degrading of living creatures to a commodity seems to me in fact to contradict the relationship of mutuality that comes across in the Bible."

Factory farmers also assure us that all of this is an inevitable stage of industrial efficiency. Leave aside the obvious reply that we could all do a lot of things in life more efficiently if we didn't have to trouble ourselves with ethical restraints. Leave aside, too, the tens of billions of dollars in annual federal subsidies that have helped megafarms undermine small family farms and the decent communities that once surrounded them and to give us the illusion of cheap products. And never mind the collateral damage to land, water, and air that factory farms cause and the more billions of dollars it costs taxpayers to clean up after them. Factory farming is a predatory enterprise, absorbing profit and externalizing costs, unnaturally propped up by political influence and government subsidies much as factory-farmed animals are unnaturally sustained by hormones and antibiotics.

Even if all the economic arguments were correct, conservatives usually aren't impressed by breathless talk of inevitable progress. I am asked sometimes how a conservative could possibly care about animal suffering in factory farms, but the question is premised on a liberal caricature of conservatism—the assumption that, for all of our fine talk about moral values, "compassionate conservatism" and the like, everything we really care about can be counted in dollars. In the case of factory farming, and the conservative's blithe tolerance of it, the caricature is too close to the truth.

Exactly how far are we all prepared to follow these industrial and technological advances before pausing to take stock of where things stand and where it is all tending? Very soon companies like Smithfield plan to have tens of millions of cloned animals in their factory farms. Other companies are at work genetically engineering chickens without feathers so that one day all poultry farmers might be spared the toil and cost of de-feathering their birds. For years, the many shills for our livestock industry employed in the "Animal Science" and "Meat Science" departments of rural universities (we used to call them Animal Husbandry departments) have been tampering with the genes of pigs and other animals to locate and expunge that part of their genetic makeup that makes them stressed in factory farm conditions—taking away the desire to protect themselves and to live. Instead of redesigning the factory farm to suit the animals, they are redesigning the animals to suit the factory farm.

Are there no boundaries of nature and elementary ethics that the conservative should be the first to see? The hubris of such projects is beyond belief, only more because of the foolish and frivolous goods to be gained—blood-free meats and the perfect pork chop.

No one who does not profit from them can look at our modern factory farms or frenzied slaughter plants or agricultural laboratories with their featherless chickens and fear-free pigs and think, "Yes, this is humanity at our finest—exactly as things should be." Devils charged with designing a farm could hardly have made it more severe. Least of all should we look for sanction in Judeo-Christian morality, whose whole logic is one of gracious condescension, of the proud learning to be humble, the higher serving the lower, and the strong protecting the weak.

Those religious conservatives who, in every debate over animal welfare, rush to remind us that the animals themselves are secondary and man must come first are exactly right—only they don't follow their own thought to its moral conclusion. Somehow, in their pious notions of stewardship and dominion, we always seem to end up with singular moral dignity but no singular moral accountability to go with it.

Lofty talk about humanity's special status among creatures only invites such questions as: what would the Good Shepherd make of our factory farms? Where does the creature of conscience get off lording it over these poor creatures so mercilessly? "How is it possible," as Malcolm Muggeridge asked in the years when factory farming began to spread, "to look for God and sing his praises while insulting and degrading his creatures? If, as I had thought, all lambs are the Agnus Dei, then to deprive them of light and the field and their joyous frisking and the sky is the worst kind of blasphemy."

The writer B.R. Meyers remarked in *The Atlantic*, "research could prove that cows love Jesus, and the line at the McDonald's drive-through wouldn't be one sagging carload shorter the next day …. Has any generation in history ever been so ready to cause so much suffering for such a trivial advantage? We deaden our consciences to enjoy—for a few minutes a day—the taste of blood, the feel of our teeth meeting through muscle."

That is a cynical but serious indictment, and we must never let it be true of us in the choices we each make or urge upon others. If reason and morality are what set human beings apart from animals, then reason and morality must always guide us in how we treat them, or else it's all just caprice, unbridled appetite with the pretense of piety. When people say that they like their pork chops, veal, or foie gras just too much ever to give them up, reason hears in that the voice of gluttony, willfulness, or at best moral complaisance. What makes a human being human is precisely the ability to understand that the suffering of an animal is more important than the taste of a treat.

Of the many conservatives who reviewed *Dominion*, every last one conceded that factory farming is a wretched business and a betrayal of human responsibility. So it should be a short step to agreement that it also constitutes a serious issue of law and public policy. Having granted that certain practices are abusive, cruel, and wrong, we must be prepared actually to do something about them.

Among animal activists, of course, there are some who go too far—there are in the best of causes. But fairness requires that we judge a cause by its best advocates instead of making straw men of the worst. There isn't much money in championing the cause of animals, so we're dealing with some pretty altruistic people who on that account alone deserve the benefit of the doubt.

If we're looking for fitting targets for inquiry and scorn, for people with an angle and a truly pernicious influence, better to start with groups like Smithfield Foods (my candidate for the worst corporation in America in its ruthlessness to people and animals alike), the National Pork Producers Council (a reliable Republican contributor), or the various think tanks in Washington subsidized by animal-use industries for intellectual cover.

After the last election, the National Pork Producers Council rejoiced, "President Bush's victory ensures that the U.S. pork industry will be very well positioned for the next four years politically, and pork producers will benefit from the long-term results of a livestock agriculture-friendly agenda." But this is no tribute. And millions of good people who live in what's left of America's small family-farm communities would themselves rejoice if the president were to announce that he is prepared to sign a bipartisan bill making some basic reforms in livestock agriculture.

Bush's new agriculture secretary, former Nebraska Gov. Mike Johanns, has shown a sympathy for animal welfare. He and the president might both be surprised at the number and variety of supporters such reforms would find in the Congress, from Republicans like Chris Smith and Elton Gallegly in the House to John Ensign and Rick Santorum in the Senate, along with Democrats such as Robert Byrd, Barbara Boxer, or the North Carolina congressman who called me in to say that he, too, was disgusted and saddened by hog farming in his state.

If such matters were ever brought to President Bush's attention in a serious way, he would find in the details of factory farming many things abhorrent to the Christian heart and to his own kindly instincts. Even if he were to drop into relevant speeches a few of the prohibited words in modern industrial agriculture (cruel, humane, compassionate), instead of endlessly flattering corporate farmers for virtues they lack, that alone would help to set reforms in motion.

We need our conservative values voters to get behind a Humane Farming Act so that we can all quit averting our eyes. This reform, a set of explicit federal cruelty statutes with enforcement funding to back it up, would leave us with farms we could imagine without wincing, photograph without prosecution, and explain without excuses.

The law would uphold not only the elementary standards of animal husbandry but also of veterinary ethics, following no more complicated a principle than that pigs and cows should be able to walk and turn around, fowl to move about and spread their wings, and all creatures to know the feel of soil and grass and the warmth of the sun. No need for labels saying "free-range" or "humanely raised." They will all be raised that way. They all get to be treated like animals and not as unfeeling machines.

On a date certain, mass confinement, sow gestation crates, veal crates, battery cages, and all such innovations would be prohibited. This will end livestock agriculture's moral race to the bottom and turn the ingenuity of its scientists toward compassionate solutions. It will remove the federal support that unnaturally serves agribusiness at the expense of small farms. And it will shift economies of scale, turning the balance in favor of humane farmers—as those who run companies like Wal-Mart could do right now by taking their business away from factory farms.

In all cases, the law would apply to corporate farmers a few simple rules that better men would have been observing all along: we cannot just take from these creatures, we must give them something in return. We owe them a merciful death, and we owe them a merciful life. And when human beings cannot do something humanely, without degrading both the creatures and ourselves, then we should not do it at all.

■ READING AND WRITING

1. How does Scully build and support his case that cruelty to animals, especially in the factory farming system, should be a conservative cause?

2. In his essay, Scully writes: "If reason and morality are what set human beings apart from animals, then reason and morality must always guide us in how we treat them, or else it's all just caprice, unbridled appetite with the pretense of piety." What do you think Scully means by this? Do you agree with him? Explain your response.

3. Where does Scully stand on the "rights" of animals? Point to specific passages from his essay to support your response.

■ DEVELOPING LONGER RESPONSES

4. Read through the essay and identify the sources that Scully uses to support his argument. Why do you think he chose these particular people and publications? How do these sources help him reach his intended audience?

Molly J. Dahm and Amy R. Shows are on the faculty of the Department of Family and Consumer Sciences at Lamar University in Beaumont, Texas. Aurelia V. Samonte works with Buckner Children and Family Services in Beaumont. They wrote this article for the Journal of American College Health *in 2009.*

ORGANIC FOODS: DO ECO-FRIENDLY ATTITUDES PREDICT ECO-FRIENDLY BEHAVIORS?

Molly J. Dahm, Aurelia V. Samonte, and Amy R. Shows

■ Consumption of Organic Foods

New research and mounting public interest have increased global awareness of organic food products. The primary consumers of organic food are women aged 30 to 45 who have children in the household and who are environmentally conscious.[1,2] However, interest in organic foods along with a sense of responsibility for the environment is growing among younger people, specifically college students, who are likely to identify issues that will influence their attitudes and activities in the future. Purchase and consumption of organic foods is another positive socially conscious behavior.[3]

One way universities in the United States have responded to students' increased interest in the environment is by adding organic foods to their menus. In fact, the presence of organic foods may ultimately factor into a student's choice of school.[4] Purchase and consumption of organic foods is one way students can practice eco-friendly behaviors. Eco-friendly behaviors might also be referred to as environmentally conscious behaviors, or "green consumption," e.g., legitimate means of exhibiting environmentally safe and responsible behaviors.[1] Other eco-friendly practices include recycling, energy conservation, water conservation, driving hybrid cars or carpooling, and ozone protection.

In this study, we examined the awareness (knowledge), attitudes, and behaviors of university students towards organic foods. We also attempted to determine if positive attitudes about organic foods and other environmental issues would predict consumption of organic foods and other healthy and eco-friendly practices.

■ Federal Standards for Organic Foods

The United States Department of Agriculture (USDA) informs consumers that the terms natural and organic are not interchangeable.[5] "Natural" refers to products without artificial flavorings, colorings, or chemical preservatives and minimal processing.[5] The USDA defines "organic foods" as products grown without the use of pesticides, synthetic fertilizers, sewage sludge, genetically modified organisms, or ionizing radiation.[5] The agency also requires that organic meat, poultry, eggs, and dairy products be produced from animals free of antibiotics or growth hormones.[6] The term "organic" is increasingly recognized as a trusted symbol of eco-friendly products.[7] Companies that handle or process organic foods for public consumption must be certified by the USDA.[5] The USDA Organic Seal (Figure 1) exhibits evidence of this certification.

Consumers who want to buy organic products should be able to correctly identify them. The USDA's label standards for organic products include 100% Organic (made with 100% organic ingredients); the word organic or the organic seal (95% organic); made with organic ingredients (minimum of 70% organic ingredients); and organic ingredients listed on the side panel (less than 70% organic ingredients).[5,6]

Other certification programs, such as Oregon's eco-labeling program and the system of integrated management (SIM) in Greece, promote eco-friendly products to consumers.[7] Loureiro et al.[8] studied consumers' level of awareness of certified products using eco-labeled apples and found that although general level of awareness about organic products was high (86%), awareness of the label meaning was limited.

FIGURE 1. USDA Organic Seal

Consumer Attitudes and Behaviors

Much of the current research about consumer attitudes and behaviors regarding organic foods has been conducted outside the United States, where scholars have noted consumer trust in organic products. In a Swedish study, attitudes towards and purchase of organic foods were strongly related to the perceived human health benefits of those foods.[2] Researchers in the United Kingdom found the term "organic" had emotional resonance for consumers in terms of personal well-being, health, benefits to the environment, and a healthy diet.[9,10]

As attitudes towards organic products evolve, values play an important but mixed role in how organic products are perceived.[11,12] Dreezens et al.[12] indicated that organic foods were viewed positively and associated with the values of welfare for all people and protection of nature. By contrast, Chryssohoidis and Krystallis[11] found that external values such as belonging to society were less important to consumers who purchased organic foods than internal values such as self-respect and enjoyment of life.

Consumer perception of appearance, taste, and texture of organic foods varies. In Northern Ireland, a focus group found organic products bland and lacking in color, yet stated that some organic foods, especially mixed vegetables, had desirable texture and flavor.[13] Researchers in the United Kingdom and Australia concluded that the taste of organic food was better than conventionally grown products[10] and that organic food had sensual qualities.[1]

As consumers develop more positive attitudes towards organic food, they are faced with purchase decisions. Studies have examined decision-making factors. Padel and Foster[9] concluded that the process is complex, and that motives and barriers may vary with product categories. Researchers have found a widespread perception of organic foods as expensive[10] and that the primary barrier to purchasing organic food was the consumer's level of personal disposable income.[14] Lockie et al.[1] suggested that increased education and household income is positively associated with the likelihood that an individual has consumed organic foods. However, other scholars have found that the main factor that hinders the purchase of organic food is limited availability of such foods.[11,15]

Consumer purchases of organic foods have increased. In 1994, Tregear et al.[18] found that 29% of the general public occasionally bought organic foods. A later study found that almost half of respondents purchased organic food on a regular basis.[13] Fruits and vegetables tend to be the first, and often the only, organic products that consumers buy.[9] Nonetheless, few consumers follow a diet that is mainly organic.[1]

■ Other Eco-Friendly Behaviors

There is some disagreement about whether there is an association between consumption of organic foods and other environmentally friendly behaviors. Davies et al.[14] found that consumers of organic foods were not necessarily concerned about the environment. However, two more recent studies found a significant relationship between environmentally friendly behaviors and organic food consumption.[1,2] In Oregon, the likelihood that a consumer will pay a premium for eco-labeled apples was positively associated with being environmentally conscious.[7] In Greece, willingness to pay for organic products was higher among consumers who placed importance on health.[8]

■ Attitudes and Behaviors of Young People

In a study of 651 high school students in a major metropolitan area, Bissonnette and Contento[3] found that American adolescents had positive attitudes about organic foods.

Students believed organic foods were healthier, tasted better, and were better for the environment. Yet their beliefs were not strong enough to urge them to act.[3]

Interest in organic foods or alternative food sources is evident in college age individuals who show an increasing enthusiasm for a healthy lifestyle and a sense of environmental responsibility.[4] Over the past 10 years, universities across the United States have introduced organic food options in response to student demand. For example, in 2000 the University of Wisconsin at Madison became the first major American public university to consistently place foods grown on local farms on the regular menu.[16]

In April 2006, the University of California-Berkeley received the nation's first organic certification on a college campus.[17] Menlo College uses nearly 100% organic foods and beverages on campus.[18] Also in 2006, Colorado State University and the University of Pennsylvania, in 2003, introduced student food venues that sell locally grown food. Oral Roberts University introduced its Green Cuisine brand in 2006, which includes organic salads, sandwiches, and packaged goods made from local food.[18,19] Thus, universities have responded to student demands for organic foods.

Because the literature is unclear whether consumer purchases follow upon knowledge and attitudes, the links between knowledge, attitudes, and behaviors with regard to organic foods (and other eco-friendly behaviors) should be explored to better understand and respond to consumer needs on college campuses.

METHOD

■ Population and Sample

The population for this study was students at a mid-size university in the southeastern United States. The sample included 443 students who were enrolled in one of the mandated entry-level political science classes. Thus, the sampling method ensured a representative sample of the student body.

■ Instrumentation

The instrument, designed by the researchers, was 4 pages long and consisted of 28 items. Consent information was included on the first page of the instrument. Completion of the survey constituted consent to participate in the study. Study protocol was approved by the university's Institutional Review Board.

The first 5 questions requested demographic information: gender, race, age, student classification, place of residence, and income level. Four questions evaluated the subjects' awareness/knowledge of organic foods and 5 questions addressed the subjects' attitudes toward organic foods. In the fnal section, 12 questions sought information about student eating behaviors in relation to organic foods and healthy lifestyle practices, and 2 multipart questions examined attitudes and behaviors regarding other eco-friendly practices (recycling, energy conservation, water conservation, driving hybrid cars or carpooling).

■ Procedures

After departmental approval was granted, researchers obtained permission from individual professors to administer the survey in each class. The average class size was 50 students. The survey was administered over a 2-week period to students present on the day of the survey. Several classes were not surveyed due to scheduling conflicts. A research assistant read procedures from a script before the surveys were distributed. Students were informed that the survey was voluntary and anonymous.

■ Statistical Analysis

Data analysis was conducted using SPSS Version 14.0 and Jump Version 5.0. Descriptive statistics described the sample and displayed frequencies of responses to survey items. Chi-square analysis was conducted to determine associations between categorical variables of interest. Linear regression tested whether student awareness/knowledge of organic foods predicted attitude about organic foods. Multiple correlation was used to examine the relationship between attitudes about organic foods and the purchase and consumption of those foods in different contexts. Linear regression and path analysis determined whether attitudes about organic foods might predict organic food purchase and consumption and healthy lifestyle practices. Finally, multiple correlation tested whether attitudes about other eco-friendly practices might predict corresponding behaviors.

RESULTS

The sample ($N = 443$) was 44.2% male and 55.8% female. The mean age of the group was 21.6 (SD ±5.01) years, with a range of 16 to 48 years. The racial/ethnic background of students was 54.6% White/Non-Hispanic, 30.6% African American, 7.0% Hispanic, 3.9% Asian, and 3.7% Other. The majority (59.5%) of the students were classified as sophomores. Approximately one third (27.4%) of the students lived on campus; the remaining students (72.6%) were commuters. Household annual income for 32.6% of the respondents was less than $20,000. Twenty-seven percent reported an annual household income of $20,001 to $50,000. The remainder (40.2%) reported annual income above $50,001.

When asked to identify the definition of the term "organic," 214 respondents (49.0%) selected the correct definition. Meanwhile, 138 (31.7%) recognized the USDA-approved organic seal. Knowledge of the correct definition of organic and recognition of the seal were significantly associated ($r_s = .161$, $p < .001$). Younger students (<21.6 years) were more likely to know the definition of organic and recognize the organic seal.

A majority of students knew that organic foods were available for purchase in grocery stores and in health food stores (72.2% and 79.0%, respectively). Few (9.7%) believed organic foods were available in restaurants. When asked in what form organic foods could be purchased (subjects could indicate all that applied), responses were as follows: produce (87.1%), grains (72.2%), dairy (53.5%), snacks (31.4%), meat (29.3%), beverages (28.2%), and candy (7.7%).

Most students (56.4%) were neutral in their opinion about organic foods, but 41.3% either "accept organic foods" or "only eat organic foods." Students ranked taste as the factor that influenced them most when selecting organic foods, followed by price, appearance, availability, and package information (Table 1). Approximately one third (31.1%) of respondents believed organic foods tasted the same as conventionally grown products, whereas 15.8% felt organic foods tasted better, and 12.3% felt organic foods tasted worse.

Only 20.7% of respondents reported they could purchase organic foods on campus, and few consumed more than 50% organic diets, no matter where they purchased foods. However, between 33.2% and 45.5% reported they purchased and consumed some organic foods on campus, in restaurants, or at home. The highest number (45.5%) purchased for consumption at home. When asked where they purchased organic foods 47.4% indicated the grocery store and 13.5% indicated a health food store. The frequencies of types of organic foods purchased were as follows: produce (40.4%), grains (28.2%), dairy (22.8%), drinks/beverages (20.8%), snacks (16.3%), and meat (13.8%). Interestingly, 50.5% of the students indicated they would support the use of organic foods on campus, and 64.0% reported they would buy organic foods if offered on campus.

There were significant positive relationships between knowledge of the definition of the term organic and opinion about organic foods (attitude) ($r_s = .103, p < .05$) and between recognition of the organic seal (knowledge) and opinion about organic foods (attitude) ($r_s = .197, p < .01$). Thus, awareness and attitude about organic foods were associated. Linear regression was used to test if the two knowledge variables predicted attitude. Results were

TABLE 1   FREQUENCY RANKINGS OF FACTORS AFFECTING PURCHASE OR CONSUMPTION OF ORGANIC FOODS

Factors	Rankings	
	Frequency	Percentage (%)
Price	193	46.5
Taste	247	59.7
Appearance	120	29.0
Package Information	46	11.2
Other	12	5.6

significant ($R^2 = .04$, $F(2, 422) = 9.73$, $p < .000$). Recognition of the seal was the strongest of the 2 predictors.

There was also a significant positive relationship between recognition of the organic seal and opinion about the taste of organic foods as compared to conventionally grown products ($r_s = .298$, $p < .01$). The relationship between the other knowledge variable (definition of organic) and attitude was not significant. Linear regression tested recognition of the organic seal as a predictor of attitude and was found to be significant ($R^2 = .08$, $F(2, 418) = 20.09$, $p < .000$). When knowledge of the definition of organic was added as a predictor and tested in a second linear regression, model fit did not change significantly, corroborating the previous conclusion that the stronger predictor of attitude was recognition of the seal.

Multiple correlation was used to examine the relationship between attitudes about organic foods and subject responses about the support and purchase of organic foods (behavior) in different contexts (Table 2). Attitude towards organic foods was found to be significantly related to (1) purchase and consumption of organic foods on campus, (2) purchase and consumption of organic foods (usually in restaurants), and (3) purchase for consumption of foods at home.

Given the significant findings of the correlational analysis and linear regression, we conducted a path analysis (Figure 2) to determine whether attitudes toward organic foods would predict the three sets of purchase and consumption behaviors. Attitude was found to be a significant predictor ($p < .01$) of all 3 behaviors. Path analysis can be used to determine the significance and magnitude of the direct effect of predictor variables on response variables. It is an empirical tool to test cause-and-effect relationships.[20]

Attitude towards organic foods was found to be significantly related to student perceptions of whether or not they lead healthy lifestyles ($r_s = .160$, $p < .01$). A second

TABLE 2   CORRELATION BETWEEN ATTITUDE TOWARDS AND CONSUMPTION OF ORGANIC FOOD

	Attitude towards organic foods	Purchase and consumption of organic foods		
		On campus	Off campus (restaurant)	Home
Attitude towards organic foods	—	$.284^{**}$	$.309^{**}$	$.298^{**}$
Purchase/consumption of organic foods				
On campus		—	$.670^{**}$	$.524^{**}$
Off campus (restaurant)			—	$.641^{**}$
Home				—

Note. $**p < .01$.

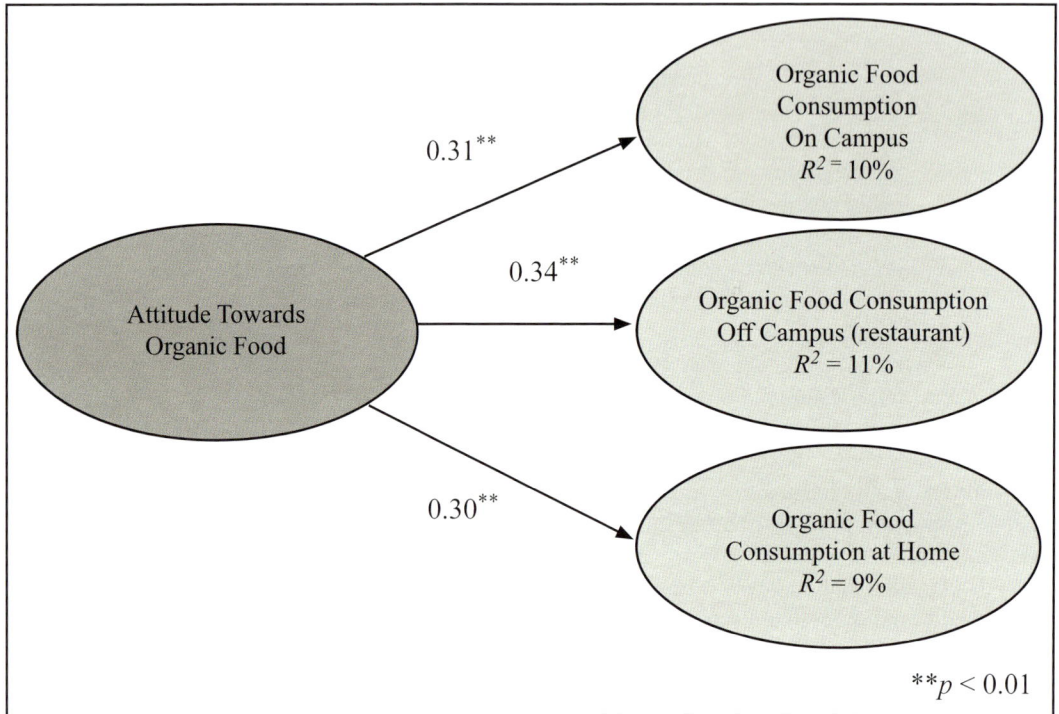

FIGURE 2. Path analysis: Direct effect of student's overall attitude towards organic foods on their food choices on-campus, off-campus, and at home.

path analysis was conducted to determine the direct effect of attitude towards organic foods on other healthy lifestyle practices. Significant path coefficients were calculated for relationships between positive attitudes towards organic foods and healthy diet ($p = .22$, $R^2 = 5.1\%$), regular exercise ($p = .14$, $R^2 = 2.1\%$), and consumption of organic foods ($p = .12$, $R^2 = 1.2\%$) only.

A final analysis examined the relationship between attitudes about other eco-friendly behaviors and the actual behaviors. Multiple correlation determined that most of the attitudes expressed about such behaviors were related to the practice of the behaviors. Further, in many instances, the respondents' attitudes about an eco-friendly behavior such as recycling and energy conservation were significantly related to supportive behaviors such as recycling, energy conservation, driving hybrid cars or carpooling, and ozone protection.

COMMENT

We found that students are relatively knowledgeable about organic food products and believe that organic foods are beneficial and necessary. Many expressed an interest in having more organic foods available on campus and indicated they would be willing to purchase organic foods if made available on campus. Contrary to the literature, we found that students were more likely to act upon the beliefs they expressed about both organic foods and eco-friendly behaviors.

Equal numbers of males and females knew the correct definition of the term organic, recognized the federal organic seal, and expressed a positive attitude towards organic foods. This finding varies somewhat from the literature, which identifies females as being more aware and having stronger attitudes about organic foods. Perhaps students, as a group, are simply more informed consumers. In future research, student responses could be compared to other types of consumers. When examining the relationship between awareness (knowledge) and attitude, we concluded that although many students selected the incorrect definition of the term organic, even these students had positive opinions in support of organic foods and other eco-friendly practices.

Most of the students in this study clustered in household income levels of under $20,000 or above $50,000. More than 30% of respondents from the upper household income levels reported that they "accept organic foods." Similar findings in the literature indicate higher levels of awareness and support for organic foods among individuals with higher incomes.[1] Future research should explore the degree to which parental/family household income affects student consumer choices. More students under the mean age of 21.6 years knew the correct definition of the term organic and recognized the organic seal. Further, twice as many younger respondents expressed positive attitudes toward organic foods as those over the mean age. This suggests that younger people may seek out organic foods in various food environments or at least feel strongly about having them available. In that case, it makes sense that university food services should integrate more organic food options into their on-campus menus.

When subjects ranked factors that influenced their buying decisions, taste was reported to be most important, followed in order by price, appearance, availability, and package information. Consumers tend to associate health benefits with organic foods. Perhaps a younger, health-minded generation of educated consumers places more emphasis on quality (taste) and value (price). Such a conclusion might also support the fact that students knew of the availability of many forms of organic foods. A future study might include a tasting panel in which student consumers identify how various factors interact to influence the buying decision.

Students indicated that they purchased organic foods for consumption at home rather than on- or off-campus. This reinforces the finding that these foods were primarily purchased at grocery stores and health food stores. Produce, grains, and dairy products were the most often purchased organic foods. We agree with the literature that health educators need to work with food service operators to develop informational materials such as table tents and posters to help students learn about other organic food options.[9]

Few students followed an all-organic diet. Most purchased and consumed "50% or less" organic foods. However, more than half reported they would support the integration of organic foods into campus menus, and even more said they would buy organic foods if offered on campus. Such findings reinforce the current move on university campuses to provide more organic food options.

Students who were able to identify the correct definition of the term organic and who recognized the USDA organic seal were more likely to have positive opinions supporting organic foods. Recognition of the organic seal was a significant predictor of the perception that organic foods tasted as good as or better than their conventionally grown counterparts. An extension of this study might involve a taste panel in which a perceptions and preferences are tested with respect to awareness and attitudes about organic foods.

The primary purpose of this study was to determine if student attitudes actually predicted corresponding behaviors with regard to organic foods. We concluded that they did. Tracking responses over time might determine if increased exposure to/availability of organic food products influences students who currently have no opinion about organic foods. We also found that students who had positive opinions about organic foods purchased and consumed such foods in different venues, most often for consumption at home. Therefore, attitude predicted behavior.

Botonaki et al.[7] suggested that consumers of organic foods are likely to engage in other healthy lifestyle practices. In our study, a positive attitude towards organic foods was significantly associated with consuming a healthy diet and exercising regularly. Health educators should further examine differences in student perceptions about healthy lifestyle practices.

Lockie et al.[1] and Magnusson et al.[2] found the consumption of organic foods and other environmentally conscious behaviors to be significantly related. In the present study, when students were asked about eco-friendly practices, there was a significant relationship between a positive attitude about these practices and the corresponding behavior. Clearly, students in this study not only felt strongly about environmental issues, but they also felt compelled towards eco-friendly practices.

CONCLUSION

In a classroom administration format or as with any self-report instrument, there is always the concern that subjects respond truthfully to the instrument items. In addition, the population characteristics of this university may be different. Thus, our findings that attitudes generally predicted behaviors must be interpreted with caution. Future studies should focus on other types of universities and track student behaviors to determine through observation whether a significant link with attitudes actually exists.

Some instrument items were forced choice, with an option to write in additional information. Forced-choice items do not accommodate the full range of possible responses even with the write-in option. For example, students with food allergies or concerns about chemical preservatives might opt for an organic diet. We may not have identified all opinions and factors relevant to the purchase and consumption of organic foods, healthy lifestyle or eco-friendly practices.

This study sampled students (young adults) from an American university, which helps to fill certain gaps in the literature. Additional research in the United States about the attitudes towards purchase and consumption of organic foods is needed.

A principle finding in this study was that students are knowledgeable about organic foods and that they support the integration of organic foods into their menu choices and diets. Although less than half of the students indicated they purchased and cc organic products in various environments, more than half of study respondents they would support the use of organic products on campus and would actually p organic foods on campus.

This sentiment is an important indicator for college and universities. There is already a demand for healthy food options on university campuses.[4,18] It seems that campus food services should evaluate not only their menu offerings, but even what they term healthy choices, in terms of organic food standards. It would be interesting to sample a portion of the respondents in this study in a year or so to determine if their attitudes have changed with regard to organic food purchase or consumption.

Our study focused on students as primary consumers; however, campuses also accommodate faculty and staff, many of whom may have opinions similar to those expressed by the students in this study. A future study might examine not only the opinions of other students on other campuses as well as other groups on campuses.

This study found that students who felt positively about organic foods were also inclined to behave accordingly. In other words, they were more likely to act on their opinions and choose to purchase and consume organic foods. Such a finding has implications for market food producers in general, in that college students are both consumers today as well as primary consumers of the future. It will be important to address this growing demand in more venues than college campuses.

REFERENCES

1. Lockie S, Lyons K, Lawrence G, Grice J. "Choosing organics: a path analysis of factors underlying the selection of organic food among Australian consumers." *Appetite*. 2004;43:135-146.
2. Magnusson M, Arvola A, Hursti U, Aberg L, Sjoden P. "Choice of organic foods is related to perceived consequences for human health and to environmentally friendly behaviour." *Appetite*. 2003;40:109-117.
3. Bissonnette M, Contento I. "Adolescents' perspectives and food choice behaviors in terms of the environmental impacts of food production practices: application of a psychosocial model." *J Nutr Educ*. 2001;33:72-82.
4. Horovitz B. "More university students call for organic, 'sustainable' food." *USAToday.com*, September 26, 2006.A.
5. "The National Organic Program." *Organic Food Standards and labels: The Facts*. Agricultural Marketing Service at United States Department of Agriculture Web site. http://www.ams.usda.gov/nop/Consumers/brochure.html. Accessed March 8, 2007.
6. "Organic faq." Organic.org Web site. http://www.organic.org/home/faq. Accessed October 17, 2006.
7. Botonaki A, Polymeros K, Tsakindou E, Mattas K. "The role of food quality certification on consumers' food choices." *Br Food J*. 2006;108:77-91.
8. Loureiro M, McCluskey J, Mittelhammer R. "Will consumers pay a premium for eco-labeled apples?" *J Consumer Affairs*. 2002;36:203-219.

9. Padel S, Foster C. "Exploring the gap between attitudes and behaviour: understanding why consumers buy or do not buy organic food." *Br Food J.* 2005;107:606-625.

10. Tregear A, Dent J, McGregor M. "The demand for organically-grown produce." *Br Food J.* 1994;96:21-26.

11 Chryssohoidis G, Krystallis, A. "Organic consumers' personal values research: testing and validating the list of values (LOV) scale and implementing a value-based segmentation task." *Food Qual Prefer.* 2005;16:585-599.

12. Dreezens E, Martijn C, Tenbult P, Kok G, de Vries N. "Food and values: an examination of values underlying attitudes toward genetically modified—and organically grown food products." *Appetite.* 2005;44:115-122.

13. Connor R, Douglas L. "Consumer attitudes to organic foods." *Nutr Food Sci.* 2001;31:254-258.

14. Davies A, Titterington A, Cochrane C. "Who buys organic food? A profile of the purchasers of organic food in Northern Ireland." *Br Food J.* 1995;97:17-24.

15. Fotopoulos, G. "Factors affecting the decision to purchase organic food." *J Eur-Marketing.* 2000;9:45-66.

16. "University of Wisconsin goes organic." *Organic Consumer Association Web site. 2006.* http://www.orgaanicconsumers.org/organic/uofw101903.cfm. Accessed October 17, 2006.

17. *Organic certification.* University of California-Berkeley Web site. http://caldining.berkeley.edu/environment.organic.cert.html. Accessed October 17, 2006.

18. Horovitz B. "Organic food spreads across campuses." *USAToday*, September 27, 2006:B2.

19. Oral Roberts Fall 2007 "Student Catalogue." *Oral Roberts University* Web site. http://www.oru.edu/catalog/ORU.hb0203.pdf. Accessed March 12, 2008.

20. Williams W, Jones M, Demment M. "A concise table for path analysis statistics." *Agron J.* 1990;82:1022-1024.

■ READING AND WRITING

1. Dahm, Samonte, and Shows wrote their article for the *Journal of American College Health*. Look online for more information about this journal and its primary audience. How are the journal's mission and audience reflected in the content and style of this article?
2. Do the conclusions presented by Dahm, Samonte, and Shows reflect your experiences with organic food? Explain your response.

■ DEVELOPING LONGER RESPONSES

3. Evaluate Dahm, Samonte, and Shows' findings. Do you consider their primary and secondary research convincing? How does the evidence they provide differ from previous essays you've read? How do the stylistic conventions of an academic journal article influence your reading experience? What are the methodological strengths and weakness of the piece? Did you find the survey questions appropriate? Were there any questions that you think should have been added? Were the charts useful in explaining the researchers' results? Given the scope that they identify, do you think this is a significant study? Do you find this type of article more or less convincing than personal narratives such as "The Pleasures of Eating" or "The Culinary Seasons of My Childhood"? Why?

■ USING RESEARCH

4. Research USC's organic food offerings. What are they? Were you aware of these offerings (or lack thereof) before your research? If organic options are available, do you regularly take advantage of them? Next, find other schools that stock local or organic food for students. What different levels of commitment to organic food in higher education do you find in your research?

Joel Salatin is a third-generation alternative farmer at Polyface Farm in Virginia's Shenandoah Valley. He and his farm have been featured in several national publications, in Michael Pollan's book The Omnivore's Dilemma, *and in the documentary film* Food, Inc. *Salatin wrote this essay for* Food, Inc.: How Industrial Food Is Making Us Sicker, Fatter, and Poorer—and What You Can Do about It, *the companion book to that film.*

DECLARE YOUR INDEPENDENCE   Joel Salatin

Perhaps the most empowering concept in any paradigm-challenging movement is simply opting out. The opt-out strategy can humble the mightiest forces because it declares to one and all, "You do not control me."

The time has come for people who are ready to challenge the paradigm of factory-produced food and to return to a more natural, wholesome, and sustainable way of eating (and living) to make that declaration to the powers that be, in business and government, that established the existing system and continue to prop it up. It's time to opt out and simply start eating better—right here, right now.

Impractical? Idealistic? Utopian? Not really. As I'll explain, it's actually the most realistic and effective approach to transforming a system that is slowly but surely killing us.

■ What Happened to Food?

First, why am I taking a position that many well-intentioned people might consider alarmist or extreme? Let me explain.

At the risk of stating the obvious, the unprecedented variety of bar-coded packages in today's supermarket really does not mean that out generation enjoys better food options than our predecessors. These packages, by and large, having passed through the food inspection fraternity, the industrial food fraternity, and the lethargic cheap-food-purchasing consumer fraternity, represent an incredibly narrow choice. If you took away everything with an ingredient foreign to our three trillion intestinal microflora, the shelves would be bare indeed. (I'm talking here about the incredible variety of microorganisms that live in our digestive tracts and perform an array of useful functions, including training our immune systems and producing vitamins like biotin and vitamin K.) In fact, if you just eliminated every product that would have been unavailable in 1900, almost everything would be gone, including staples that had been chemically fertilized, sprayed with pesticides, or ripened with gas.

Rather than representing newfound abundance, these packages wending their way to store shelves after spending a month in the belly of Chinese merchant marines are actually the meager offerings of a tyrannical food system. Strong words? Try buying real milk—as in raw. See if you can find meat processed in the clean open air under sterilizing sunshine. Look for pot pies made with local produce and meat. How about good old unpasteurized apple cider? Fresh cheese? Unpasteurized almonds? All these staples that our great-grandparents relished and grew healthy on have been banished from today's supermarket.

They've been replaced by an array of pseudo-foods that did not exist a mere century ago. The food additives, preservatives, colorings, emulsifiers, corn syrups, and unpronounceable ingredients listed on the colorful packages bespeak a centralized control mindset that actually reduces the options available to fill Americans' dinner plates. Whether by intentional design or benign ignorance, the result has been the same—the criminalization and/or demonization of heritage foods.

The mindset behind this radical transformation of American eating habits expresses itself in at least a couple of ways.

One is the completely absurd argument that without industrial food, the world would starve. "How can you feed the world?" is the most common question people ask me when they tour Polyface Farm. Actually, when you consider the fact that millions of people, including many vast cities, were fed and sustained using traditional farming methods until just a few decades ago, the answer is obvious. America has traded seventy-five million buffalo, which required no tillage, petroleum, or chemicals, for a mere forty-two million head of cattle. Even with all the current chemical inputs, our production is a shadow of what it was 500 years ago. Clearly, if we returned to herbivorous principles five centuries old, we could double our meat supply. The potential for similar increases exists for other food items.

The second argument is about food safety. "How can we be sure that food produced on local farms without centralized inspection and processing is really safe to eat?" Here, too, the facts are opposite to what many people assume. The notion that indigenous food is unsafe simply has no scientific backing. Milk-borne pathogens, for example, became a significant health problem only during a narrow time period between 1900 and 1930, before refrigeration but after unprecedented urban expansion. Breweries needed to be located near metropolitan centers, and adjacent dairies fed herbivore-unfriendly brewery waste to cows. The combination created real problems that do not exist in grass-based dairies practicing good sanitation under refrigeration conditions.

Lest you think the pressure to maintain the industrialized food system is all really about food safety, consider that all the natural-food items I listed above can be given away, and the donors are considered pillars of community benevolence. But as soon as money changes hands, all these wonderful choices become "hazardous substances," guaranteed to send our neighbors to the hospital with food poisoning. Maybe it's not human health but corporate profits that are really being protected.

Furthermore, realize that many of the same power brokers (politicians and the like) encourage citizens to go out into the woods on a 70-degree fall day; gun-shoot a deer with possible variant Creutzfeld-Jacob's disease (like mad cow for deer); drag the carcass a mile through squirrel dung, sticks, and rocks; then drive parade-like through town in the blazing afternoon sun with the carcass prominently displayed on the hood of the Blazer. The hunter takes the carcass home, strings it up in the backyard tree under roosting birds for a week, then skins it out and feeds the meat to his children. This is all considered noble and wonderful, even patriotic. Safety? It's not an issue.

The question is, who decides what food is safe? In our society, the decisions are made by the same type of people who decided in the Dred Scott ruling that slaves were not human beings. Just because well-educated, credentialed experts say something does not make it true. History abounds with expert opinion that turned out to be dead wrong. Ultimately, food safety is a personal matter of choice, of conscience. In fact, if high-fructose corn syrup is hazardous to health—and certainly we could argue that it is—then half of the government-sanctioned food in supermarkets is unsafe. Mainline soft drinks would carry a warning label. Clearly, safety is a subjective matter.

■ RECLAIMING FOOD FREEDOM

Once we realize that safety is a matter of personal choice, individual freedom suddenly—and appropriately—takes center stage. What could be a more basic freedom than the freedom to choose what to feed my three-trillion-member internal community?

In America I have the freedom to own guns, speak, and assemble. But what good are those freedoms if I can't choose to eat what my body wants in order to have the energy to shoot, preach, and worship? The only reason the framers of the American Constitution and Bill of Rights did not guarantee freedom of food choice was that they couldn't envision a day when neighbor-to-neighbor commerce would be criminalized…when the bureaucratic-industrial food fraternity would subsidize corn syrup and create a nation of diabetes sufferers, but deny my neighbor a pound of sausage from my Thanksgiving hog killin'.

People tend to have short memories. We all assume that whatever is must be normal. Industrial food is not normal. Nothing about it is normal. In the continuum of human history, what western civilization has done to its food in the last century represents a mere blip. It is a grand experiment on an ever-widening global scale. We have not been here before. The three trillion members of our intestinal community have not been here before. If we ate like humans have eaten for as long as anyone has kept historical records, almost nothing in the supermarket would be on the table.

A reasonable person, looking at the lack of choice we now suffer, would ask for a Food Emancipation Proclamation. Food has been enslaved by so-called inspectors that deem the most local, indigenous, heritage-based, and traditional foods unsafe and make them illegal. It has been enslaved by a host-consuming agricultural parasite called "government farm subsidies." It has been enslaved by corporate-subsidized research that declared for four decades that feeding dead cows to cows was sound science—until mad cows came to dinner.

The same criminalization is occurring on the production side. The province of Quebec has virtually outlawed outdoor poultry. Ponds, which stabilize hydrologic cycles and have forever been considered natural assets, are now considered liabilities because they encourage wild birds, which could bring avian influenza. And with the specter of a

National Animal Identification System being rammed down farmers' throats, small flocks and herds are being economized right out of existence.

On our Polyface Farm nestled in Virginia's Shenandoah Valley, we have consciously opted out of the industrial production and marketing paradigms. Meat chickens move every day in floorless, portable shelters across the pasture, enjoying bugs, forage, and local grain (grown free of genetically modified organisms). Tyson-style, inhumane, fecal factory chicken houses have no place here.

The magical land-healing process we use, with cattle using mob-stocking, herbivorous, solar conversion, lignified carbon sequestration fertilization, runs opposite the grain-based feedlot system practiced by mainline industrial cattle production. We move the cows every day from paddock to paddock, allowing the forage to regenerate completely through its growth curve, metabolizing solar energy into biomass.

Our pigs aerate anaerobic, fermented bedding in the hay feeding shed, where manure, carbon, and corn create a pig delight. We actually believe that honoring and respecting the "pigness" of the pig is the first step in an ethical, moral cultural code. By contrast, today's industrial food system views pigs as merely inanimate piles of protoplasmic molecular structure to be manipulated with whatever cleverness the egocentric human mind can conceive. A society that views its plants and animals from that manipulative, egocentric, mechanistic mindset will soon come to view its citizens in the same way. How we respect and honor the least of these is how we respect and honor the greatest of these.

The industrial pig growers are even trying to find the stress gene so it can be taken out of the pig's DNA. That way the pigs can be abused but won't be stressed about it. Then they can be crammed in even tighter quarters without cannibalizing and getting sick. In the name of all that's decent, what kind of ethics encourages such notions?

In just the last couple of decades, Americans have learned a new lexicon of squiggly Latin words: camphylobacter, lysteria, E. coli, salmonella, bovine spongiform encephalopathy, avian influenza. Whence these strange words? Nature is speaking a protest, screaming to our generation: "Enough!" The assault on biological dignity has pushed nature to the limit. Begging for mercy, its pleas go largely unheeded on Wall Street, where Conquistadors subjugating weaker species think they can forever tyrannize without an eventual payback. But the rapist will pay—eventually. You and I must bring a nurturing mentality to the table to balance the industrial food mindset.

Here at Polyface, eggmobiles follow the cows through the grazing cycle. These portable laying hen trailers allow the birds to scratch through the cows' dung and harvest newly uncovered crickets and grasshoppers, acting like a biological pasture sanitizer. This biomimicry stands in stark contrast to chickens housed beak by wattle in egg factories, never allowed to see sunshine or chase a grasshopper.

We have done all of this without money or encouragement from those who hold the reins of food power, government or private. We haven't asked for grants. We haven't asked for permission. In fact, to the shock and amazement of our urban friends, our farm is considered a Typhoid Mary by our industrial farm neighbors. Why? Because we don't medicate, vaccinate, genetically adulterate, irradiate, or exudate like they do. They fear our methods because they've been conditioned by the powers that be to fear our methods.

The point of all this is that if anyone waits for credentialed industrial experts, whether government or nongovernment, to create ecologically, nutritionally, and emotionally friendly food, they might as well get ready for a long, long wait. For example, just imagine what a grass-finished herbivore paradigm would do to the financial and power structure of America. Today, roughly seventy percent of all grains go through herbivores, which aren't supposed to eat them and, in nature, never do. If the land devoted to that production were converted to perennial prairie polycultures under indigenous biomimicry management, it would topple the grain cartel and reduce petroleum usage, chemical usage, machinery manufacture, and bovine pharmaceuticals.

Think about it. That's a lot of economic inertia resisting change. Now do you see why the Farm Bill that controls government input into our agricultural system never changes by more than about two percent every few years? Even so-called conservation measures usually end up serving the power brokers when all is said and done.

■ Opting Out

If things are going to change, it is up to you and me to make the change. But what is the most efficacious way to make the change? Is it through legislation? Is it by picketing the World Trade Organization talks? Is it by dumping cow manure on the parking lot at McDonald's? Is it by demanding regulatory restraint over the aesthetically and aromatically repulsive industrial food system?

At the risk of being labeled simplistic, I suggest that the most efficacious way to change things is simply to declare our independence from the figurative kings in the industrial system. To make the point clear, here are the hallmarks of the industrial food system:

- Centralized production

- Mono-speciation

- Genetic manipulation

- Centralized processing

- Confined animal feeding operations

- Things that end in "cide" (Latin for death)

- Ready-to-Eat food

- Long-distance transportation

- Externalized costs—economy, society, ecology

- Pharmaceuticals

- Opaqueness

- Unpronounceable ingredients

- Supermarkets

- Fancy packaging

- High fructose corn syrup

- High liability insurance

- "No Trespassing" signs

Reviewing this list shows the magnitude and far-reaching power of the industrial food system. I contend that it will not move. Entrenched paradigms never move...until outside forces move them. And those forces always come from the bottom up. The people who sit on the throne tend to like things the way they are. They have no reason to change until they are forced to do so.

The most powerful force you and I can exert on the system is to opt out. Just declare that we will not participate. Resistance movements from the antislavery movement to women's suffrage to sustainable agriculture always have and always will begin with opt-out resistance to the status quo. And seldom does an issue present itself with such a daily—in fact, thrice daily—opportunity to opt out.

Perhaps the best analogy in recent history is the home-school movement. In the late 1970s, as more families began opting out of institutional educational settings, credentialed educational experts warned us about the jails and mental asylums we'd have to build to handle the educationally and socially deprived children that home-schooling would produce. Many parents went to jail for violating school truancy laws. A quarter-century later, of course, the paranoid predictions are universally recognized as wrong. Not everyone opts for home-schooling, but the option must be available for those who want it. In the same way, an opt-out food movement will eventually show the Henny Penny food police just how wrong they are.

■ Learn to Cook Again

I think the opt-out strategy involves at least four basic ideas.

First, we must rediscover our kitchens. Never has a culture spent more to remodel and techno-glitz its kitchens, but at the same time been more lost as to where the kitchen is and what it's for. As a culture, we don't cook any more. Americans consume nearly a quarter of all their food in their cars, for crying out loud. Americans graze through the kitchen, popping precooked, heat-and-eat, bar-coded packages into the microwave for eating-on-the-run.

That treatment doesn't work with real food. Real heritage food needs to be sliced, peeled, sautéed, marinated, pureed, and a host of other things that require true culinary skills. Back in the early 1980s when our farm began selling pastured poultry, nobody even asked for boneless, skinless breast. To be perfectly sexist, every mom knew how to cut up a chicken. That was generic cultural mom information. Today, half of the moms don't know that a chicken even has bones.

I was delivering to one of our buying club drops a couple of months ago, and one of the ladies discreetly pulled me aside and asked: "How do you make a hamburger?" I thought I'd misunderstood, and asked her to repeat the question. I bent my ear down close to hear her sheepishly repeat the same question. I looked at her incredulously and asked: "Are you kidding?"

"My husband and I have been vegetarians. But now that we realize we can save the world by eating grass-based livestock, we're eating meat, and he wants a hamburger. But I don't know how to make it." This was an upper-middle-income, college-educated, bright, intelligent woman.

The indigenous knowledge base surrounding food is largely gone. When "scratch" cooking means actually opening a can, and when church and family reunion potlucks include buckets of Kentucky Fried Chicken, you know our culture has suffered a culinary information implosion. Big time. Indeed, according to marketing surveys roughly seventy percent of Americans have no idea what they are having for supper at 4:00 pm. That's scary.

Whatever happened to planning the week's menus? We still do that at our house. In the summer, our Polyface interns and apprentices enjoy creating a potluck for all of us Salatins every Saturday evening. All week they connive to plan the meal. It develops throughout the week, morphs into what is available locally and seasonally, and always culminates in a fellowship feast.

As a culture, if all we did was rediscover our kitchens and quit buying prepared foods, it would fundamentally change the industrial food system. The reason I'm leading this discussion with the option is because too often the foodies and greenies seem to put the onus for change on the backs of farmers. But this is a team effort, and since farmers do not even merit Census Bureau recognition, non-farmers must ante up to the responsibility for the change. And both moms and dads need to reclaim the basic food preparation knowledge that was once the natural inheritance of every human being.

■ Buy Local

After rediscovering your kitchen, the next opt-out strategy is to purchase as directly as possible from your local farmer. If the money pouring into industrial food dried up tomorrow, that system would cease to exist. Sounds easy, doesn't it? Actually, it is. It doesn't take any legislation, regulation, taxes, agencies, or programs. As the money flows to local producers, more producers will join them. The only reason the local food system is still minuscule is because few people patronize it.

Even organics have been largely co-opted by industrial systems. Go to a food co-op drop, and you'll find that more than half the dollars are being spent for organic corn chips, treats, and snacks. From far away.

Just for fun, close your eyes and imagine walking down the aisle of your nearby Wal-Mart or Whole Foods. Make a note of each item as you walk by and think about what could be grown within one hundred miles of that venue. I recommend this exercise when speaking at conferences all over the world, and it's astounding the effect it has on people. As humans, we tend to get mired in the sheer monstrosity of it all. But if we break it down into little bits, suddenly the job seems doable. Can milk be produced within one hundred miles of you? Eggs? Tomatoes? Why not?

Not everything can be grown locally, but the lion's share of what you eat certainly can. I was recently in the San Joaquin Valley looking at almonds—square miles of almonds. Some eighty-five percent of all the world's almonds are grown in that area. Why not grow a variety of things for the people of Los Angeles instead? My goodness, if you're going to irrigate anyway, why not grow things that will be eaten locally rather than things that will be shipped to some far corner of the world. Why indeed? Because most people aren't asking for local. Los Angeles is buying peas from China so almonds can be shipped to China.

Plenty of venues exist for close exchange to happen. Farmers' markets are a big and growing part of this movement. They provide a social atmosphere and a wide variety of fare. Too often, however, their politics and regulations stifle vendors. And they aren't open every day for the convenience of shoppers.

Community-supported agriculture (CSA) is a shared-risk investment that answers some of the tax and liability issues surrounding food commerce. Patrons invest in a portion of the farm's products and receive a share every week during the season. The drawback is the paperwork and lack of patron choice.

Food boutiques or niche retail facades are gradually filling a necessary role because most farmers' markets are not open daily. The price markup may be more, but the convenience is real. These allow farmers to drop off products quickly and go back to farming or other errands. Probably the biggest challenge with these venues is their overhead relative to scale.

Farmgate sales, especially near cities, are wonderful retail opportunities. Obviously, traveling to the farm has its drawbacks, but actually visiting the farm creates an accountability and transparency that are hard to achieve in any other venue. To acquire food on the farmer's own turf creates a connection, relationship, and memory that heighten the intimate dining experience. The biggest hurdle is zoning laws that often do not allow neighbors to collaboratively sell. (My book *Everything I Want to Do Is Illegal* details the local food hurdles in greater detail.)

Metropolitan buying clubs (MBCs) are developing rapidly as a new local marketing and distribution venue. Using the Internet as a farmer-to-patron real-time communication avenue, this scheme offers scheduled drops in urban areas. Patrons order via the Internet from an inventory supplied by one or more farms. Drop points in their neighborhoods offer easy access. Farmers do not have farmers' market politics or regulations to deal with, or sales commissions to pay. This transaction is highly efficient because it is nonspeculative—everything that goes on the delivery vehicle is preordered, and nothing comes back to the farm. Customizing each delivery's inventory for seasonal availability offers flexibility and an info-dense menu.

Many people ask, "Where do I find local food, or a farmer?" My answer: "They are all around. If you will put as much time into sourcing your local food as many people put into picketing and political posturing, you will discover a whole world that Wall Street doesn't know exists." I am a firm believer in the Chinese proverb: "When the student is ready, the teacher will appear." This nonindustrial food system lurks below the radar in every locality. If you seek, you will find.

■ Buy What's in Season

After discovering your kitchen and finding your farmer, the third opt-out procedure is to eat seasonally. This includes "laying by" for the off season. Eating seasonally does not mean denying yourself tomatoes in January if you live in New Hampshire. It means procuring the mountains of late-season tomatoes thrown away each year and canning, freezing, or dehydrating them for winter use.

In our basement, hundreds of quarts of canned summer produce line the pantry shelves. Green beans, yellow squash, applesauce, pickled beets, pickles, relish, and a host of other delicacies await off-season menus. I realize this takes time, but it's the way for all of us to share bioregional rhythms. To refuse to join this natural food ebb and flow is to deny connectedness. And this indifference to life around us creates a jaundiced view of our ecological nest and our responsibilities within it.

For the first time in human history, a person can move into a community, build a house out of outsourced material, heat it with outsourced energy, hook up to water from an unknown source, send waste out a pipe somewhere else, and eat food from an unknown source. In other words, in modern America we can live without any regard to the ecological life raft that undergirds us. Perhaps that is why many of us have become indifferent to nature's cry.

The most unnatural characteristic of the industrial food system is the notion that the same food items should be available everywhere at once at all times. To have empty grocery shelves during inventory downtime is unthinkable in the supermarket world. When we refuse to participate in the nonseasonal game, it strikes a heavy blow to the infrastructure, pipeline, distribution system, and ecological assault that upholds industrial food.

■ Plant a Garden

My final recommendation for declaring your food independence is to grow some of your own. I am constantly amazed at the creativity shown by urban-dwellers who physically embody their opt-out decision by growing something themselves. For some, it may be a community garden where neighbors work together to grow tomatoes, beans, and squash. For others, it may be three or four laying hens in an apartment. Shocking? Why? As a culture, we think nothing of having exotic tropical birds in city apartments. Why not use that space for something productive, like egg layers? Feed them kitchen scraps and gather fresh eggs every day.

Did someone mention something about ordinances? Forget them. Do it anyway. Defy. Don't comply. People who think nothing of driving around Washington, D.C., at eighty miles an hour in a fifty-five speed limit zone often go apoplectic at the thought of defying a zoning- or building-code ordinance. The secret reality is that the government is out of money and can't hire enough bureaucrats to check up on everybody anyway. So we all need to just begin opting out and it will be like five lanes of speeders on the beltway—who do you stop?

Have you ever wanted to have a cottage business producing that wonderful soup, pot pie, or baked item your grandmother used to make? Well, go ahead and make it, sell it to your neighbors and friends at church or garden club. Food safety laws? Forget them. People getting sick from food aren't getting it from their neighbors; they are getting it from USDA-approved, industrially produced, irradiated, amalgamated, adulterated, reconstituted, extruded, pseudo-food laced with preservatives, dyes, and high fructose corn syrup.

If you live in a condominium complex, approach the landlord about taking over a patch for a garden. Plant edible landscaping. If all the campuses in Silicon Valley would plant edible varieties instead of high maintenance ornamentals, their irrigation water would actually be put to ecological use instead of just feeding hedge clippers and lawn mower engines. Urban garden projects are taking over abandoned lots, and that is a good thing. We need to see more of that. Schools can produce their own food. Instead of hiring Chemlawn, how about running pastured poultry across the yard? Students can butcher the chickens and learn about the death-life-death-life cycle.

Clearly, so much can be done right here, right now, with what you and I have. The question is not, "What can I force someone else to do?" The question is "What am I doing today to opt out of the industrial food system?" For some, it may be having one family sit-down, locally-sourced meal a week. That's fine. We haven't gotten where we've gotten overnight, and we certainly won't extract ourselves from where we are overnight.

But we must stop feeling like victims and adopt a proactive stance. The power of many individual right actions will then compound to create a different culture. Our children deserve it. And the earthworms will love us—along with the rest of the planet.

■ READING AND WRITING

1. If the industrial food system is going to change, Salatin writes, "it is up to you and me to make the change." And the best way to do this, he says, is to "declare your independence" from the status quo. How can we do this, according to Salatin? What specifically does he mean by "opting out"?
2. How would you characterize the tone of Salatin's essay? Point to passages in the text that Salatin uses to establish this tone. Do you find the tone compelling? Is it effective? Explain.
3. How does Salatin address the two major concerns he mentions about his proposal—that the world will not be able to feed itself without industrial food and that locally grown food is not always safe? Do you think his handling of these concerns is sufficient?

■ DEVELOPING LONGER RESPONSES

4. Write a formal letter to Salatin in which you raise any questions you have about his proposal—about its feasibility, for example, or its effectiveness.

■ RESEARCH AND WRITING PROJECTS

© Peter Menzel / menzelphoto.com

1. **IMAGE 2.3,** like those on pages 71 and 88, is from the book *Hungry Planet: What the World Eats* by Peter Menzel and Faith D'Aluisio. Here, the Ahmed family of Cairo, Egypt, poses with a week's supply of food, which cost them 387.85 Egyptian Pounds, or $68.53. If you look closely, you can see some packaged and apparently processed foods mixed in with the fresh produce. Several of the readings in this chapter mention the worldwide reach of America's industrial food system, but none fully explores the issue. Using library and internet resources, research the following question: How does the U.S. industrial food system—including factory farms—affect the availability, quality, and cost of food in other parts of the world? Use your research to compile an annotated bibliography of at least six informative and reliable sources that you can use in a later writing project.

2. Working with a group of classmates, investigate and catalog the sources of the food served on the University of South Carolina campus—from dining halls to fast-food outlets. Some questions to keep in mind as you conduct your research: What companies supply the meals that are offered on campus? Where do they get the food to produce these meals? Does any of the food come from local resources (farms, ranches, or farmer's markets)? If not, why not? With your group, use your research findings to compose a report on the state of USC's food supply. Later in the semester, your instructor might ask you to develop an argument based on your research and your report.

3. Nearly every essay in this chapter speaks, in one way or another, of the need for Americans to return to the kitchen, to learn how to cook meals from scratch to avoid processed foods. Research this issue to find out if there are any organized movements—in schools, churches, or communities, for example—whose goal it is to teach Americans, especially children, to cook. Use your research, and your own experience, to write a policy argument that proposes an effective way to teach cooking skills.

4. Reread the section titled "Learn to Cook Again" in Joel Salatin's essay. With the principles Salatin states in mind, plan a meal you could cook using your own kitchen (or whatever available means you have to cook). Start by seeking out recipes and local ingredients (you might interview family members for the former and visit a local farmer's market for the latter). Then, plan your meal and prepare a menu and explanation of how the meal fits Salatin's ideas about leaving the industrial food system behind.

5. In the early 1980s, Alice Waters made history by including the first proper-noun meat on a menu: Niman Ranch beef. Since then, many restaurants have followed suit to indicate their commitment to the ideals of a loosely defined food revolution. Finding a chef's eating or food philosophy isn't just reserved for idealists. Even fast food restaurants demonstrate their beliefs through menu design. For instance, McDonald's boasts "Extra Value Meals" and a "Dollar Menu," indicating

its appeals to cost consciousness. For this assignment, write an essay in which you analyze a local restaurant's menu and how the document reveals the establishment's eating or food philosophy. Here are some questions to help you get started:

■ What is the name of the restaurant? What type of cuisine does it offer? Is it a chain restaurant? Is it a themed restaurant?

■ Who are the customers? Who is the restaurant's target demographic?

■ What assumptions does the menu make about your values or beliefs? How do these assumptions show up in the menu?

■ How much writing is on the menu? What does the writing focus on? Are there descriptions of how dishes are prepared? Does the menu include where the food comes from?

■ Are there any images on the menu? If so, what do they look like? Where are the images placed?

■ How would you describe the tone, style, and emotion of the menu? Is it playful? Serious? Succinct? Verbose? Accessible? Difficult to understand? How does the menu achieve its effect?

■ What story does the menu tell about how food should be eaten? Is eating about having fun? Connecting with friends and family? Fueling the body? Supporting local economies? Sustaining the environment? Saving money? Enjoying an unmatched experience? Be sure to link the menu's philosophy with concrete visual and textual details of the menu.

3

Reading Green

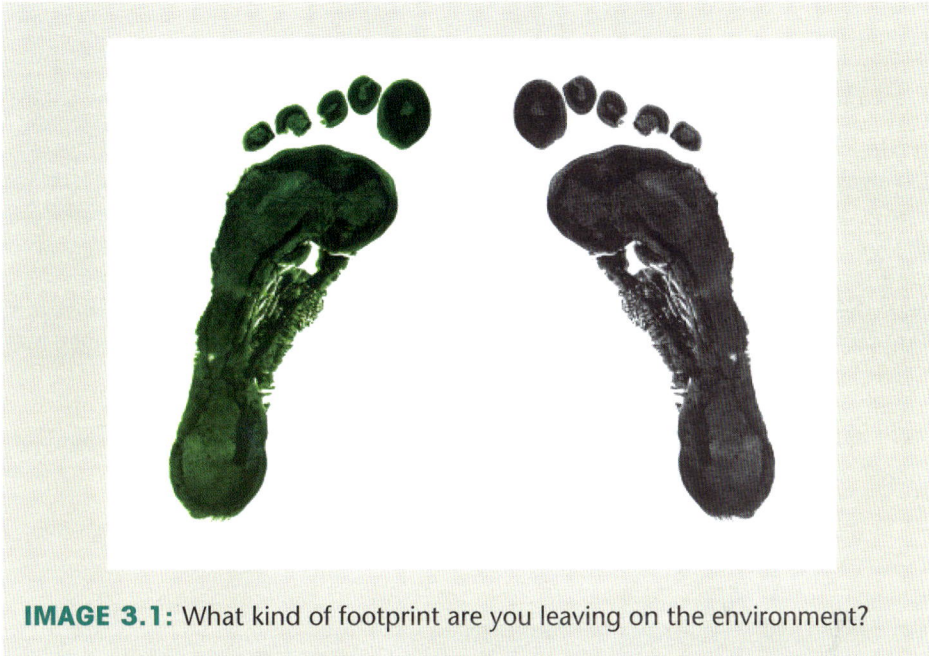

IMAGE 3.1: What kind of footprint are you leaving on the environment?

Though experts may debate the best way to address the threats to our environment, most agree that the situation is dire and that we cannot maintain our present course. Against this backdrop, this chapter provides a path through the myriad perspectives on environmental issues. Rooted in philosophy, science, politics, history, pop culture, and personal experience, the texts collected in the pages that follow consider the environmental crises we face and argue about how and why we should try to do something to protect the planet—and ourselves.

One of the world's greatest and most influential living scientists, biologist Edward O. Wilson has written numerous books and won two Pulitzer Prizes. "For the Love of Life" is the penultimate chapter of his 2002 book The Future of Life, which one reviewer called "a meditation on the splendor of our biosphere and the dangers we pose to it."

FOR THE LOVE OF LIFE Edward O. Wilson

Have you ever wondered how we will be remembered a thousand years from now, when we are as remote as Charlemagne? Many would be satisfied with a list that includes the following: *the technoscientific revolution continued, globalized, and unstoppable; computer capacity approaching that of the human brain; robotic auxiliaries proliferating; cells rebuilt from molecules; space colonized; population growth slackening; the world democratized; international trade accelerated; people better fed and healthier than ever before; life span stretched; religion holding firm.*

In this buoyant vision of the twenty-first century, what might we have overlooked about our place in history? What are we neglecting and at risk of forever losing? The answer most likely in the year 3000 is: *much of the rest of life, and part of what it means to be a human being.*

A few technophiles, I expect, will beg to differ. What, after all, in the long term does it mean to be human? We have traveled this far; we will go on. As to the rest of life, they continue, we should be able to immerse fertilized eggs and clonable tissues of endangered species in liquid nitrogen and use them later to rebuild the destroyed ecosystems. Even that may not be necessary: in time entirely new species and ecosystems, better suited to human needs than the old ones, can be created by genetic engineering. *Homo sapiens* might choose to redesign itself along the way, the better to live in a new biological order of our own making.

Such is the extrapolated endpoint of technomania applied to the natural world. The compelling response, in my opinion, is that to travel even partway there would be a dangerous gamble, a single throw of the dice with the future of life on the table. To revive or synthesize the thousands of species needed—probably millions when the still largely unknown microorganisms have been cataloged—and put them together in functioning ecosystems is beyond even the theoretical imagination of existing science. Each species is adapted to particular physical and chemical environments within the habitat. Each species has evolved to fit together with certain other species in ways biologists are only beginning to understand. To synthesize ecosystems on bare ground or in empty water is no more practicable than the reanimation of deep-frozen human corpses. And to redesign the human genotype better to fit a ruined biosphere is the stuff of science horror fiction. Let us leave it there, in the realm of imagination.

Another reason exists not to take the gamble, not to let the natural world slip away. Suppose, for the sake of argument, that new species can be engineered and stable ecosystems built from them. With that distant potential in mind, should we go ahead, and for short-term gain, allow the original species and ecosystems to slip away? Yes? Erase Earth's living history? Then also burn the libraries and art galleries, make cordwood of the musical instruments, pulp the musical scores, erase Shakespeare, Beethoven, and Goethe, and the Beatles too, because all these—or at least fairly good substitutes—can be re-created.

The issue, like all great decisions, is moral. Science and technology are what we can do; morality is what we agree we should or should not do. The ethic from which moral decisions spring is a norm or standard of behavior in support of a value, and value in turn depends on purpose. Purpose, whether personal or global, whether urged by conscience or graven in sacred script, expresses the image we hold of ourselves and our society. In short, ethics evolve through discrete steps, from self-image to purpose to value to ethical precepts to moral reasoning.

A conservation ethic is that which aims to pass on to future generations the best part of the nonhuman world. To know this world is to gain a proprietary attachment to it. To know it well is to love and take responsibility for it.

Each species—American eagle, Sumatran rhinoceros, flat-spined three-toothed land snail, furbish lousewort, and on down the roster of ten million or more still with us—is a masterpiece. The craftsman who assembled them was natural selection, acting upon mutations and recombinations of genes, through vast numbers of steps over long periods of time. Each species, when examined closely, offers an endless bounty of knowledge and aesthetic pleasure. It is a living library. The number of genes prescribing a eukaryotic life form such as a Douglas fir or a human being runs into the tens of thousands. The nucleotide pairs composing them—in other words, the genetic letters that encode the life-giving enzymes—vary among species from one billion to ten billion. If the DNA helics in one cell of a mouse, a typical animal species, were placed end on end and magically enlarged to have the same width as wrapping string, they would extend for over nine hundred kilometers, with about four thousand nucleotide pairs packed into every meter. Measured in bits of pure information, the genome of a cell is comparable to all editions of the *Encyclopedia Britannica* published since its inception in 1768.

The creature at your feet dismissed as a bug or a weed is a creation in and of itself. It has a name, a million-year history, and a place in the world. Its genome adapts it to a special niche in an ecosystem. The ethical value substantiated by close examination of its biology is that the life forms around us are too old, too complex, and potentially too useful to be carelessly discarded.

Biologists point to another ethically potent value; the genetic unity of life. All organisms have descended from the same distant ancestral life form. The reading of the genetic codes has shown thus far that the common ancestor of all living species was similar to present-day bacteria and Achaeans, single-celled microbes with the simplest known anatomy and molecular composition. Because of this single ancestry, which arose on Earth over 3.5 billion years ago, all species today share certain fundamental molecular traits. Their tissue is divided into cells, whose enveloping lipid membranes regulate exchange with the outside environment. The molecular machinery that generates energy is similar. The genetic information is stored in DNA, transcribed into RNA, and translated into proteins. Finally, a large array of mostly similar protein catalysts, the enzymes, accelerate all the life processes.

Still another intensely felt value is stewardship, which appears to arise from emotions programmed in the very genes of human social behavior. Because all organisms have descended from a common ancestor, it is correct to say that the biosphere as a whole began to think when humanity was born. If the rest of life is the body, we are the mind. Thus, our place in nature, viewed from an ethical perspective, is to think about the creation and to protect the living planet.

As cognitive scientists have focused on the nature of the mind, they have come to characterize it not just as a physical entity, the brain at work, but more specifically as a flood of scenarios. Whether set in the past, present, or future, whether based on reality or entirely fictive, these free-running narratives are all churned out with equal facility. The present is constructed from the avalanche of sensations that pour into the wakened brain. Working at a furious pace, the brain summons memories to screen and make sense of the incoming chaos. Only a minute part of the information is selected for higher-order processing. From that part, small segments are enlisted through symbolic imagery to create the white-hot core of activity we call the conscious mind.

During the story-building process the past is reworked and then returned to storage. The repeated cycles allow the brain to hold on to only small but shrinking fragments of these former conscious states. Over a lifetime the details of real events are increasingly distorted by editing and supplementation. Across generations the most important among them turn into history, and finally legend and myth.

Each culture has its own creation myth, the primary functions of which are to place the tribe that contrived it at the center of the universe, and to portray history as a noble epic. The ultimate epic unfolding through science is the genetic history both of *Homo sapiens* and of all our antecedents. Traced back far enough through time, across more than three billion years, all organisms on Earth share a common ancestry. That genetic unity is a fact-based history confirmed with increasing exactitude by the geneticists and paleontologists who reconstruct evolutionary genealogy. If *Homo sapiens* as a whole must have a creation myth—and emotionally in the age of globalization it seems we must—none is more solid and unifying for the species than evolutionary history. That is another value favoring stewardship of the natural world.

To summarize: a sense of genetic unity, kinship, and deep history are among the values that bond us to the living environment. They are survival mechanisms for ourselves and our species. To conserve biological diversity is an investment in immortality.

Do other species therefore have inalienable rights? There are three reaches of altruism possible from which a response can be made. The first is anthropocentrism: nothing matters except that which affects humanity. Then pathocentrism: intrinsic rights should be extended to chimpanzees, dogs, and other intelligent animals for whom we can legitimately feel empathy. And finally biocentrism: all kinds of organisms have an intrinsic right at least to exist. The three levels are not as exclusive as they first seem. In real life they often coincide, and when in life-or-death conflict, they can be ordered in priority as follows: first humanity, next intelligent animals, and then other forms of life.

The influence of the biocentric view, expressed institutionally through quasi-religious movements such as Deep Ecology and the Epic of Evolution, is growing worldwide. The philosopher Holmes Rolston III tells a story that can serve as a parable of this trend. For years, trailside signs at a sub alpine campground in the Rocky Mountains he occasionally visited read, "Please leave the flowers for others to enjoy." When the wooden signs began to erode and flake, they were replaced by new ones that read, "Let the flowers live!"

It is not so difficult to love nonhuman life, if gifted with knowledge about it. The capacity, even the proneness to do so, may well be one of the human instincts. The phenomenon has been called biophilia, defined as the innate tendency to focus upon life and lifelike forms, and in some instances to affiliate with them emotionally. Human beings sharply distinguish the living from the inanimate. We esteem novelty and diversity in other organisms. We are thrilled by the prospect of unknown creatures, whether in the deep sea, the unbroken forest, or remote mountains. We are riveted by the idea of life on other planets. Dinosaurs are our icons of vanished biodiversity. More people visit zoos in the United States than attend professional sports events. Their favorite site in the National Zoo of Washington, D.C., is the insect exhibit, representing maximum novelty and diversity.

A prominent component of biophilia is habitat selection. Studies conducted in the relatively new field of environmental psychology during the past thirty years point consistently to the following conclusion: people prefer to be in natural environments, and especially in savanna or park-like habitats. They like a long depth of view across a relatively smooth, grassy ground surface dotted with trees and copses. They want to be near a body of water, whether ocean, lake, river, or stream. They try to place their habitations on a prominence, from which they can safely scan the savanna and watery environment. With nearly absolute consistency, these landscapes are preferred over urban settings that are either bare or clothed in scant vegetation. To a relative degree people dislike woodland views that possess restricted depth of vision, a disordered complexity of vegetation, and rough ground structures—in short, forests with small, closely spaced trees and dense undergrowth. They want a topography and openings that improve their line of sight.

People prefer to look out over their ideal terrain from a secure position framed by the semi-enclosure of a domicile. Their choice of home and environs, if made freely, combines a balance of refuge for safety and a wide visual prospect for exploration and foraging. There may be small gender differences: among Western landscape painters at least, women stress refuges with small prospect spaces, and men stress large prospect spaces. Women also tend to place human figures in or near the refuges, while men place them more consistently in the open spaces beyond.

The ideal natural habitat is intuitively understood by landscape architects and real-estate entrepreneurs. Even when it offers no practical value, the setting commands a relatively high price, reaching its maximum if also located conveniently near cities.

I once described the principle of the ideal habitat to a wealthy friend as we looked down from his New York penthouse to the open woodland and lake of Central Park. His terrace, I also noticed, was ringed by potted plants. I thought of him as a convincing experimental subject. It has since often occurred to me that to see most clearly the manifestations of human instinct, it is useful to start with the rich, who among us enjoy the widest range of options in response, and most readily follow their emotional and aesthetic inclinations.

No direct evidence has yet been sought for a genetic basis of the human habitat preference, but its presence is suggested by a consistency in its manifestation across cultures, including those in North America, Europe, Korea, and Nigeria.

A similar convergence occurs in the aesthetics of tree form. Subjects in cross-cultural psychological tests prefer moderate-sized and sturdy trees with broad, layered canopies close to the ground. The species considered most attractive include acacias, which are dominant elements of healthy African savannas.

Tree aesthetics brings us to the question of the origin of the biophilic instincts. The human habitat preference is consistent with the "savanna hypothesis," that humanity originated in the savannas and transitional forests of Africa. Almost the full evolutionary history of the genus *Homo,* including *Homo sapiens* and its immediate ancestors, was spent in or near these habitats or others similar to them. If that amount of time, about two millions years, were to be compressed into a span of seventy years, humanity occupied the ancestral environment for sixty-nine years and eight months, whereupon some of the populations took up agriculture and moved into villages to spend the last 120 days.

The savanna hypothesis extended to include behavior stipulates that *Homo sapiens* is likely to be genetically specialized for the ancestral environment so that today, even in the most sequestered stone-and-glass cities, we still prefer it. Part of human nature is a residue of bias in mental development that causes us to gravitate back to savannas or their surrogates.

The savanna hypothesis of habitat preference may strike some readers as evolutionism run amok. But is the idea really so strange? Not at all: just a glance at the world of animal behavior suggests otherwise. Every species that moves under its own power, from protozoans to chimpanzees, instinctively seeks the habitat it must occupy in order to survive and reproduce. The behavioral steps for which it is genetically programmed are usually complex and exactly executed. The study of habitat selection is an important branch of ecology, and no species ever lets down the researcher who chooses to examine this part of its life cycle. To take one of a multitude of excellent examples, the African mosquito *Anopheles gambiae* is a species specialized to feed on human blood. (As a result it is a carrier of the malignant malarial parasite *Plasmodium falciparum*.) Each female, in order to complete her life cycle, finds her way from the stagnant pool of her birth and larval growth to a nearby village. In the daytime she hides in crevices of the house. At night she flies directly to one of the inhabitants, moving upwind through a plume of the chemically distinctive odor of the human body. She accomplishes all this with no experience and a brain the size of a grain of salt.

So it should be no great surprise that human beings, a biological species dependent on certain natural environments until very recently in its evolutionary history, should retain an aesthetic preference for savannas and transitional woodland among an array of natural and artificial environments laid before them. In general, what we call aesthetics may be just the pleasurable sensations we get from the particular stimuli to which our brains are inherently adapted.

To say that there is an instinct, or more accurately an array of instincts, that can be labeled biophilia is not to imply that the brain is hardwired. We do not ambulate like robots to the nearest lakeshore meadow. Instead, the brain is predisposed to acquire certain preferences as opposed to others. Psychologists who study mental development say that we are hereditarily *prepared* to learn certain behaviors and *counter-prepared* to learn others. The vast majority of humans, to use a familiar example, are prepared to learn the lyrics of a song but counter-prepared to learn calculus. We delight in the first and are fearful and begrudging of the second. Also, true to the pattern of instinct thus broadly defined, there are sensitive periods during childhood and early maturity in which learning and distaste are most easily picked up. In a manner also true to the conception, the timing varies among categories of behavior. Fluency in language comes earlier than fluency in mathematics.

The critical stages in the acquisition of biophilia have been worked out by psychologists during studies of childhood mental development. Under the age of six, children tend to be egocentric, self-serving, and domineering in their responses to animals and nature. They are also most prone to be uncaring or fearful of the natural world and of all but a few familiar animals. Between six and nine, children become interested in wild creatures for the first time, and aware that animals can suffer pain and distress. From nine to twelve their knowledge and interest in the natural world rises sharply, and between thirteen and seventeen they readily acquire moral feeling toward animal welfare and species conservation.

A single study in the United States devoted to the subject suggests that a parallel sequence unfolds in the development of habitat preference. Children between the ages of eight and eleven, when given a choice of environmental photographs spread before them, favored savanna over hardwood forest, north-temperate conifer forest, rainforest, and desert. In contrast, older children preferred hardwood forest and savanna equally—in other words, habitats with which they had the most direct experience during their adolescence. Both of these environments were chosen over the remaining three. From this one set of data at least, the evidence supports the savanna hypothesis. In other words, children are evidently predisposed to favor the ancestral human habitat, but then increasingly favor the environment in which they have grown up.

Another sequence occurs in the way children explore the environment. At four they confine themselves to the immediate vicinity of their home and to small creatures readily found there, the "worms, chipmunks and pigeons" of neighboring yards and streets, as David Sobel expressed it in *Children's Special Places*. At eight to eleven they head for nearby woods, fields, ditches, and other unclaimed spots they can claim as their own. There they often build some kind of shelter such as a tree house, fort, or cave where they can read magazines, eat lunch, conspire with a friend or two, play games, and spy on the world. If natural wild environments are available, so much the better, but they are not essential. In urban East Harlem, children were observed building forts in culverts, alleyways, basements, abandoned warehouses, railroad right-of-ways, and hedges.

The secret places of childhood, whether a product of instinct or not, at the very least predispose us to acquire certain preferences and to undertake practices of later value in survival. The hideaways bond us with place, and they nourish our individuality and self-esteem. They enhance joy in the construction of habitation. If played out in natural environments, they also bring us close to the earth and nature in ways that can engender a lifelong love of both. Such was my own experience as a boy of eleven to thirteen, when I sought little Edens in the forest of Alabama and Florida. On one occasion I built a small hut of saplings in a remote off-trail spot. Unfortunately, I didn't notice until later that some of the saplings were poison oak, a virulent relative of poison ivy. That was the last of my secret-house constructions, but my love of the natural world nevertheless grew even stronger.

If biophilia is truly part of human nature, if it is truly an instinct, we should be able to find evidence of a positive effect of the natural world and other organisms on health. In fact, the annals of physiology and medicine contain abundant and diverse studies affirming just such a connection, at least when health is broadly defined, to use the words of the World Health Organization, as "a state of complete physical, mental and social well-being and not merely the absence of disease and infirmity." The following results of published studies are representative:

- A population of 120 volunteers were shown a stressful movie, followed by videotapes of either natural or urban settings. By their own subjective rating, they recovered from the feeling of stress more quickly while experiencing the natural settings. Their opinion was supported by four standard physiological measures of stress: heartbeat, systolic blood pressure, facial muscle tension, and electrical skin conductance. The results suggest, although don't prove, the involvement of the parasympathetic nerves, that part of the autonomic system whose activation induces a state of relaxed awareness. The same result was obtained in a different group of student volunteers stressed by a difficult mathematical examination, and then shown videotapes that stimulated automobile rides through natural as opposed to urban settings.

- Studies of response prior to surgery and dental work have consistently revealed a significant reduction of stress in the presence of plants and aquaria. Natural environments viewed through windows or merely displayed in wall-mounted pictures produce the same effect.

- Post-surgical patients recover more quickly, suffer fewer minor complications, and need smaller dosages of painkillers if given a window view of open terrain or waterscape.

- In one Swedish study covering fifteen years of records, clinically anxious psychiatric patients responded positively to wall pictures of natural environments, but negatively, occasionally even violently, to most other decorations (especially those containing abstract art).

- Comparable studies in prisons revealed that inmates provided window views of nearby farmlands and forest, as opposed to prison yards, reported fewer stress-related symptoms such as headaches and indigestion.

- In a different category, the popular notion that owning pets reduces stress-related problems has been well supported by research conducted independently in Australia, England, and the United States. In one Australian study, which factored out variation in exercise levels, diet, and social class, pet ownership accounted for a statistically significant reduction of cholesterol, triglycerides, and systolic blood pressure. In a parallel U.S. study, survivors of heart attacks (myocardial infarction) who owned dogs had a survival rate six times higher than those who did not. The same benefit was not, I am sorry to report, enjoyed by cat owners.

The implications of biophilia for preventive medicine are substantial. The biophilic instinct can be counted as one of humanity's fortunate irrationalities, like women's choice to have fewer children when economically secure, that deserve to be understood better and put to more practical use. It is a remarkable fact that while average life expectancy in the leading industrialized countries has risen to nearly eighty years, the contribution of preventive medicine, including the design of healthful and curative environments, has remained far below potential. Obesity, diabetes, melanoma, asthma, depression, hip fracture, and breast cancer have risen in frequency since 1980. Further, despite advances in scientific knowledge and public awareness, neither coronary atherosclerosis among young people nor acute myocardial infarction among the middle-ages and old has declined. All of these conditions can be delayed or even avoided by preventive measures that include, in most cases and to the point I wish to make, a reconnection to the natural world. As such they are cost-effective, amounting to no more than salvage of natural habitats, improvements in landscape design, and relocation of windows in public buildings.

Of course nature has a dark side too. The face it presents to humanity is not always friendly. Throughout most of human deep history there have been predators eager to snatch us for dinner; venomous snakes ready with a fatal, defensive strike to the ankle; spiders and insects that bite, sting, and infect; and microbes designed to reduce the human body to malodorous catabolic chemicals. The reverse side of nature's green-and-gold is the black-and-scarlet of disease and death. The companion of biophilia is therefore biophobia. Like the responses of biophilia, those of biophobia are acquired by prepared learning. They vary in intensity among individuals according to heredity and experience. At one end of the scale are mild distaste and feelings of apprehension. At the other end are full-blown clinical phobias that fire the sympathetic nervous system and produce panic, nausea, and cold sweat. The innate biophobic intensities are most readily evoked by sources of peril that have existed in the natural world throughout humanity's evolutionary past. They include heights, close spaces, running water, snakes, wolves, rats and mice, bats, spiders, and blood. In contrast, prepared learning is unknown in response to knives, frayed electric wires, automobiles, and guns, although far deadlier today than the ancient perils of humankind, are too recent in evolutionary history to have been targeted by genetically prepared learning.

The defining properties of hereditary predisposition are multiple. One negative experience may be enough to trigger the response and permanently instill the fear. The critical stimulus can be unexpected and very simple—for example, the abrupt approach of an animal face, or the writhing of a serpent or serpent-like object nearby. The likelihood of imprinting is enhanced by already existing stressful conditions that surround the event. The learning can even be vicarious: just witnessing panic in another person or listening to a scary story can induce it in some people.

Those in whom the fear has been implanted respond almost instantly and subconsciously to subliminal images. When psychologists flashed pictures of snakes or spiders to subjects for only fifteen to thirty milliseconds, intervals too brief to be processed by the conscious mind, those previously conditioned adversely to these animals reacted with automatic muscle changes in the face within less than half a second. Although the response was easily detectable by the researchers, the subjects remained unaware that anything had happened at all.

Because aversive responses are so well defined, it has been possible to apply standard tests used in human genetics to determine whether variation in them among people has at least a partly genetic basis. The measure of choice is heritability, the standard used in studies of personality, obesity, neuroticism, and other traits that display complex variation in human populations. Heritability of a given trait is the percentage of variation among individuals in a population due to differences in genes among the individuals, as opposed to the percentage caused by differences in their environment. The heritability of innate aversion to snakes, spiders, insects, and bats respectively has been estimated to be about 30 percent, a common figure for human behavioral traits in general. The heritability of proneness to agoraphobia, an extreme aversion to crowds or open areas, is about 40 percent.

Another characteristic of prepared aversion is the existence of a sensitive period, which as in biophilic behavior is the interval in the normal life cycle when learning is easiest and the trait most apt to be established. In the case of ophidiophobia (snake), arachnophobia (spider), and other animal phobias, the onset occurs during childhood, with about 70 percent of cases occurring by ten years of age. In contrast, agoraphobia is an affliction of adolescents and young adults, triggered in 60 percent of the cases between fifteen and thirty years of age.

If elements of the natural world can sometimes paralyze modern humans by the evocation of ancient instincts, human instinct can and does wreak havoc on the natural world. Finding themselves surrounded by forests that once covered most of Earth's habitable land, Neolithic peoples set out ten thousand years ago to convert them into cropland, pasture, corrals, and scattered woodlots. What they could not chop down, they burned. Successive generations, their populations growing, continued the process until today only half the original cover is left. They needed the food, of course, but there is another way of looking at the relentless deforestation. People then as now instinctively wanted the ancestral habitat. So they proceeded to create savanna crafted to human needs. *Homo sapien* did not evolve to be a forest dweller, like chimpanzees, gorillas, and other great apes. Rather, it became a specialist of open spaces. The aesthetically ideal environment of today's transformed world is the much-treasured pastoral landscape, for better or worse our ersatz savanna.

Where does attachment to that habitat leave wilderness? No question in environmental ethics cuts more deeply. Before agriculture and villages were invented, people lived in or very close to nature. They were part of it, and had no need for the concept of wilderness. Pastoral settlers drew a line between cultivated and virgin land. As they pushed back virgin land and built more complex societies with the aid of agricultural surpluses, they sharpened the distinction. Those in more advanced cultures imagined themselves to be above the untamed world around them. They were destined, they thought, to dwell among the gods. The word "wilderness" acquired the meaning expressed in its Old English progenitor *wil(d) dēornes:* wild, savage. To pastoral and urban sensibilities, it was the impenetrable dark woods, the mountain fastness, the thorn bush desert, the open sea, and any other part of the world that had not been and might never be tamed. It was the realm of beasts, savages, evil spirits, magic, and the menacing, amorphous unknown.

The European conquest of the New World established the concept of wilderness as a frontier region waiting to be rolled back. The image was most clearly formed in the United States, whose early history is geographically defined as a westward march across an undeveloped and fertile continent.

Then came a tipping point. By the time the American frontier closed, around 1890, wilderness had become a scarce resource at risk of being eliminated altogether and hence worth saving. American environmentalism was born, rising upon the new conservation ethic created by Henry David Thoreau, John Muir, and other nineteenth-century prophets. It spread slowly through the United States, Europe, and elsewhere. It argued that humanity would be foolish to wager its future on a wholly transformed planet. Wild lands in particular, the early environmentalists said, have a unique value for humankind. The warrior king of the movement was Theodore Roosevelt, who declared, "I hate a man who skins the land."

What is a wilderness today in our largely humanized world? What it has always been: a space that sustains itself, was here before humanity, and where, in the words of the Wilderness Act of 1964, "the Earth and its community of life are untrammeled by man and where man himself is a visitor who does not remain." The true great wildernesses of the world include the rainforests of the Amazon, the Congo, and New Guinea; the evergreen coniferous forests of northern North America and Eurasia; and Earth's ancient deserts, polar regions, and open seas.

A few contrarians like to claim that true wilderness is a thing of the past. They point out, correctly, that very few places on land have remained untrodden by human feet. Moreover, 5 percent of Earth's land surface is burned every year, and the plumes of nitrous oxide produced travel most of the way around the world. Greenhouse gases thicken, global temperatures rise, and glaciers and montane forests retreat up mountain peaks. With the exception of a few places in tropical Asia and Africa, terrestrial environments everywhere have lost most of their largest mammals, birds, and reptiles, destabilizing the populations of many other kinds of plants and animals. As the remnant wild areas shrink, they are invaded by more and more alien species, diminishing the native plants and animals yet more. The smaller the area of the natural reserves, the more we are forced to intervene to avoid the partial collapse of their ecosystems.

All true. But to claim that the surviving wildernesses are less than the name implies, and have in some sense become part of the human domain, is false. The argument is specious. It is like flattening the Himalayas to the level of the Ganges Delta by saying that all the planet's surface is but a geometer's plane. Walk from a pasture into a tropical rainforest, sail from a harbor marina to a coral reef, and you will see the difference. The glory of the primeval world is still there to protect and savor.

The exact perception of wilderness is a matter of scale. Even in disturbed environments, with most of their native plants and vertebrates long vanished, bacteria, protozoans, and miniature invertebrates still maintain the ancient substratum. The micro-wildernesses are more accessible than full-scale wildernesses. They are usually only minutes away, waiting to be visited by microscope instead of jetliner. A single tree in a city park, harboring thousands of species, is an island, complete with miniature mountains, valleys, lakes, and subterranean caverns. Scientists have only begun to explore these compacted worlds. Educators have made surprisingly little use of them in introducing the wonders of life to students. Micro aesthetics based upon them is still an unexplored wilderness to the creative mind.

A strong case can be made for the creation of micro-reserves. A one-hectare patch of rainforest still clinging to a Honduran hillside, a road strip of native grasses in Iowa, and a muddy natural pond on the edge of a Florida golf course are to be valued and preserved even if the large native organisms that once lived in and around them have disappeared.

Still, while micro-reserves are infinitely better than nothing at all, they are no substitute for macro- and mega-reserves, where full-blown biotas with sizable animals continue to live. People can acquire an appreciation for savage carnivorous nematodes and shape-shifting rotifers in a drop of pond water, but they need life on the large scale to which the human intellect and emotion most naturally respond. No one of my acquaintance, except a few microbiologists, would visit a town dump upon being told it harbors a dazzling variety of bacteria. But tourists and locals alike travel to the dumps of sub-arctic Canadian towns to watch scavenging polar bears.

To the multiple valorizations of wild environments can be added mystery. Without mystery life shrinks. The completely known is a numbing void to all active minds. Even a laboratory rat seeks the advantage of the maze.

So we are drawn to the natural world, aware that it contains structure and complexity and length of history as well, at orders of magnitude greater than anything yet conceived in human imagination. Mysteries solved within it merely uncover more mysteries beyond. For the naturalist every entrance into a wild environment rekindles an excitement that is childlike in spontaneity, often tinged with apprehension—in short, the way life ought to be lived, all the time.

I will offer one such personal remembrance out of hundreds forever fresh in my mind. It is the summer of 1965, in the Dry Tortugas, at the tip of the Florida Keys. I stand at the water's edge on Garden Key, with Fort Jefferson at my back, looking across a narrow channel to Bush Key, where the littoral scrub and mangrove swamp are alive with thousands of nesting sooty terns. I have a boat, and I will go there soon, but right now I have an inexplicable urge to swim across instead. The channel is about a hundred feet across, maybe less, and the tidal current from the Gulf of Mexico to Florida Bay is for the moment too slow to pose a risk. There will be no problem if I choose to swim, it seems. Then I look more closely at the moving water. How deep is the channel center? What might come up from below to meet me? A barracuda? I saw a five-footer circling the nearby dock pilings that morning. And what do I know about the local sharks? Hammerheads and bull sharks are common in deeper water, for sure, and have been known to attack humans. Great whites are occasionally seen. Shark attacks in this region are very rare, yet—would I be the dramatic exception? Now, reflecting as I hesitate, I feel an urge not just to cross, but to dive and explore the bottom of the channel. I want to know it inch by inch as I know the soil surface of the islands I have been studying, to see what else lives there and comes in sporadically from the Gulf.

The impulse to swim fades as quickly as it arose, but I make a resolution to come back someday and become an intimate of the channel and its inhabitants and to bond with this place on which I have randomly fixated, to make it part of my life. There is something crazy about the episode, but also something real, primal, and deeply satisfying.

At some time in our lives—for the naturalist always—we long for the gate to the paradisiacal world. It is the instinctive after-image that comes to us in daydreams, and a wellspring of hope. Its mysteries, if ignited in our minds and solved, grant more control over existence. If ignored, they leave an emotional void. How did such a strange quality of human nature come about? No one knows for sure, but evolutionary genetics tells us that even if just one person in a thousand survived because of a genetic predisposition to explore the unknown and persevere in daunting circumstances, then over many generations, natural selection would have installed the predisposition in the whole human race to wonder and take the dare.

We need nature, and particularly its wilderness strongholds. It is the alien world that gave rise to our species, and the home to which we can safely return. It offers choices our spirit was designed to enjoy.

■ READING AND WRITING

1. Wilson cites the World Health Organization's definition of health: "a state of complete physical, mental, and social well-being and not merely the absence of disease and infirmity." According to Wilson, how does biophilia promote this state of being? What do you think is the environment's role in promoting the health of humans?

2. Wilson recounts philosopher Holmes Rolston III's telling of a brief story: "For years, trailside signs at a sub alpine campground in the Rocky Mountains ... read, 'Please leave the flowers for others to enjoy.' When the wooden signs began to erode and flake, they were replaced by new ones that read, 'Let the flowers live!'" What does this anecdote mean? How does Wilson use it to explain the nature of biocentrism?

■ USING RESEARCH

3. Wilson writes that "micro-wildernesses are more accessible than full-scale wildernesses. They are usually only minutes away, waiting to be visited by the microscope instead of jetliner." By way of example, Wilson likens a single tree in a city park to an island. With this metaphor in mind, explore the USC campus, your backyard, or a local park, forest,

or lake. What micro-wildernesses make up your local environment? Your instructor may ask you to work with a small group or as a class to develop a list of these locations and discuss how they might introduce you and others to what Wilson characterizes as "the wonders of life."

Maywa Montenegro, an editor at Seed magazine, likes to write about agriculture, biodiversity, and sustainable development. Terry Glavin, a journalist, editor, and author of numerous books, teaches in the Creative Writing Department at University of British Columbia and maintains the blog "Chronicles and Dissent." They wrote this piece for the October 2008 print edition of Seed; it was published on Seed's website in July 2010.

IN DEFENSE OF DIFFERENCE

Maywa Montenegro and Terry Glavin

In January 2008, at the St. Innocent Russian Orthodox Cathedral in Anchorage, Alaska, friends and relatives gathered to bid their last farewell to Marie Smith Jones, a beloved matriarch of her community. At 89 years old, she was the last fluent speaker of the Eyak language. In May 2007 a cavalry of the Janjaweed—the notorious Sudanese militia responsible for the ongoing genocide of the indigenous people of Darfur—made its way across the border into neighboring Chad. They were hunting for 1.5 tons of confiscated ivory, worth nearly $1.5 million, locked in a storeroom in Zakouma National Park. Around the same time, a wave of mysterious frog disappearances that had been confounding herpetologists worldwide spread to the US Pacific Northwest. It was soon discovered that Batrachochytrium dendrobatidis, a deadly fungus native to southern Africa, had found its way via such routes as the overseas trade in frog's legs to Central America, South America, Australia, and now the United States. One year later, food riots broke out across the island nation of Haiti, leaving at least five people dead; as food prices soared, similar violence erupted in Mexico, Bangladesh, Egypt, Cameroon, Ivory Coast, Senegal and Ethiopia.

All these seemingly disconnected events are the symptoms, you could say, of a global epidemic of sameness. It has no precise parameters, but wherever its shadow falls, it leaves the landscape monochromatic, monocultural, and homogeneous. Even before we've been able to take stock of the enormous diversity that today exists—from undescribed microbes to undocumented tongues—this epidemic carries away an entire human language every two weeks, destroys a domesticated food-crop variety every six hours, and kills off an entire species every few minutes. The fallout isn't merely an assault to our aesthetic or even ethical values: As cultures and languages vanish, along with them go vast and ancient storehouses of accumulated knowledge. And as species disappear, along with them go not just valuable genetic resources, but critical links in complex ecological webs.

Experts have long recognized the perils of biological and cultural extinctions. But they've only just begun to see them as different facets of the same phenomenon, and to tease out the myriad ways in which social and natural systems interact. Catalyzed in part by the urgency that climate change has brought to all matters environmental, two progressive movements, incubating already for decades, have recently emerged into fuller view.

Joining natural and social scientists from a wide range of disciplines and policy arenas, these initiatives are today working to connect the dots between ethnosphere and biosphere in a way that is rapidly leaving behind old unilateral approaches to conservation. Efforts to stanch extinctions of linguistic, cultural, and biological life have yielded a "biocultural" perspective that integrates the three. Efforts to understand the value of diversity in a complex systems framework have matured into a science of "resilience." On parallel paths, though with different emphases, different lexicons, and only slightly overlapping clouds of experts, these emergent paradigms have created space for a fresh struggle with the tough questions: What kinds of diversity must we consider, and how do we measure them on local, regional, and global scales? Can diversity be buffered against the streamlining pressures of economic growth? How much diversity is enough? From a recent biocultural diversity symposium in New York City to the first ever global discussion of resilience in Stockholm, these burgeoning movements are joining biologist with anthropologist, scientist with storyteller, in building a new framework to describe how, why, and what to sustain.

The biological diversity crisis is often called the "Sixth Extinction" because an event of this magnitude has occurred only five times in the history of life on Earth. The last was at the end of the Cretaceous period, when the dinosaurs disappeared. In the past couple hundred years, humans have increased species extinction rates by as much as 10,000 times the background rates that have been typical over Earth's history. This is a crash that, within the scientific community, is causing a slow panic and a wide belief that the dangers of biodiversity loss are woefully underestimated by most everyone outside of science. Yet even those who grasp extinction's severity haven't made much of a noticeable contribution to its containment. On May 16, 2008, the Zoological Society of London released a report suggesting that since contemporary environmentalism emerged with the declaration of the first Earth Day in 1970, close to one-third of all the wild species on Earth have disappeared. Language conservationists have fared no better: Of the world's roughly 6,800 languages, fully half—though some experts say closer to 90 percent—are expected to disappear before the end of the century.

Our collective failure to recognize and impede this rampant winnowing of diversity can in part be blamed on the sheer rapidity with which it has advanced. Since only 1900, the human population has increased by a factor of four, water use by a factor of nine, carbon dioxide emissions by 17, marine-fish catch by 35, and industrial output by 40. It's this expanding human footprint, and the global commerce on which it depends, that unifies the stories of Marie Smith Jones, the Janjaweed horsemen, the disappearing frogs, and the food riots. The transnational flow of people and products, media and information, crops and commodities has never in the history of the planet been so heavy or so fast. But as globalized trade expands across horizons, it both uproots local cultures and kills off vulnerable species of animals and plants. If it's not the literal extinction of a language when its last speaker dies or the spread of a devastating invasive fungus, it's the trafficking of such exotic commodities as elephant tusks, which only get more precious as the animals' numbers dwindle. A world increasingly calibrated on consumption, efficiency, and convenience is perhaps most apparent in modern industrial agriculture, which churns out mass quantities of food but also demands ever greater uniformity and standardization. And deep flaws within the system are beginning to show. This year a potent mix of drought, flooding, high fuel prices, and an increased developing-world demand for meat caused supplies of many staple crops to plummet and their prices to surge. But as scientists and farmers consider how to breed and engineer the next generation of higher-yielding, climate-resilient plants, they confront an alarmingly shallow gene pool. Addressing the audience at the World Food Summit in May, Alexander Müller, assistant director-general of the UN Food and Agriculture Organization, warned that most of the global food supply had narrowed to just a dozen crops and 14 animal species. According to the FAO, three-quarters of the world's critically important food-crop varieties have disappeared during the 20th century, and hundreds of locally adapted livestock breeds are on the verge of doing so. "The erosion of biodiversity for food and agriculture severely compromises global food security," said Müller.

The tether between linguistic, cultural, and biological extinction is, however, far more complex than its common, top-down driver of globalization. Once set in motion, the extinctions themselves also become drivers, creating a dense network of positive feedback loops. That we are beginning to understand the intricacies of these relationships is due in no small measure to the work of Italian-born anthropologist and linguist Luisa Maffi. Thirty years ago, fresh out of the University of Rome, Maffi was doing fieldwork in Somalia when she first began to surmise a connection between language and ecology. She moved to the University of California at Berkeley and began working toward a PhD in anthropology doing research on ethnomedicine in Chiapas, Mexico. It was in Chiapas that Maffi had a kind of epiphany.

The way Maffi tells the story, she was interviewing Tzeltal Mayan people waiting in line at a medical clinic in the village of Tenejapa when she met a man who had walked for hours, carrying his two-year-old daughter, who was suffering from diarrhea. It turned out that the man had only a dim memory of the "grasshopper leg herb" that was once well known as a perfectly effective diarrhea remedy in the Tzeltal ethnomedical pharmacopeia. Because he'd nearly forgotten the words for the herb, he'd lost almost any trace of the herb's utility, or even of its existence.

This is when the full impact of current global trends dawned on her, Maffi recalls. It's not just species or languages that are vanishing from the world. The world is losing knowledge, too, of the most useful and precious kinds. If the world was losing local knowledge, what else was slipping away?

Maffi began to cast her net broadly, reaching out to indigenous leaders, academics in the natural and social sciences, development experts, and, of course, linguists. In 1996 she and her colleagues organized a pivotal conference at Berkeley, "Endangered Knowledge, Endangered Environments," and one year later, Maffi founded Terralingua, an international organization dedicated to research, education, and advocacy for "linguistic human rights." Thanks in large part to Maffi, the term "biocultural diversity" started showing up with increasing frequency in the lexicon of a wide variety of scientists and academics concerned with the phenomenon of extinction.

The biocultural perspective is now gaining a high profile on the international scene. Last October, when United Nations Environment Program (UNEP) released its Global Outlook 4 report, reiterating the scientific consensus that, ultimately, humans are to blame for current global extinctions, UNEP for the first time made an explicit connection between the ongoing collapse of biological diversity and the rapid, global-scale withering of cultural and linguistic diversity: "Global social and economic change is driving the loss of biodiversity and disrupting local ways of life by promoting cultural assimilation and homogenization," the report noted. "Cultural change, such as loss of cultural and spiritual values, languages, and traditional knowledge and practices, is a driver that can cause increasing pressures on biodiversity...In turn, these pressures impact human well-being."

A second major milestone—arguably even more significant—came earlier this year, when more than 300 leading thinkers in nature conservation, linguistics, anthropology, and biology gathered at the American Museum of Natural History in New York City for a symposium entitled "Sustaining Cultural and Biological Diversity in a Rapidly Changing World: Lessons for Global Policy." Co-organized by the museum's Center for Biodiversity Conservation, Maffi's Terralingua, and a handful of other groups, the symposium was an attempt to begin rectifying what those involved identified as two gaping handicaps: a "mutual isolation" between the natural and social sciences and a "limited appreciation of the relevance of the vast variety of approaches to human-environment relationships that have developed across the world's diverse cultures." Through four days of panels, presentations, and informal "ubuntu" sessions (in the spirit of the African "humanity towards others" ethic), the forum highlighted a renewed interest in transdisciplinary fields such as enthnolinguistics, ethnozoology, ethnobotany, ethnobiology, and ethnoecology— all of which focus on documenting, describing, and understanding how other peoples perceive, use, and manage their environments.

The symposium ended on a firm and high note: a formal resolution to be put before the International Union for the Conservation of Nature (IUCN) when it convenes this October in Barcelona, Spain. The resolution calls on the IUCN—which until now has focused solely on nonhuman aspects of conservation—to begin integrating into its policies and programs efforts to preserve cultural diversity.

"If it all happens the way we want, this would be a really huge shift," says Eleanor Sterling, director of the Center for Biodiversity Conservation. "It would mean a focus not just on biodiversity, but also on how people have traditionally shaped the land. It would be a major shift in the way the world thinks about what it is we're trying to conserve."

Maffi agrees that if the Barcelona resolution is adopted, it will completely change the way the IUCN operates. A key contributor to the biodiversity sections of last year's UNEP Global Outlook report, Maffi says the concept of biocultural diversity appears to have finally hit its stride. "When I think about where we were 12 years ago," Maffi says, "this sort of thing just wasn't what people were talking about. It was difficult to open a clearing for these discussions to take place. But now we are getting to this important understanding that nature and culture are one thing. It's gone from being a really obscure issue to having an important place in international forums."

It is one thing, of course, to recognize on paper that culture and nature, language and landscape, are intimately connected. Discerning what those relationships are, in a rigorous manner, is infinitely more challenging, and it's the sort of research that Maffi and others are just delving into. Some patterns, however, have already emerged—the most remarkable being a striking geographic overlap: Epicenters of global biodiversity, it turns out, tend to be situated in exactly the same places as the epicenters of high cultural, linguistic, and food-crop diversity. One of these so-called "megadiversity" hotspots sits on the borderlands of Burma, India, and China, in the tropical forests of the Eastern Himalayas. In just one small corner of the region, more than 30 Tibeto-Burman languages are spoken; in the gardens of just three small villages within one tribal district, more than 150 domesticated food-plant varieties are under cultivation.

Indeed, if it were possible for a person to hover over the Earth and to somehow detect biocultural richness, they would see, on every continent save Antarctica, regions where nature and culture seem to have spilled all their riches in concentrated drops. Why this overlap exists, however, makes for an ongoing riddle, for the lines of cause and effect can—and often do—run in many directions. Habitat loss through deforestation, for example, is widely known to result in language death and mass extinction of animal and plant species. But sometimes, as in the case of Canada's pine forests, the causality is inverted. Over the past decade, mountain pine beetles have killed off about 7 million hectares of British Columbia's forests—an area roughly equal in size to the state of New York. But the story really begins with smallpox, which swept through the interior about 150 years ago, decimating tribal communities that had for thousands of years regularly burned the forests in order to regulate berry production and deer abundance. When that management scheme came to an end, the result was a landscape of dense forests and even-aged stands of pine. A government policy of fire suppression, coupled with fewer winter cold snaps, and the pine forests became increasingly susceptible to insect infestations and massive fires.

That the Earth is becoming more homogeneous—less of a patchwork quilt and more of a melting pot—is only partly due to the extinction of regionally unique languages or life forms. The greater contributing factor is invasiveness. According to the 2005 Millennium Ecosystem Assessment report, as rapidly as regionally unique species are dying out, rates of species introductions in most regions of the world actually far exceed current rates of extinction. Similarly, the spread of English, Spanish, and, to a lesser extent, Chinese, into all corners of the world easily dwarfs the rate of global language loss. This spread of opportunistic species and prodigal tongues thrives on today's anthropogenic conduits of commerce and communications.

Bringing new organisms or new languages into a community nearly always results in an increase of global homogeneity. Its effect on diversity is, however, more complex, raising an important point about the very concept of diversity: It makes sense only as a matter of scale. If, for example, you introduce several weedy species to an African veldt, you will increase local biodiversity. Introduce English into a multidialect Alaskan community, and you will increase local linguistic diversity—you are, after all, just adding more to the mix. But gains in local diversity due to new introductions are likely to be short-lived. Just as languages often become overwhelmed by more dominant ones, invasive plants, animals, and microbes often eventually outcompete and replace native life. If even one native grass or one native dialect perishes as a result of these introductions—as is almost always the case—global biodiversity suffers. Thus, homogeneity, while not synonymous with extinction, reflects both extinctions in the past and ones likely to ensue.

But what, ultimately, is the value in diversity? What merits the colossal efforts required to preserve it? According to biologist E.O. Wilson's often-cited "biophilia" hypothesis, humans have an innate attraction to other kinds of creatures and a desire to live in a world of diverse and abundant forms of life. Pose questions on the value of diversity to a group of people, and some will certainly emerge as biophiles, citing the intrinsic worth of other life forms and other ways of knowing, and therefore, their inherent right to exist. Others will take a more utilitarian tack, mentioning the carbon sink services of a forest or the role of local languages as records of human history. Still others will be hard-pressed to find any value at all. But amid the philosophical, the pragmatic, and the nonexistent, there's a new paradigm emerging to describe the importance of diversity. For a small group of forward-thinking biologists, ecologists, physicists, and economists who assembled earlier this year in Stockholm, the answer is simple: It's all about resilience.

Resilience theory, and the nascent field of resilience science associated with it, begins with the basic premise that human and natural systems act as strongly coupled, integrated systems. These so-called "social-ecological" systems are understood to be in constant flux and highly unpredictable. And unlike standard ecological theory, which holds that nature responds to gradual changes in a correspondingly steady fashion, resilience thinking holds that systems often respond to stochastic events—things like storms or fires—with dramatic shifts into completely different states from which it is difficult, if not impossible, to recover. Numerous studies of rangelands, coral reefs, forests, lakes, and even human political systems show this to be true: A clear lake, for instance, seems hardly affected by fertilizer runoff until a critical threshold is passed, at which point the pond abruptly turns murky. A reef dominated by hard coral can, in the aftermath of a hurricane, flip into a state dominated by algae. A democratic nation stricken by drought, disease, or stock market crashes can descend into political chaos.

It's the ability of a system—whether a tide pool or township—to withstand environmental flux without collapsing into a qualitatively different state that is formally defined as "resilience." And that is where diversity enters the equation. The more biologically and culturally variegated a system is, the more buffered, or resilient, it is against disturbance. Take the Caribbean Sea, where a wide variety of fish once kept algae on the coral reef in check. Because of overfishing in recent years, these grazers gradually gave way to sea urchins, which continued to keep algae levels down. Then in 1983 a pathogen moved in and decimated the urchin population, sending the reef into a state of algal dominance. Thus, the loss of diversity through overfishing eroded the resilience of the system, making it vulnerable to an attack it likely could have withstood in the past.

For Crawford "Buzz" Holling, widely acknowledged as the father of resilience theory and founding director of the Resilience Alliance, a small international network of academics who collaborate to explore the dynamics of social-ecological systems, this year marked a definite coming of age of an idea. At the first annual Resilience 2008 summit, held at the newly opened Resilience Center at the University of Stockholm, Holling delivered the keynote address to more than 600 scientists, policymakers, and artists, convened for a four-day brainstorm session. As was the case at the AMNH symposium just weeks earlier, the focus was on how to move from theory to practice. And once one starts thinking through the lens of resilience, the policy implications are indeed enormous. Economics necessarily morphs into its social-ecological analogue, "ecological economics"—so that a city seeking to expand its boundaries, for example, must consider not only costs and benefits in human terms, but also the same calculus as applied to the environment. Efficiency at the expense of diversity becomes anathema, so that a company struggling to stay afloat thinks twice before replacing five human workers with one seemingly smarter machine. Redundancy is encouraged, rather than quashed, on the grounds that more genes and more memes ultimately provide insurance against a time when changing conditions overwhelm the dominant paradigm of the day. There is no "sacred balance" in nature, says Holling. "That is a very dangerous idea."

Resilience science can get bogged down in its own specific lexicon: a cloud of "adaptive capacities," "functional groups," and "self-organizing principles." But pull back from the jargon and the essence is simple: Homogeneous landscapes—whether linguistic, cultural, biological, or genetic—are brittle and prone to failure. The evidence peppers human history, as Jared Diamond so meticulously catalogued in his aptly named book, Collapse. Whether it was due to a shifting climate that devastated a too-narrow agricultural base, a lack of cultural imagination in how to deal with the problem, or a devastating combination of the two, societies insufficiently resilient enough to cope with the demands of a changing environment invariably crumbled. The idea is perhaps best summed up in the pithy standard, "What doesn't bend, breaks."

By the reckoning of ecological economist Robert Costanza, the value of all Earth's ecosystem services amounts to a staggering $33 trillion. When this figure was published in Nature back in 1997 the impact rippled widely—for the first time people had a sense of what an intact biosphere contributes to the economy, and, on the flip side, what the fallout of its destruction would be. Decelerating the biological and the cultural extinctions we now understand to be close affiliates is the only logical response to this kind of calculation. And yet no one seems to have even a vague figure in mind when it comes to a goal. Just how much diversity—biological, linguistic, or social—is enough?

The first difficulty is inherent in the question itself: "Enough for what?" To be resilient against 75 percent of environmental change? Against 90 percent? Enough to fulfill how much of the aesthetic, utilitarian, and scientific value it encompasses? The second problem, more concrete though equally intractable, is that in 2008 we still have only a partial record of the biological and linguistic diversity that exists on the planet. On geneticist Craig Venter's recent two-year cruise aboard the Sorcerer II, he more than doubled all the genes known so far to science. During an interview upon returning, Venter said, "We're finding as many as 40,000 new species of bacteria in a barrel of seawater. And that's not counting viruses. There may be as many as 400,000 of those." Wilson estimates that humans have named only about 1.5 to 1.8 million species, among a total number that scientists put somewhere between 3.6 and 112 million. While no reliable data concerning the level of documentation of the world's languages exists, a plausible estimate is that fewer than 10 percent are "well documented," meaning that they have comprehensive grammars, extensive dictionaries, and abundant texts in a variety of genres and media. The remaining 90 percent are, to varying degrees, underdocumented, or, for all intents and purposes, not documented at all.

Perhaps the closest anyone has come to an explicit goal for conserving diversity is the "2010 Biodiversity Target," a decision approved in 2002 by the 188 (now 191) member nations of the UN Convention on Biological Diversity. Its aim is ambitious: "to achieve by 2010 a significant reduction of the current rate of biodiversity loss at the global, regional, and national level as a contribution to poverty alleviation and to the benefit of all life on earth." But despite marked progress, including the 2006 incorporation of the objective into the UN Millennium Development Goals and a recent redoubled commitment to it by global leaders at the 2008 World Biodiversity Summit in Bonn, by the UN's own reckoning, the target is unlikely to be met by 2010 without "unprecedented additional efforts." A less lofty, though perhaps more feasible, approach has focused on the shoring up of the world's biological hot spots. With organizations such as Conservation International and the World Wildlife Fund, Wilson has spent the past several years advocating for the urgent protection of 25 tracts of land that account for only 1.4 percent of the Earth's terrestrial surface but house 44 percent of its plant species and more than one-third of all species of birds, mammals, reptiles, and amphibians. He estimates that the cost of this project would amount to around $25 billion—or roughly 5 percent of the US defense budget for 2008. Given the clear geographic overlap between biodiversity and language hotspots—and more crucially, what Maffi and others are identifying as the coevolution of language and ecology—that $25 billion could quite possibly be the best bargain on Earth.

The emergent paradigms of biocultural diversity and resilience science are not, however, without their detractors. In a 2005 paper, University of Chicago linguist and evolutionary biologist Salikoko Mufwene said he wondered whether bioculturalists weren't "simply being paternalistic and not making an effort to learn what has led speakers to give up their languages." He argued that people routinely exchange their native languages for perfectly rational social and economic benefits, and "ethnolinguistic segregation" is no remedy to the economic conditions at the root of language loss. "The embarrassment," he said, "is that language rights advocates have given little thought to the revolution that is entailed by their discourse."

Perhaps Mufwene has a point. After all, more than 96 percent of the world's languages are spoken by just 4 percent of its people. If all the planet's endangered tongues disappeared tomorrow, hardly anyone, relatively speaking, would notice. And who, really, would mourn the loss of a few million undiscovered microbes? We might accept that some extinction is the justifiable trade-off for the many advantages of a globalized society—that to maintain a world rapidly becoming hotter, smaller, and more crowded, the luxuries of heterogeneity may have to go.

That argument might be more convincing if our current trajectory didn't look so precarious. For all that modern, industrialized civilization has produced—from more-abundant food and better medicines to near-instantaneous communications—it is built on what Jules Pretty calls a fundamental "deceit." In a session on the opening day of the AMNH symposium, Pretty, who heads the biological sciences department at University of Essex, told the audience, "There is an underlying assumption in much of the literature that the world can be saved from these problems that we face—poverty, lack of food, environmental problems—if we bring consumption levels across the world up to the same levels [of] North America and Europe." But this sort of convergence, says Pretty, would require the resources of six to eight planets. "How can we move from convergence to divergence, and hence diversity?"

Traditional environmentalism, with its tendency to erect impermeable theoretical barriers between nature and culture, between the functions of artificial and natural selection, hasn't been able to accommodate the perspective necessary to see larger patterns at work. Its distinction—as the writer Lewis Lapham recently put it—"between what is 'natural' (the good, the true, the beautiful) and what is 'artificial' (wicked, man-made, false)" has obscured their profound interrelatedness. Whether expressed as biocultural diversity or as diverse social-ecological systems, the language of these new paradigms reframes the very concept of "environment." Explicit in both terms is a core understanding that as human behavior shapes nature in every instant, nature shapes human behavior. Also explicit is that myth, legend, art, literature, and science are not only themselves reflections of the environment, passed through the filter of human cognition, but that they are indeed the very means we have for determining the road ahead.

READING AND WRITING

1. A causal argument, "In Defense of Difference" begins with a problem and then makes a series of claims about causes and consequences. What is the problem at the heart of this argument? How do Montenegro and Glavin try to make their readers understand and care about this problem?

2. Montenegro and Glavin introduce two terms that are vital to their argument: "biocultural diversity" and "resilience theory." How do they define these terms? How are they related?

3. What, according to this text, are some of the consequences of what Montenegro and Glavin call a "world increasingly calibrated on consumption, efficiency, and convenience"?

USING RESEARCH

4. In their piece, which was first published in 2008, Montenegro and Glavin write: "Perhaps the closest anyone has come to an explicit goal for conserving diversity is the '2010 Biodiversity Target,' a decision approved in 2002 by the 188 (now 191) member nations of the UN Convention on Biological Diversity. Its aim is ambitious: 'to achieve by 2010 a significant reduction of the current rate of biodiversity loss at the global, regional, and national level as a contribution to poverty alleviation and to the benefit of all life on earth.'" Using resources available online and through the library, find out the status of this effort. Did the world hit the '2010 Biodiversity Target'?

DEVELOPING LONGER RESPONSES

5. In their piece, Montenegro and Glavin ask, "what, ultimately, is the value in diversity?" Write a brief essay in which you answer this question.

IMAGE 3.2

The irreverent and infamous graffiti artist known as Banksy created this poster—featuring iconic Disney characters from the 1967 film *Jungle Book*—for the environmental organization Greenpeace, as part of a campaign against deforestation. It was also made into stickers and included in the 2006 book called *Banksy: Wall and Piece*. You can see more of Banksy's work at http://www.banksy.co.uk/.

■ READING AND WRITING

1. Based on the content of the *Jungle Book* image that Banksy produced, who do you think is the poster's intended audience? Who might Greenpeace be trying to reach with this particular text? What messages does the poster convey? Do you think this text presents an effective argument?

■ USING RESEARCH

2. Find out more about both Banksy and Greenpeace. After conducting this research, explain why you think Greenpeace would use the work of an artist like Banksy to help advance its causes.

3. Working with a group of classmates, find another example of a pop culture icon (this can include fictional characters, celebrities, sports figures, and the like) being used to advance a social or political cause. Discuss with your group why you think this particular icon was matched with the issue at hand. Do you think this pairing was effective? Was it persuasive? Explain your responses.

Though he died nearly a century ago, naturalist and writer John Muir, according to a Sierra Club biography, is still teaching Americans "the importance of experiencing and protecting our natural heritage. … His personal and determined involvement in the great conservation questions of the day was and remains an inspiration for environmental activists everywhere." "The American Forests," from which this piece was excerpted, was first published in August 1897 in the Atlantic Monthly.

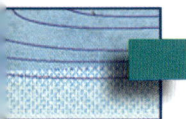

excerpts from
THE AMERICAN FORESTS   John Muir

The forests of America, however slighted by man, must have been a great delight to God; for they were the best he ever planted. The whole continent was a garden, and from the beginning it seemed to be favored above all the other wild parks and gardens of the globe. To prepare the ground, it was rolled and sifted in seas with infinite loving deliberation and forethought, lifted into the light, submerged and warmed over and over again, pressed and crumpled into folds and ridges, mountains and hills, subsoiled with heaving volcanic fires, ploughed and ground and sculptured into scenery and soil with glaciers and rivers,—every feature growing and changing from beauty to beauty, higher and higher. And in the fullness of time it was planted in groves, and belts, and broad, exuberant, mantling forests, with the largest, most varied, most fruitful, and most beautiful trees in the world. Bright seas made its border with wave embroidery and icebergs; gray deserts were outspread in the middle of it, mossy tundras on the north, savannas on the south, and blooming prairies and plains; while lakes and rivers shone through all the vast forests and openings, and happy birds and beasts gave delightful animation. Everywhere, everywhere over all the blessed continent, there were beauty, and melody, and kindly, wholesome, foodful abundance.

These forests were composed of about five hundred species of trees, all of them in some way useful to man, ranging in size from twenty-five feet in height and less than one foot in diameter at the ground to four hundred feet in height and more than twenty feet in diameter,—lordly monarchs proclaiming the gospel of beauty like apostles. For many a century after the ice-ploughs were melted, nature fed them and dressed them every day; working like a man, a loving, devoted, painstaking gardener; fingering every leaf and flower and mossy furrowed bole; bending, trimming, modeling, balancing, painting them with the loveliest colors; bringing over them now clouds with cooling shadows and showers, now sunshine; fanning them with gentle winds and rustling their leaves; exercising them in every fibre with storms, and pruning them; loading them with flowers and fruit, loading them with snow, and ever making them more beautiful as the years rolled by. Wide-branching oak and elm in endless variety, walnut and maple, chestnut and beech, ilex and locust, touching limb to limb, spread a leafy translucent canopy along the coast of the Atlantic over the wrinkled folds and ridges of the Alleghanies,—a green billowy sea in summer, golden and purple in autumn, pearly gray like a steadfast frozen mist of interlacing branches and sprays in leafless, restful winter.

To the southward stretched dark, level-topped cypresses in knobby, tangled swamps, grassy savannas in the midst of them like lakes of light, groves of gay sparkling spice-trees, magnolias and palms, glossy-leaved and blooming and shining continually. To the northward, over Maine and the Ottawa, rose hosts of spiry, rosiny evergreens,—white pine and spruce, hemlock and cedar, shoulder to shoulder, laden with purple cones, their myriad needles sparkling and shimmering, covering hills and swamps, rocky headlands and domes, ever bravely aspiring and seeking the sky; the ground in their shade now snow-clad and frozen, now mossy and flowery; beaver meadows here and there, full of lilies and grass; lakes gleaming like eyes, and a silvery embroidery of rivers and creeks watering and brightening all the vast glad wilderness.

Thence westward were oak and elm, hickory and tupelo, gum and liriodendron, sassafras and ash, linden and laurel, spreading on ever wider in glorious exuberance over the great fertile basin of the Mississippi, over damp level bottoms, low dimpling hollows, and round dotting hills, embosoming sunny prairies and cheery park openings, half sunshine, half shade; while a dark wilderness of pines covered the region around the Great Lakes. Thence still westward swept the forests to right and left around grassy plains and deserts a thousand miles wide: irrepressible hosts of spruce and pine, aspen and willow, nut-pine and juniper, cactus and yucca, caring nothing for drought, extending undaunted from mountain to mountain, over mesa and desert, to join the darkening multitudes of pines that covered the high Rocky ranges and the glorious forests along the coast of the moist and balmy Pacific, where new species of pine, giant cedars and spruces, silver firs and sequoias, kings of their race, growing close together like grass in a meadow, poised their brave domes and spires in the sky three hundred feet above the ferns and the lilies that enameled the ground; towering serene through the long centuries, preaching God's forestry fresh from heaven.

Here the forests reached their highest development. Hence they went wavering northward over icy Alaska, brave spruce and fir, poplar and birch, by the coasts and the rivers, to within sight of the Arctic Ocean. American forests! the glory of the world! Surveyed thus from the east to the west, from the north to the south, they are rich beyond thought, immortal, immeasurable, enough and to spare for every feeding, sheltering beast and bird, insect and son of Adam; and nobody need have cared had there been no pines in Norway, no cedars and deodars on Lebanon and the Himalayas, no vine-clad selvas in the basin of the Amazon. With such variety, harmony, and triumphant exuberance, even nature, it would seem, might have rested content with the forests of North America, and planted no more.

So they appeared a few centuries ago when they were rejoicing in wildness. The Indians with stone axes could do them no more harm than could gnawing beavers and browsing moose. Even the fires of the Indians and the fierce shattering lightning seemed to work together only for good in clearing spots here and there for smooth garden prairies, and openings for sunflowers seeking the light. But when the steel axe of the white man rang out in the startled air their doom was sealed. Every tree heard the bodeful sound, and pillars of smoke gave the sign in the sky.

I suppose we need not go mourning the buffaloes. In the nature of things they had to give place to better cattle, though the change might have been made without barbarous wickedness. Likewise many of nature's five hundred kinds of wild trees had to make way for orchards and cornfields. In the settlement and civilization of the country, bread more than timber or beauty was wanted; and in the blindness of hunger, the early settlers, claiming Heaven as their guide, regarded God's trees as only a larger kind of pernicious weeds, extremely hard to get rid of. Accordingly, with no eye to the future, these pious destroyers waged interminable forest wars; chips flew thick and fast; trees in their beauty fell crashing by millions, smashed to confusion, and the smoke of their burning has been rising to heaven more than two hundred years. After the Atlantic coast from Maine to Georgia had been mostly cleared and scorched into melancholy ruins, the overflowing multitude of bread and money seekers poured over the Alleghanies into the fertile middle West, spreading ruthless devastation ever wider and farther over the rich valley of the Mississippi and the vast shadowy pine region about the Great Lakes. Thence still westward the invading horde of destroyers called settlers made its fiery way over the broad Rocky Mountains, felling and burning more fiercely than ever, until at last it has reached the wild side of the continent, and entered the last of the great aboriginal forests on the shores of the Pacific.

Surely, then, it should not be wondered at that lovers of their country, bewailing its baldness, are now crying aloud, "Save what is left of the forests!" Clearing has surely now gone far enough; soon timber will be scarce, and not a grove will be left to rest in or pray in. The remnant protected will yield plenty of timber, a perennial harvest for every right use, without further diminution of its area, and will continue to cover the springs of the rivers that rise in the mountains and give irrigating waters to the dry valleys at their feet, prevent wasting floods and be a blessing to everybody forever. [...]

[…] Emerson says that things refuse to be mismanaged long. An exception would seem to be found in the case of our forests, which have been mismanaged rather long, and now come desperately near being like smashed eggs and spilt milk. Still, in the long run the world does not move backward. The wonderful advance made in the last few years, in creating four national parks in the West, and thirty forest reservations, embracing nearly forty million acres; and in the planting of the borders of streets and highways and spacious parks in all the great cities, to satisfy the natural taste and hunger for landscape beauty and righteousness that God has put, in some measure, into every human being and animal, shows the trend of awakening public opinion. The making of the far-famed New York Central Park was opposed by even good men, with misguided pluck, perseverance, and ingenuity; but straight right won its way, and now that park is appreciated. So we confidently believe it will be with our great national parks and forest reservations. There will be a period of indifference on the part of the rich, sleepy with wealth, and of the toiling millions, sleepy with poverty, most of whom never saw a forest; a period of screaming protest and objection from the plunderers, who are as unconscionable and enterprising as Satan. But light is surely coming, and the friends of destruction will preach and bewail in vain.

The United States government has always been proud of the welcome it has extended to good men of every nation, seeking freedom and homes and bread. Let them be welcomed still as nature welcomes them, to the woods as well as to the prairies and plains. No place is too good for good men, and still there is room. They are invited to heaven, and may well be allowed in America. Every place is made better by them. Let them be as free to pick gold and gems from the hills, to cut and hew, dig and plant, for homes and bread, as the birds are to pick berries from the wild bushes, and moss and leaves for nests. The ground will be glad to feed them, and the pines will come down from the mountains for their homes as willingly as the cedars came from Lebanon for Solomon's temple. Nor will the woods be the worse for this use, or their benign influences be diminished any more than the sun is diminished by shining. Mere destroyers, however, tree-killers, spreading death and confusion in the fairest groves and gardens ever planted, let the government hasten to cast them out and make an end of them. For it must be told again and again, and be burningly borne in mind, that just now, while protective measures are being deliberated languidly, destruction and use are speeding on faster and farther every day. The axe and saw are insanely busy, chips are flying thick as snowflakes, and every summer thousands of acres of priceless forests, with their underbrush, soil, springs, climate, scenery, and religion, are vanishing away in clouds of smoke, while, except in the national parks, not one forest guard is employed.

All sorts of local laws and regulations have been tried and found wanting, and the costly lessons of our own experience, as well as that of every civilized nation, show conclusively that the fate of the remnant of our forests is in the hands of the federal government, and that if the remnant is to be saved at all, it must be saved quickly.

Any fool can destroy trees. They cannot run away; and if they could, they would still be destroyed,—chased and hunted down as long as fun or a dollar could be got out of their bark hides, branching horns, or magnificent bole backbones. Few that fell trees plant them; nor would planting avail much towards getting back anything like the noble primeval forests. During a man's life only saplings can be grown, in the place of the old trees— tens of centuries old—that have been destroyed. It took more than three thousand years to make some of the trees in these Western woods,—trees that are still standing in perfect strength and beauty, waving and singing in the mighty forests of the Sierra. Through all the wonderful, eventful centuries since Christ's time—and long before that—God has cared for these trees, saved them from drought, disease, avalanches, and a thousand straining, leveling tempests and floods; but he cannot save them from fools,—only Uncle Sam can do that.

READING AND WRITING

1. Muir's piece is remarkable in its use of highly descriptive language. Why do you think he makes such an effort to vividly describe the forests? How does this language help him persuade readers of his claim?

DEVELOPING LONGER RESPONSES

2. Think about the forests, mountains, swamps, beaches, valleys, or lakes (among other possible natural landscapes) that make up your local surroundings. With one of these sites in mind, write a short passage in which you imitate Muir's descriptive prose.

USING RESEARCH

3. Muir's "The American Forests" was originally published in 1897, but its message—that we need to better manage our natural resources—does not seem so dated. Using online search engines or the library's databases, find a modern editorial or letter to the editor that shares a message similar to Muir's. What similarities do you notice? Why do you think this message stands the test of time?
4. Research the state of America's forests at the time Muir was writing (including percentage of forested land, percentage of protected forests, threats to the forests, and the like) and compare your findings with conditions today. What has changed in the past century? Has anything remained the same?

In these excerpts from her 1999 memoir Ecology of a Cracker Childhood, *author and environmental activist Janisse Ray writes eloquently of her family's deep-rooted ties to the longleaf pine forests of southern Georgia and of her fears about the destruction of these irreplaceable ecosystems.*

excerpts from
ECOLOGY OF A CRACKER CHILDHOOD
Janisse Ray

■ Introduction

In south Georgia everything is flat and wide. Not empty. My people live among the mobile homes, junked cars, pine plantations, clearcuts, and fields. They live among the lost forests.

The creation ends in south Georgia, at the very edge of the sweet earth. Only the sky, widest of the wide, goes on, flatness a gainst flatness. The sky appears so close that, with a long-enough extension ladder, you think you could touch it, and sometimes you do, when clouds descend in the night to set a fine pelt of dew on the grasses, leaving behind white trails of fog and mist.

At night the stars are thick and bright as a pint jar of fireflies, the moon at full a pearly orb, sailing through them like an egret. By day the sun, close in a paper sky, laps moisture from the land, then gives it back, always an exchange. Even in drought, when each dawn a parched sun cracks against the horizon's griddle, the air is thick with water.

It is a land of few surprises. It is a land of routine, of cycle, and of constancy. Many a summer afternoon a black cloud builds to the southwest, approaching until you hear thunder and spot lightning, and even then there's time to clear away tools and bring in the laundry before the first raindrops spatter down. Everything that comes you see coming.

That's because the land is so wide, so much of it open. It's wide open, flat as a book, vulnerable as a child. It's easy to take advantage of, and yet it is also a land of dignity. It has been the way it is for thousands of years, and it is not wont to change.

I was born from people who were born from people who were born from people who were born here. The Crackers crossed the wide Altamaha into what had been Creek territory and settled the vast, fire-loving uplands of the coastal plains of southeast Georgia, surrounded by a singing forest of tall and widely spaced pines whose history they did not know, whose stories were untold. The memory of what they entered is scrawled on my bones, so that I carry the landscape inside like an ache. The story of who I am cannot be severed from the story of the flatwoods.

To find myself among what has been and what remains, I go where my grandmother's name is inscribed on a clay hill beside my grandfather. The cemetery rests in a sparse stand of remnant longleaf pine, where clumps of wiregrass can still be found. From the grave I can see a hardwood drain, hung with Spanish moss, and beyond to a cypress swamp, and almost to the river, but beyond that, there is only sky.

◼ Child of Pine

When my parents had been married five years and my sister was four, they went out searching among the pinewoods through which the junkyard had begun to spread. It was early February of 1962, and the ewes in the small herd of sheep that kept the grass cropped around the junked cars were dropping lambs.

On this day, Candlemas, with winter half undone, a tormented wind bore down from the north and brought with it a bitter wet cold that cut through my parents' sweaters and coats and sliced through thin socks, stinging their skin and penetrating to the bone. Tonight the pipes would freeze if the faucets weren't left dripping, and if the fig tree wasn't covered with quilts, it would be knocked back to the ground.

It was dark by six, for the days lengthened only by minutes, and my father had gone early to shut up the sheep. Nights he penned them in one end of his shop, a wide, tin-roofed building that smelled both acrid and sweet, a mixture of dry dung, gasoline, hay, and grease. That night when he counted them, one of the ewes was missing. He had bought the sheep to keep weeds and snakes down in the junkyard, so people could get to parts they needed; now he knew all the animals by name and knew also their personalities. Maude was close to her time.

In the hour they had been walking, the temperature had fallen steadily. It would soon be dark. Out of the grayness Mama heard a bleating cry.

"Listen," she said, touching Daddy's big arm and stopping so suddenly that shoulder-length curls of dark hair swung across her heart-shaped face. Her eyes were a deep, rich brown, and she cut a fine figure, slim and strong, easy in her body. Her husband was over six feet tall, handsome, his forehead wide and smart, his hair thick and wiry as horsetail.

Again came the cry. It sounded more human than sheep, coming from a clump of palmettos beneath a pine. The sharp-needled fronds of the palmettos stood out emerald against the gray of winter, and the pine needles, so richly brown when first dropped, had faded to dull sienna. Daddy slid his hands—big, rough hands—past the bayonet-tipped palmetto fronds, their fans rattling urgently with his movements, him careful not to rake against saw-blade stems. The weird crying had not stopped. He peered in.

It was a baby. Pine needles cradled a long-limbed newborn child with a duff of dark hair, its face red and puckered. And that was me, his second-born. I came into their lives easy as finding a dark-faced merino with legs yet too wobbly to stand.

My sister had been found in a big cabbage in the garden; a year after me, my brother was discovered under the grapevine, and a year after that, my little brother appeared beside a huckleberry bush. From as early as I could question, I was told this creation story. If they'd said they'd found me in the trunk of a '52 Ford, it would have been more believable.

I was raised on a junkyard on the outskirts of a town called Baxley, the county seat of Appling, in rural south Georgia. [...]

■ Below the Fall Line

The landscape that I was born to, that owns my body: the uplands and lowlands of southern Georgia. The region lies below what's called the fall line, a half-imaginary demarcation avouched by a slight dip in the land, above which the piedmont climbs to the foothills of the Blue Ridge, then up that mountain chain to the eastern continental divide. The fall line separates the piedmont from the Atlantic coastal plain—a wide flat plateau of piney-woods that sweeps to a marble sea.

My homeland is about as ugly as a place gets. There's nothing in south Georgia, people will tell you, except straight, lonely roads, one-horse towns, sprawling farms, and tracts of planted pines. It's flat, monotonous, used-up, hotter than hell in summer and cold enough in winter that orange trees won't grow. No mountains, no canyons, no rocky streams, no waterfalls. The rivers are muddy, wide and flat, like somebody's feet. The coastal plain lacks the stark grace of the desert or the umber panache of the pampas. Unless you look close, there's little majesty.

It wasn't always this way. Even now, in places, in the Red Hills near Thomasville, for example, and on Fort Stewart Military Reservation near Hinesville, you can see how south Georgia used to be, before all the old longleaf pine forests that were our sublimity and our majesty were cut. Nothing is more beautiful, nothing more mysterious, nothing more breathtaking, nothing more surreal.

Longleaf pine is the tree that grows in the upland flatwoods of the coastal plains. Miles and miles of longleaf and wiregrass, the ground cover that coevolved with the pine, once covered the left hip of North America—from Virginia to the Florida peninsula, west past the Mississippi River: longleaf as far in any direction as you could see. In a longleaf forest, miles of trees forever fade into a brilliant salmon sunset and reappear the next dawn as a battalion marching out of fog. The tip of each needle carries a single drop of silver. The trees are so well spaced that their limbs seldom touch and sunlight streams between and within them. Below their flattened branches, grasses arch their tall, richly dun heads of seeds, and orchids and lilies paint the ground orange and scarlet. Purple liatris gestures across the landscape. Our eyes seek the flowers like they seek the flash of birds and the careful crossings of forest animals.

You can still see this in places.

Forest historians estimate that longleaf covered 85 of the 156 million acres in its southeastern range. By 1930, virtually all of the virgin longleaf pine had been felled. Now, at the end of the twentieth century, about two million acres of longleaf remain. Most is first-and second-growth, hard-hit by logging, turpentining, grazing, and the suppression of fire.

Less than 10,000 acres are virgin—not even 0.001 percent of what was. There's none known in Virginia, none in Louisiana, non in Texas, none in South Carolina. About 200 old-growth acres remain in Mississippi, about 300 in Alabama, and almost 500 in North Carolina, in four separate tracts. The rest survives in Georgia and Florida. An estimated 3,000 acres of old-growth in Georgia lie on private land, precariously, and the largest holding of virgin longleaf, about 5,000 acres, belongs to Eglin Air Force Base in Florida.

In a 1995 National Biological Service assessment of biological loss, ecologist Reed Noss classified the longleaf/wiregrass community as "critically endangered." Ninety-eight percent of the presettlement longleaf pine barrens in the southeastern coastal plains were lost by 1986, he said. Natural stands—meaning not planted—have been reduced by about 99 percent.

Apocalyptic.

This was not a loss I knew as a child. *Longleaf* was a word I never heard. But it is a loss that as an adult shadows every step I take. I am daily aghast at how much we have taken, since it does not belong to us, and how much as a people we have suffered in consequence.

Not long ago I dreamed of actually cradling a place, as if something so amorphous and vague as a region, existing mostly in imagination and idea, suddenly took form. I held its shrunken relief in my arms, a baby smelted from a plastic topography map, and when I gazed down into its face, as my father had gazed into mine, I saw the pine flatwoods of my homeland.

■ Clearcut

If you clear a forest, you'd better pray continuously. While you're pushing a road through and rigging the cables and moving between trees on the dozer, you'd better be talking to God. While you're cruising timber and marking trees with a blue slash, be praying; and pray while you're peddling the chips and logs and writing Friday's checks and paying the diesel bill—even if it's under your breath, a rustling at the lips. If you're manning the saw head or the scissors, snipping the trees off at the ground, going from one to another, approaching them brusquely and laying them down, I'd say, pray extra hard; and pray hard when you're hauling them away.

God doesn't like a clearcut. It makes his heart turn cold, makes him wince and wonder what went wrong with his creation, and sets him to thinking about what spoils the child.

You'd better be pretty sure that the cut is absolutely necessary and be at peace with it, so you can explain it to God, for it's fairly certain he's going to question your motives, want to know if your children are hungry and your oldest boy needs asthma medicine—whether you deserve forgiveness or if you're being greedy and heartless. You'd better pay good attention to the saw blade and the runners and the falling trees; when a forest is falling, it's easy for God to determine to spank. Quid pro quo.

Don't ever look away or daydream and don't, no matter what, plan how you will spend your tree money while you are in among toppling trees.

For a long time God didn't worry about the forests. Some trees got cut, which was bad enough, of course, and he would be sick about the cutting awhile, but his children needed houses and warmth, so he stepped in right after they had gone and got some seeds in the ground. The clear-cutting had come so fast he'd been unprepared. One minute the loggers were axmen, with their crosscut saws and oxen and rafts, and when he looked again, they were in helicopters.

When people started to replant, it was a good thing, but there was no way to re-create a forest. Not quickly. And the trees would just be cut again.

Before God knew it, his trees were being planted in rows, like corn, and harvested like corn. That was 1940, when the tree farming started, but it seems like yesterday to God.

Not longleaf. It was quirky in habit, its taproot cumbersome to deal with and slow-growing, so most of the tree farmers abandoned it. They could plant slash or loblolly and in twenty-five years be able to cut again.

Plant for the future, the signs said.

To prepare ground, they chopped, disked, rootraked, herbicided, windrowed. In wetter soils they bedded, plowing and heaping the soil into wide racks with drainage furrows between. The land was laid bare as a vulture's pate, and the scriveners came on their tree-planting tractors, driving down new words to replace the old one, *forest*.

The trees were planted close, five or six feet between, in phalanxes. They were all the same age and size, unlike the woodland that had been, with its old-growth and its saplings, as well as every age in between. The old forest had snags where woodpeckers fed and it had pine cones eager to burst open on bare ground.

Because slash and loblolly are intolerant of fire, the tree farmers, with Smokey as mascot, kept fire back. Within ten years a canopy would close, and the commercial plantation was dark within, darker than you can imagine a forest being. The limbs and needles of the overcrowded pines drank every inch of sky. Any native vegetation that survived land preparation did not survive loss of light.

The diversity of the forest decreased exponentially the more it was altered. In autumn, the flatwoods salamander no longer crossed the plantation to breed, and the migrating redstart no longer stopped, and the pine snake was not to be found. The gopher frog was a thirsty pool of silence.

Pine plantations dishearten God. In them he aches for blooming things, and he misses the sun trickling through the tree crowns, and he pines for the crawling, spotted, scale-backed, bushy-tailed, leaf-hopping, chattering creatures. Most of all he misses the bright-winged, singing beings he cast as angels.

The wind knocking limbs together is a jeremiad.

God likes to prop himself against a tree in a forest and study the plants and animals. They all please him. He has to drag himself through a pine plantation, looking for light on the other side, half-crazy with darkness, half-sick with regret. He refuses to go into clearcuts at all. He thought he had given his children everything their hearts would desire; what he sees puts him in a quarrelsome mood, wondering where he went wrong.

READING AND WRITING

1. Ray characterizes herself as a "child of pine" and re-tells the "creation stories" told to her and her sister about how they came into the world. What are these "creation stories" and why do you think Ray includes them in her memoir? What do they tell you about her? How do these make her message more concrete and compelling?
2. Ray's piece is an excerpt from a memoir, not an argumentative essay. Nevertheless, it does present a point of view. What ideas do you think Ray is trying to convey to her readers about the environment?

DEVELOPING LONGER RESPONSES

3. Ray explains that her Georgia homeland "is about as ugly as a place gets," but that "[i]t wasn't always that way." With Ray's descriptions of the now disappearing longleaf pines in mind, write a eulogy for a vanished environment in which you use thoughtful plotting and vivid description to bring to life a place that was important to you in some way. For example, you could write a eulogy for local farmland that has been developed, for a tree that's been knocked over in a storm, or for the lake house where you vacationed with your parents. The idea is to remember and mourn a place that no longer exists for you. This "vanishing" can be tangible (like a once pristine beach that has been lost to erosion) or it can be emotional (like your childhood home, which, though still standing, is no longer the place it was to you then).

Activists Derrick Jensen and Stephanie McMillan teamed to produce the graphic novel As the World Burns: 50 Simple Things You Can Do to Stay in Denial in 2007. Jensen has written several books and in 2008 was named one of Utne Reader's "50 Visionaries Who Are Changing Your World." McMillan began syndicating her political cartoons in 1999, and a book based on her comic strip "Minimum Security" was published in 2005. Seven Stories Press, which published As the World Burns, offers this description of the book on its website: "Two of America's most talented activists team up to deliver a bold and hilarious satire of modern environmental policy in this fully illustrated graphic novel. The U.S. government gives robot machines from space permission to eat the earth in exchange for bricks of gold. A one-eyed bunny rescues his friends from a corporate animal-testing laboratory. And two little girls figure out the secret to saving the world from both of its enemies (and it isn't by using energy-efficient light bulbs or biodiesel fuel). As the World Burns will inspire you to do whatever it takes to stop ecocide before it's too late." Jensen and McMillan continue to create and publish an As the World Burns serial graphic novel online at http://sevenstories.com/astheworldburns.

excerpt from
AS THE WORLD BURNS: 50 SIMPLE THINGS YOU CAN DO TO STAY IN DENIAL
Derrick Jensen and Stephanie McMillan

You mean big industries can make lots of money by building dams for aluminum smelting, choking the life out of rivers and killing the fish, plus tearing up great swaths of Africa for mining bauxite?

Wow!

Big money for builders, miners and manufacturers!

Fabulous!

We see this so often.
50 SIMPLE THINGS YOU CAN DO TO SAVE THE EARTH!
CAN STREAMING VIDEO STOP GLOBAL WARMING?
LET TIKI THE PENGUIN GUIDE YOU! FIND OUT HOW KIDS CAN STOP GLOBAL WARMING!
YAHOO CELEBRATES 35 YEARS OF EARTH DAY WITH "10 SIMPLE WAYS YOU CAN SAVE THE WORLD IN A DAY!"
GREEN YOUR EVERYDAY ONLINE SHOPPING AND STOP GLOBAL WARMING!
Wouldn't it be wonderful if life were this simple, the problems we face so easily solvable? Every cell in my body wants for recycling to save the day, wants for shorter showers to save enough water for the rivers to run free.
But they won't. You know that. Fish and turtles and beavers and frogs and bears know that. Everybody knows that.
Sometimes we forget.

Another important one is to avoid products with a lot of packaging.

I can still buy things, right? I just avoid the ones with packaging...

That's it exactly! You can save 1,200 pounds of carbon dioxide if you cut down your garbage by 10 percent!

The next one is to adjust your thermostat. Moving your thermostat down just two degrees in winter and up two degrees in summer could save about 2,000 pounds of CO_2 a year.

We did it! We saved the planet!

That's if every person in the United States does every one of these things.

But they will! If we just tell them. This isn't so hard! We can do it!

There's just one thing. Total carbon emissions for the United States is 7.1 billion tons.

If every man, woman and child did all of the things on the list from the movie ~ and you know there is precisely zero chance that every man, woman and child in the United States will do this...

I don't like where this is going

That would only be about a 21 percent reduction in carbon emissions. And since total carbon emissions go up about two percent per year, that whole reduction would disappear in about...

sigh.

READING AND WRITING

1. Look closely at the hand-drawn images in *As the World Burns*. What do you notice about the style of the drawings? How are the humans characterized? The animals? How does the artist represent big corporations? What messages about human impact on the environment (and about environmentalism itself) do these images convey?
2. Do you think the graphic novel is an effective genre for argumentation? Explain your response.

DEVELOPING LONGER RESPONSES

3. *As the World Burns* uses a combination of images and texts to make a claim about the human impact on the environment and about our attempts to repair what damage we've done. With some of the strategies of the graphic novel in mind, compose a multimodal essay in which you use images and text in combination to make a claim about an environmental issue. Have a specific claim in mind and seek out (or take) photographs that, when read in a careful progression, help articulate your argument. Carefully write and pair short captions for each image and put them into a narrative form.

USING RESEARCH

4. Using your library's resources or the web, research the definitional criteria for satire. (What is a satire? What are the essential criteria of the genre?) Based on these criteria, do you think this excerpt from *As the World Burns* qualifies as a satire? How so? Do you think the text is effective?

Anne Marie Todd is an associate professor of communication studies at San Jose State University. Her essay "Prime Time Subversion" was published in the 2002 collection Enviropop: Studies in Environmental Rhetoric and Popular Culture.

PRIME-TIME SUBVERSION: THE ENVIRONMENTAL RHETORIC OF THE SIMPSONS Anne Marie Todd

On April 19, 1987, America was introduced to the Simpsons, the title family of the first animated prime-time television series since the 1960s. Described by its creator and executive producer Matt Groening as "a celebration of the American family at its wildest" (Steiger, 1999, p. 1), *The Simpsons* offered a critical view of mainstream social and cultural norms. In a television world dominated by upper-middle-class storybook families like the Huxtables of *The Cosby Show*, *The Simpsons* presented a satirical documentary of a more complex family whose characters and plots related more directly to the familial experience of America's television audience. In fact, *The Simpsons* first aired on prime-time television opposite *The Cosby Show*, assuming a revolutionary position toward mainstream television and the network establishment. The series exhibited a realism that appealed to a widely diverse audience and established *The Simpsons* as a fixture of American prime-time. When the show debuted, it quickly became the FOX Network's highest rated program (Korte, 1997, p.1). The success of *The Simpsons* is evident in the show's impressive popularity with a heterogeneous audience that spans generations. The program has also won critical acclaim, and has received numerous awards, including the Peabody Award (1997), the People's Choice Award (1990-1991) and several Emmies (Steiger, 1999, p.2). As Steiger argued, *The Simpsons'* "vicious social satire" and subtle profound "pop-culture allusions" had a "considerable impact on the television landscape of the nation" (p. 2).

Multiple layers of profound social and cultural commentary distinguish *The Simpsons* from conventional television programs. "The critical humor, self-reflexiveness, intertextuality and form" of *The Simpsons* solidify the literary significance of the series' postmodern commentary (Korte, 1997, p. 3). Such rhetorical elements help establish the Simpson family as an icon of American popular culture. In 1998, *Time* magazine listed Bart Simpson on behalf of the entire series as one of the key cultural and most influential figures of the twentieth century (Steiger, 1999, p.2). The realism of the characters and plot lines of *The Simpsons* give the series a dramatic quality; the Simpsons' family adventures expose the nuances of American family life while simultaneously informing the social and cultural experience of the television audience.

Critical and popular acclaim for *The Simpsons* distinguishes the series as a rich multi-dimensional text for rhetorical analysis. In countless interviews, Matt Groening has described *The Simpsons* as a show that rewards its audience for paying attention (Korte,

1997, p. 9). As the most counter-cultural cartoon to hit prime-time, the series is ripe for rhetorical inquiry into its potential as a vehicle for critical political and social commentary. *The Simpsons* contributes significantly to critical analysis of popular culture, particularly in the study of television media, because the show is more literary and complex than regular television programming (Korte, 1997, p. 7). In a decade, *The Simpsons* has secured immense popularity, and its established prime-time slot confirms the magnitude of the show's viewing audience. With its copious literary and cinematic references and interminable political commentary, *The Simpsons* is indisputably embedded in American culture, and thus offers a lens into the rhetorical dimensions of human experience. Rhetorical analysis of popular culture is indispensable in the exposition of the social, cultural, and political motivations of human action. Our understanding of meaning and our comprehension of rhetorical symbols are best achieved through the explication of human motives. Rhetorical analysis of popular culture discloses how communication of symbols in the interpretation of personal experience promotes a persuasive rhetoric that engenders critical commentary regarding the social and cultural dimensions of human experience.

This chapter explicates the meaning and significance of *The Simpsons'* social commentary through two mediums of rhetorical criticism. The first method of analysis utilizes Kenneth Burke's (1959) comic frame to determine the meaning of the show's multi-textual rhetoric. Analysis of televisual communication requires an enhanced application of the comic form through a second mode of inquiry, the explication of the symbolism of *The Simpsons'* visual argument. The show presents a unique rhetorical form that exhibits profound pop-cultural influence, and in particular makes a significant impression on American environmental consciousness. This analysis begins with an explication of the utility of the comic frame and visual argument as prolific tools of rhetorical criticism. The synthesis of these two approaches engenders an enriched analysis, which articulates *The Simpsons'* intertextual environmental rhetoric. Next, the convergence of comic and visual critical practices is examined, which illuminates the symbolic elements of the show's environmental rhetoric. The abundance of episodic material, teeming with rich dialogue and resplendent visuals, rendered focusing this analysis an enigmatic task. As a directive for this criticism, two predominant metaphors are explored: Springfield's nuclear power plant as an icon of irresponsible energy use and the figurative role of nonhuman characters in the series. This project's conclusion articulates the coherent ecological message in *The Simpsons'* rhetoric, and thus renders a conclusive evaluation of the show's televisual environmental commentary. Specifically, I propose that the show's rhetoric presents a strong environmental message regarding the relationship between humans and the rest of nature.

This message is most clearly articulated in the show's rhetorical strategies, which reveal a pervasive ecological criticism of human activity, produced through comedy and visual argument—rhetorical tools that successfully engage the audience in *The Simpsons'* critical environmental commentary. This rhetorical criticism examines the first ten seasons of the series in recognition of the rhetorical force with which these animated social texts exhibit the interface of environmental communication and popular culture. The analysis was conducted by viewing various collected videotapes of the series' first ten seasons (4/9/87-5/16/99)—approximately 80 percent of the episodes—and supplemented with data from Matt Groening's two-volume guide to the show. The ten years of episodes in the sample provide hundreds of rhetorical propositions of ecological tone. Conducting a satisfactory analysis of all such references in the confines of this chapter is impossible. Thus, I focused primarily (almost exclusively) on the show's principal environmental symbols and themes. As a result, the discussion focuses on only a few entire episodes, significant plot lines, familiar environmental theses, and explicit recurring rhetorical symbols. By focusing on the dominant characteristics of *The Simpsons'* environmental communication, I endeavored to limit the scope of criticism, and thus foster a more informed evaluation of the overall environmental message of the show. Ultimately, these televised visual and linguistic images disclose the show itself as an expression of environmental activism, and expose the salience of *The Simpsons'* environmental rhetoric.

■ The Comic Frame: Transcending the Social Order through Symbolic Action

In *A Rhetoric of Motives* (1950), Kenneth Burke describes the study of rhetoric as the understanding of human motives, and his theory of symbolic action provides the basis for innumerable conceptions of the study of rhetoric. Contextualizing the comic frame within a theory of rhetoric as symbolic action, Arne Madsen cites Burke's definition of humans as symbol-using creatures that construct responses to everyday experiences. That is, human action involves using and manipulating symbols to respond to interpretations of experience (Madsen, 1993, p. 166). In this way, rhetorical criticism relies on the explication of symbols to understand human responses to experience. The rhetorical critic must analyze such behavior in order to understand human motives and to comprehend how the manipulation of symbols influences human behavior. Burke expounds on this concept of symbolic rhetoric as an explanation for human motivation in *Language as Symbolic Action* (1966). He argues that human communication involves the expression of symbolic meaning in order to directly influence the behavior and conduct of one's audience (Burke, 1966, p. 28). That is, we use symbols to construct arguments, and conceptually plan courses of action based on our interpretation of our experience.

This discussion of the symbolic expression of motives provides a context for Burke's presentation of the comic frame in *Attitudes Toward History* (1959). He introduces the comic frame as a means to enhance scholars' understanding of human motivations and foster better evaluation of the social and cultural meaning of symbolic action. The comic frame enables individuals to "be observers of themselves, while acting [to create] maximum consciousness. One would 'transcend himself by noting his own foibles'" (Burke, 1959, p. 171). Burke envisioned that applying the comic frame would create social consciousness to expose the impotence of the status quo—the existing social order—and create public awareness to address the failings of the social system. The comic frame fosters more than an ironic self-awareness, but also constructs a position of semi-detachment, where one is able to reflect and comment on human foibles without guilt, shame, or other negative emotion, or without undue involvement in the human comedy. Toward this end, Burke established the utility of frames as tools for rhetorical criticism; he described frames as the perspectives that direct all interpretations of human experience. That is, frames provide symbolic structure that enables human beings to impose order upon their personal and social experiences. Rhetorical criticism involves the dual-purposed application of frames to episodes of human experience—frames function as blueprints for actions that fix social attitudes according to a particular perspective. Frames also embody attitudes and motives, empowering scholars to determine various social and cultural forms of symbolic action (Burke, 1959, p. 20). In this way, the comic frame enriches rhetorical criticism by revealing the flaws of the present system, enabling alternative discourse to gain public recognition.

Comedy provides the means to criticize one's own complicity in the dominant social order. By acknowledging the failings of the bureaucratic system, humans create discursive space for self-analysis. Such personal criticism involves a discourse that promotes historically marginalized opinions within the public sphere. Thus, the comic frame is rhetorically powerful on two levels: through recognition of human error as the cause of social ills, and through the spiritual and moral identification with humanity. By creating social distance between reformers and the clown as a scapegoat, the comic frame also conveys a preference for a social upbraiding, rather than malicious immolation, to promote the rapprochement engendered by comic consciousness. *The Simpsons* utilizes the comic frame to identify the incongruity of human action and the symbolic interpretation of the ecological context of our experience.

■ Popular Culture Imagery As Social Commentary: the Rhetoric of Visual Argument

The coherence of the environmental message of *The Simpsons* is enriched by the show's televisual rhetorical form. The series' animated realism informs traditional methods of rhetorical criticism by illuminating tactics of visual argument. Contemporary rhetorical theory, guided by Susanne Langer, Kenneth Burke, Ernest Bormann and others, emphasizes the symbolic form of rhetorical discourse (Klumpp & Hollihan, 1989, p. 88). Accordingly, the persuasive force of rhetoric is rooted in the motivational power of symbol, located in the relationship between rhetoric and the reality of the social order. The rhetorical critic's objective is to illuminate and evaluate persuasive messages (Andrews, 1990, p. 14) and thus determine the ways in which rhetorical discourse functions as symbolic action in response to different rhetorical situations. Rhetorical criticism is concerned with the persuasiveness of discourse through the "creation of social forms in human symbolic behavior" (Klumpp & Hollihan, 1989, p. 88). That is, the salience of rhetorical propositions is largely based on the correspondence of the symbolic value of a discourse with the established meaning of the existing social order. Stating the case for visual communication, Blair (1996) argues that "the concept of visual argument is an extension of rhetoric's paradigm into a new domain...[R]hetoric in a broader sense is the use of symbols to communicate...[A]ny form of persuasion, including visual persuasion, belongs within rhetoric's province" (p. 37). With the emergence of visual communication as an acknowledged persuasive force, rhetorical critics must identify ways to evaluate the meaning of visual arguments.

Contemporary analysis of the social and cultural context of human communication must account for the increased mediation of rhetorical messages. Analysis of televised communication acts requires amplified discursive frames to evaluate the complex argumentation strategies fostered by expanded media formats. Television media enjoy a substantially larger audience than traditional rhetorical settings, and thus must account for the diverse experiences of television viewers. In addition, televised messages are informed by the broader context of rhetorical symbols and are thus enabled to offer critical commentary on the social, cultural, and political experience of the American viewing public. Gronbeck (1995) offers a defense of visual argument, and argues that rhetorical meaning requires interpretation to decode the symbols of a message. He posits that symbolic meaning is not exclusively linguistic, and visual, aural, and other symbolic systems can offer propositions that affirm or deny social and cultural experience (p. 539).

Visual media are capable of symbolic expression because they are rooted in a particularly rich context of social, cultural and political influences. The complexities of the existing social order are manifest in the stream of televised visual images—elemental, socio-cultural interpretations of human experience. Effective visual communication exhibits rich and visual symbolism that incorporates signs and symbols of conventionalized images (Blair, 1996, p. 25). The symbolic form of visual argument is deeply rooted in the context of pop culture, a rubric for the innumerable vernacular of consumer cultural images. For this reason, visual arguments enjoy an appeal that eludes verbal communication: ocular recognition of pictorial images evokes meaning that is rooted in the memory of personal experience. Visual messages persuade because they provoke "unconscious identification," which are not possible with the linguistic basis of verbal images (Blair, 1996, p. 34). Thus, visual images persuade because they give meaning to personal experience by connecting thematic elements of shared social experience (whether televised experience or actual, real experience) to individual perception. Audience members incorporate the symbolic meaning of the visual image(s) into their personal value system, affecting their individual and social worldviews (Blair, 1996, p. 34). The symbolism of visual images remains ambiguous without a stabilizing linguistic text. Thus, the rhetorical force of one visual image appeals to a heterogeneous audience because pictorial symbols adapt to individualized experience, and encompass many meanings.

Visual argument is gaining particular ascendance as a rhetorical device with the technological improvement of visual communication, notably the advent of digital technology and the remarkable realism of computer animation. A rhetoric of visual discourse employs aesthetic symbols to inform social action. Visual tactics of communication rely on personal allegiances and affinities, which evoke dramatic reactions based on the rhetorical force of the visual image. Individual interpretation entails the personal association of familiar visual images within a normalizing social context. Such personal interpretation makes individual actions meaningful because the actions are grounded in a social context, and the social context in turn guides individual behavior according to established social and cultural norms. Visual argument facilitates social change by compelling individuals to modify their behavior to accommodate the symbolic norms of visual discourse. Visual images resonate with personal experience, facilitating the production of social meaning. Furthermore, visual argument enjoys an element of realism that makes its interpretation of human experience uniquely persuasive to individuals who can understand the context of the rhetorical message.

The Simpsons is an animated cartoon rather than a show filmed with real actors in an actual physical setting. The animation creates an air of detachment from real life, in addition to the detachment created by the comic frame. Animation is a particularly salient medium to television viewers who can suspend belief for plot development (which they would not be able to do with real characters). At the same time, the show establishes a personal connection with viewers because the characters are believable.

Television programming is provocative because it engages the audience through the mediation of social situations, which imparts socially constructed norms under the guise of actual experiential knowledge. Television, particularly animation, misrepresents reality, masquerading as lived experience, in order to manipulate social contexts that provide meaning for personal experience, and guide individual action.

◼ The Environmental Politics of the Springfield Nuclear Power Plant

"Both overshadowing and enlightening" (Steiger, 1999, p. 4), Springfield's nuclear power plant is owned and operated by the miserly Montgomery Burns, the town's wealthiest citizen. Homer is an employee of the plant, and holds the title of safety inspector despite his egregious lack of training. A Springfield institution, the plant is prominently featured in the show as a visual scenic element or as a comedic factor in plot development. The plant's prominence as a visual symbol of the show's environmental message is exhibited in the longer version of the show's opening sequence. The camera moves in over a hillside for a view of the picturesque town, marred only by the centrally positioned image of the plant's twin smokestacks, which billow thick clouds of dark gray smoke. The rampant pollution billowing from the smokestacks juxtaposed to the unsullied town landscape is a disturbing image. This disturbing introduction exemplifies the show's dark humor, and the potent combination of visual argument and comic frame. The negative symbolic image of the plant's egregious emissions, the dark gray billowing smoke, is reinforced by its contrast with the depiction of the town, which is animated in unrealistically bright colors. The plant symbolizes the show's environmental commentary by exhibiting a wide range of ecological implications of nuclear power, in general, and of specific conditions in the building itself.

The power plant's interior affords a setting for further visual commentary regarding the pervasive negligence that characterizes company standards for disposing of nuclear waste. A recurring joke in interior scenes is the visual image of open barrels leaking bright green radioactive waste. The plant's inner recesses are overrun with barrels strewn about the halls and open areas of the plant. Painfully bright green waste, a caricature of radioactive refuse, leaks out of the barrels and even out of the trash can in the plant's coffee room (Gewirtz, 1991). The confluence of visual argument with the comic frame establishes the symbolic meaning of the leaking waste as an animated eyesore. The pervasive images of waste enhance the visual argument symbolized in the barrels. The images position the environmental rhetoric within a burlesque comic frame, which reveals the absurdity of the publicly ignored biohazard. That is, the conspicuous barrels reveal the neglect exhibited by their inadequate disposal of the barrels, and the obvious environmental hazard that they pose. The entire scene indicates the derelict administration of safety concerns.

The plant's employees remain oblivious to the adverse situation. Their blasé attitudes enhance the situation's comedic appeal. The more egregious methods of waste disposal demonstrate the comedic effect of the employees' general apathy. Lenny and Karl, Homer's coworkers, push wheelbarrows of nuclear waste down the hallways. As Lenny and Karl discuss proper locations and methods for disposal, one of the wheelbarrows crashes into a cement column and overturns. Lenny and Karl look at each other, shrug their shoulders, and continue down the hall. The waste from the overturned container spreads ominously through the passage, while the workers resume their labor, apparently unaware of the toxic spill. That the employees rarely notice the plant's production of waste adds humorous appeal to this visual image, and contributes to the show's rhetorical condemnation of unsound disposal practices. *The Simpsons* mocks the nuclear safety precautions typified in the overwhelming lack of concern for the hazards of radioactive waste. Leaking radioactive waste is a visual symbol intended to evoke criticism of the pervasive human disregard for the environment.

This social criticism is made more explicit within a burlesque comedic frame, in a parody of safety videos on nuclear energy. *The Simpsons* relies on the burlesque comic frame to render its explicit criticism of current standard practices of nuclear waste disposal. In Springfield's caricature of pro-nukes propaganda, Smilin' Joe Fission describes the preferred method of disposal for nuclear waste: "I'll just put it where nobody'll find it for a million years" (Kogen & Wolodarsky, 1990). This parody represents the typical "out of sight, out of mind" strategy for waste disposal, and attacks the general disregard for the environmental consequences of nuclear waste disposal. The show uses humor to reveal the ridiculousness of such careless disposal strategies—clarifying the obvious problems with improper disposal, and subsequent disregard for the possible environmental consequences. *The Simpsons* employs a comic frame to expose the failings of the social order, and to criticize the audiences' complicity in the normalization of such environmentally unsafe methods. By making light of the impact of nuclear accidents and contamination of the environment, the show forces the audience to adopt a critical eye regarding real social practices that mirror the environmental negligence of the citizens of Springfield. In this way, the show's writers comment on the general human view of the environment and the anthropocentric methods that govern the power plant's safety code.

Through the comic frame, *The Simpsons* carefully balances harsh criticism of American bureaucratic institutions and sardonic commentary of individual consumptive habits. "The comic frame inherently bypasses the extremes of the bureaucratic mindset... Further, the comic frame allows observation of oneself, recognizing one's own failures and limitations" (Madesen, 1993, p. 171). Members of the audience recognize themselves in the show's characters, gaining perspective on the limits and failures of their own actions. Through this self-observation, the comic frame engenders enlightened criticism of the symbolic relationships that ground social action. The comic frame enables *The Simpsons* to rhetorically connect the economic motivations for environmental exploitation with the normalizing power of profit-driven bureaucratic social institutions that foster individual anthropocentric practices. The nuclear plant symbolizes tension between economic and environmental concerns. The plant represents the exploitation of environmental resources for wealth and power. Mr. Burns' priorities, exhibited in his operation of the plant, exemplify the attitude of economic elites and resource barons toward environmental concerns. Burns' methods of operation reveal the assumptions of characters represented by his prototype that environmental concerns are irreconcilable with economic interests. Furthermore, Burns uses his money and power to manipulate the image of his plant in order to make the environmental pollution more salient to the public.

At times *The Simpsons* abandons this charitable attitude in favor of a rhetoric well beyond the boundaries of Burke's comic frame, adopting a satiric or even burlesque style. *The Simpsons'* successful use of the burlesque comic frame is nowhere more evident than in the second season when Bart and Lisa catch a three-eyed fish while fishing near the Springfield Nuclear Reactor (Simon & Swartzwelder, 1990). When the event becomes public, a federal safety inspection team investigates the plant's emissions. In proper burlesque form, the episode chronicles the ludicrous findings of the inspection team: gum used to seal a crack in the coolant tower, a plutonium rod used as a paper-weight, monitoring stations unattended, and nuclear waste shin-deep in the hallways. The Feds threaten to shut down the power plant unless Burns makes significant improvements. Rather than bring his plant up to standard, Burns runs for governor, intending to use his elected power to keep the plant open. Inevitably confronted with Blinky, the three-eyed fish—a travesty of the ecological impacts of nuclear pollution, Burns hires spin doctors to boost his public image. In a brilliant burlesque dialogue, Burns exacerbates Blinky's parodic symbolism with his dramatic interpretation of the fish's mutation as an evolutionary advance, based on the outlandish premise that three eyes are better than two.

> *Mr. Burns*: I'm here to talk to you about my little friend, here. Blinky. Many of you consider him to be a hideous genetic mutation. Well, nothing could be further from the truth. But don't take my word for it, let's ask an actor portraying Charles Darwin what he thinks.
>
> *Darwin*: Hello, Mr. Burns.
>
> *Burns*: Oh, hello Charles. Be a good fellow and tell our viewers about your theory of natural selection.
>
> *Darwin*: Glad to, Mr. Burns. You see, every so often Mother Nature changes her animals, giving them bigger teeth, sharper claws, longer legs, or in this case, a third eye. And if these variations turn out to be an improvement, the new animals thrive and multiply and spread across the face of the earth.

Burns: So you're saying this fish might have an advantage over other fish, that it may in fact be a kind of super-fish.

Darwin: I wouldn't mind having a third eye, would you? (Simon & Swartzwelder, 1990, in Groening, 1997, p. 38).

Mr. Burns' narrative continues the farcical tone of this episode, and performs a lampoon of evolutionary theory. Appealing to the authority of (an actor playing) Charles Darwin, Burns dismisses Blinky's (the so-called super-fish) state as a "hideous" blunder by Mother Nature. He characterizes Blinky's extra eye as an improvement on Mother Nature's original creation, and explains the mutation as the result of the evolutionary process of natural selection that begets superfish like Blinky. This imparts an explicit visual argument in the image of the fish, and articulates a profound contradiction to the verbal text uttered by Mr. Burns. The triply endowed animated fish visually "voices" opposition to Mr. Burns' claims, and through its own vivid image conveys the heinous maltreatment suffered by innumerable other animals in the same predicament in another location. The burlesque form of this episode exposes the outlandish excuses for the plant's pollution, and offers insightful ecological commentary on several levels. Human pollution is characterized as an improvement on nature, and human progress is viewed as an integral part of human evolution. These references articulate specific criticism of current environmental regulations, specifically the lax enforcement of the regulations concerning the dumping, safe storage, and disposal of nuclear waste. Furthermore, this episode condemns the manipulation of political and economic power to disguise ecological accountability and to shift blame for environmental problems. The show comments on the lack of adherence to safety standards for the plant, and criticizes the apathetic acceptance of unenforced environmental inspections. Finally, this episode explicitly criticizes media spin-doctors who distort the impacts of ecological degradation caused by wealthy corporations such as the nuclear power plant. *The Simpsons* artfully employs a burlesque comic frame to condemn the established social order that promotes media distortion of public knowledge, while encouraging self-criticism for viewers to recognize their own fallibility in the show's parody of the disingenuous politics of the resource elites.

As an icon of televised popular culture, *The Simpsons* offers critical social commentary on human experience. The show remarks on the cultural, social, and political ramifications of human activity, in recognizing the limitations of exploitative human existence. "*The Simpsons* works to encourage, critique, demanding that viewers be active in their consumption" (Korte, 1997, p. 3). *The Simpsons* characterizes human activity in an incriminating light, questioning established social institutions and normalized behaviors of the dominant societal frames. The show fosters social change by providing the audience the opportunity to recognize the shortcomings of their own living practices and alter their behavior accordingly. This self-critical observation fosters a charitable attitude toward the motivations of others. The comic frame thus promotes cooperative discussion, rather than tragic blame assignment that offers no possibility for social transcendence. Certainly comic framing exposes the bureaucratic power in everyday life and creates an ironic awareness of hierarchical absurdities, but the comic frame remains charitable rather than tragic, always assuming that negotiation of environmental issues is possible. Some environmental issues, however, inevitably have tragic consequences and may be impossible to reconcile. The comic frame endows us with a sense of social awareness, but it does not necessarily promote social activism. Toward this end, *The Simpsons* offers a critical view of the dominant attitude toward nature and exposes the dangers of human-centered practices. The show's rhetorical message fosters social transformation through comedy—revealing the negative social value of anti-environmentalism in a humorous light, which conveys the potential for positive social change. The comic frame offers a dynamic vision of humanity, and thus precludes the defeatism promoted by a static view of human activity that forecloses the possibility of cooperative action. As a televised communication medium, *The Simpsons* encourages the audience to engage in such dramatistic analysis to infer the implications of the show's humorous message.

■ Springfield's Other Creatures: the Role and Fate of Animals in the Simpsons

Through the comic frame, *The Simpsons* exposes the ecological implications of numerous types of human-animal relationships, and comments on socially accepted practices of animal exploitation. The series offers countless opportunities for rhetorical criticism, but to maintain the close focus of this project, this section analyzes two episodes which provide the richest comedic visual text for an informed rhetorical analysis: the show's portrayal of eating and wearing animals.

In perhaps its most vivid expression of ecological commentary, *The Simpsons* chronicles Lisa's social transformation to a vegetarian lifestyle after she correlates the cute baby lamb she met at the petting zoo with the lamb chop on her dinner plate (Cohen, 1995). When her new lifestyle becomes public, Lisa is constantly under attack, most notably at school, where she is shown an outdated film encouraging the consumption of meat. A production of the beef industry, the film presents a comical depiction of the production of meat that scorns children who do not abide by the dominant social norms that compel consumption of animals. While the film offers a humorous view of dietary norms, it has a dark humor appeal because the film parody exhibits strident similarities with the meat industry's propaganda in the real world. Lisa is further ridiculed at Homer's barbecue where she is scorned for serving gazpacho, a vegetarian soup. The barbecue scene should resonate with vegetarian viewers as a depiction of the ubiquitous resistance to the provision of a vegetarian-friendly menu that offers meatless options in widely diverse social situations. At the barbecue, Lisa endures ridicule from her family as well as the guests, and she retaliates by attempting to vandalize the pig roasting on the rotisserie grill. Lisa's efforts to plunder the barbecue are themselves botched, propelling the entire barbecue—pig, pit, and all—on an airborne trajectory, ruining the year's most momentous social event, in Homer's estimation. The slapstick humor of the barbecue scene employs Burke's comedic frame, and facilitates the self-observation of the audience, questioning socially constructed dietary norms. Through humor, the cookout scene reveals the calamity of intolerance of diverse lifestyles; both Lisa and Homer—representing opposite extremes of the dietary conflict—exhibited a remarkable lack of tolerance for the eating preferences of their counterparts. This egotistic clash destroyed the carnivorous and vegetarian options, demonstrating the need for socially accommodating conditions to facilitate mutual satisfaction.

As the episode continues, Lisa endures an inner conflict about whether she should pursue her individual preferences or admit defeat in a culture inundated with propaganda pushing consumption of meat. Succumbing to this social pressure to eat flesh, Lisa eats a hot dog at the Kwik-E-Mart, but is informed it is a tofu hot dog, so she has not yet compromised her personal environmental code. She then meets Paul and Linda McCartney, who school Lisa in the etiquette of good vegetarianism, respecting others' choices, yet remaining vigilant in one's protest of animal consumption. Lisa's earlier inner conflict is resolved as she reconciles her personal convictions with tolerance for the personal decisions of others. Through Lisa's struggle to resist dominant social norms, this episode sheds light on the inherent incongruity between individual experience and socially constructed normative practices. This is an essential use of the comic frame: to divest one's own fallibility and attain an enriched perspective of the established order and its incumbent social and cultural values.

The concurrence of visual argument and the application of the comic frame in *The Simpsons* establish the potency of this program's environmental message. The episodic commentary on Lisa's vegetarianism exemplifies the rich text of the show as a productive multi-dimensional environmental commentary. At a base level, the show critiques social and cultural norms that vigorously condone the rampant consumption of animals. Through the narration of Lisa's struggle for a dietary choice, this episode reveals the marginalized perspective of vegetarians, which is relegated to the periphery of public discourse by the hegemonic culture of consumption. At another level, this narrative employs the comedic frame to humorously interpret the discrimination suffered by vegetarians and other dissidents against animal cruelty, for instance. The show offers a comedic interpretation of the marginalization of individuals who publicly hold counter-cultural ideals and are ridiculed and ostracized for their lifestyles. This episode reveals the personal suffering of marginalized individuals to promote a culture of social tolerance, and also articulates a formative experience that facilitates the social identification of dissident individuals through common experience who persevere in the knowledge that they are not alone. Through this comedic frame, *The Simpsons* presents a critical view of human exploitation of animals, enabling the audience to perceive the excessiveness of common practices. The program enjoys such significant persuasive influence because fundamentally the show is self-critical, exerting subtle rhetorical messages to promote positive social change.

Another preeminent episode critically comments on the subordinate position of nonhuman animals perpetuated by the extermination of animals expressly for the sartorial value of their coats. Mr. Burns represents the socially established and extremely affluent upper class. He demonstrates an unbridled consumptive appetite, and his social practices are marked by exploitative tactics of manipulation that establish his disregard for persons of inferior social status (all of Springfield). Mr. Burns enjoys the privileged position of a resource elite and exhibits his privilege through excessively wasteful habits that neglect ecological conservation. Aside from his customary exploitative disposition, Mr. Burns displays a unique perspective for rhetorical analysis in his flagrant desire to destroy animals for their fur (Scully, 1995). To realize his special penchant for a fur tuxedo, Burns steals the Simpsons' litter of twenty-five puppies. This episode's literary allusion to *101 Dalmatians* is testament to *The Simpsons'* profound pop-cultural allegory, and points to the significance of the synthesis of visual argument and the comic frame in this pop-cultural, televisual text.

The episode's predominant feature is a musical number performed by Mr. Burns extolling the virtue of wearing fur. Lisa and Bart observe Burns' performance from a window where they learn of his plans for their puppies. As external witnesses to Burns' theatrics, Lisa and Bart are a cruelty-conscious counterpoint to Burns' exploitative extravagance. The children possess a contrapuntal function to Burns' gleeful display—that is, they represent a socially conscious stance in disapproval of Burns' plans to exorcise the puppies. Bart and Lisa, who remain mostly silent spectators precluded from occupying space inside Mr. Burns' room, offer a critical perspective to the television audience through visual argument. Viewers identify with the spatial positioning of Bart and Lisa's visual images because Bart and Lisa's positioning as critical observers parallels the audience's relation to the animated reality of Springfield as critical observers. Bart and Lisa, as critical observers of Burns' flaunted excessive consumerism, serve as intermediaries to the contested practice of fur consumption. Through their mediating role and the spatial position of their visual images, the Simpson children perform an argumentative function. Bart and Lisa are positioned in physical opposition to Mr. Burns' stage (his closet), in a visual representation of social criticism against fur. The symbolic force of the children's visual images comes from the rhetorical power of their counterpoint to Burns. In addition, their discursive space on the second stage of the television itself, their spatial position, empowers the television audience to adopt similar roles as critical observers. The rhetorical tactics of the visual argument of this scene should ideally foster critical commentary regarding the ecological implications of killing animals for their pelts, and thus induce environmentally conscious change.

Mr. Burns provides a verbal text to add meaning to the pictorial, spatial arguments of the scene. He offers the perspective of guiltless consumption that is associated with the implications of environmental degradation. Unconcerned with socially responsible behavior, Mr. Burns sings a song that offers a riotous commentary on the fur trade. "See My Vest" is a hysterical musical number in which Mr. Burns models his wardrobe, making the argument for human wearing of animals. The song is a litany of animal skins and appendages including the title item, a vest "made from real gorilla chest." Mr. Burns describes the softness of his sweater made from "authentic Irish Setter," the elegance of his vampire bat evening-wear, and the warmth of his "grizzly bear underwear." He sings of his "albino African endangered rhino" slippers, his poodle beret, his loafers made of gophers, the hat that was his cat, and his plethora of turtlenecks (literally). Mr. Burns ends the song celebrating the magnificence of his "greyhound fur tuxedo," adding two dogs should be saved for "matching clogs" (Scully, 1995, in Groening, 1997, p. 172).

Burns celebrates his successful acquisition of his impressive collection of clothing exclusively tailored from genuine animal pelts. He sings a lyrical commentary on the pleasure of owning such luxurious garments, and emphasizes the authenticity of these literally "wild" fabrics. The application of the comic frame is evident in the witty rhyming scheme coupled with the lyrical revelry of such outlandish social practices. The comic effect of Burns' eccentric performance is enhanced by the conflation of his morbid subject matter and his jubilant attitude. Burns plays the clown in this episode, performing a comic ritual that highlights social discrepancies, which warrant conscious action. The incongruity of the song's textual and musical elements articulates comedy's usefulness to identify the absurdity of normative social practice. Burns' whimsical inflection belies the literal meaning of his words, and exposes the absurdity of his message. In this way, Burns presents a farcical rendition of human consumption that fosters meaningful critical commentary through the composition of Burns' comedic message and the visual argument of Bart and Lisa's spatial position.

The Simpsons' environmental rhetoric demonstrates the power of the comic frame in pop-culture analysis, enabling the audience to see through "the obfuscation of the bureaucratic, while opening space for discourse by the minority and marginalized voices in society" (Madsen, 1993, p. 171). The comic frame exhibits a two-pronged approach for effective rhetorical commentary: exposing social ills while creating a new discursive space to incorporate marginalized opinions into the public sphere. Through comedic expression, *The Simpsons* presents a complicated environmental message. That message presents enlightened criticism of the hegemonic assumptions of the existing social order, while simultaneously maintaining a self-critical attitude that facilitates a re-conceptualization of social and cultural relationships that grounds social action.

■ Nature As Ideology:
The Simpsons' Prime-Time Eco-Critique

This detailed investigation into the meaning of *The Simpsons* seeks to identify the show's environmental message. Granted, most viewers might not impart such significance from thirty minutes of their prime-time experience. Determining the audience's understanding of the environmental message is admittedly difficult. Such critical analysis is crucial, however, to increasing public awareness of mediated discourse. Madsen describes the critic's ultimate task to alter social frames, which increases the chance for constructive social change (Madsen, 1993, p. 170). Such endeavors help foster more informed television audience members who recognize their situation as passive subjects to the manipulation of media messages to influence and direct their behavior as consumers. *The Simpsons'* antics "mirror even our culture's most unrecognized aspects in all its tiny facets. So even if the viewer does not manage to grasp all the messages transmitted by the series' characters, he or she is always very likely to at least decode some of them" (Steiger, 1999, p. 13). *The Simpsons'* success results from a combination of rhetorical elements, which projects more than mere entertainment into America's living rooms (Steiger, 1999, p. 3). In this way, the show educates its audience while maintaining popular appeal through its humorous, animated form. The series has transferred the expression of political opinion from traditional sources such as radio, and newspapers, to television (Steiger, 1999, p. 13).

The powerful symbolic influence of *The Simpsons* is enhanced through its unique synthesis of comedic and visual rhetorical elements. Televisual media enables a critical look at the complexities of human experience through the manipulation of verbal, acoustic and visual dramatic elements. The combination of these different sense experiences creates a powerfully realistic portrayal of familiar human situations. "By animating *The Simpsons*, Groening managed to reach a higher degree of realism, while he is still entertaining and thus appealing to his audience" (Steiger, 1999, p. 4). The complex symbolism of comic and visual media presents a multidimensional perspective of reality that enjoys powerful rhetorical appeal. Televised reality enjoys an attractiveness that enables persuasive arguments against dominant social and cultural norms. The realism of televisual media is particularly persuasive when offering critical commentary against institutions and practices familiar to America's television audience. *The Simpsons* presents an alternative epistemology that critiques the environmental practices sanctioned by dominant social norms. Through the complex manipulation of multidimensional rhetorical elements, the series reveals the ecological impacts of human activity. The subversive symbolism of *The Simpsons'* environmental rhetoric functions as enlightened criticism of cultural norms of consumption, which exonerate society's ecocidal practices.

The Simpsons presents a strong ideological message about nature as a symbol—as an object for human exploitation. The characters of *The Simpsons* display an overall disregard for the environment, are separated from nature, and often oppose nature. The show portrays the mainstream culture in which the environment has a solely utilitarian value and exists exclusively for human purposes. Through humorous exaggeration, *The Simpsons* offers critical commentary on humanity and points out the danger of destroying the environment. The series' message is revolutionary because it portrays the counterculture of environmental activism as an alternative to anthropocentrism. *The Simpsons'* activism is communicated effectively through the juxtaposition of characters that represent the extremes on an ecological spectrum. Homer represents anthropocentrism, the quintessential exploitative human. Homer's character has a powerful dramatic function: increasing viewers' awareness by evoking reactions to his naivete to media influence of popular culture (Steiger, 1999, p. 5).

Lisa counters Homer's egregious anthropocentrism and symbolizes an environmental ethic of caring for nonhuman creatures. Lisa represents a moral center to the show, which enables her to reveal the irony of her father's anthropocentric actions. When Lisa bemoans the crashing of an oil tanker on Baby Seal Beach, Homer comforts her and reveals his anthropocentric perspective: "It'll be okay, honey. There's lots more oil where that came from" (Appel, 1996). Homer, not considering the ecological implications of the oil spill, instead thinks of the effects on human access to resources.

Through humor, each character's commentary functions differently; Lisa presents a moral force that opposes Homer's flagrant anthropocentrism and effectively points out the absurdity of human action. In this way, the show offers the chance for positive social change. The comic frame permits observation of ourselves, while maintaining the possibility for action by increasing societal consciousness (Carlson, 1986, p. 447). *The Simpsons* is a subversive look at the state of human existence, but is effective because of its chosen methods of rhetorical commentary. The visual communication of the show makes its criticism palatable. The show's writers are well aware that the "pastel colors of animation often blind the censors to their biting critiques of the world" (Korte, 1997, p. 7). "Combining entertainment and subversion, *The Simpsons* angers some people as much as it amuses others...Joe Rhodes of *Entertainment Weekly* notes that '*The Simpsons* at its heart... is guerrilla TV, a wicked satire masquerading as a prime-time cartoon'" (Korte, 1997, p. 9). Through its unique rhetorical methods, *The Simpsons* describes the environmental harms of social ills. Through the humorous interpretations of Springfield's environmental hazards and the moral force of Lisa's portrayal of environmental activism, the show offers an alternative solution to exploitative human practices.

    The Simpsons functions as a form of environmental activism and thus reveals popular culture's effectiveness as a medium for ecological commentary. The show increases public awareness of environmental issues, and educates the television audience while entertaining them. "Unlike many shows on TV, *The Simpsons* works to encourage critique, demanding that viewers be active in their consumption" (Korte, 1997, p. 3). Through humor, the show reveals the anthropocentrism of human activity in such a way that otherwise harsh criticism is palatable and potentially effects social change. By pointing out the humorous fallacies in human action, the series offers a significant look at the life of the typical American family, and in this way profoundly impacts the attitudes and beliefs of the television audience. The crude animation of *The Simpsons* transcends conventional boundaries of environmental rhetoric. The series embodies a powerful social force by presenting a multidimensional message that critically comments on institutions and practices of the normative social and cultural context, and engages the audience through rhetorical appeals to viewers' personal experiences.

REFERENCES

Andrews, J.R. (1990). *The Practice of Rhetorical Criticism.* White Plains, NY: Longman.

Appel, R. (1996, November 24). Bart after dark (D. Polcino, Director). In J.L. Brooks, M. Groening, & S. Simon (Executive Producers), *The Simpsons.* New York: Twentieth Century Fox Film Corporation.

Blair, J.A. (1996). The possibility and actuality of visual arguments. *Argumentation and Advocacy.* 33, 23-29.

Burke, K. (1950). *A Rhetoric of Motives.* Berkeley: University of California Press.

Burke, K. (1959). *Attitudes Toward History.* Boston: Beacon Press.

Burke, K. (1966). *Language as Symbolic Action: Essays on Life, Literature, and Method.* Berkeley: University of California Press.

Carlson, A.C. (1986). Gandhi and the comic frame: "Ad bellum purificandum". *Quarterly Journal of Speech*, 72, 446-445.

Cohen, D.S. (1995, October 15). Lisa the vegetarian (M. Kirkland, Director). In J.L. Brooks, M. Groening, & S. Simon (Executive Producers), *The Simpsons*. New York: Twentieth Century Fox Film Corporation.

Gewirtz, J. (1991, October 17). Homer defined (M. Kirkland, Director). In J.L. Brooks, M. Groening, S. Simon (Executive Producers), *The Simpsons*. New York: Twentieth Century Fox Film Corporation.

Groening, M. (1997). *The Simpsons: A Complete Guide to our Favorite Family*. R. Richmond & A. Coffman (Eds.), Harper Perennial: New York.

Groening, M. (1999). *The Simpsons Forever: A Complete Guide to our Favorite Family... Continued*. S.M. Gimple (Ed.), Harper Perennial: New York.

Gronbeck, B.E. (1995). Unstated propositions: Relationships among verbal, visual and acoustic languages. In S. Jackson (Ed.), *Argumentation and Values* (pp. 539-542). Annandale, VA: Speech Communication Association.

Klumpp, J.F. & Hollihan, T. (1989). Rhetorical criticism as moral action. *Quarterly Journal of Speech*, 75, 84-97.

Kogen, J. & Wolodarsky, W. (1990, January 21). Homer's odyssey (W. Archer, Director). In J.L. Brooks, M. Groening, & S. Simon (Executive Producers), *The Simpsons*. New York: Twentieth Century Fox Film Corporation.

Korte, D. (1997). *The Simpsons* as quality television. *The Simpsons Archive* [On-line]. Available: http://www.snpp.com/other/papers/dk.paper.html

Madsen, A. (1993). The comic frame as a corrective to bureaucratization: A dramatistic perspective on argumentation. *Argumentation and Advocacy*, 29, 64-177.

Scully, M. (1995, April 9). Two dozen and one greyhounds (B. Anderson, Director). In J.L. Brooks, M. Groening, & S. Simon (Executive Producers), *The Simpsons*. New York: Twentieth Century Fox Film Corporation.

Simon, S. & Swartzwelder, J. (1990, November 1). Two Cars in every Garage and Three Eyes on every Fish (W. Archer, Director). In J.L. Brooks, M. Groening, & S. Simon (Executive Producers), *The Simpsons*. New York: Twentieth Century Fox Film Corporation.

Steiger, G. (1999). *The Simpsons* - just funny or more? *The Simpsons Archive* [On-line]. Available: http://www.snpp.com/other/papers/gs.paper.html

READING AND WRITING

1. What is Todd's analytical argument about *The Simpsons*? What support does she marshal to make this case? What details does she use from the episodes themselves? Do you find her analysis persuasive?

DEVELOPING LONGER RESPONSES

2. Todd makes much of the character Lisa Simpson's ability to create social commentary on human treatment of animals and the environment. Watch an episode or two of *The Simpsons* (you might consider watching "Lisa the Vegetarian" from season 7, which Todd describes in her essay), and write a short essay in which you describe Lisa's environmental ethos. What characteristics does she possess? Do these characteristics endear her and her beliefs to you? Why or why not?

USING RESEARCH

3. Todd's essay was originally published in a collection titled *Enviropop: Studies in Environmental Rhetoric and Popular Culture*. Look this book up online (you might try Amazon.com or Google Books) and examine the table of contents and any summaries or descriptions you can find. Based on this research and your reading of Todd's piece, explain who you think Todd's target audience is.

4. Todd argues in part that *The Simpsons* uses humor to offer up a cutting cultural critique of the way we treat the environment. Do some online searching to find another humorous text (this could be a clip from a TV show, a film, or a stand-up act, among other possibilities) that makes a claim about an environmental issue. Bring this text to class and present it to your classmates, explaining the argument you see emerging there.

Kevin Bullis is the energy editor for the journal Technology Review, where this article was published in early 2010. In it, Bullis explains the controversial topic of geoengineering, the use of risky technologies to try to undue some of the damage we have caused the planet.

THE GEOENGINEERING GAMBIT   Kevin Bullis

Rivers fed by melting snow and glaciers supply water to over one-sixth of the world's population—well over a billion people. But these sources of water are quickly disappearing: the Himalayan glaciers that feed rivers in India, China, and other Asian countries could be gone in 25 years. Such effects of climate change no longer surprise scientists. But the speed at which they're happening does. "The earth appears to be changing faster than the climate models predicted," says Daniel Schrag, a professor of earth and planetary sciences at Harvard University, who advises President Obama on climate issues.

Atmospheric levels of carbon dioxide have already climbed to 385 parts per million, well over the 350 parts per million that many scientists say is the upper limit for a relatively stable climate. And despite government-led efforts to limit carbon emissions in many countries, annual emissions from fossil-fuel combustion are going up, not down: over the last two decades, they have increased 41 percent. In the last 10 years, the concentration of carbon dioxide in the atmosphere has increased by nearly two parts per million every year. At this rate, they'll be twice preindustrial levels by the end of the century. Meanwhile, researchers are growing convinced that the climate might be more sensitive to greenhouse gases at this level than once thought. "The likelihood that we're going to avoid serious damage seems quite low," says Schrag. "The best we're going to do is probably not going to be good enough."

This shocking realization has caused many influential scientists, including Obama advisors like Schrag, to fundamentally change their thinking about how to respond to climate change. They have begun calling for the government to start funding research into geoengineering—large-scale schemes for rapidly cooling the earth.

Strategies for geoengineering vary widely, from launching trillions of sun shields into space to triggering vast algae blooms in oceans. The one that has gained the most attention in recent years involves injecting millions of tons of sulfur dioxide high into the atmosphere to form microscopic particles that would shade the planet. Many geoengineering proposals date back decades, but until just a few years ago, most climate scientists considered them something between high-tech hubris and science fiction. Indeed, the subject was "forbidden territory," says Ronald Prinn, a professor of atmospheric sciences at MIT. Not only is it unclear how such engineering feats would be accomplished and whether they would, in fact, moderate the climate, but most scientists worry that they could have disastrous unintended consequences. What's more, relying on geoengineering to cool the earth, rather than cutting greenhouse-gas emissions, would commit future generations to maintaining these schemes indefinitely. For these reasons, mere discussion of geoengineering was considered a dangerous distraction for policy makers considering how to deal with global warming. Prinn says that until a few years ago, he thought its advocates were "off the deep end."

It's not just a fringe idea anymore. The United Kingdom's Royal Society issued a report on geoengineering in September that outlined the research and policy challenges ahead. The National Academies in the United States are working on a similar study. And John Holdren, the director of the White House Office of Science and Technology Policy, broached the idea soon after he was appointed. "Climate change is happening faster than anyone previously predicted," he said during one talk. "If we get sufficiently desperate, we may try to engage in geoengineering to try to create cooling effects." To prepare ourselves, he said, we need to understand the possibilities and the possible side effects. Even the U.S. Congress has now taken an interest, holding its first hearings on geoengineering in November.

Geoengineering might be "a terrible idea," but it might be better than doing nothing, says Schrag. Unlike many past advocates, he doesn't think it's an alternative to reducing greenhouse-gas emissions. "It's not a techno-fix. It's not a Band-Aid. It's a tourniquet," he says. "There are potential side effects, yes. But it may be better than the alternative, which is bleeding to death."

■ Sunday Storms

The idea of geoengineering has a long history. In the 1830s, James Espy, the first federally funded meteorologist in the United States, wanted to burn large swaths of Appalachian forest every Sunday afternoon, supposing that heat from the fires would induce regular rainstorms. More than a century later, meteorologists and physicists in the United States and the Soviet Union separately considered a range of schemes for changing the climate, often with the goal of warming up northern latitudes to extend growing seasons and clear shipping lanes through the Arctic. In 1974 a Soviet scientist, Mikhail Budyko, first suggested what is today probably the leading plan for cooling down the earth: injecting gases into the upper reaches of the atmosphere, where they would form microscopic particles to block sunlight. The idea is based on a natural phenomenon. Every few decades a volcano erupts so violently that it sends several millions of tons of sulfur—in the form of sulfur dioxide   more than 10 kilometers into the upper reaches of the atmosphere, a region called the stratosphere. The resulting sulfate particles spread out quickly and stay suspended for years. They reflect and diffuse sunlight, creating a haze that whitens blue skies and causes dramatic sunsets. By decreasing the amount of sunlight that reaches the surface, the haze also lowers its temperature. This is what happened after the 1991 eruption of Mount Pinatubo in the Philippines, which released about 15 million tons of sulfur dioxide into the stratosphere. Over the next 15 months, average temperatures dropped by half a degree Celsius. (Within a few years, the sulfates settled out of the stratosphere, and the cooling effect was gone.)

Photograph by Mauricio Alejo

Photograph by Mauricio Alejo

Scientists estimate that compensating for the increase in carbon dioxide levels expected over this century would require pumping between one million and five million tons of sulfur into the stratosphere every year. Diverse strategies for getting all that sulfur up there have been proposed. Billionaire investor Nathan Myhrvold, the former chief technology officer at Microsoft and the founder and CEO of Intellectual Ventures, based in Bellevue, Washington, has thought of several, one of which takes advantage of the fact that coal-fired power plants already emit vast amounts of sulfur dioxide. These emissions stay close to the ground, and rain washes them out of the atmosphere within a couple of weeks. But if the pollution could reach the stratosphere, it would circulate for years, vastly multiplying its impact in reflecting sunlight. To get the sulfur into the stratosphere, Myhrvold suggests, why not use a "flexible, inflatable hot-air-balloon smokestack" 25 kilometers tall? The emissions from just two coal-fired plants might solve the problem, he says. He estimates that his solution would cost less than $100 million a year, including the cost of replacing balloons damaged by storms.

Not surprisingly, climate scientists are not ready to sign off on such a scheme. Some problems are obvious. No one has ever tried to build a 25-kilometer smokestack, for one thing. Moreover, scientists don't understand atmospheric chemistry well enough to be sure what would happen; far from alleviating climate change, shooting tons of sulfates into the stratosphere could have disastrous consequences. The chemistry is too complex for us to be certain, and climate models aren't powerful enough to tell the whole story.

"We know Pinatubo cooled the earth, but that's not the question," Schrag says. "Average temperature is not the only issue." You've also got to account for regional variations in temperature and effects on precipitation, he explains—the very things that climate models are notoriously bad at accounting for. Prinn concurs: "If we lower levels of sunlight, we are unsure of the exact response of the climate system to doing that, for the same reason that we don't know exactly how the climate will respond to a particular level of greenhouse gases." He adds, "That's the big issue. How can you engineer a system you don't fully understand?"

The actual effects of Mount Pinatubo were, in fact, complex. Climate models at the time predicted that by decreasing the amount of sunlight hitting the surface of the earth, the haze of sulfates produced in such an eruption would reduce evaporation, which in turn would lower the amount of precipitation worldwide. Rainfall did decrease—but by much more than scientists had expected. "The year following Mount Pinatubo had by far the lowest amount of rainfall on record," says Kevin Trenberth, a senior scientist at the National Center for Atmospheric Research in Boulder, CO. "In fact, it was 50 percent lower than the previous low of any year." The effects, however, weren't uniform; in some places, precipitation actually increased. A human-engineered sulfate haze could have similarly unpredictable results, scientists warn.

Even in a best-case scenario, where side effects are small and manageable, cooling the planet by deflecting sunlight would not reduce the carbon dioxide in the atmosphere, and elevated levels of that gas have consequences beyond raising the temperature. One is that the ocean absorbs more carbon dioxide and becomes more acidic as a result. That harms shellfish and some forms of plankton, a key source of food for fish and whales. The fishing industry could be devastated. What's more, carbon dioxide levels will continue to rise if we don't address them directly, so any sunlight-reducing technology would have to be continually ratcheted up to compensate for their warming effects.

And if the geoengineering had to stop—say, for environmental or economic reasons—the higher levels of greenhouse gases would cause an abrupt warm-up. "Even if the geoengineering worked perfectly," says Raymond Pierrehumbert, a professor of geophysical sciences at the University of Chicago, "you're still in the situation where the whole planet is just one global war or depression away from being hit with maybe a hundred years' worth of global warming in under a decade, which is certainly catastrophic. Geoengineering, if it were carried out, would put the earth in an extremely precarious state."

■ Smarter Sulfates

Figuring out the consequences of various geoengineering plans and developing strategies to make them safer and more effective will take years, or even decades, of research. "For every dollar we spend figuring out how to actually do geoengineering," says Schrag, "we need to be spending 10 dollars learning what the impacts will be."

To begin with, scientists aren't even sure that sulfates delivered over the course of decades, rather than in one short volcanic blast, will work to cool the planet down. One key question is how microscopic particles interact in the stratosphere. It's possible that sulfate particles added repeatedly to the same area over time would clump together. If that happened, the particles could start to interact with longer-wave radiation than just the wavelengths of electromagnetic energy in visible light. This would trap some of the heat that naturally escapes into space, causing a net heating effect rather than a cooling effect. Or the larger particles could fall out of the sky before they had a chance to deflect the sun's heat. To study such phenomena, David Keith, the director of the Energy and Environmental Systems Group at the University of Calgary, envisions experiments in which a plane would spray a gas at low vapor pressure over an area of 100 square kilometers. The gas would condense into particles in the stratosphere, and the plane would fly back through the particle cloud to take measurements. Systematically altering the size of the particles, the quantity of particles in a given area, the timing of their release, and other variables could reveal key details about their microscale interactions.

Yet even if the behavior of sulfate particles can be understood and managed, it's far from clear how injecting them into the stratosphere would affect vast, complex climate systems. So far, most models have been crude; only recently, for example, did they start taking into account the movement of ice and ocean currents. Sulfates would cool the planet during the day, but they'd make no difference when the sun isn't shining. As a result, nights would probably be warmer relative to days, but scientists have done little to model this effect and study how it could affect ecosystems. "Similarly, you could affect the seasons," Schrag says: the sulfates would lower temperatures less during the winter (when there's less daylight) and more during the summer. And scientists have done little to understand how stratospheric circulation patterns would change with the addition of sulfates, or precisely how any of these things could affect where and when we might experience droughts, floods, and other disasters.

If scientists could learn more about the effects of sulfates in the stratosphere, it could raise the intriguing possibility of "smart" geoengineering, Schrag says. Volcanic eruptions are crude tools, releasing a lot of sulfur in the course of a few days, and all from one location. But geoengineers could choose exactly where to send sulfates into the stratosphere, as well as when and how fast.

"So far we're thinking about a very simplistic thing," Schrag says. "We're talking about injecting stuff in the stratosphere in a uniform way." The effects that have been predicted so far, however, aren't evenly distributed. Changes in evaporation, for example, could be devastating if they caused droughts on land, but if less rain falls over the ocean, it's not such a big deal. By taking advantage of stratospheric circulation patterns and seasonal variations in weather, it might be possible to limit the most damaging consequences. "You can pulse injections," he says. "You could build smart systems that might cancel out some of those negative effects."

Rather than intentionally polluting the stratosphere, a different and potentially less risky approach to geoengineering is to pull carbon dioxide out of the air. But the necessary technology would be challenging to develop and put in place on large scale.

In his 10th-floor lab in the Manhattan neighborhood of Morningside Heights, Klaus Lackner, a professor of geophysics in the Department of Earth and Environmental Engineering at Columbia University, is experimenting with a material that chemically binds to carbon dioxide in the air and then, when doused in water, releases the gas in a concentrated form that can easily be captured. The work is at an early stage. Lackner's carbon-capture devices look like misshapen test-tube brushes; they have to be hand dipped in water, and it's hard to quickly seal them into the improvised chamber used to measure the carbon dioxide they release. But he envisions automated systems—millions of them, each the size of a small cabin—scattered over the countryside near geologic reservoirs that could store the gases they capture. A system based on this material, he calculates, could remove carbon dioxide from the air a thousand times as fast as trees do now. Others at Columbia are working on ways to exploit the fact that peridotite rock reacts with carbon dioxide to form magnesium carbonate and other minerals, removing the greenhouse gas from the atmosphere. The researchers hope to speed up these natural reactions.

It's far from clear that these ideas for capturing carbon will be practical. Some may even require so much energy that they create a net increase in carbon dioxide. "But even if it takes us a hundred years to learn how to do it," Pierrehumbert says, "it's still useful, because CO_2 naturally takes a thousand years to get out of the atmosphere."

■ The Seeds of War

Several existing geoengineering schemes, though, could be attempted relatively cheaply and easily. And even if no one knows whether they would be safe or effective, that doesn't mean they won't be tried.

FIVE GEOENGINEERING SCHEMES

Researchers and entrepreneurs have proposed approaches ranging from the relatively cheap and simple to the elaborate. Here are the ones that have received the most attention so far.

SULFATE INJECTION

Aircraft, or a hose suspended by hundreds of wing-shaped balloons, could inject aerosols into the upper atmosphere. The particles would reflect light and shade the earth.
Pros: It could be cheap and fast-acting, cooling the earth in months.
Cons: It could cause droughts. Injections might need to continue for hundreds of years.

CLOUD BRIGHTENING

Tiny droplets made by spraying an extremely fine mist of seawater into low-lying clouds could make them reflect more sunlight than ordinary clouds.
Pros: Shading could be targeted—to stop the melting of Arctic Sea ice, for example.
Cons: Scientists don't know how it would affect precipitation and temperatures over land, where it would matter most.

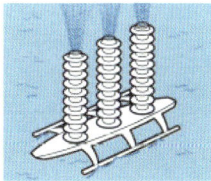

OCEAN FERTILIZATION

Adding iron or other nutrients to the ocean could promote algae blooms, which would capture carbon dioxide and store some of it deep in the ocean.
Pros: It would directly address the root of climate change: carbon dioxide in the atmosphere.
Cons: At best, it could offset an eighth of the greenhouse-gas emissions attributed to humans, and it could harm ecosystems.

SPACE SHADES

Trillions of disks launched into space could reflect incoming sunlight.
Pros: Space-based systems don't pollute the atmosphere. Once in place, they would cool the earth quickly.
Cons: The technology could take decades to develop. And launching trillions of disks is fantastically expensive.

ARTIFICIAL TREES

Various chemical reactions can be used to capture carbon dioxide from the atmosphere for permanent storage.
Pros: In the long run, this could reduce atmospheric concentrations of carbon dioxide. There is no obvious limit to how much of the greenhouse gas could be stored.
Cons: It could be very expensive and energy intensive, and it would take a long time to reduce temperatures.

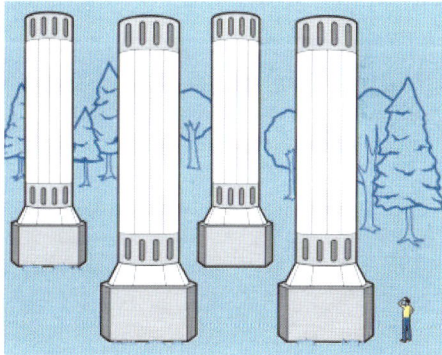

David Victor, the director of the Laboratory on International Law and Regulation at the University of California, San Diego, sees two scenarios in which it might happen. First, "the desperate Hail Mary pass:" "A country quite vulnerable to changing climate is desperate to alter outcomes and sees that efforts to cut emissions are not bearing fruit.

Crude geoengineering schemes could be very inexpensive, and thus this option might even be available to a Trinidad or Bangladesh—the former rich in gas exports and quite vulnerable, and the latter poor but large enough that it might do something seen as essential for survival." And second, "the Soviet-style arrogant engineering scenario:" "A country run by engineers and not overly exposed to public opinion or to dissenting voices undertakes geoengineering as a national mission—much like massive building of poorly designed nuclear reactors, river diversion projects, resettlement of populations, and other national missions that are hard to pursue when the public is informed, responsive, and in power." In either case, a single country acting alone could influence the climate of the entire world.

How would the world react? In extreme cases, Victor says, it could lead to war. Some countries might object to cooling the earth, especially if higher temperatures have brought them advantages such as longer growing seasons and milder winters. And if geoengineering decreases rainfall, countries that have experienced droughts due to global warming could suffer even more.

No current international laws or agreements would clearly prevent a country from unilaterally starting a geoengineering project. And too little is known now for a governing body such as the United Nations to establish sound regulations—regulations that might in any case be ignored by a country set on trying to save itself from a climate disaster. Victor says the best hope is for leading scientists around the world to collaborate on establishing as clearly as possible what dangers could be involved in geoengineering and how, if at all, it might be used. Through open international research, he says, we can "increase the odds—not to 100 percent—that responsible norms would emerge."

■ Ready or Not

In 2006, Paul Crutzen, the Dutch scientist who won the Nobel Prize in chemistry for his discoveries about the depletion of the stratospheric ozone layer, wrote an essay in the journal *Climatic Change* in which he declared that efforts to reduce greenhouse-gas emissions "have been grossly unsuccessful." He called for increased research into the "feasibility and environmental consequences of climate engineering," even though he acknowledged that injecting sulfates into the stratosphere could damage the ozone layer and cause large, unpredictable side effects. Despite these dangers, he said, climatic engineering could ultimately be "the only option available to rapidly reduce temperature rises."

At the time, Crutzen's essay was controversial, and many scientists called it irresponsible. But since then it has served to bring geoengineering into the open, says David Keith, who started studying the subject in 1989. After a scientist of Crutzen's credentials, who understood the stratosphere as well as anyone, came out in favor of studying sulfate injection as a way to cool the earth, many other scientists were willing to start talking about it.

Among the most recent converts is David Battisti, a professor of atmospheric sciences at the University of Washington. One problem in particular worries him. Studies of heat waves show that crop yields drop off sharply when temperatures rise 3 °C to 4 °C above normal—the temperatures that MIT's Prinn predicts we might reach even with strict emissions controls. Speaking at a geoengineering symposium at MIT this fall, Battisti said, "By the end of the century, just due to temperature alone, we're looking at a 30 to 40 percent reduction in [crop] yields, while in the next 50 years demand for food is expected to more than double."

Battisti is well aware of the uncertainties that surround geoengineering. According to research he's conducted recently, the first computer models that tried to show how shading the earth would affect climate were off by 2 °C to 3 °C in predictions of regional temperature change and by as much as 40 percent in predictions of regional rainfall. But with a billion people already malnourished, and billions more who could go hungry if global warming disrupts agriculture, Battisti has reluctantly conceded that we may need to consider "a climate-engineering patch." Better data and better models will help clarify the effects of geoengineering. "Give us 30 or 40 years and we'll be there," he said at the MIT symposium. "But in 30 to 40 years, at the level we're increasing CO_2, we're going to need this, whether we're ready or not."

■ READING AND WRITING

1. What, according to this piece, is geoengineering? (Include some examples of geoengineering proposals in your response.) Why is geoengineering a controversial subject?

2. Bullis writes, "Many geoengineering proposals date back decades, but until just a few years ago, most climate scientists considered them something between high-tech hubris and science fiction." Why, according to Bullis, have these proposals been pushed to the fringes for so long? What has changed in recent years to bring geoengineering into more acceptable scientific and political discussions? What do you think the future holds for these approaches to dealing with climate change?

3. If you haven't already, read Edward O. Wilson's "For the Love of Life," which opens this chapter. Based on that essay, how do you think Wilson might respond to the concept of geoengineering? Would he consider it a good idea? Explain your response.

■ DEVELOPING LONGER RESPONSES

4. Among journalists, scientists, and policymakers, the critical question surrounding geoengineering is not, "How we would do it?" but rather, "Should we do it?" Write a short essay in which you characterize the ethical dilemmas attached to geoengineering. Write your own responses to these dilemmas. If we had the technology to cool the planet through geoengineering, should we do it? Why or why not?

IMAGE 3.3

"Technology can be good for the environment," Stewart Brand writes in "Reframing the Problems." Based on your reading of Brand's piece and "The Geoengineering Gambit" by Kevin Bullis, how might this be the case? Why might some environmentalists be wary of such a statement?

In the fall of 1968, Stewart Brand founded, edited, and published the Whole Earth Catalog, a pioneering resource that changed the way many people thought about the environment (parts of the catalog are available online at http://www.wholeearth.com/index.php). "Reframing the Problems" is an excerpt from Brand's 2000 book The Clock of the Long Now: Time and Responsibility, which "challenges readers to get outside themselves and combat the short-term irresponsible thinking that has led to environmental destruction and social chaos," according to a Publisher's Weekly review.

REFRAMING THE PROBLEMS   Stewart Brand

In 1996, a suddenly growing multibillion-dollar California foundation asked me and others to write a short paper on the question, "What are the most serious environmental problems confronting humankind at the beginning of the twenty-first century?" Figuring I would have nothing original to add to that list, I decided to write the piece from the perspective of the Clock of the Long Now. *Looking from outside the present time gave a sideways rather than end-on view of the current environmental problems and invited rethinking them in terms of eventual practical solutions rather than only how great a threat they pose. I think the paper fits in at this point in the discussion, where the uses and advantages of long-view thinking are explored. The foundation (now the third-largest in America) is endowed with the wealth of David Packard, cofounder of Hewlett-Packard, the brilliantly successful electronics firm based in Palo Alto, California.*

To the David and Lucile Packard Foundation:

My contribution may be to bend your question a little. Environmental problems these days come in a pretty familiar litany of pretty familiar names. The World Population problem. Climate Change problem. Loss of Biodiversity. Ocean Fisheries. Freshwater Aquifers. North/South Economic Disparity. Rain Forests. Agricultural and Industrial Pollution. Identifying these issues and making them everyone's concern has been a major triumph of environmental science and activism in the late twentieth century.

I propose that the Packard Foundation could make a contribution beyond even the splendid effect of its funding by helping to rethink—reframe—the very structure of how environmental problems are stated. This is a common practice among inventive engineers such as the late Mr. Packard. When a design problem resists solution, reframe the problem in such a way that it invites solution.

An example of spontaneous reframing occurred in 1969, when the Apollo program began returning color photographs of the Earth from space. Everyone saw the photographs and saw that we occupied a planet that was beautiful, all one, very finite, and possibly fragile. The environmental movement took off from that moment—the first Earth Day was in 1970. That effect of the American space program was never intended or anticipated. Indeed, nearly all environmentalists in the sixties (except Jacques Cousteau) actively fought against the space program, saying that we had to solve Earth's problems before exploring space.

What might be some further helpful reframings?

(1) *Civilization's shortening attention span is mismatched with the pace of environmental problems.*

What with accelerating technology and the short-horizon perspective that goes with burgeoning market economics (next quarter) and the spread of democracy (next election), we have a situation where steady but gradual environmental degradation escapes our notice. The slow, inexorable pace of ecological and climatic cycles and lag times bear no relation to the hasty cycles and lag times of human attention, decision, and action. We can't slow down all of human behavior, and shouldn't, but we might slow down parts.

Now is the period in which people feel they live and act and have responsibility. For most of us *now* is about a week, sometimes a year. For some traditional tribes in the American northeast and Australia *now* is seven generations back and forward (175 years each direction). Just as the Earth photographs gave us a sense of *the big here*, we need things that give people a sense of *the long now*.

Candidate now-lengtheners might include: abiding charismatic artifacts; extreme longitudinal scientific studies; very large, slow, ambitious projects; human life extension (with delayable childbearing); some highly durable institutions; reward systems for slow responsible behavior; honoring patience and sometimes disdaining rush; widespread personal feeling for the span of history; planning practices that preserve options for the future.

In a sense, the task here is to make the world safe for hurry by slowing some parts way down.

(2) *Natural systems can be thought of pragmatically as "natural infrastructure."*

One area in which governments and other institutions seem comfortable thinking in the long term is the realm of infrastructure, even though there is no formal economics of infrastructure benefits and costs. (There should be and could be.) We feel good about investing huge amounts in transportation systems, utility grids, and buildings.

Infrastructure thinking is directly transferable to natural systems. Lucky for us, we don't have to build the atmosphere that sustains us, the soils, the aquifers, the wild fisheries, the forests, the rich biological complexity that keeps the whole thing resilient. All we have to do is defend these systems—from ourselves. It doesn't take much money. It doesn't even take much knowledge, though knowledge certainly helps.

A bracing way to think about this matter would be to seriously take on the project of terraforming Mars—making it comfortable for life. Then think about reterraforming Earth if we lose the natural systems that previously built themselves here. The fact is that humans are now so powerful that we are in effect terraforming Earth. Rather poorly so far. We can't undo our power; it will only increase. We can terraform more intelligently—with a light, slow hand, and with the joy and pride that goes with huge infrastructure projects. Current efforts by the Army Corps of Engineers to restore the Florida Everglades, for example, have this quality.

(3) *Technology can be good for the environment.*

My old biology teacher, Paul Ehrlich, has a formula declaring that environmental degradation is proportional to "population times affluence times technology." It now appears that the coming of information technology is reversing that formula, so that better technology and more affluence leads to less environmental harm—*if* that is one of the goals of the society.

"Doing more with less"—Buckminister Fuller's "ephemeralization"—is creating vastly more efficient industrial and agricultural processes, with proportionately less impact on natural systems. It is also moving ever more of human activity into an *infosphere* less harmfully entwined with the biosphere.

Given its roots, the Packard Foundation is particularly well suited to evaluate and foster what a Buddhist engineer might call *right technology*. It would be helpful to assemble a roster of existing environmentally benign technologies. Satellites for communication and remote sensing come to mind. So does Jim Levelock's gas chromatograph (which detected atmospheric chlorofluorocarbons)—invented for Hewlett-Packard, as I recall.

The foundation might support activities such as Eric Drexler's Foresight Institute, which is aiming to shape nanotechnology (molecular engineering) toward cultural and environmental responsibility. It might support services on the Internet that distribute information and discussion about the environmental impacts of new and anticipated technologies and their interactions. Good effects should be investigated as well as ill effects.

(4) *Feedback is the primary tool for tuning systems, especially at the natural/artificial interface.*

German military officers are required to eat what their troops eat and after they eat. That single tradition assures that everyone's meals are excellent and timely, and it enhances unit morals, and respect for the officers. The feedback cycle is local and immediate, not routed through bureaucratic specialists or levels of hierarchy.

In similar fashion, factories, farms, and cities that pollute rivers and water tables could be required to release their outflows upstream of their own water intake rather than downstream.

The much-lamented "tragedy of the commons" is a classic case of pathological feedback—where each individual player is rewarded rather than punished for wasting the common resource. In fact, healthy self-governing commons systems are frequent in the world and in history, as examined in Elinor Ostrum's *Governing the Commons*. The commons she dissects include communally held mountain meadows and forests in Switzerland, irrigation cooperatives in Japan and Spain, and jointly managed fisheries in Turkey, Sri Lanka, and Nova Scotia. The successful ones are maintained (and maintainable) neither by the state nor the market but by a local set of community feedbacks adroitly tuned to ensure the system's long-term health and prosperity. Ostrum detects eight design principles that keep a wide variety of common systems self-balancing. They are: clear boundaries;

locally appropriate rules; collective agreement; monitoring; graduated sanctions; conflict-resolution mechanisms; rights to organize; nested enterprises.

The Packard Foundation could encourage feedback analysis of environmental problems and help devise local-feedback solutions.

(5) *Environmental health requires peace, prosperity, and continuity.*

War, especially civil war, destroys the environment and displaces caring for the environment for generations. Widespread poverty destroys the environment and undermines all ability to think and act for the long term.

Environmental activists and peace activists are still catching on that they are natural partners, and both remain averse to business boosters who might aid prosperity. Peacekeeping soldiers are not in the mix at all. But for a culture and its environment to come into abiding equanimity you need all four—eco-activists, peace activists, marketeers, and honest cops—each of them with a light touch, comfort with collaboration, and eagerness to replace themselves with local talent. An example of productive joining of regional business and environmental goals is the Ecotrust project at Willapa Bay, Washington.

By its funding choices and guidelines, Packard Foundation could foster "jointness" in world-saving endeavors. In support of the long now, it could promote people, ideas, and organizations that are in for the long haul.

■ READING AND WRITING

1. In his letter to the Packard Foundation, Brand calls for a reframing "of the very structure of how environmental problems are stated." What does he mean by this? How does he say this "reframing" will help? What examples does he give to support his position?

2. Brand argues for, among other things, "what a Buddhist engineer might call *right technology*." What does he mean by this? After you've established his definition, read "The Geoengineering Gambit" by Jeff Bullis. Do you think the technologies Bullis describes there fit the definition advocated by Brand?

■ USING RESEARCH

3. Brand suggests that the first color photographs of the Earth from space, taken by Apollo 11 in 1969, sparked the environmental movement. This effect, he says, was an unintended benefit of the U.S. space program. Go online to find those first images of Earth (search for "NASA photo ID

AS11-44-6552" and "NASA photo ID AS11-36-5355" to find the most
famous of these pictures). Spend some time looking at what you find.
What details do you notice? How are the photographs composed? Why
do you think these images motivated people to action? What might have
been so compelling or persuasive about them four decades ago?

4. In an interview with *Seed* magazine titled "A Manifesto for the Planet,"
Brand makes a distinction between environmentalists he calls "Greens"
and "Turquoises." What is the difference between the two? Using
resources from the web and from your library, write a short essay in
which you distinguish one environmental movement from another.
Based on what you've discovered, which approach seems the most
useful or perhaps the most necessary to you?

■ RESEARCH AND WRITING PROJECTS

1. In "Ecology of a Cracker Childhood," Janisse Ray describes the powerful influence that the rural south Georgia landscape had on her life. She connects her vivid experiences as a child in the pine flatwoods to her identity, all the while making an argument about the practice of clear-cutting. Using the library's resources and the internet, find one or two similar personal essays that make arguments about the environment. Then, after reading these, compose a personal essay of your own that uses a personal experience to make an argument about an environmental issue. After you have decided on a topic, think about the following questions:

   ■ What specific argument do you want to make about your experience? (In other words, what is your purpose in writing about this particular place?)

   ■ What kind of reaction do you want from your audience? What do you want them to take from your essay?

   ■ What is the best way to connect with your audience? (Think, for example, about the things you want your audience to see, hear, smell, and feel about your subject.)

2. Environmental issues, like just about anything else that stirs emotions and debate, are reported on and written about in vastly different ways online, on television and radio, and in print. Why? Because the sources of that coverage—be they bloggers, news media, businesses, special interest groups, or others—tailor their coverage to appeal to their audiences and to achieve specific purposes. For this assignment, write an essay in which you analyze and compare how two media websites covered (or are covering) the same environmental issue or development. Please note that this is not a traditional compare-and-contrast assignment in which you simply report the surface similarities and differences between two subjects. Your focus should be on analyzing the rhetorical choices the two web sources make as they try to inform, move, and persuade their audiences. Some of the choices will be similar and others different.

You should make note of that and also explain how and why these differences matter, based on the purpose each website. To choose a topic, you might select an environmental issue or development that interests you (destruction of the Guatemalan rain forests, for example) and then find two websites that take different approaches to the topic. Or, you might go immediately to two web sources that you know have very different agendas (such as Greenpeace and Fox News) and then examine their coverage of specific environmental issues.

3. Kevin Bullis, in "The Geoengineering Gambit," engages in explanatory writing—that is, he introduces and explains information and ideas with which the audience may not be familiar. Explanatory writing, as the name implies, has a specific purpose: It is meant to help readers understand something new. The news media engage in explanatory writing every day as they try to help their audiences make sense of what's going on in the world. Using the reading you've done and your class discussions as background, select a green technology that interests you and conduct research to learn as much as you can about the technology. Then, write an essay in which you explain the technology to an audience unfamiliar with it. As you consider a topic, think broadly about what "green" means. You might, for example, write about a technology used to aid the oil cleanup in the Gulf of Mexico. Or you might explain a set of new smart phone apps that purport to help the environment in some way. Whatever you decide, your goal is to help your readers understand your topic as well as you do after you have conducted your research.

4. If you're not familiar with them, service learning projects are meant to bring students and their communities closer together to benefit both. These projects—sometimes they encompass entire courses—give students the opportunity to put what they're learning in college to work beyond campus. Ideally, this sharing of knowledge, skills, and concern for the common good works both ways: Students enrich their learning experiences, while the organizations they work with get help they need to better serve the community. In an English or writing course, such projects might include proposal, grant, or letter writing; website development; publicity (pamphlets, public service announcements, and the like); or other tasks that put students' communication skills

to good use. This assignment asks you to develop a proposal for an environmentally oriented service learning project, and it involves several steps (you should work closely with your instructor on each one):

■ First, identify an environmental organization on campus or in your community that is open to working with service learning students.

■ Then, research the organization to learn as much as you can about it—including its history, mission, and methods. You'll probably be able to find some information online or through your library, but you should also consider visiting the organization—or attending a meeting—so you can talk to leaders and other members. (Be certain to consult your instructor before you plan a visit.)

■ After you've learned about the organization, identify areas of need that you think fit your time and skills.

■ Finally, develop a proposal for the work you would do for the organization. Your instructor will provide more specific details, but, in general, your proposal should include: a summary of the organization's mission, membership, and activities, and needs; a clear explanation of the project you would like to undertake; and a brief explanation of how your project would help the organization.

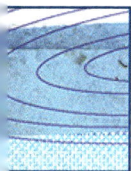

CHAPTER 4

A Woman's Place?

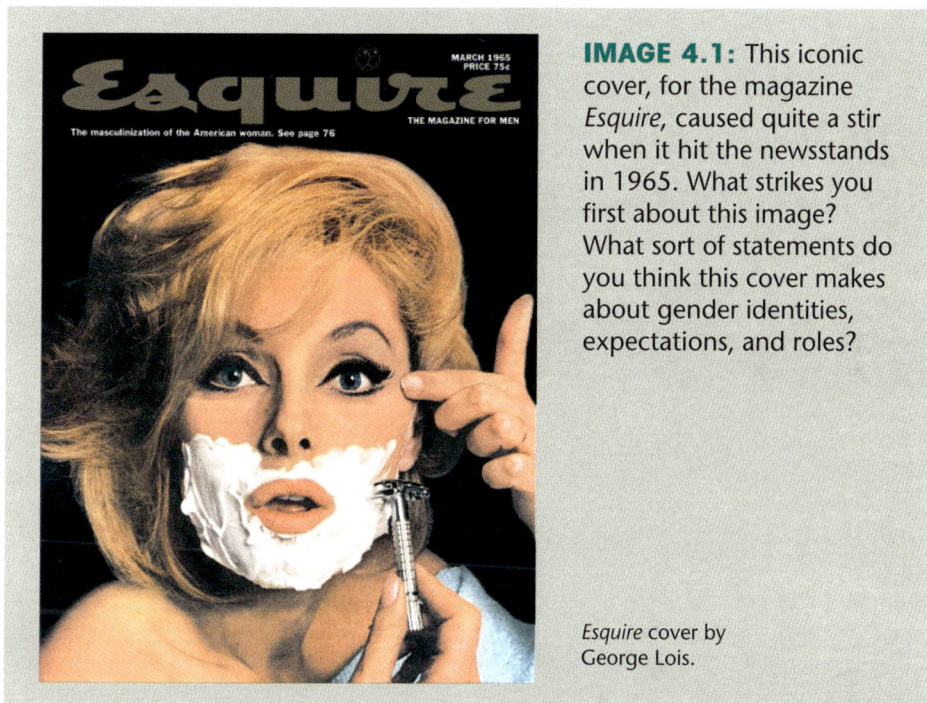

IMAGE 4.1: This iconic cover, for the magazine *Esquire*, caused quite a stir when it hit the newsstands in 1965. What strikes you first about this image? What sort of statements do you think this cover makes about gender identities, expectations, and roles?

Esquire cover by George Lois.

Gender is a difficult concept—one that often blends intensely personal issues with overtly political, religious, and cultural agendas. Rather than attempt to explain the many perspectives on the subject, the readings in this chapter offer stories and opinions in a variety of genres about girls and women and how they deal with gender-based traditions and expectations. Why this particular focus? The article that opens the chapter offers one reason: "Women hold up half the sky," Nicholas Kristof and Sheryl WuDunn write, alluding to an untapped source of social and economic power that can transform the world. Individually, these texts use people and personal experience to imply compelling arguments. Taken together, they provide a vivid and often moving introduction to one facet of gender studies.

237

Nicholas D. Kristof is a New York Times *Op-Ed columnist and Sheryl WuDunn is a former* Times *correspondent who works in finance and philanthropy. This essay, published August 23, 2009, in the* Times, *is adapted from their new book* Half the Sky: Turning Oppression Into Opportunity for Women Worldwide. *You can learn more about* Half the Sky *at www.halftheskymovement.org*

THE WOMEN'S CRUSADE
Nicholas D. Kristof and Sheryl WuDunn

IN THE 19TH CENTURY, the paramount moral challenge was slavery. In the 20th century, it was totalitarianism. In this century, it is the brutality inflicted on so many women and girls around the globe: sex trafficking, acid attacks, bride burnings and mass rape.

Yet if the injustices that women in poor countries suffer are of paramount importance, in an economic and geopolitical sense the opportunity they represent is even greater. "Women hold up half the sky," in the words of a Chinese saying, yet that's mostly an aspiration: In a large slice of the world, girls are uneducated and women marginalized, and it's not an accident that those same countries are disproportionately mired in poverty and riven by fundamentalism and chaos. There's a growing recognition among everyone from the World Bank to the U.S. military's Joint Chiefs of Staff to aid organizations like CARE that focusing on women and girls is the most effective way to fight global poverty and extremism. That's why foreign aid is increasingly directed to women. The world is awakening to a powerful truth: Women and girls aren't the problem; they're the solution.

One place to observe this alchemy of gender is in the muddy back alleys of Pakistan. In a slum outside the grand old city of Lahore, a woman named Saima Muhammad used to dissolve into tears every evening. A round-faced woman with thick black hair tucked into a head scarf, Saima had barely a rupee, and her deadbeat husband was unemployed and not particularly employable. He was frustrated and angry, and he coped by beating Saima each afternoon. Their house was falling apart, and Saima had to send her young daughter to live with an aunt, because there wasn't enough food to go around.

"My sister-in-law made fun of me, saying, 'You can't even feed your children,'" recalled Saima when Nick met her two years ago on a trip to Pakistan. "My husband beat me up. My brother-in-law beat me up. I had an awful life." Saima's husband accumulated a debt of more than $3,000, and it seemed that these loans would hang over the family for generations. Then when Saima's second child was born and turned out to be a girl as well, her mother-in-law, a harsh, blunt woman named Sharifa Bibi, raised the stakes.

"She's not going to have a son," Sharifa told Saima's husband, in front of her. "So you should marry again. Take a second wife." Saima was shattered and ran off sobbing. Another wife would leave even less money to feed and educate the children. And Saima herself would be marginalized in the household, cast off like an old sock. For days Saima walked around in a daze, her eyes red; the slightest incident would send her collapsing into hysterical tears.

It was at that point that Saima signed up with the Kashf Foundation, a Pakistani microfinance organization that lends tiny amounts of money to poor women to start businesses. Kashf is typical of microfinance institutions, in that it lends almost exclusively to women, in groups of 25. The women guarantee one another's debts and meet every two weeks to make payments and discuss a social issue, like family planning or schooling for girls. A Pakistani woman is often forbidden to leave the house without her husband's permission, but husbands tolerate these meetings because the women return with cash and investment ideas.

Saima took out a $65 loan and used the money to buy beads and cloth, which she transformed into beautiful embroidery that she then sold to merchants in the markets of Lahore. She used the profit to buy more beads and cloth, and soon she had an embroidery business and was earning a solid income—the only one in her household to do so. Saima took her elder daughter back from the aunt and began paying off her husband's debt.

When merchants requested more embroidery than Saima could produce, she paid neighbors to assist her. Eventually 30 families were working for her, and she put her husband to work as well—"under my direction," she explained with a twinkle in her eye. Saima became the tycoon of the neighborhood, and she was able to pay off her husband's entire debt, keep her daughters in school, renovate the house, connect running water and buy a television.

"Now everyone comes to me to borrow money, the same ones who used to criticize me," Saima said, beaming in satisfaction. "And the children of those who used to criticize me now come to my house to watch TV."

Today, Saima is a bit plump and displays a gold nose ring as well as several other rings and bracelets on each wrist. She exudes self-confidence as she offers a grand tour of her home and work area, ostentatiously showing off the television and the new plumbing. She doesn't even pretend to be subordinate to her husband. He spends his days mostly loafing around, occasionally helping with the work but always having to accept orders from his wife. He has become more impressed with females in general: Saima had a third child, also a girl, but now that's not a problem. "Girls are just as good as boys," he explained.

Saima's new prosperity has transformed the family's educational prospects. She is planning to send all three of her daughters through high school and maybe to college as well. She brings in tutors to improve their schoolwork, and her oldest child, Javaria, is ranked first in her class. We asked Javaria what she wanted to be when she grew up, thinking she might aspire to be a doctor or lawyer. Javaria cocked her head. "I'd like to do embroidery," she said.

As for her husband, Saima said, "We have a good relationship now." She explained, "We don't fight, and he treats me well." And what about finding another wife who might bear him a son? Saima chuckled at the question: "Now nobody says anything about that." Sharifa Bibi, the mother-in-law, looked shocked when we asked whether she wanted her son to take a second wife to bear a son. "No, no," she said. "Saima is bringing so much to this house. ... She puts a roof over our heads and food on the table."

Sharifa even allows that Saima is now largely exempt from beatings by her husband. "A woman should know her limits, and if not, then it's her husband's right to beat her," Sharifa said. "But if a woman earns more than her husband, it's difficult for him to discipline her."

WHAT SHOULD we make of stories like Saima's? Traditionally, the status of women was seen as a "soft" issue—worthy but marginal. We initially reflected that view ourselves in our work as journalists. We preferred to focus instead on the "serious" international issues, like trade disputes or arms proliferation. Our awakening came in China.

After we married in 1988, we moved to Beijing to be correspondents for The New York Times. Seven months later we found ourselves standing on the edge of Tiananmen Square watching troops fire their automatic weapons at prodemocracy protesters. The massacre claimed between 400 and 800 lives and transfixed the world; wrenching images of the killings appeared constantly on the front page and on television screens.

Yet the following year we came across an obscure but meticulous demographic study that outlined a human rights violation that had claimed tens of thousands more lives. This study found that 39,000 baby girls died annually in China because parents didn't give them the same medical care and attention that boys received—and that was just in the first year of life. A result is that as many infant girls died unnecessarily every week in China as protesters died at Tiananmen Square. Those Chinese girls never received a column inch of news coverage, and we began to wonder if our journalistic priorities were skewed.

A similar pattern emerged in other countries. In India, a "bride burning" takes place approximately once every two hours, to punish a woman for an inadequate dowry or to eliminate her so a man can remarry—but these rarely constitute news. When a prominent dissident was arrested in China, we would write a front-page article; when 100,000 girls were kidnapped and trafficked into brothels, we didn't even consider it news.

Amartya Sen, the ebullient Nobel Prize-winning economist, developed a gauge of gender inequality that is a striking reminder of the stakes involved. "More than 100 million women are missing," Sen wrote in a classic essay in 1990 in The New York Review of Books, spurring a new field of research. Sen noted that in normal circumstances, women live longer than men, and so there are more females than males in much of the world. Yet in places where girls have a deeply unequal status, they vanish. China has 107 males for every 100 females in its overall population (and an even greater disproportion among newborns), and India has 108. The implication of the sex ratios, Sen later found, is that about 107 million females are missing from the globe today. Follow-up studies have calculated the number slightly differently, deriving alternative figures for "missing women" of between 60 million and 107 million.

Girls vanish partly because they don't get the same health care and food as boys. In India, for example, girls are less likely to be vaccinated than boys and are taken to the hospital only when they are sicker. A result is that girls in India from 1 to 5 years of age are 50 percent more likely to die than boys their age. In addition, ultrasound machines have allowed a pregnant woman to find out the sex of her fetus—and then get an abortion if it is female.

The global statistics on the abuse of girls are numbing. It appears that more girls and women are now missing from the planet, precisely because they are female, than men were killed on the battlefield in all the wars of the 20th century. The number of victims of this routine "gendercide" far exceeds the number of people who were slaughtered in all the genocides of the 20th century.

For those women who live, mistreatment is sometimes shockingly brutal. If you're reading this article, the phrase "gender discrimination" might conjure thoughts of unequal pay, underfinanced sports teams or unwanted touching from a boss. In the developing world, meanwhile, millions of women and girls are actually enslaved. While a precise number is hard to pin down, the International Labor Organization, a U.N. agency, estimates that at any one time there are 12.3 million people engaged in forced labor of all kinds, including sexual servitude. In Asia alone about one million children working in the sex trade are held in conditions indistinguishable from slavery, according to a U.N. report. Girls and women are locked in brothels and beaten if they resist, fed just enough to be kept alive and often sedated with drugs—to pacify them and often to cultivate addiction. India probably has more modern slaves than any other country.

Another huge burden for women in poor countries is maternal mortality, with one woman dying in childbirth around the world every minute. In the West African country Niger, a woman stands a one-in-seven chance of dying in childbirth at some point in her life. (These statistics are all somewhat dubious, because maternal mortality isn't considered significant enough to require good data collection.) For all of India's shiny new high-rises, a woman there still has a 1-in-70 lifetime chance of dying in childbirth. In contrast, the lifetime risk in the United States is 1 in 4,800; in Ireland, it is 1 in 47,600. The reason for the gap is not that we don't know how to save lives of women in poor countries. It's simply that poor, uneducated women in Africa and Asia have never been a priority either in their own countries or to donor nations.

ABBAS BE, A BEAUTIFUL teenage girl in the Indian city of Hyderabad, has chocolate skin, black hair and gleaming white teeth—and a lovely smile, which made her all the more marketable.

Money was tight in her family, so when she was about 14 she arranged to take a job as a maid in the capital, New Delhi. Instead, she was locked up in a brothel, beaten with a cricket bat, gang-raped and told that she would have to cater to customers. Three days after she arrived, Abbas and all 70 girls in the brothel were made to gather round and watch as the pimps made an example of one teenage girl who had fought customers. The troublesome girl was stripped naked, hogtied, humiliated and mocked, beaten savagely and then stabbed in the stomach until she bled to death in front of Abbas and the others.

Abbas was never paid for her work. Any sign of dissatisfaction led to a beating or worse; two more times, she watched girls murdered by the brothel managers for resisting. Eventually Abbas was freed by police and taken back to Hyderabad. She found a home in a shelter run by Prajwala, an organization that takes in girls rescued from brothels and teaches them new skills. Abbas is acquiring an education and has learned to be a bookbinder; she also counsels other girls about how to avoid being trafficked. As a skilled bookbinder, Abbas is able to earn a decent living, and she is now helping to put her younger sisters through school as well. With an education, they will be far less vulnerable to being trafficked. Abbas has moved from being a slave to being a producer, contributing to India's economic development and helping raise her family.

Perhaps the lesson presented by both Abbas and Saima is the same: In many poor countries, the greatest unexploited resource isn't oil fields or veins of gold; it is the women and girls who aren't educated and never become a major presence in the formal economy. With education and with help starting businesses, impoverished women can earn money and support their countries as well as their families. They represent perhaps the best hope for fighting global poverty.

In East Asia, as we saw in our years of reporting there, women have already benefited from deep social changes. In countries like South Korea and Malaysia, China and Thailand, rural girls who previously contributed negligibly to the economy have gone to school and received educations, giving them the autonomy to move to the city to hold factory jobs. This hugely increased the formal labor force; when the women then delayed childbearing, there was a demographic dividend to the country as well. In the 1990s, by our estimations, some 80 percent of the employees on the assembly lines in coastal China were female, and the proportion across the manufacturing belt of East Asia was at least 70 percent.

The hours were long and the conditions wretched, just as in the sweatshops of the Industrial Revolution in the West. But peasant women were making money, sending it back home and sometimes becoming the breadwinners in their families. They gained new skills that elevated their status. Westerners encounter sweatshops and see exploitation, and indeed, many of these plants are just as bad as critics say. But it's sometimes said in poor countries that the only thing worse than being exploited in a sweatshop is not being exploited in a sweatshop. Low-wage manufacturing jobs disproportionately benefited women in countries like China because these were jobs for which brute physical force was not necessary and women's nimbleness gave them an advantage over men—which was not the case with agricultural labor or construction or other jobs typically available in poor countries. Strange as it may seem, sweatshops in Asia had the effect of empowering women. One hundred years ago, many women in China were still having their feet bound. Today, while discrimination and inequality and harassment persist, the culture has been transformed. In the major cities, we've found that Chinese men often do more domestic chores than American men typically do. And urban parents are often not only happy with an only daughter; they may even prefer one, under the belief that daughters are better than sons at looking after aging parents.

WHY DO MICROFINANCE organizations usually focus their assistance on women? And why does everyone benefit when women enter the work force and bring home regular pay checks? One reason involves the dirty little secret of global poverty: some of the most wretched suffering is caused not just by low incomes but also by unwise spending by the poor—especially by men. Surprisingly frequently, we've come across a mother mourning a child who has just died of malaria for want of a $5 mosquito bed net; the mother says that the family couldn't afford a bed net and she means it, but then we find the father at a nearby bar. He goes three evenings a week to the bar, spending $5 each week.

Our interviews and perusal of the data available suggest that the poorest families in the world spend approximately 10 times as much (20 percent of their incomes on average) on a combination of alcohol, prostitution, candy, sugary drinks and lavish feasts as they do on educating their children (2 percent). If poor families spent only as much on educating their children as they do on beer and prostitutes, there would be a breakthrough in the prospects of poor countries. Girls, since they are the ones kept home from school now, would be the biggest beneficiaries. Moreover, one way to reallocate family expenditures in this way is to put more money in the hands of women. A series of studies has found that when women hold assets or gain incomes, family money is more likely to be spent on nutrition, medicine and housing, and consequently children are healthier.

In Ivory Coast, one research project examined the different crops that men and women grow for their private kitties: men grow coffee, cocoa and pineapple, and women grow plantains, bananas, coconuts and vegetables. Some years the "men's crops" have good harvests and the men are flush with cash, and other years it is the women who prosper. Money is to some extent shared. But even so, the economist Esther Duflo of M.I.T. found that when the men's crops flourish, the household spends more money on alcohol and tobacco. When the women have a good crop, the households spend more money on food. "When women command greater power, child health and nutrition improves," Duflo says.

Such research has concrete implications: for example, donor countries should nudge poor countries to adjust their laws so that when a man dies, his property is passed on to his widow rather than to his brothers. Governments should make it easy for women to hold property and bank accounts—1 percent of the world's landowners are women—and they should make it much easier for microfinance institutions to start banks so that women can save money.

OF COURSE, IT'S FAIR to ask: empowering women is well and good, but can one do this effectively? Does foreign aid really work? William Easterly, an economist at New York University, has argued powerfully that shoveling money at poor countries accomplishes little. Some Africans, including Dambisa Moyo, author of "Dead Aid," have said the same thing. The critics note that there has been no correlation between amounts of aid going to countries and their economic growth rates.

Our take is that, frankly, there is something to these criticisms. Helping people is far harder than it looks. Aid experiments often go awry, or small successes turn out to be difficult to replicate or scale up. Yet we've also seen, anecdotally and in the statistics, evidence that some kinds of aid have been enormously effective. The delivery of vaccinations and other kinds of health care has reduced the number of children who die every year before they reach the age of 5 to less than 10 million today from 20 million in 1960.

In general, aid appears to work best when it is focused on health, education and microfinance (although microfinance has been somewhat less successful in Africa than in Asia). And in each case, crucially, aid has often been most effective when aimed at women and girls; when policy wonks do the math, they often find that these investments have a net economic return. Only a small proportion of aid specifically targets women or girls, but increasingly donors are recognizing that that is where they often get the most bang for the buck.

In the early 1990s, the United Nations and the World Bank began to proclaim the potential resource that women and girls represent. "Investment in girls' education may well be the highest-return investment available in the developing world," Larry Summers wrote when he was chief economist of the World Bank. Private aid groups and foundations shifted gears as well. "Women are the key to ending hunger in Africa," declared the Hunger Project. The Center for Global Development issued a major report explaining "why and how to put girls at the center of development." CARE took women and girls as the centerpiece of its anti-poverty efforts. "Gender inequality hurts economic growth," Goldman Sachs concluded in a 2008 research report that emphasized how much developing countries could improve their economic performance by educating girls.

Bill Gates recalls once being invited to speak in Saudi Arabia and finding himself facing a segregated audience. Four-fifths of the listeners were men, on the left. The remaining one-fifth were women, all covered in black cloaks and veils, on the right. A partition separated the two groups. Toward the end, in the question-and-answer session, a member of the audience noted that Saudi Arabia aimed to be one of the Top 10 countries in the world in technology by 2010 and asked if that was realistic. "Well, if you're not fully utilizing half the talent in the country," Gates said, "you're not going to get too close to the Top 10." The small group on the right erupted in wild cheering.

Policy makers have gotten the message as well. President Obama has appointed a new White House Council on Women and Girls. Perhaps he was indoctrinated by his mother, who was one of the early adopters of microloans to women when she worked to fight poverty in Indonesia. Secretary of State Hillary Rodham Clinton is a member of the White House Council, and she has also selected a talented activist, Melanne Verveer, to direct a new State Department Office of Global Women's Issues. On Capitol Hill, the Senate Foreign Relations Committee has put Senator Barbara Boxer in charge of a new subcommittee that deals with women's issues.

Yet another reason to educate and empower women is that greater female involvement in society and the economy appears to undermine extremism and terrorism. It has long been known that a risk factor for turbulence and violence is the share of a country's population made up of young people. Now it is emerging that male domination of society is also a risk factor; the reasons aren't fully understood, but it may be that when women are marginalized the nation takes on the testosterone-laden culture of a military camp or a high-school boys' locker room. That's in part why the Joint Chiefs of Staff and international security specialists are puzzling over how to increase girls' education in countries like Afghanistan—and why generals have gotten briefings from Greg Mortenson, who wrote about building girls' schools in his best seller, "Three Cups of Tea." Indeed, some scholars say they believe the reason Muslim countries have been disproportionately afflicted by terrorism is not Islamic teachings about infidels or violence but rather the low levels of female education and participation in the labor force.

SO WHAT WOULD an agenda for fighting poverty through helping women look like? You might begin with the education of girls—which doesn't just mean building schools. There are other innovative means at our disposal. A study in Kenya by Michael Kremer, a Harvard economist, examined six different approaches to improving educational performance, from providing free textbooks to child-sponsorship programs. The approach that raised student test scores the most was to offer girls who had scored in the top 15 percent of their class on sixth-grade tests a $19 scholarship for seventh and eighth grade (and the glory of recognition at an assembly). Boys also performed better, apparently because they were pushed by the girls or didn't want to endure the embarrassment of being left behind.

Another Kenyan study found that giving girls a new $6 school uniform every 18 months significantly reduced dropout rates and pregnancy rates. Likewise, there's growing evidence that a cheap way to help keep high-school girls in school is to help them manage menstruation. For fear of embarrassing leaks and stains, girls sometimes stay home during their periods, and the absenteeism puts them behind and eventually leads them to drop out. Aid workers are experimenting with giving African teenage girls sanitary pads, along with access to a toilet where they can change them. The Campaign for Female Education, an organization devoted to getting more girls into school in Africa, helps girls with their periods, and a new group, Sustainable Health Enterprises, is trying to do the same.

And so, if President Obama wanted to adopt a foreign-aid policy that built on insights into the role of women in development, he would do well to start with education. We would suggest a $10 billion effort over five years to educate girls around the world. This initiative would focus on Africa but would also support—and prod—Asian countries like Afghanistan and Pakistan to do better. This plan would also double as population policy, for it would significantly reduce birthrates—and thus help poor countries overcome the demographic obstacles to economic growth.

But President Obama might consider two different proposals as well. We would recommend that the United States sponsor a global drive to eliminate iodine deficiency around the globe, by helping countries iodize salt. About a third of households in the developing world do not get enough iodine, and a result is often an impairment in brain formation in the fetal stages. For reasons that are unclear, this particularly affects female fetuses and typically costs children 10 to 15 I.Q. points. Research by Erica Field of Harvard found that daughters of women given iodine performed markedly better in school. Other research suggests that salt iodization would yield benefits worth nine times the cost.

We would also recommend that the United States announce a 12-year, $1.6 billion program to eradicate obstetric fistula, a childbirth injury that is one of the worst scourges of women in the developing world. An obstetric fistula, which is a hole created inside the body by a difficult childbirth, leaves a woman incontinent, smelly, often crippled and shunned by her village—yet it can be repaired for a few hundred dollars. Dr. Lewis Wall, president of the Worldwide Fistula Fund, and Michael Horowitz, a conservative agitator on humanitarian issues, have drafted the 12-year plan—and it's eminently practical and built on proven methods. Evidence that fistulas can be prevented or repaired comes from impoverished Somaliland, a northern enclave of Somalia, where an extraordinary nurse-midwife named Edna Adan has built her own maternity hospital to save the lives of the women around her. A former first lady of Somalia and World Health Organization official, Adan used her savings to build the hospital, which is supported by a group of admirers in the U.S. who call themselves Friends of Edna Maternity Hospital.

gitimate concerns about how well humanitarian aid is spent, investments
.izing salt and maternal health all have a proven record of success. And the
st: all three components of our plan together amount to about what the U.S.
'akistan since 9/11—a sum that accomplished virtually nothing worthwhile
istanis or for Americans.

F THE MANY aid groups that for pragmatic reasons has increasingly focused on women is Heifer International, a charitable organization based in Arkansas that has been around for decades. The organization gives cows, goats and chickens to farmers in poor countries. On assuming the presidency of Heifer in 1992, the activist Jo Luck traveled to Africa, where one day she found herself sitting on the ground with a group of young women in a Zimbabwean village. One of them was Tererai Trent.

Tererai is a long-faced woman with high cheekbones and a medium brown complexion; she has a high forehead and tight cornrows. Like many women around the world, she doesn't know when she was born and has no documentation of her birth. As a child, Tererai didn't get much formal education, partly because she was a girl and was expected to do household chores. She herded cattle and looked after her younger siblings. Her father would say, "Let's send our sons to school, because they will be the breadwinners." Tererai's brother, Tinashe, was forced to go to school, where he was an indifferent student. Tererai pleaded to be allowed to attend but wasn't permitted to do so. Tinashe brought his books home each afternoon, and Tererai pored over them and taught herself to read and write. Soon she was doing her brother's homework every evening.

The teacher grew puzzled, for Tinashe was a poor student in class but always handed in exemplary homework. Finally, the teacher noticed that the handwriting was different for homework and for class assignments and whipped Tinashe until he confessed the truth. Then the teacher went to the father, told him that Tererai was a prodigy and begged that she be allowed to attend school. After much argument, the father allowed Tererai to attend school for a couple of terms, but then married her off at about age 11.

Tererai's husband barred her from attending school, resented her literacy and beat her whenever she tried to practice her reading by looking at a scrap of old newspaper. Indeed, he beat her for plenty more as well. She hated her marriage but had no way out. "If you're a woman and you are not educated, what else?" she asks.

Yet when Jo Luck came and talked to Tererai and other young women in her village, Luck kept insisting that things did not have to be this way. She kept saying that they could achieve their goals, repeatedly using the word "achievable." The women caught the repetition and asked the interpreter to explain in detail what "achievable" meant. That gave Luck a chance to push forward. "What are your hopes?" she asked the women, through the interpreter. Tererai and the others were puzzled by the question, because they didn't really have any hopes. But Luck pushed them to think about their dreams, and reluctantly, they began to think about what they wanted.

Tererai timidly voiced hope of getting an education. Luck pounced and told her that she could do it, that she should write down her goals and methodically pursue them. After Luck and her entourage disappeared, Tererai began to study on her own, in hiding from her husband, while raising her five children. Painstakingly, with the help of friends, she wrote down her goals on a piece of paper: "One day I will go to the United States of America," she began, for Goal 1. She added that she would earn a college degree, a master's degree and a Ph.D.—all exquisitely absurd dreams for a married cattle herder in Zimbabwe who had less than one year's formal education. But Tererai took the piece of paper and folded it inside three layers of plastic to protect it, and then placed it in an old can. She buried the can under a rock where she herded cattle.

Then Tererai took correspondence classes and began saving money. Her self-confidence grew as she did brilliantly in her studies, and she became a community organizer for Heifer. She stunned everyone with superb schoolwork, and the Heifer aid workers encouraged her to think that she could study in America. One day in 1998, she received notice that she had been admitted to Oklahoma State University.

Some of the neighbors thought that a woman should focus on educating her children, not herself. "I can't talk about my children's education when I'm not educated myself," Tererai responded. "If I educate myself, then I can educate my children." So she climbed into an airplane and flew to America.

At Oklahoma State, Tererai took every credit she could and worked nights to make money. She earned her undergraduate degree, brought her five children to America and started her master's, then returned to her village. She dug up the tin can under the rock and took out the paper on which she had scribbled her goals. She put check marks beside the goals she had fulfilled and buried the tin can again.

In Arkansas, she took a job working for Heifer—while simultaneously earning a master's degree part time. When she had her M.A., Tererai again returned to her village. After embracing her mother and sister, she dug up her tin can and checked off her next goal. Now she is working on her Ph.D. at Western Michigan University.

Tererai has completed her course work and is completing a dissertation about AIDS programs among the poor in Africa. She will become a productive economic asset for Africa and a significant figure in the battle against AIDS. And when she has her doctorate, Tererai will go back to her village and, after hugging her loved ones, go out to the field and dig up her can again.

There are many metaphors for the role of foreign assistance. For our part, we like to think of aid as a kind of lubricant, a few drops of oil in the crankcase of the developing world, so that gears move freely again on their own. That is what the assistance to Tererai amounted to: a bit of help where and when it counts most, which often means focusing on women like her. And now Tererai is gliding along freely on her own—truly able to hold up half the sky.

■ READING AND WRITING

1. Summarize the central elements of Kristof and WuDunn's argument, including the problems they present, the solutions they suggest, and the evidence they use to persuade their audience.

2. How do Kristof and WuDunn intertwine appeals rooted in pathos and logos to advance their argument? Point to specific examples in your response.

3. Why, according to Kristof and WuDunn, are microfinance loans such an effective way to help improve the lives of poor families in some parts of the world? Why do microfinance organizations lend almost exclusively to women?

4. What is the portrait of men that emerges from this article? Consider that images of non-white or poor men as criminal, lazy, or foolish have frequently had the effect of inflaming racism and violence. In portraying the abuse of third-world women, does this article risk representing men in ways that align with dangerous stereotypes? How could Kristof and WuDunn make their argument in a different way?

■ USING RESEARCH

5. Find and explore Kristof and WuDunn's website *Half the Sky* at www.halftheskymovement.org. How is this site, and the effort supported by Kristof and WuDunn, an example of what Elie Wiesel calls, in "Am I My Brother's Keeper?" in Chapter 1, transforming knowledge into responsibility?

The excerpt that follows is Chapter 8 of Catharine E. Beecher's highly successful 1842 book A Treatise on Domestic Economy, For the Use of Young Ladies at Home, and At School, *"the first complete guide to house-keeping published in America," according to the University of Virginia website* Uncle Tom's Cabin and American Culture. *The website points out that Harriet Beecher Stowe, "who later collaborated with Catharine on another domestic manual, put her sister's expertise to use in 1851, when she asked Catharine to move in and take charge of her household while she finished writing* Uncle Tom's Cabin*." (Editor's note: Beecher's frequent use of what we today would consider unnecessary commas may make reading her chapter feel like a grind. While you should note this as a good example of how our use of punctuation has evolved over the past century and a half, you also may wish to ignore the commas as you read.)*

ON THE PRESERVATION OF A GOOD TEMPER IN A HOUSEKEEPER Catharine E. Beecher

THERE is nothing, which has a more abiding influence on the happiness of a family, than the preservation of equable and cheerful temper and tones in the housekeeper. A woman, who is habitually gentle, sympathizing, forbearing, and cheerful, carries an atmosphere about her, which imparts a soothing and sustaining influence, and renders it easier for all to do right, under her administration, than in any other situation.

The writer has known families, where the mother's presence seemed the sunshine of the circle around her; imparting cheering and vivifying power, scarcely realized, till it was withdrawn. Every one, without thinking of it, or knowing why it was so, experienced a peaceful and invigorating influence, as soon as he entered the sphere illumined by her smile, and sustained by her cheering, kindness and sympathy. On the contrary, many a good housekeeper, (good in every respect but this,) by wearing a countenance of anxiety and dissatisfaction, and by indulging in the frequent use of sharp and reprehensive tones, more than destroys all the comfort which otherwise would result from her system, neatness, and economy.

There is a secret, social sympathy, which every mind, to a greater or less degree, experiences with the feelings of those around, as they are manifested by the countenance and voice. A sorrowful, a discontented, or an angry, countenance, produces a silent, sympathetic influence, imparting a sombre shade to the mind, while tones of anger or complaint still more effectually jar the spirits.

No person can maintain, a quiet and cheerful frame of mind, while tones of discontent and displeasure are sounding on the car. We may gradually accustom ourselves to the evil, till it is partially diminished; but it always is an evil, which greatly interferes with the enjoyment of the family state. There are sometimes cases where the entrance of the mistress of a family seems to awaken a slight apprehension, in every mind around, as if each felt in danger of a reproof, for something either perpetrated or neglected. A woman, who should go around her house with a small stinging snapper, which she habitually applied to those whom she met, would be encountered with feelings very much like to those which are experienced by the inmates of a family, where the mistress often uses her countenance and voice, to inflict similar penalties for duties neglected.

Yet, there are many allowances to be made for housekeepers, who sometimes imperceptibly and unconsciously fall into such habits. A woman, who attempts to carry out any plans of system, order, and economy, and who has her feelings and habits conformed to certain rules, is constantly liable to have her plans crossed and her taste violated, by the inexperience, or inattention of those about her. And no housekeeper, whatever may be her habits can escape the frequent recurrence of negligence or mistake, which interferes with her plans. It is probable, that there is no class of persons, in the world, who have such incessant trials of temper, and temptations to be fretful, as American housekeepers. For a housekeeper's business is not, like that of the other sex, limited to a particular department, for which previous preparation is made. It consists of ten thousand little disconnected items, which, can never be so systematically arranged, that there is no daily jostling, somewhere. And in the best-regulated families, it is not infrequently the case, that some act of forgetfulness or carelessness, from some member, will disarrange the business of the whole day, so that every hour will bring renewed occasion for annoyance. And the more strongly a woman realizes the value of time, and the importance of system and order, the more will she be tempted to irritability and complaint.

The following considerations, may aid in preparing a woman to meet such daily crosses, with even a cheerful temper and tones.

In the first place, a woman, who has charge of a large household, should regard her duties as dignified, important, and difficult. The mind is so made, as to be elevated and cheered by a sense of far-reaching influence and usefulness. A woman, who feels that she is a cipher, and that it makes little difference how she perform her duties, has far less to sustain and invigorate her than one, who truly estimates the importance of her station. A man, who feels that the destinies of a nation are turning on the judgement and skill with which he plans and executes, has a pressure of motive, and an elevation of feeling, which are great safeguards from all that is low, trivial, and degrading.

So, an American mother and housekeeper, who looks at her position in the aspect presented in the previous pages, and who rightly estimates the long train of influences which will pass down to thousands, whose destinies, from generation to generation, will be modified by those decisions of her will, which regulated the temper, principles, and habits, of her family, must be elevated above petty temptations, which would otherwise assail her.

Again, a housekeeper should feel that she really has great difficulties to meet and overcome. A person, who wrongly thinks there is little danger, can never maintain so faithful a guard, as one who rightly estimates the temptations which beset her. Nor can one, who thinks that they are trifling difficulties which she has to encounter, and trivial temptations, to which she must yield, so much enjoy the just reward of conscious virtue and self-control, as one who takes an opposite view of the subject.

A third method, is, for a woman deliberately to calculate on having her best-arranged plans interfered with, very often; and to be in such a state of preparation, that the evil will not come unawares. So complicated are the pursuits, and so diverse the habits of the various members of a family, that it is almost impossible for every one to avoid interfering with the plans and taste of a housekeeper, in some one point or another. It is, therefore, most wise, for a woman to keep the loins of her mind ever girt, to meet such collisions with a cheerful and quiet spirit.

Another important rule, is, to form all plans and arrangements in consistency with the means at command, and the character of those around. A woman, who has a heedless husband, and young children, and incompetent domestics, ought not to make such plans, as one may properly form, who will not, in so many directions, meet embarrassment. She must aim at just so much as she can probably secure, and no more; and thus she will usually escape much temptation, and much of the irritation of disappointment.

The fifth, and a very important, consideration, is, that system, economy, and neatness, are valuable, only so far as they tend to promote the comfort and well-being of those affected. Some women seem to act under the impression, that these advantages must be secured, at all events, even. if the comfort of the family be the sacrifice. True, it is very important that children grow up in habits of system, neatness, and, order; and it is very desirable that the mother give them every incentive, both by precept and example: but it is still more important, that they grow up with amiable tempers, that they learn to meet the crosses of life with patience and cheerfulness; and nothing has a greater influence to secure this, than a mother's example. Whenever, therefore, a woman cannot accomplish her plans of neatness and order, without injury to her own temper, or to the temper of others, she ought to modify and reduce them, until she can.

The sixth method, relates to the government of the tones of voice. In many cases, when a woman's domestic arrangements are suddenly and seriously crossed, it is impossible, not to feel some irritation. But it is always possible to refrain from angry tones. A woman can resolve, that, whatever happens she will not speak, till she can do it in a calm and gentle manner. Perfect silence is a safe resort, when such control cannot be attained, as enables a person to speak calmly; and this determination, persevered in, will eventually be crowned with success.

Many persons seem to imagine, that tones of anger are needful, in order to secure prompt obedience. But observation has convinced the writer that they are never necessary; that in all cases, reproof, administered in calm tones, would be better. A case will be given in illustration.

A young girl had been repeatedly charged to avoid a certain arrangement in cooking. On one day, when company was invited to dine, the direction was forgotten, and the consequence was, an accident, which disarranged every thing, seriously injured the principal dish, and delayed dinner for an hour. The mistress of the family entered the kitchen, just as it occurred, and at a glance, saw the extent of the mischief. For a moment, her eyes flashed, and her cheeks glowed; but she held her peace. After a minute or so, she gave directions, in a calm voice, as to the best mode of retrieving the evil, and then left, without a word said to the offender.

After the company left, she sent for the girl, alone, and in a calm and kind manner pointed out the aggravations of the case, and described the trouble which had been caused to her husband, her visitors, and herself. She then portrayed the future evils which would result from such habits of neglect and inattention, and the modes of attempting to overcome them; and then offered a reward for the future, if, in a given time, she succeeded in improving in this respect. Not a tone of anger was uttered; and yet the severest scolding of a practised Xantippe could not have secured such contrition, and determination to reform, as was gained by this method.

But similar negligence is often visited by a continuous stream of complaint and reproof, which, in most cases, is met, either by sullen silence, or impertinent retort, while anger prevents any contrition, or any resolution of future amendment.

It is very certain, that some ladies do carry forward a most efficient government, both of children and domestics, without employing tones of anger; and therefore they are not indispensable, nor on any account desirable.

Though some ladies, of intelligence and refinement, do fall unconsciously into such a practice, it is certainly very unlady-like, and in very bad taste, to scold; and the further a woman departs from all approach to it, the more perfectly she sustains her character as a lady.

Another method of securing equanimity, amid the trials of domestic life, is, to cultivate a habit of making allowances for the difficulties, ignorance, or temptations, of those who violate rule or neglect duty. It is vain, and most unreasonable, to expect the consideration and care of a mature mind, in childhood and youth; or that persons, of such limited advantages as most domestics have enjoyed, should practise proper self-control, and possess proper habits and principles.

Every parent, and every employer, needs daily to cultivate the spirit expressed in the Divine prayer, "forgive us our trespasses, as we forgive those who trespass against us." The same allowances and forbearance, which we supplicate from our Heavenly Father, and desire from our fellow men, in reference to our own deficiencies, we should, constantly aim to extend to all, who cross our feelings and interfere with our plans.

The last, and most important, mode of securing a placid and cheerful temper and tones, is by a right view of the doctrine of a superintending Providence. All persons are too much in the habit of regarding the more important events of life, as exclusively under the control of Perfect Wisdom. But the fall of a sparrow, or the loss of a hair, they do not feel to be equally the result of His directing agency. In consequence of this, Christian persons, who aim at perfect and cheerful submission to heavy afflictions, and who succeed, to the edification of all about them, are sometimes sadly deficient under petty crosses. If a beloved child be laid in the grave, even if its' death resulted from the carelessness of a domestic, or of a physician, the eye is turned from the subordinate agent, to the Supreme Guardian of all, and to Him they bow, without murmur or complaint. But if a pudding be burnt, or a room badly swept, or an errand forgotten, then vexation and complaint are allowed, just as if these events were not appointed by Perfect Wisdom, as much as the sorer chastisement.

A woman, therefore, needs to cultivate the habitual feeling, that all the events of her nursery and kitchen, are brought about by the permission of our Heavenly Father, and that fretfulness or complaint, in regard to these, is, in fact, complaining and disputing at the appointments of God, and is really as sinful, as unsubmissive murmurs amid the sorer chastisements of His hand. And a woman, who cultivates this habit of referring all the minor trials of life to the wise and benevolent agency of a Heavenly Parent, and daily seeks His sympathy and aid, to enable her to meet them with a quiet and cheerful spirit, will soon find it the perennial spring of abiding peace and content.

■ READING AND WRITING

1. Based on your reading of this piece, define the term "housekeeper" as Beecher would have her audience understand it. Why, according to Beecher, is an "equable and cheerful temper" so important for a housekeeper"?

2. Write a brief summary of Beecher's list of "considerations [that] may aid in preparing a woman to meet ... [her] daily crosses, with even a cheerful temper and tones."

3. Beecher's treatise includes certain assumptions that distinguish the types of housework available to and expected of women of different classes. Where do you see these assumptions playing out in her chapter? How do these assumptions complicate Beecher's implied definitions of "woman" and "housekeeper"?

■ DEVELOPING LONGER RESPONSES

4. After reading Beecher's piece and "Meet the Radical Homemakers" by Shannon Hayes (at the end of this chapter), write a brief essay in which you distinguish between the 1842 model of a "housekeeper" and the 2010 version of a "homemaker."

> Marge Piercy has written seventeen volumes of poetry, seventeen novels, and a critically acclaimed memoir, Sleeping with Cats. According to her website, she has been a prominent player in many of "the major progressive political battles of our time, including the anti-Vietnam war and the women's movements," as well as protests against the war in Iraq. "What's that smell in the kitchen?" is from her 1982 collection Circles on the Water: Selected Poems of Marge Piercy and points to the gendered expectations that still loom over the home kitchen.

WHAT'S THAT SMELL IN THE KITCHEN?
Marge Piercy

All over America women are burning dinners.
It's lambchops in Peoria; it's haddock
in Providence; it's steak in Chicago
tofu delight in Big Sur; red
rice and beans in Dallas.
All over America women are burning
food they're supposed to bring with calico
smile on platters glittering like wax.
Anger sputters in her brainpan, confined
but spewing out missiles of hot fat.
Carbonized despair presses like a clinker
from a barbecue against the back of her eyes.
If she wants to grill anything, it's
her husband spitted over a slow fire.
If she wants to serve him anything
it's a dead rat with a bomb in its belly
ticking like the heart of an insomniac.
Her life is cooked and digested,
nothing but leftovers in Tupperware.
Look, she says, once I was roast duck
on your platter with parsley but now I am Spam.
Burning dinner is not incompetence but war.

■ DEVELOPING LONGER RESPONSES

1. Piercy's poem stands out in this book in genre and style. After studying "What's that smell in the kitchen?" amplify Piercy's argument and rewrite the poem as an essay. Try to remain true to Piercy's theme as you make this transformation.

■ USING RESEARCH

2. After reading Piercy's poem, watch writer Sarah Haskins's take on women and cooking. (You can Google the search terms *sarah haskins target women feeding your family*). How does what one writer has called "the rhetoric of kitchen oppression" play out in Piercy's poem and Haskins' video? How does each author view the relationship between women and food? How does each make her argument? Do you find these texts persuasive? Why or why not?

Nancy Bauer, associate professor and chair of philosophy at Tufts University, is the author of Simone de Beauvoir, Philosophy, and Feminism *and is currently completing a new book,* How to Do Things With Pornography. *She wrote this piece in June 2010 for the* New York Times *blog called* The Stone, *described by the newspaper as "a forum for contemporary philosophers on issues both timely and timeless."*

LADY POWER   Nancy Bauer

If you want to get a bead on the state of feminism these days, look no further than the ubiquitous pop star Lady Gaga. Last summer, after identifying herself as a representative for "sexual, strong women who speak their mind," the 23-year-old Gaga seemed to embrace the old canard that a feminist is by definition a man-hater when she told a Norwegian journalist, "I'm not a feminist. I hail men! I love men!" But by December she was praising the journalist Ann Powers, in a profile in The Los Angeles Times, for being "a little bit of a feminist, like I am." She continued, "When I say to you, there is nobody like me, and there never was, that is a statement I want every woman to feel and make about themselves." Apparently, even though she loves men—she hails them!—she is a little bit of a feminist because she exemplifies what it looks like for a woman to say, and to believe, that there's nobody like her.

There is nobody like Lady Gaga in part because she keeps us guessing about who she, as a woman, really is. She has been praised for using her music and videos to raise this question and to confound the usual exploitative answers provided by "the media." Powers compares Gaga to the artist Cindy Sherman: both draw our attention to the extent to which being a woman is a matter of artifice, of artful self-presentation. Gaga's gonzo wigs, her outrageous costumes, and her fondness for dousing herself in what looks like blood, are supposed to complicate what are otherwise conventionally sexualized performances.

In her "Telephone" video, which has in its various forms received upwards of 60 million YouTube hits since it was first posted in March, Gaga plays a model-skinny and often skimpily dressed inmate of a highly sexualized women's prison who, a few minutes into the film, is bailed out by Beyoncé. The two take off in the same truck Uma Thurman drove in "Kill Bill"—à la Thelma and Louise by way of Quentin Tarantino—and stop at a diner, where they poison, first, a man who stares lewdly at women and, then, all the other patrons (plus—go figure—a dog). Throughout, Gaga sings to her lover about how she's too busy dancing in a club and drinking champagne with her girlfriends to talk to or text him on her telephone.

Is this an expression of Lady Gaga's strength as a woman or an exercise in self-objectification? It's hard to decide. The man who drools at women's body parts is punished, but then again so is everyone else in the place. And if this man can be said to drool, then we need a new word for what the camera is doing to Gaga's and Beyoncé's bodies for upwards of 10 minutes. Twenty years ago, Thelma and Louise set out on their road trip to have fun and found out, as they steadily turned in lipstick and earrings for bandannas and cowboy hats, that the men in their world were hopelessly unable to distinguish between what a woman finds fun and what she finds hateful, literally death-dealing. The rejection by Gaga and Beyoncé of the world in which they are—to use a favorite word of Gaga's—"freaks" takes the form of their exploiting their hyperbolic feminization to mow down everyone in their way, or even not in their way.

The tension in Gaga's self-presentation, far from being idiosyncratic or self-contradictory, epitomizes the situation of a certain class of comfortably affluent young women today. There's a reason they love Gaga. On the one hand, they have been raised to understand themselves according to the old American dream, one that used to be beyond women's grasp: the world is basically your oyster, and if you just believe in yourself, stay faithful to who you are, and work hard and cannily enough, you'll get the pearl. On the other hand, there is more pressure on them than ever to care about being sexually attractive according to the reigning norms. The genius of Gaga is to make it seem obvious—more so than even Madonna once did—that feminine sexuality is the perfect shucking knife. And Gaga is explicit in her insistence that, since feminine sexuality is a social construct, anyone, even a man who's willing to buck gender norms, can wield it.

Gaga wants us to understand her self-presentation as a kind of deconstruction of femininity, not to mention celebrity. As she told Ann Powers, "Me embodying the position that I'm analyzing is the very thing that makes it so powerful." Of course, the more successful the embodiment, the less obvious the analytic part is. And since Gaga herself literally embodies the norms that she claims to be putting pressure on (she's pretty, she's thin, she's well-proportioned), the message, even when it comes through, is not exactly stable. It's easy to construe Gaga as suggesting that frank self-objectification is a form of real power.

If there's anything that feminism has bequeathed to young women of means, it's that power is their birthright. Visit an American college campus on a Monday morning and you'll find any number of amazingly ambitious and talented young women wielding their brain power, determined not to let anything—including a relationship with some needy, dependent man—get in their way. Come back on a party night, and you'll find many of these same girls (they stopped calling themselves "women" years ago) wielding their sexual power, dressed as provocatively as they dare, matching the guys drink for drink—and then hook-up for hook-up.

Lady Gaga idealizes this way of being in the world. But real young women, who, as has been well documented, are pressured to make themselves into boy toys at younger and younger ages, feel torn. They tell themselves a Gaga-esque story about what they're doing. When they're on their knees in front of a worked-up guy they just met at a party, they genuinely do feel powerful—sadistic, even. After all, though they don't stand up and walk away, they in principle could. But the morning after, students routinely tell me, they are vulnerable to what I've come to call the "hook-up hangover." They'll see the guy in the quad and cringe. Or they'll find themselves wishing in vain for more—if not for a prince (or a vampire, maybe) to sweep them off their feet, at least for the guy actually to have programmed their number into his cell phone the night before. When the text doesn't come, it's off to the next party.

What's going on here? Women of my generation—I have a Gaga-savvy daughter home for the summer from her first year of college—have been scratching our heads. When we hear our daughters tell us that in between taking A.P. Statistics and fronting your own band you may be expected to perform a few oral sexual feats, we can't believe it. Some critics of "hook-up culture" have suggested, more or less moralistically, that the problem is that all this casual sex is going to mess with girls' heads. But whatever you think of casual sex, it's not new. What's mind-boggling is how girls are able to understand engaging in it, especially when it's unidirectional, as a form of power.

Jean-Paul Sartre, taking a cue from Hegel's master-slave dialectic, proposed in "Being and Nothingness" that what moves human beings to do things that don't quite square with one another is that we are metaphysical amalgams. Like everything else in the world, we have a nature: we're bodily, we can't control what happens around us, and we are constantly the objects of other people's judgments. Sartre called this part of ourselves "being-in-itself." But at the same time we're subjects, or what he, following Hegel, called "being-for-itself": we make choices about what we do with our bodies and appetites, experience ourselves as the center of our worlds and judge the passing show and other people's roles in it. For Sartre, the rub is that it's impossible for us to put these two halves of ourselves together. At any given moment, a person is either an object or a subject.

The Cartesian dualism that drives Sartre's understanding of human beings as metaphysically divided from themselves is decidedly out of fashion these days. Most contemporary philosophers of all stripes reject the idea that we possess selves that are made of more than one type of metaphysical stuff. But we shouldn't forget that the claim at the heart of Sartre's picture is thoroughly phenomenological: it's not so much that people are split as that they experience themselves as such. Notoriously, Sartre was convinced that we are inclined to deal with the schism by acting in "bad faith." On occasion we find ourselves pretending that we're pure subjects, with no fixed nature, no past, no constraints, no limits. And at other times we fool ourselves into believing that we're pure objects, the helpless victims of others' assessments, our own questionable proclivities, our material circumstances, our biology. Sartre's view gives us a way to understand how a girl might construe her sexually servicing a random guy or shaking her thong-clad booty at a video camera as an act of unadulterated self-expression and personal power. But this interpretation comes at the cost of an epistemic superiority complex, according to which young women are hiding from themselves the ugly truth about what they're "really" doing.

Leave it to Simone de Beauvoir to take her lifelong partner Sartre to task on this very point. If you have it in your head that "The Second Sex" is just warmed-over Sartre, look again. When it comes to her incredibly detailed descriptions of women's lives, Beauvoir repeatedly stresses that our chances for happiness often turn on our capacity for canny self-objectification. Women are—still—heavily rewarded for pleasing men. When we make ourselves into what men want, we are more likely to get what we want, or at least thought we wanted. Unlike Sartre, Beauvoir believed in the possibility of human beings' encountering each other simultaneously as subjects and as objects. In fact, she thought that truly successful erotic encounters positively demand that we be "in-itself-for-itself" with one another, mutually recognizing ourselves and our partners as both subjects and objects. The problem is that we are inclined to deal with the discomfort of our metaphysical ambiguity by splitting the difference: men, we imagine, will relentlessly play the role of subjects; women, of objects. Thus our age-old investment in norms of femininity and masculinity. The few times that Beauvoir uses the term "bad faith" she's almost always lamenting our cleaving to gender roles as a way of dealing with what metaphysically ails us, rather than, à la Sartre, scolding women for doing the best they can in an unjust world.

The goal of "The Second Sex" is to get women, and men, to crave freedom—social, political and psychological—more than the precarious kind of happiness that an unjust world intermittently begrudges to the people who play by its rules. Beauvoir warned that you can't just will yourself to be free, that is, to abjure relentlessly the temptations to want only what the world wants you to want. For her the job of the philosopher, at least as much as the fiction writer, is to re-describe how things are in a way that competes with the status quo story and leaves us craving social justice and the truly wide berth for self-expression that only it can provide.

Lady Gaga and her shotgun companions should not be seen as barreling down the road of bad faith. But neither are they living in a world in which their acts of self-expression or self-empowerment are distinguishable, even in theory, from acts of self-objectification. It remains to be seen whether philosophers will be able to pick up the gauntlet that's still lying on the ground more than half a century after Beauvoir tossed it down: whether we can sketch a vision of a just world seductive enough to compete with the allures of the present one.

■ READING AND WRITING

1. What, according to Bauer, is the source of "our age-old investment in norms of femininity and masculinity"?

2. When she writes of the situation facing "a certain class of comfortably affluent young women today," Bauer points to what she calls the "genius of Gaga." What is this "genius"? How does it complicate traditional views of femininity as well as common definitions of feminism?

3. Bauer claims that "[w]omen are—still—heavily rewarded for pleasing men. When we make ourselves into what men want, we are more likely to get what we want, or at least thought we wanted." What kind of evidence does Bauer provide to support this claim? How does she use this point to advance her central argument?

■ **USING RESEARCH**

4. In her essay, Bauer mentions a comparison between Lady Gaga and the artist Cindy Sherman: both, according to this comparison, draw our attention to the "artful self-presentation" of being a woman. Use the resources available through the library and the internet to investigate this comparison: Who is Cindy Sherman? How would you characterize her art? Do you think she and Lady Gaga—and their respective projects—are similar? After doing this research, do you find the comparison Bauer uses in her essay accurate?

IMAGE 4.3: "Women are—still—heavily rewarded for pleasing men. When we make ourselves into what men want, we are more likely to get what we want, or at least thought we wanted," Nancy Bauer writes in "Lady Power." Based on your reading in this chapter and on your own experience, do you agree with Bauer that women still become what the men in their lives want? What evidence can you point to in order to support your response?

Mary Kay Blakely teaches magazine writing at the University of Missouri Journalism School and has been a contributing editor to Ms. *magazine since 1981. She has written essays on social and political issues for* The New York Times, The Washington Post, Mother Jones, *and many other publications. She is also the author of the critically acclaimed memoirs* Wake Me When It's Over *and* American Mom: Motherhood, Politics, and Humble Pie, *in which this essay appeared.*

A WRESTLING MOM   Mary Kay Blakely

A writer I much admire said in an essay about the trials of being the feminist mother of sons that it *pained* her to see her adolescent son suffer abuse from thuggish friends for sticking up for the rights of gay sailors and American Indians. Good God, I thought, those are the joyful moments for a feminist mother. The painful moments come when she hears her son issue a wolf whistle or talk about joining the army.

My sons have wanted to join the army, to be like Tom Cruise in *Top Gun*. They have wanted to swagger. Like Clint Eastwood, they've hankered after the respect and awe a man gets when he leaves a wake of death behind him. I have seen these macho personas come and go with my sons. So I didn't take all these theatrical characters too seriously—Indiana Jones, Luke Skywalker, Rocky Balboa. They usually didn't survive beyond the year. One did, however, and I realized after the third year that it was probably a keeper. It was not a part of my son I had grown, and it did not cheer me. Of all the role models I imagined for my sons, Hulk Hogan was not one of them.

"It's not the same as TV, Mom," Ryan said. Wrestle-Mania was just theatre, he said. "It's a joke. That isn't real wrestling." His passion for this sport would eventually engage me in a male culture for which I would never have imagined developing an affinity.

Every Friday morning during his senior year of high school, Ryan stood before the bathroom mirror carefully knotting his tie. A strictly jeans and T-shirt guy at age eighteen, he followed the high school athlete's tradition of wearing ties to notify classmates: I have a game today. Friends would wish him luck in the halls, but few would attend the afternoon meet. Unlike the football and basketball teams, wrestlers attract about the same size audience as, say, the chess club. It did not matter. His teammates and coaches—the close fraternity he aimed to please most—would observe every move. A sparse population of parents would make up in volume what we lacked in numbers.

The button at his neck fell a half-inch short of its mark, although his eyes withheld any pleasure at the measurable results of all the iron he'd pumped. Nor did his eyes concede any regret when he combed his hair around the swollen, tender tip of his "cauliflower" ear, in full bloom again this season. Admitting neither vanity nor chagrin to the mirror, a young wrestler strives to become utterly unconscious of his body—its muscle, its pain, its hunger, its sweat. It was the wrestler's mom, approaching the end of an eighteen-year intimacy with this body and this boy, who openly admired and winced through mornings such as these.

"How do I look?" he asked, more out of habit than any need for my approval. He patted his black tie familiarly. "Like a pallbearer with a tic," I replied. He laughed.

In fact, I thought he looked splendid, but saying so would have been meaningless that day. We had come to the outer edge of unconditional love, and wrestling taught both of us what some of the future conditions might be. For a boy who'd always known how to charm parents and teachers out of final ultimata, for whom friendship and fun came easily but deadlines and due dates were hard, I suspected he loved this sport precisely because it was so merciless. Give in to temptation, skip a practice, allow a distraction, underestimate an opponent—you lose. In a six-minute match, there is no room for excuses. Preparing for a test that would take him to the limits of his strength and his will, he had no use for easy praise that day.

Before he left the bathroom, he weighed himself one last time, apparently to see if combing his hair had worked off another ounce. Wrestlers are relentless dieters—if you're good at 152 pounds, they maintain, you should be dynamite at 145. Despite the saunas and workouts in layers of polyurethane, there would be high anxiety when, stripped down to mere ounces of clothing, he stepped on the scale to qualify for the meet. "Enjoy your Thanksgiving dinner," his head coach advised in November. "It will be your last full meal for three months." Not making weight was the worst kind of defeat, providing opponents the free points of a forfeit and disappointing teammates with a failure of will.

All family dinners became testy events during wrestling season. His scorn for calories interrupted my long habits of the heart, equating food with love. Rejection was inevitable. "What's *in* this?" he asked suspiciously before applying his fork to his plate. "How many grams of fat?" For someone who once thought there was no greater heaven than helping himself to a full bag of Chips Ahoy, a stick of celery held little bliss. That morning, he had a glass of water for breakfast. He would probably skip lunch.

"Are you coming today?" he asked before heading out the door, aware of my conflicts with work. Four years ago, I hadn't comprehended the urgency of his repeated invitations to the meets. As a single mom, I preferred other ways of spending our limited "quality time" together than by losing circulation in the bleachers twice a week. Initially, duty rather than enthusiasm brought me to the gym. It's hard for my family and friends to believe I became a sweaty-palmed fan of high school wrestling.

The team had already begun their stretching exercises when I took my seat in the bleachers that afternoon. Ryan sat in the center of the circle with the two other captains, Enrique and Will, surrounded by their black, white, Asian, and Hispanic teammates—all dressed in red. Like a military drill team, they moved in unison to the captains' calls: "Down…up…again…up…left…up…down…" The goofball antics that regularly erupted during practices were not indulged here. Under the scrutiny of opponents with names like the Rams, Bears, Wreckers, Vikings, or Warriors, the Greenwich Cardinals gave nothing away.

Although their movements were graceful and disciplined, adolescence lent a distinctly amateur quality to their performance: there was always a limb flailing here or there with a too-large foot. Already my throat swelled with involuntary emotion, like that buried patriotism that reveals itself when a parade marches by. An almost primal longing for a united humanity surfaced as I watched this colorfully diverse team moving in a single, unified direction.

The youngest wrestlers, smaller by half than most of the fans in the bleachers, approached the mat first. The lightweights, usually in their first varsity season, were all limbs. In any position, their eight entangled appendages resembled a dense thicket of pickup sticks. During Ryan's first season four years ago, I could never tell exactly what he was supposed to be doing down there. My cheers were feeble, limited to "Go, Ry!" But where? To what end? The rapid development in a boy between fourteen and eighteen can give a mother the bends, however prepared she may think she is for the coming man.

I had, of course, observed the results of his body-building, but until I attended a wrestling match I'd never watched him use this power on another person. At eighteen, he had the capacity to level most of the people in the gymnasium. There was a part of him that loved this power; there was a part of me that regretted it. I couldn't witness this obvious strength in my son, his joy in using it, without thinking about the ways it would change his social relationships with women. His habitual friendliness with strangers on the sidewalk, with clerks in stores and cafés, was not as readily returned anymore. Some women—not because of any thing he had done but what had been done to them—automatically feared him. The "collateral" damage of violence against women: it costs all men smiles on the street.

When the weight class below him was called to the mat, Ryan shed his warmup sweats and secured the straps of his singlet. One of the reasons he kept inviting me to his meets, I finally understood, was that he wanted to announce: "This is who I am now. See me." And see I did. Confronted by all that lycra and muscle, the various states of dress and undress, the mothers in the bleachers hardly knew where to rest their eyes. When I looked away from my own son, I soon realized that I was admiring the son of another mother, perhaps the one sitting next to me. I looked down at my feet and thought about human sexuality. I wondered if it was the same for fathers who observed their daughters in bikinis for the first time. It was hard to know the appropriate way to acknowledge the stunning physical changes in a child of the other sex, and yet not to acknowledge those changes was to ignore the most important development issues of the moment.

He put on his headgear and then began the sideline dance that wrestlers do, the loose-limbed hop from foot to foot that simultaneously pumps them up and calms them down. His eyes were focused utterly inward, concentrating on some private vision inside his head. If he knew I was watching, if he knew how much I studied and enjoyed this unselfconscious, rhythmic, juice-up dance, he would stop instantly, as if he had been caught exploring his face for morning stubble in the bathroom mirror. I thought if he kept up this freedom of expression, there was a good chance he'd be spared the urge to beat drums as a Wild Man twenty-some years from now.

For all the mockery Robert Bly's tribal rituals in suburban America have inspired, he has hit a cultural nerve in his argument for exclusively male companionship and ritual. In a lecture four years ago, Bly implied that a single mother's close relationships with sons—especially firstborns—often made it difficult for them to come to terms with the aggressive and competitive parts of themselves. He suggested there were some truths men must learn that mothers cannot teach them. Ryan learned things in the company of his coaches and teammates that I could never have taught him. This recognition brought an element of pain, as separation invariably does.

The week before, still pumped up after an invigorating victory, a phrase commonly used in the locker room slipped out in the car: it was too bad his best friend had to lose to that "fuckin' fairy" from Darien. He was sorry the minute he'd said the F-word—not the first one, which has thoroughly saturated the culture. ("The word 'fuck' is uttered 102 times during the film *The Last Boy Scouts*," according to the *Harper's* Index). No, it was the second F-word that prompted the apology. Only in the environment of the car did he remember that our extended family of friends included several fairies. The word meant nothing, he assured me. It was army.

"It's only language," I reminded him, "...only the stuff we think with." I knew crudeness was a prerequisite in the world of the locker room; he knew sexism and homophobia were enemies in mine. His defection didn't seem so innocent, so temporary, to me because this phrase was acquired during his first real experience with power. How that power was defined, for and against whom, had everything to do with how it would eventually be used. Still largely unconscious of the bigotry that began with a word, he didn't want it to matter. "Trust me," I said. "Words matter."

If my son had some discomforting moments with the language requirements of a feminist mom, I had a few unsettling months with the service obligations of a wrestling son. According to tradition, the captains' moms were responsible for raising funds for the team. Consequently, I spent most of my Saturdays that winter in the corridor outside the gymnasium serving chili-dogs with the other mothers. We were real estate managers, bank cashiers, journalists…women who had not served coffee to the men in our offices for the last ten years. Yet there we were, catering to sons who stood on the brink of "emancipated minor," fully aware that serving men leads not to gratitude but to oblivion.

I had some difficulties with the unfair assumption that a captain's dad belongs in the bleachers while a captain's mom is happiest behind the refreshment stand. Nevertheless, I felt a peculiar satisfaction fulfilling my chili-dog duties. Maybe it was a fit of nostalgia, savoring every ritual of our last season together. Or maybe it was the greater generosity one generation affords to the next. Fifteen years ago, I was a consultant for the Amax Coal Company when the first women employees entered the mines, amid great hostility and resistance. "I can get behind this liberation stuff for my daughters," one of the miners confessed privately, "but not for my wife."

My thoughts were suddenly interrupted by loud hollering below. The two coaches leaped up from their seats and were leaning over the edge of the mat as the referee crouched low, eyeball-to-eyeball with the wrestlers on the floor. Before I could join the rallying shouts, a hand slapped the mat, a whistle blew. The wrestler in blue jumped up ecstatically. A defeated Cardinal sat on the mat in limp disbelief. He threw off his headgear angrily, then quickly picked it up and left the mat before tripping into the penalty points of unsportsmanlike conduct. The head coach shrugged and raised a pair of helpless hands—sign language for "shit happens." Slipping out of his wet singlet, he put on the T-shirt bearing this month's slogan: "PAIN—It is better to give than to receive." A junior varsity player was bounced from the bench to make room for the higher ranked, defeated teammate. Membership had its privileges.

Whenever a Cardinal left the mat in despair, a grim and wordless exchange rippled through the eyes in the bleachers. It was a humbling moment to witness a son in defeat, to contemplate how much more loomed ahead, how powerless we were to prevent it. Every mother I know has battled the irrational craving to spare her children disappointment and heartache. When Ryan exploded in enraged frustration on the golf course last summer, one of my relatives advised me to teach him our family philosophy that it's just as honorable to be a good loser as it is to be a gracious winner. "I can't teach him that," I said, empathizing with his suffering. "It isn't true."

The two wrestling team alumni who came to every meet were whispering some private, last-minute advice to Ryan before he stepped onto the mat. Pete and Pat—whom the Cardinals referred to as "Pete and Repeat" and who might be eligible to found the first chapter of Adult Children of Wrestling Moms—still arranged their business and social lives around the high school team, not yet having found a fraternity as satisfying as this in the outside world. I was grateful for the straightforward affection they gave my son. Whatever the content of their private conversations, it introduced me to what complete comprehension looked like on his face. It was not an expression I'd ever seen at home.

The coaches met him at the edge of the mat. They had the credibility and authority—all but expired for most of the parents in the bleachers—to demand discipline and give orders. It was a challenge to feel entirely happy about this natural turn of events. I couldn't help wishing this authority were directing him, "Do your homework! Think about your future!" But instead I heard, "I know you can *kill* this guy! I want to see it in the first period!"

As Ryan crouched into his stance, my heartbeat accelerated, my skin dampened, my own muscles became taut. Sitting in the bleachers was an aerobic experience for me. As usual, I sat myself next to the Puebla women, Enrique's mother and two sisters, who taught the tweedier New England residents how to behave at a wrestling meet. The team loved them: "You can really *hear* them," the coach said.

I liked to sit next to the Pueblas because I never had to feel like an emotionally embarrassing relative in their company. Enrique's mother Marcia, one of my fund-raising teammates at the refreshment stand this year, spoke only Spanish while I spoke only English. We understood each other's sign language and facial expressions adequately enough to conduct our chili-dog business, but our communication in the bleachers was seamless. She screamed, I screamed, we all screamed.

An aggressive takedown in the first period resulted in a reversal. Alarm flashed into Ryan's face and stayed there. As he fought with everything he had—every muscle straining against the hold, every fiber of his being resisting defeat—the Cardinal fans tried to out-shout the deafening cheers from our opponents. The buzzer sounded, ending the period in the nick of time.

Unless someone got a bloody nose—a painless and welcome time out—it was usually necessary for one of the wrestlers to tie his shoe between periods. It was a lengthy process, tightening laces and wrapping the ankles, then taking a drink for revival. It was usually the losing wrestler who discovered he needed to relace a shoe, who needed to break the momentum of his opponent and rally his own. Perilously close to defeat, Ryan painstakingly attended his shoe. My thoughts drifted back to the first time he dressed himself, the gorgeous look of satisfaction on his three-year-old face…until he got to those damn shoes. Defeated by a shoelace, he cried in frustration. Vulnerable again, the lone figure bent in concentration on the mat raised an identical lump in my throat. If he lost his match that day, I knew he would not let himself cry.

After a second punishing round, his total exhaustion was evident: spent muscles, sweaty limbs, airless lungs, a worried face. With time running out, the third period was always the most reckless. Already, mat burns colored his cheeks, blood trickled from his mouth; his ear, I thought, must have been swelling under his headgear. He said he never felt these injuries when they were happening. I did. For the last four years, emergency rooms had been a regular feature of my existence. In these stark, tiled rooms of reverberating tensions, there were no crowds, no cheers, no coaches. Emergency rooms were where mothers wrestled alone against monstrous fears.

I thought back to the prior December when Ryan's teammate, Will, grabbed my elbow before I paid my admission at the Staples High School tournament and reported that Ryan had just been taken out on a stretcher. My heart squeezed fiercely as images of broken necks, brain damage, and comas flooded my brain. "It's only his arm," Will assured me. Only an arm, only an ear…only the young can be so cavalier about their bodies. Armies are made up of youth for a reason. Ryan was a casualty of friendly fire that day: The injury happened during warm-ups with a teammate. When he lost consciousness after severely dislocating his right elbow, the trainer called an ambulance.

Fifteen minutes later, after a record number of moving violations on I-95, I reached Norwalk Hospital. Despite my wish to remain calm, I had trouble with simple interrogatory sentences at the information desk: "My son, Staples High School, about fifteen minutes ago—his arm (a spastic gesture to my right elbow)…is he here?" The nurse looked quizzically, then brightened.

"Oh, you mean *Ryan*." She smiled and pointed down a long corridor. A burly paramedic pushing an ambulance gurney noted my hesitation in the hallway. I repeated my garbled question. "Oh," he said, grinning, "you want *Ryan*." He accompanied me to his room.

Obviously no longer unconscious, my son was propped up in his bed, a very pale Cardinal in a nest of white sheets. The doctor, still smiling from some joke that preceded my arrival, picked up a pair of scissors to free the wounded arm from his pullover jacket. Their amiable chatter concluded abruptly.

"No way!" Ryan said, the color returning to his face. He sat bolt upright and insisted on pulling it over his head. When the doctor rejected that suggestion as too painful and risky, the paramedic, a former high school wrestler, came to the defense of his fellow jock.

"Doc, you can't cut his jacket—read this," he said, pointing to the word embroidered on the right shoulder: "Captain." The doctor looked at me, the only nonmember of this religion.

"Knock him out," I said. "Cut the jacket."

The patient prevailed. It took three of us to slip the jacket, undamaged, over his head and arm. It seemed a foolish kind of bravery, risking enormous pain to salvage a symbol. But in the whiplash emotions of his final wrestling season, nothing stayed the same. As the fear of permanent physical injury receded into the background, I recognized the enduring psychological benefits he'd earned from this sport. If wrestling gave him one oddball ear and six weeks in a sling, it also produced a confident, witty, capable young man, the Ryan instantly recognized by the hospital staff. He was willing to put his body between the scissors and the "Captain" because, he reminded me, "words matter."

Going into that third reckless period, he knew he needed a pin. Handicapped by the limited flexibility of this now-bandaged arm and a longer limbed opponent, he had trouble securing the leg he needed for a take-down. With thirty seconds to go, he lunged for a knee in a sudden rush of adrenalin. Now he was in a cradle, now he was out, now he had freed his arm, now he was on top pressing down…three inches to go, two inches, oh-my-God-*one*-inch! My laryngitis would inform me later that much of the thunderous noise in the bleachers came from me. He got his pin, seven seconds to spare.

Tradition required each wrestler, after the referee raised the winner's arm, to shake the hand of the opponent's coach. Although Ryan might not yet have mastered the good loser part of our family's honorable equation, his relatives would have been pleased to have seen him in the role of gracious winner. On the way back across the mat to his own bench he always stopped, win or lose, to hug his opponent. This hug was no formality but full of emotion. After four years of rising up in the same weight class together and witnessing each other's most glorious and humiliating moments, his mortal enemies from other schools had become his friends. During long breaks at all-day tournaments, they empathized with injuries and bad seasons, traded tips about summer camps and clinics, talked scholarships and women. The hug said "congratulations" or "sorry I had to pin you." In his last year, it had the bittersweet tinge of "so long."

Like the handshake of peace at the end of a church service, each team lined up after the final match and walked in a single file across the gym, shaking or slapping each hand from the opposite direction. Only once, when a racial slur tipped the defeated Cardinals beyond a strained control, did the handshake erupt in a brawl. Wrestling on a multi-racial team required coming to terms with every myth about racial superiority or inferiority. On the mat, you could hardly know a man better, be closer, understand more thoroughly that his immediate goals are exactly the same as your own.

Maybe it was this quality that wrestling had given my son—the camaraderie and experience of navigating the high tensions of an interracial world—that caused my palms to sweat so. The civil wars among our children, race against race, are so heartbreaking. Watching this handshake of peace, it became excruciatingly clear that if all of us would only do the same—if we would only mobilize our wills not to give in to temptation, skip a practice, allow a distraction, underestimate an opponent, or be careless with language—we would not have to keep losing the next generation to wars.

As the team rolled up the mats, the moms in the bleachers conferred on final plans for the annual awards banquet. Moving as far away from chili-dogs as possible we agreed on a Chinese menu, then decided to hire a caterer to serve it. We packed our gear—the video cameras, the coolers of Gatorade, the ace bandages and aspirin and ice packs we were never without. If we were entirely sane, we would not need these semi-barbaric rituals to break our hearts and thrill our souls. But we were not entirely sane. We would be back next week.

■ READING AND WRITING

1. In her memoir, Blakely refers to herself as a feminist. Based on what you have read, how do you think she defines that term? How do you define it?

2. Blakely's title works on multiple levels—yes, she becomes a "wrestling mom" to her son's team, but there's more. What is Blakely wrestling with in this excerpt? How does she work through these issues?

3. What does this text say about environment—people, places, interactions—and gender? Do you agree with Blakeley's position? Explain.

4. Who do you think is Blakeley's intended audience? What does she do in her text to connect with this audience?

Charles Hirshberg is a journalist and author whose work has appeared in The Washington Post, The Los Angeles Times, *and* Life *magazine, and who has written three books about popular music. The following essay was first published in May 2002 in* Popular Science *and later collected in* The Best American Science and Nature Writing, 2003.

MY MOTHER, THE SCIENTIST   Charles Hirshberg

In 1966, Mrs. Weddle's first grade class at Las Lomitas Elementary School got its first homework assignment: We were to find out what our fathers did for a living, then come back and tell the class. The next day, as my well-scrubbed classmates boasted about their fathers, I was nervous. For one thing, I was afraid of Mrs. Weddle: I realize now that she was probably harmless, but to a shy, elf-size, nervous little guy she looked like a monstrous, talking baked potato. On top of that, I had a surprise in store, and I wasn't sure how it would be received.

"My daddy is a scientist," I said, and Mrs. Weddle turned to write this information on the blackboard. Then I dropped the bomb: "And my mommy is a scientist!"

Twenty-five pairs of first-grade eyes drew a bead on me, wondering what the hell I was talking about. It was then that I began to understand how unusual my mother was.

Today, after more than four decades of geophysical research, my mother, Joan Feynman, is getting ready to retire as a senior scientist at NASA's Jet Propulsion Laboratory. She is probably best known for developing a statistical model to calculate the number of high-energy particles likely to hit a spacecraft over its lifetime, and for her method of predicting sun spot cycles. Both are used by scientists worldwide. Beyond this, however, my mother's career illustrates the enormous change in how America regards what was, only a few decades ago, extremely rare: a scientist who's a woman and also a mother.

To become a scientist is hard enough. But to become one while running a gauntlet of lies, insults, mockeries, and disapproval—this was what my mother had to do. If such treatment is unthinkable (or, at least, unusual) today, it is largely because my mother and other female scientists of her generation proved equal to every obstacle thrown in their way.

My introduction to chemistry came in 1970, on a day when my mom was baking challah bread for the Jewish New Year. I was about 10, and though I felt cooking was unmanly for a guy who played shortstop for Village Host Pizza in the Menlo Park, California, Little League, she had persuaded me to help. When the bread was in the oven, she gave me a plastic pill bottle and a cork. She told me to sprinkle a little baking soda into the bottle, then a little vinegar, and cork the bottle as fast as I could. There followed a violent and completely unexpected pop as the cork flew off and walloped me in the forehead. Exploding food: I was ecstatic! "That's called a chemical reaction," she said, rubbing my shirt clean. "The vinegar is an acid and the soda is a base, and that's what happens when you mix the two."

After that, I never understood what other kids meant when they said that science was boring.

One of my mother's earliest memories is of standing in her crib at the age of about 2, yanking on her 11-year-old brother's hair. This brother, her only sibling, was none other than Richard Feynman, destined to become one of the greatest theoretical physicists of his generation: enfant terrible of the Manhattan Project, pioneer of quantum electrodynamics, father of nanotechnology, winner of the Nobel Prize, and so on. At the time, he was training his sister to solve simple math problems and rewarding each correct answer by letting her tug on his hair while he made faces. When he wasn't doing that, he was often seen wandering around Far Rockaway, New York, with a screwdriver in his pocket, repairing radios—at age 11, mind you.

My mother worshipped her brother, and there was never any doubt about what he would become. By the time she was 5, Richard had hired her for 2 cents a week to assist him in the electronics lab he'd built in his room. "My job was to throw certain switches on command," she recalls. "I had to climb up on a box to reach them. Also, sometimes I'd stick my finger in a spark gap for the edification of his friends." At night, when she called out for a glass of water, Riddy, as he was called, would demonstrate centrifugal force by whirling it around in the air so that the glass was upside down during part of the arc. "Until, one night," my mother recalls, "the glass slipped out of his hand and flew across the room."

Richard explained the miraculous fact that the family dog, the waffle iron, and Joan herself were all made out of atoms. He would run her hand over the corner of a picture frame, describe a right triangle and make her repeat that the sum of the square of the sides was equal to the square of the hypotenuse. "I had no idea what it meant," she says, "but he recited it like a poem, so I loved to recite it too." One night, he roused her from her bed and led her outside, down the street, and onto a nearby golf course. He pointed out washes of magnificent light that were streaking across the sky. It was the aurora borealis. My mother had discovered her destiny.

That is when the trouble started. Her mother, Lucille Feynman, was a sophisticated and compassionate woman who had marched for women's suffrage in her youth. Nonetheless, when 8-year-old Joanie announced that she intended to be a scientist, Grandma explained that it was impossible. "Women can't do science," she said, "because their brains can't understand enough of it." My mother climbed into a living room chair and sobbed into the cushion. "I know she thought she was telling me the inescapable truth. But it was devastating for a little girl to be told that all of her dreams were impossible. And I've doubted my abilities ever since."

The fact that the greatest chemist of the age, Marie Curie, was a woman gave no comfort. "To me, Madame Curie was a mythological character," my mother says, "not a real person whom you could strive to emulate." It wasn't until her 14th birthday—March 31, 1942—that her notion of becoming a scientist was revived. Richard presented her with a book called *Astronomy*. "It was a college textbook. I'd start reading it, get stuck, and then start over again. This went on for months, but I kept at it. When I reached page 407,

I came across a graph that changed my life." My mother shuts her eyes and recites from memory: "'Relative strengths of the Mg+ absorption line at 4,481 angstroms ... from *Stellar Atmospheres* by Cecilia Payne.' Cecilia Payne! It was scientific proof that a woman was capable of writing a book that, in turn, was quoted in a text. The secret was out, you see."

My mother taught me about resonances when I was about 12. We were on a camping trip and needed wood for a fire. My brother and sister and I looked everywhere, without luck. Mom spotted a dead branch up in a tree. She walked up to the trunk and gave it a shake. "Look closely," she told us, pointing up at the branches. "Each branch waves at a different frequency." We could see that she was right. So what? "Watch the dead branch," she went on. "If we shake the tree trunk in just the right rhythm, we can match its frequency and it'll drop off." Soon we were roasting marshmallows.

The catalog of abuse to which my mother was subjected, beginning in 1944 when she entered Oberlin College, is too long and relentless to fully record. At Oberlin, her lab partner was ill-prepared for the advanced-level physics course in which they were enrolled, so my mother did all the experiments herself. The partner took copious notes and received an A. My mother got a D. "He understands what he's doing," the lab instructor explained, "and you don't." In graduate school, a professor of solid state physics advised her to do her Ph.D. dissertation on cobwebs, because she would encounter them while cleaning. She did not take the advice; her thesis was titled "Absorption of infrared radiation in crystals of diamond-type lattice structure." After graduation, she found that the "Situations Wanted" section of The New York Times was divided between Men and Women, and she could not place an ad among the men, the only place anyone needing a research scientist would bother to look.

At that time, even the dean of women at Columbia University argued that "sensible motherhood" was "the most useful and satisfying of the jobs that women can do." My mother tried to be a sensible mother and it damn near killed her. For three years, she cooked, cleaned, and looked after my brother and me, two stubborn and voluble babies.

One day in 1964 she found herself preparing to hurl the dish drain through the kitchen window and decided to get professional help. "I was incredibly lucky," she remembers, "to find a shrink who was enlightened enough to urge me to try to get a job. I didn't think anyone would hire me, but I did what he told me to do." She applied to Lamont-Doherty Observatory and, to her astonishment, received three offers. She chose to work part-time, studying the relationship between the solar wind and the magnetosphere. Soon she would be among the first to announce that the magnetosphere—the part of space in which Earth's magnetic field dominates and the solar wind doesn't enter—was open-ended, with a tail on one side, rather than having a closed-teardrop shape, as had been widely believed. She was off and running.

My mother introduced me to physics when I was about 14. I was crazy about bluegrass music, and learned that Ralph Stanley was coming to town with his Clinch Mountain Boys. Although Mom did not share my taste for hillbilly music, she agreed to take me. The highlight turned out to be fiddler Curly Ray Cline's version of "Orange Blossom Special," a barn burner in which the fiddle imitates the sound of an approaching and departing train. My mother stood and danced a buck-and-wing and when, to my great relief, she sat down, she said, "Great tune, huh? It's based on the Doppler effect." This is not the sort of thing one expects to hear in reference to Curly Ray Cline's repertoire. Later, over onion rings at the Rockybilt Cafe, she explained: "When the train is coming, its sound is shifting to higher frequencies. And when the train is leaving, its sound is shifting to lower frequencies. That's called the Doppler shift. You can see the same thing when you look at a star: if the light source is moving toward you, it shifts toward blue; if it's moving away, it shifts toward red. Most stars shift toward red because the universe is expanding."

I cannot pretend that, as a boy, I liked everything about having a scientist for a mother. When I saw the likes of Mrs. Brady on TV, I sometimes wished I had what I thought of as a mom with an apron. And then, abruptly, I got one.

It was 1971 and my mother was working for NASA at Ames Research Center in California. She had just made an important discovery concerning the solar wind, which has two states, steady and transient. The latter consists of puffs of material, also known as coronal mass ejections, which, though long known about, were notoriously hard to find. My mother showed they could be recognized by the large amount of helium in the solar wind. Her career was flourishing. But the economy was in recession and NASA's budget was slashed. My mother was a housewife again. For months, as she looked for work, the severe depression that had haunted her years before began to return.

Mom had been taught to turn to the synagogue in times of trouble, and it seemed to make especially good sense in this case, because our synagogue had more scientists in it than most Ivy League universities. Our rabbi, a celebrated civil rights activist, was arranging networking parties for unemployed eggheads. But when my mother asked for an invitation to one of these affairs, he accused her of being selfish. "After all-there are men out of work just now."

"But Rabbi," she said, "it's my life."

I remember her coming home that night, stuffing food into the refrigerator, then pulling out the vacuum cleaner. She switched it on, pushed it back and forth across the floor a few times, then switched it off and burst into tears. In a moment, I was crying too and my mother was comforting me. We sat there a long time.

"I know you want me here," she told me. "But I can either be a part-time mama, or a full-time madwoman."

A few months later, Mom was hired as a research scientist at the National Center for Atmospheric Research, and we moved to Boulder, Colorado. From then on, she decided to "follow research funding around the country, like Laplanders follow the reindeer herds." She followed it to Washington, D.C., to work for the National Science Foundation, then to the Boston College Department of Physics, and finally, in 1985, to JPL, where she's been ever since. Along the way, she unlocked some of the mysteries of the aurora. Using data from Explorer 33, she showed that auroras occur when the magnetic field of the solar wind interacts with the magnetic field of the Earth.

In 1974, she became an officer of her professional association, the American Geophysical Union, and spearheaded a committee to ensure that women in her field would be treated fairly. She was named one of JPL's elite senior scientists in 1999 and the following year was awarded NASA's Exceptional Scientific Achievement Medal.

Soon she'll retire, except that retirement as my mother the scientist envisions it means embarking on a new project: comparing recent changes in Earth's climate with historic ones. "It's a pretty important subject when you consider that even a small change in the solar output could conceivably turn Long Island into a skating rink—just like it was some 10,000 years ago."

The first thing I did when I came home from Mrs. Weddle's class that day in 1966 was to ask my mother what my father did. She told me that he was a scientist, and that she was a scientist too. I asked what a scientist was, and she handed me a spoon. "Drop it on the table," she said. I let it fall to the floor. "Why did it fall?" she asked. "Why didn't it float up to the ceiling?" It had never occurred to me that there was a "why" involved. "Because of gravity," she said. "A spoon will always fall, a hot-air balloon will always rise." I dropped the spoon again and again until she made me stop. I had no idea what gravity was, but the idea of "Why?" kept rattling around in my head. That's when I made the decision: the next day, in school, I wouldn't just tell them what my father did. I'd tell them about my mother too.

■ READING AND WRITING

1. "To become a scientist is hard enough," Hirshberg writes. "But to become one while running a gauntlet of lies, insults, mockeries, and disapproval—this was what my mother had to do." How does Hirshberg use his mother's story to compose an argument about gender? What is his claim?
2. Reread the italicized sections of the essay. What does Hirshberg achieve by setting these sections apart from the rest of the narrative? How do these sections support his argument?
3. How would you characterize Hirshberg's ethos? How does he convey this ethos to his audience?

■ DEVELOPING LONGER RESPONSES

4. Hirshberg and Shirin Ebadi both write memoirs about women and their work. After reading each of these texts, write a brief essay in which you explain the rhetorical advantages and disadvantages of using memoir to present an argument.

Nawal El Saadawi is a psychiatrist and the celebrated author of more than 40 works of fiction and non-fiction. The novel Memoirs of a Woman Doctor, *like many of her books, reveals what she calls "the double exploitation of Egyptian women—both their general, social oppression and their private oppression, through …marriage." El Saadawi has said that* Memoirs of a Woman Doctor, *from which this piece is excerpted, portrays the circumstances and characteristics of "an Egyptian woman such as myself," but that "the work is still fiction." The novel was first published in serial format and was censored when it was published in one volume.*

excerpt from
MEMOIRS OF A WOMAN DOCTOR
Nawal el-Saadawi

The conflict between me and my femininity began very early on, before my female characteristics had became pronounced and before I knew anything about myself, my sex and my origins, indeed before I knew the nature of the cavity which had housed me before I was expelled into the wide world.

All I did know at that time was that I was a girl. I used to hear it from my mother all day long. 'Girl!' she would call, and all it meant to me was that I wasn't a boy and I wasn't like my brother.

My brother's hair was cut short but otherwise left free and uncombed, while mine was allowed to grow longer and longer and my mother combed it twice a day and twisted it into plaits and imprisoned the ends of it in ribbons and rubber bands.

My brother woke up in the morning and left his bed just as it was, while I had to make my bed and his as well.

My brother went out into the street to play without asking my parents' permission and came back whenever he liked, while I could only go out if and when they let me.

My brother took a bigger piece of meat than me, gobbled it up and drank his soup noisily and my mother never said a word. But I was different: I was a girl. I had to watch every movement I made, hide my longing for the food, eat slowly and drink my soup without a sound.

My brother played, jumped around and turned somersaults, whereas if I ever sat down and allowed my skirt to ride as much as a centimeter up my thighs, my mother would pierce me with a glance like an animal immobilizing its prey and I would cover up those shameful parts of my body.

Shameful! Everything in me was shameful and I was a child of just nine years old.

I felt sorry for myself and locked myself in my room and cried. The first real tears I shed in my life weren't because I'd done badly at school or broken something valuable but because I was a girl. I wept over my femininity even before I knew what it was. The moment I opened my eyes on life, a state of enmity already existed between me and my nature.

I jumped down the stairs three at a time so as to be in the street before I'd counted ten. My brother and some of the boys and girls who lived nearby were waiting for me to play cops and robbers. I'd asked my mother's permission. I loved playing games and running as fast as I could. I felt an overwhelming happiness as I moved my head and arms and legs in the air or broke into a series of leaps and bounds, constrained only by the weight of my body which was dragged down earthwards time and again.

Why had God created me a girl and not a bird flying in the air like that pigeon? It seemed to me that God must prefer birds to girls. But my brother couldn't fly and this consoled me a little. I realized that despite his great freedom he was as incapable as I was of flying. I began to search constantly for weak spots in males to console me for the powerlessness imposed on me by the fact of being female.

I was bounding ecstatically along when I felt a violent shudder running through my body. My head spun and I saw something red. I didn't know what had happened to me. Fear gripped my heart and I left the game. I ran back to the house and locked myself in the bathroom to investigate the secret of this grave event in private.

I didn't understand it at all. I thought I must have been struck down by a terrible illness. I went to ask my mother about it in fear and trembling and saw laughter and happiness written all over her face. I wondered in amazement how she could greet this affliction with such a broad smile. Noticing my surprise and confusion, she took me by the hand and led me to my room. Here she told me women's bloody tale.

I took to my room for four days running. I couldn't face my brother, my father or even the house-boy. I thought they must all have been told about the shameful thing that had happened to me: my mother would doubtless have revealed my new secret. I locked myself in, trying to come to terms with this phenomenon. Was this unclean procedure the only way for girls to reach maturity? Could a human being really live for several days at the mercy of involuntary muscular activity? God must really hate girls to have tarnished them with this curse. I felt that God had favoured boys in everything.

I got up from the bed, dragged myself over to the mirror and looked at the two little mounds sprouting on my chest. If only I could die! I didn't recognize this body which sprang a new shame on me every day, adding to my weakness and my preoccupation with myself. What would grow on my body next? What other new symptom would my tyrannical femininity break out in?

I hated being female. I felt as if I was in chains—chains forged from my own blood tying me to the bed so that I couldn't run and jump, chains produced by the cells of my own body, chains of shame and humiliation. I turned in on myself to cover up my miserable existence.

I no longer went out to run and play. The two mounds on my chest were growing bigger. They bounced gently as I walked. I was unhappy with my tall slender frame, folding my arms over my chest to hide it and looking sadly at my brother and his friends as they played.

I grew. I grew taller than my brother even though he was older than me. I grew taller than the other children of my age. I withdrew from their midst and sat alone thinking. My childhood was over, a brief, breathless childhood. I'd scarcely been aware of it before it was gone, leaving me with a mature woman's body carrying deep inside it a ten-year-old child.

I saw the doorman's eyes and teeth shining in his black face as he came up to me; I was sitting alone on his wooden bench letting my eyes follow the movements of my brother and his friends in the street. I felt the rough edge of his galabiya brushing my leg and breathed in the strange smell of his clothes. I edged away in disgust. As he came closer again, I tried to hide my fear by staring fixedly at my brother and his companions as they played, but I felt his coarse rough fingers stroking my leg and moving up under my clothes. I jumped up in alarm and raced away from him. This horrible man had noticed my womanhood as well! I ran all the way up to our flat and my mother asked what the matter was. But I couldn't tell her anything, perhaps out of a feeling of fear or humiliation or a mixture of the two. Or perhaps because I thought she'd scold me and that would put an end to the special affection between us that made me tell her my secrets.

I no longer went out in the street, and I didn't sit on the wooden bench any more. I fled from those strange creatures with harsh voices and moustaches, the creatures they called men. I created an imaginary private world for myself in which I was a goddess and men were stupid, helpless creatures at my beck and call. I sat on a high throne in this world of mine, arranging the dolls on chairs, making the boys sit on the floor and telling stories to myself. Alone with my imagination and my dolls, nobody ruffled the calm of my life, except my mother with her never-ending orders for me to do tasks around the flat or in the kitchen: the hateful, constricted world of women with its permanent reek of garlic and onions. I'd scarcely retreated into my own little world when my mother would drag me into the kitchen saying, 'You're going to be married one day. You must learn how to cook. You're going to be married…' Marriage! Marriage! That loathsome word which my mother mentioned every day until I hated the sound of it. I couldn't hear it without having a mental picture of a man with a big see-through belly with a table of food inside it. In my mind the smell of the kitchen was linked with the smell of a husband and I hated the word husband just as I hated the smell of the food we cooked.

My grandmother's chatter broke off as she looked at my chest. I saw her diseased old eyes scrutinizing the two sprouting buds and evaluating them. Then she whispered something to my mother and I heard my mother saying to me, 'Put on your cream dress and go and say hello to your father's guest in the sitting-room.'

I caught a whiff of conspiracy in the air. I was used to meeting most of my father's friends and bringing them coffee. Sometimes I sat with them and heard my father telling them how well I was doing in school. This always made me feel elated and I thought that since my father had acknowledged my intelligence he would extricate me from the depressing world of women, reeking of onions and marriage.

But why the cream dress? It was new and I hated it. It had a strange gather at the front which made my breasts look larger. My mother looked at me inquiringly and asked, 'Where's your cream dress?'

'I won't wear it,' I replied angrily.

She noticed the stirrings of rebellion in my eyes and said regretfully, 'Smooth down your eyebrows then.'

I didn't look at her, and before opening the sitting-room door I ruffled up my eyebrows with my fingers.

I greeted my father's friend and sat down. I saw a strange, frightening face and eyes examining me relentlessly as my grandmother's had done shortly before.

'She's first in her group at primary school this year,' said my father.

I didn't notice any admiration in the man's eyes at these words but I saw his inquiring glances roaming all over my body before coming to rest on my chest. Scared, I stood up and ran out of the room as if a devil was after me. My mother and grandmother met me eagerly at the door and asked in unison, 'What did you do?'

I let out a single cry in their faces and ran to my room, slamming the door behind me. Then I went over to the mirror and stared at my chest. I hated them, these two protrusions, these two lumps of flesh which were determining my future! How I wished I could cut them off with a sharp knife! But I couldn't. All I could do was hide them by flattening them with a tight corset.

The heavy long hair I carried around everywhere on my head held me up in the morning, got in my way in the bath and made my neck burning hot in the summer. Why wasn't it short and free like my brother's? His didn't weigh his head down or hinder his activities. But it was my mother who controlled my life, my future and my body right down to every strand of my hair. Why? Because she'd given birth to me? But why did that give her some special merit? She went about her normal life like any other woman and conceived me involuntarily in a random moment of pleasure. I'd arrived without her knowing or choosing me, and without my choosing her. We'd been thrust arbitrarily on one another as mother and daughter. Could any human being love someone who'd been forced upon them? And if my mother loved me instinctively in spite of herself, what credit did that do her? Did it make her any better than a cat which sometimes loves its kittens and at other times devours them? I sometimes thought the harsh way she treated me hurt me more than if she'd eaten me! If she really loved me and wanted my happiness above her own, then why did her demands and desires always work against my happiness? How could she possibly love me when she put chains on my arms and legs and round my neck every day?

For the first time in my life I left the flat without asking my mother's permission. My heart was pounding as I went down the street, though my provocative act had given me a certain strength. As I walked, a sign caught my eye: 'Ladies' Hairdresser'. I had only a second's hesitation before going in.

I watched the long tresses squirm in the jaws of the sharp scissors and then fall to the ground. Were these what my mother called a woman's crowning glory? Could a woman's crown fall shattered to the ground like this because of one moment of determination? I was filled with a great contempt for womankind: I had seen with my own eyes that women believe in worthless trivia. This contempt gave me added strength. I walked back home with a firm step and stood squarely in front of my mother with my newly cropped hair.

My mother gave a shrill cry and slapped my face hard. Then she hit me again and again while I stood where I was as if rooted to the spot. My challenging of authority had turned me into an immovable force, my victory over my mother had transformed me into a solid mass, unaffected by the assault. My mother's hand struck my face and then drew back each time, as if it had hit a granite boulder.

Why didn't I cry? I usually burst into tears at the slightest snub or the gentlest of slaps. But the tears didn't come. My eyes stayed open, looking into my mother's eyes boldly and firmly. She went on slapping me for a while, then collapsed back on to the sofa, repeating in bewilderment, 'You must have gone mad!'

I felt sorry for her when I saw her features crumbling in helpless defeat. I had a strong urge to hug and kiss her and break down and cry in her arms, and say to her, 'It's not good for me always to do as you say.'

But I took my eyes away from hers so she wouldn't realize I'd witnessed her defeat, and ran off to my room. I looked in the mirror and smiled at my short hair, the light of victory in my eyes.

For the first time in my life I understood the meaning of victory; fear led only to defeat, and victory demanded courage. My fear of my mother had vanished; that great aura which had made me terrified of her had fallen away. I realized that she was just an ordinary woman. The slaps she delivered were the strongest thing about her but they no longer scared me—because they didn't hurt any more.

I hated our flat except for the room where my books were. I loved school except for the home economics period. I loved all the days of the week except Friday.

I took part in all school activities and joined the drama society, the debating society, the athletics club, and the music and art clubs. Even that wasn't enough for me so I got together with some friends and we set up a society that I called the Friendship Club. Why, I'm not sure, except that deep down inside I had an overwhelming longing for companionship, for profound, all-embracing companionship with no strings attached, for vast groups of people to be with me, talk to me, listen to me and soar up to the heavens with me.

It seemed to me that whatever heights I reached, I wouldn't be content, the flame burning within me wouldn't be extinguished. I began to hate the repetitiveness and similarity of lessons: I would read the material once and once only—to go over it again would stifle me, kill me. I wanted something new, new…all the time.

I wasn't aware of him at first when he came into my room where I sat reading and stood beside me. Then he said, 'Don't you want to relax for a bit?'

I'd been reading for ages and felt tired so I smiled and said, 'I'd like to go for a walk in the fresh air.'

'Put on your coat and let's go.'

I quickly pulled on my coat and ran to catch up with him. I was on the point of slipping my hand into his and running along together as we used to do when we were children. But then I caught his eye and suddenly remembered how many years it had been since I had last played like a child, years during which my legs had forgotten how to run and become used to moving slowly like grown-ups' legs. I put my hand in my coat pocket and walked slowly at his side.

'You've grown,' he said.

'So have you.'

'Do you remember when we used to play together?'

'You always beat me when we had races.'

'You always won at marbles.'

We laughed uproariously. The air flooded into my chest and invigorated me, making me feel as if I was recapturing something denied to me in my over-regimented childhood.

'I bet I'd win if we had a race now.'

'No, I'll beat you,' I said confidently.

'Let's see.'

We marked out a line on the ground and stood side by side. He shouted, 'One…two… three…' and we shot forward. I was about to reach the goal first when he grabbed my clothes from behind. I stumbled and fell and he fell beside me. Still panting, I looked up at him and saw him staring at me in a funny way which made the blood rush to my cheeks. I watched his arm reach out in the direction of my waist and he whispered in a rough voice, 'I'm going to kiss you.'

I was convulsed by a strange and violent trembling. For a moment which passed like lightning through my feelings, I wished he would stretch out his arm further and hold me tight, but then this odd secret desire was transformed into a wild fury.

My anger only made him more persistent and he held on to me with an iron grip. I don't know where I got the strength, but I threw off his arm and it flailed in the air while I brought my hand down hard across his face.

I turned over and over in bed in utter confusion. Strange sensations swept through me and images flashed before my eyes. One of them lodged itself in front of me and wouldn't go away: my cousin lying on the ground beside me, his arm nearly round my waist and his strange glances boring into my head. I closed my eyes and was borne along by my fantasy in which his arms moved tightly around me and his lips pressed firmly down on mine.

I buried my head under the covers, unable to believe that I'd slapped him with the hand I was now picturing quivering in his. I pulled the covers tightly over my head to shut out my strange dream but it crept back, so I put the pillow over my head and pressed it down as hard as I could to suffocate the stubborn ghost, until sleep finally overtook me.

I opened my eyes the following morning. The sunlight had chased away the darkness and all the phantoms that prowled in its shadows. I opened the window and the fresh air blew in, chasing away the last clinging traces of the night's dreams. I smiled scornfully at the cowardly part of me which trembled with fear at the stronger part when I was awake, but then crept into my bed at night and filled the darkness around me with fantasies and illusions.

In my final year at secondary school I came out top of my group…I sat wondering what to do…

I hated my femininity, resented my nature and knew nothing about my body. All that was left for me was to reject, to challenge, to resist! I would reject my femininity, challenge my nature, resist all the desires of my body; prove to my mother and grandmother that I wasn't a woman like them, that I wouldn't spend my life in the kitchen peeling onions and garlic, wasting all my days so that my husband could eat and eat.

I was going to show my mother that I was more intelligent than my brother, than the man she'd wanted me to wear the cream dress for, than any man, and that I could do everything my father did and more.

■ READING AND WRITING

1. Though it is a work of fiction, Saadawi's excerpt clearly introduces an argument about gender and femininity. What do you think that argument is? How does Saadawi use her protagonist to voice the argument?
2. Early in the excerpt, Saadawi's protagonist says, "I wept over my femininity even before I knew what it was." What kinds of expectations and obstacles does she face? What are the origins of these hurdles?
3. Saadawi's narrative is rich with imagery. List some of these images in the text and discuss their rhetorical effectiveness.

■ DEVELOPING LONGER RESPONSES

4. Read Shirin Ebadi's "From the Living Room to the Courtroom" elsewhere in this chapter and write a brief essay in which you compare Ebadi's piece with Saadawi's. Think about the genre of each text, the arguments, and the rhetorical choices the authors make in their efforts to persuade.

Shirin Ebadi, a lawyer and activist, won the Nobel Peace Price in 2003 for her efforts to promote democracy and human rights in Iran, especially for her focus on the rights of women and children. The Washington Post *called her 2006 book* Iran Awakening: A Memoir of Revolution and Hope *"a riveting account of a brave, lonely struggle to take Islamist jurists to task for betraying the promises of their own revolution" in Iran. "From the Living Room to the Courtroom," a chapter from that memoir, vividly recounts her struggle and the victims of injustice Ebadi risked her career and her safety to help.*

FROM THE LIVING ROOM TO THE COURTROOM Shirin Ebadi, with Azadeh Moaveni

Leila Fathi disappeared one sunny day in the summer of 1996 while picking wildflowers in the hills behind her village, near the northwestern Kurdish city of Sanandaj. Her parents, like many in the region, struggled to get by, and eleven-year-old Leila was collecting the wild plants and flowers the family would then dry and sell in the local bazaar. She and her cousin had set out with their woven baskets in the late morning and had interrupted their picking to play among the tall grasses. Growing up near Sanandaj, where people picnicked outdoors, held weddings under the open sky, and danced alongside the riverbanks, they ran about as though the hills were an extension of their tiny living room, with nothing like the intuitive watchfulness of urban children. Bent over filling her skirt with petals, Leila didn't notice the three men approaching. They emerged from the back side of the hill, moving quietly until they were almost atop her, and then closed in swiftly. One twisted her thin arms behind her back, while another tried to clasp her thrashing legs together. Her cousin managed to escape, and he hid behind a tree, watching the men drag a fighting, kicking Leila over to a slope. He watched them tear off her peasant skirt and rape her, strike a fatal blow to her head, and then hurl her battered body over a cliff in the craggy hillside.

The local police arrested the three men, but after the prime suspect confessed to the crime, he mysteriously hung himself in prison. Odd that in a prison where inmates are not even allowed to wear watches, he had conveniently found a meter of braided rope, just the length for hanging. The other two suspects denied complicity, but the court found them guilty of rape and sentenced them to death.

I mentioned earlier that under the Islamic penal code instituted after the revolution, a man's life is worth twice that of a woman. In most Islamic countries, laws determining compensation apply only in financial cases, such as inheritance. The Islamic Republic, however, applies compensation, or "blood money" provisions, in criminal cases. Under Islamic law, the family of a victim of homicide or manslaughter has the right to choose between legal punishment and financial compensation, referred to as blood money. Many Islamic scholars hold that blood money should be blind to gender, but Iran practices a discriminatory interpretation. Under the Iranian code, the worth of a woman's life equals half of a man's, a point that often leads to grotesque legal judgments that effectively punish the victim. In this instance, the judge ruled that the "blood money" for the two men was worth more than the life of the murdered nine-year-old girl, and he demanded that her family come up with thousands of dollars to finance their executions.

Leila's father sold all of his few worldly possessions, including the little clay hut where his family slept. Homeless but convinced that they would at least reclaim their honor, they offered the money to the court. It was not enough. The family took to sleeping at the shrine of Ayatollah Khomeini, a vast mausoleum on the road to Qom, while trying to raise the remaining cash. First Leila's father volunteered to sell a kidney, but his organ was rejected because of his past drug abuse. Next Leila's brother offered his up, but the doctor refused because he was handicapped by polio. "Why," asked the doctor, "are you two so insistent on selling your kidneys?" Out poured the tale. They could not return to their village, they explained, stained by the shame of Leila's rape. Family honor rests on the virtue of women, and nothing less than the perpetrators' execution could erase their shame.

Horrified by this bizarre tale, the doctor wrote to the head of the judiciary and threatened to report the case to an international organization, Doctors Without Borders, unless the state treasury made up the difference needed for the execution. The judiciary chief agreed, but in a further unbelievable twist, just days before the scheduled execution one of the convicts escaped from prison, and, in the meantime, Leila's disconsolate family had erected a ramshackle cloth tent on the sidewalk outside the courthouse. The family was shocked to learn that the court had reopened the case. Perhaps it was because the ambiguities inherent in the Iranian legal system mean that even a closed case always remains subject to further review. Perhaps, as Leila's family claimed, it was because one of the accused used a relative, a conservative member of parliament to influence the outcome. The case was unraveling.

It was at this point that I heard about the case and decided to take a look at the file. At first I was skeptical. Criminal justice in the post-revolutionary legal system was flawed; it denied female victims of violence equal restitution. But the case of Leila's family suggested that it was effectively pathological, capable of destroying the livelihoods of those who petitioned for justice on behalf of their victimized loved ones. I paid a visit to the family at their tent outside the courthouse, and after listening to their account of the long, sordid tale, I agreed to represent them.

The outlines of the case were stark, and I constructed a simple, elegant defense: it was unjust for a girl to be raped and killed, and for her family to have lost every possession and become homeless through the legal proceedings that followed; it was unjust that the victims were now being victimized further by the law. "Do not criticize Islamic law," the judge sternly warned me in court. "I'm only asking if justice has been served," I retorted.

As the session neared its close, someone whispered in my ear that Leila's brothers had concealed kitchen knives in their coats and were planning to attack the remaining defendant as he left the court. I asked for a recess and called the boys out into the hall.

"Please," I said, "please give me a chance to see what I can do in court first."

Both of them sat on a bench and wept. "If we had paid a professional assassin *half* of what we paid the court," one of them cried, "Justice would have been carried out. Now we're homeless, while one of them is free and the other is about to walk."

"I know," I whispered. "I know. But let's try."

Over the course of the proceedings, the court acquitted both defendants, overturned the acquittals, and then relaunched the investigation. The family's grief slowly descended into madness. Leila's mother took to sitting outside the courthouse in a white funeral shroud, holding a placard that described her daughter's violation. During one trial, she threatened to set herself on fire, and began screaming profanities at the court. As though the whole proceeding was not dramatic enough, the judge held her in contempt of court and filed legal charges against her that took us weeks of mediation to settle.

It would tire your patience if I detailed the legal proceedings any further, but suffice it to say that the case was not resolved, and remains open to this day. I did not succeed in getting the legal system to mete out anything approximating justice, but I do think we accomplished something else: we made a national showcase of the flaws in Iranian law concerning the rights of women and children. The case swiftly turned into a public issue, so much so that candidates in Leila's province ran on platforms that included stances on her case. The Iranian press took on Leila's story as an egregious illustration of the social problems of the Islamic Republic.

The trial reverberated long after the final court session. It played itself out in the newspapers as well as the courtroom, and the publicity established my reputation as a lawyer whose work focused on the rights of women and children. I learned very quickly that one of the most powerful tools at the disposal of the legally powerless was the media. My prominence in turn made me more effective at defending my clients, because the judge knew that both he and the judiciary would be forced to justify their decision in the court of public opinion. Oftentimes they simply did not care, but at those times I reminded myself that raising people's awareness of their rights was in itself a contribution.

In the course of the dark months when I watched Leila's family fall apart in despair, as the case garnered more attention, I was struck by how few women even knew that the legal system discriminated against them so severely. Most women had some sense of the laws governing child custody and divorce, because at some point exiting a marriage occurs to many. But by and large, murder or accidental death did not touch the lives of the majority of women; they had no occasion to hear or learn about what sort of fate might lay in store for them, what sort of legal morass awaited them, should they be so unlucky as to have an incident like Leila's befall their family.

I decided to write an article for the magazine *Iran-t Farda*, in approachable language, rather than in an overly intellectual or legalistic style, that would set out in stark terms women's inferior status in the penal code. The section of the code devoted to blood money, *diyeh*, holds that if a man suffers an injury that damages his testicles, he is entitled to compensation equal to a woman's life. I put it this way in my article: if a professional woman with a PhD is run over in the street and killed and an illiterate thug gets one of his testicles injured in a fight, the value of her life and his damaged testicle are equal. There is a vulgar expression in Persian that conveys deep contempt for someone "You're not even worth one of my testicles." I politely invoked this in my article, to explain in terms no Iranian could mistake just how outrageous these laws were, how they treated women as non-people. In the end I posed a question: Is this really how the Islamic Republic regards its women?

The article both titillated and electrified literate Tehran. The editor had published it eagerly, aware that it would, like much of the magazine's content, provoke the hard-line judiciary. The issue sold out immediately, and people showed up at the magazine's offices, begging for even a photocopy of the article. I was stunned. I had expected that it might circulate widely, but I'd never thought it would resound this way throughout the city. A hard-line member of parliament threatened me publicly, telling reporters, "Someone stop this woman, or we'll shut her up ourselves." When I heard this, I realized for the first time that the system might actually fear me and the growing public resonance with my work.

In 1996, the year Leila's case went to court, the Islamic regime tolerated little criticism of its repressive ways. The suppression of political dissent had mellowed some from the early, brutal days of the revolution, when the papers were full of the photos and names of the summarily executed, but the system still punished any perceived challenge to its authority severely. We lived with daily examples of even prominent grand ayatollahs who had been defrocked (unheard of in Shia Islam) or placed under house arrest for speaking out against executions and harsh forms of criminal punishment, such as the chopping off of hands. If the system was willing to disgrace and effectively imprison distinguished senior theologians who had participated actively in the revolution, why should it hesitate for a moment in punishing me, a nonrevolutionary, a non-cleric, and, as a woman, a nonperson?

I was nervous. While I was arguing Leila's case, the judge repeatedly accused me of speaking against Islam and its sacred laws. In the politico-religious worldview of such traditionalists, a person who challenges Islam is easily considered an apostate. And the power of interpretation—the power to differentiate between a respectful criticism of a worldly law and an attack on a holy tenet—was in their hands. I was fighting on their battlefield. And I could not simply pull out a copy of the Universal Declaration of Human Rights and wave it in the faces of clerics who found seventh-century penal practice instructive. To argue that Leila's family should not have to finance the execution of her killer or to argue that a woman's life should equal a man's before the law, I too had to draw on Islamic principles and precedents in Islamic law.

My two daughters were growing old enough that they came home from school each day with a barrage of questions. *Thud.* They would toss their backpacks in the hallway. *Thud thud.* They would run down the hall, fingers sticky from a snack on the way home. Navigating the Islamic Republic as a woman was getting more tricky, and so was navigating Islamic Republic motherhood. Maman, is it really wrong for me to go in front of my male cousins without a veil? Maman, is America truly the source of all that is toxic in the world? Maman, was Mossadegh really a bad man? It was a delicate balance, trying to teach my daughters progressive values and the emptiness behind the revolutionary dogma they were fed in school, while ensuring that they learned and superficially obeyed all that dogma anyway, so the could pass through the education system. "A lot of this is simply wrong," I would usually say, "but you need to study it anyway, so you can pass your exams and go to college."

My husband, Javad, as usual, left these delicate lessons to me. Just as he left the cooking, the shopping, the cleaning, the balancing of the checkbook, and the shuttling of the girls to and from their classes to me. With the caseload I was taking on, balancing the attention the girls needed at home and my work was getting harder. And now the girls didn't need just bedtime stories anymore. They needed our guidance in dealing with adolescence in Tehran, with all its lures and chaos. "Just tell me if you need any help," Javad would say. And that struck me as most unfair of all, because I certainly never waited for him to ask, "Shirin *jan*, can you please cook dinner tonight?" I cooked dinner every single night because it was obvious to me that it was my responsibility. This was the running theme of our arguments. He wanted me to tell him what to do, and I thought he should figure it out without being told.

Between my practice in the morning and working on articles in the evening, I had started my next book, a treatise on the rights of refugees. Before I started my legal practice, the book writing kept my mind engaged, but now, combined with representing clients, it resulted in an often overwhelming workload. I managed to keep the household running smoothly only by planning well in advance. There was really no such institution as takeout, and the expectations of an Iranian wife include that she will cook. Leaving a sink full of dirty dishes or a hamper full of laundry is simply not an option. If I needed to travel or take a short trip for work, I arranged all the family's meals in advance. They would know to look on the top shelf of the refrigerator for that evening's cutlet, and then in the freezer for the meals labeled for the following days of the week. I even made just the right amount of fresh salad dressing and put that in the refrigerator too. I don't mean to suggest that I was a brilliant housewife or a superb cook; by Iranian standards I'm sure I could have been faulted on an array of small details and neglects. But from the beginning I had run a household that was cozier than clinically spotless, and the family was accustomed to this informality. Perhaps it was a shade fatalistic, the sometimes casual approach I took to the present. But ever since my brother-in-law Fuad's execution, when the gravity of death first touched me, I'd found preoccupation with the minutiae of daily life meaningless. If we all ultimately die, and turn to dust in the ground, should it ever truly upset us if the floor hasn't been swept quite recently enough. This didn't mean that I wasn't concerned with the details of my children's lives; it just meant that I distinguished carefully which details mattered.

To bridge my worry about spending so much time away from the house, I made a point of bringing my work home in the evening and involving the girls in what I was thinking or writing about each day. Better that they be drawn into my orbit of preoccupations, I figured, than wonder why I was so absorbed in things beyond them. I suppose deep down I hoped they would inherit my beliefs, my sensitivity to injustice, and my compulsion to push the boundaries.

The night the voting results came in for the 1996 parliamentary elections, I gathered my daughters around me on the sofa and narrated to them. Sometimes I tried to tell them about my work, to make abstract concepts such as women's rights come alive through the characters who passed through their lives. They knew, for example, that my friend Shahla Sherkat had four years ago started a women's publication called *Zanan*. It was Shahla who'd first called to tell me about Leila's case and asked whether I could offer their family legal advice. In a way, my daughters could trace the evolution in women's role through my life and the lives of those they knew as close family friends. Before 1992, I couldn't even get a permit to work as an attorney. Shahla directed a government-owned weekly aimed at conservative, religious women. The same year I secured a license and began taking on cases, Shahla started up *Zanan*, which at first tentatively and then more forcefully took up the issues that a broader spectrum of women in Iran faced each day. Sometimes she referred cases to me; sometimes I wrote articles for her magazine.

Our budding activism was premised on a few basic facts: we lived under an Islamic Republic that was neither going anywhere nor inclined to recast its governing ethos as secular; the legal system was underpinned by Islamic law; and every facet of a woman's place in society—from access to birth control to divorce rights to compulsory veiling—was determined by interpretations of the Koran.

If we wanted to make a tangible difference in the lives of the women around us and in the lives of people like Leila and her family, we had no choice but to advocate for female equality in an Islamic framework. In this, our personal sensibilities and political worldview were wholly irrelevant. It so happened that I believed in the secular separation of religion and government because, fundamentally, Islam, like any religion, is subject to interpretation. It can be interpreted to oppress women or interpreted to liberate them. In an ideal world, I would choose not to be vulnerable to the caprice of interpretation, because the ambiguity of theological debates spirals back to the seventh century; there will never be a definitive resolution, as that is the nature and spirit of Islamic interpretation, a debate that will grow and evolve with the ages but never be resolved. I am a lawyer by training, and know only too well the permanent limitations of trying to enshrine inalienable rights in sources that lack fixed terms and definitions. But I am also a citizen of the Islamic Republic, and I know the futility of approaching the question any other way. My objective is not to vent my own political sensibilities but to push for a law that would save a family like Leila's from becoming homeless in their quest to finance the executions of their daughter's convicted murderers. If I'm forced to ferret through musty books of Islamic jurisprudence and rely on sources that stress the egalitarian ethics of Islam, then so be it. Is it harder this way? Of course it is. But is there an alternative battlefield? Desperate wishing aside, I cannot see one.

One summer morning in 1997, as I leafed through a newspaper in my office, I came across a story about a battered child who had died in a local hospital after suffering repeated blows to the head. The photo that ran with the story showed a bent little girl with thin limbs covered in cigarette burns. The photo was so painful to look at that I quickly folded it over and read on. The little girl was named Arian Golshani. After her parents' divorce, the court granted custody of Arian to her father, a brutal man with a police record for fraud and drug addiction. According to the neighbors, the father kept Arian in dungeon-like conditions. The nine-year-old weighed only thirty-three pounds, her arms had been broken several times and plastered with makeshift casts at home, and after the schoolteacher called her father to inquire about the cigarette burn marks all over her body, she was kept home from school for months. Arian's mother went to the court and pleaded for custody; she explained her daughter's condition, explained that her ex-husband was guilty of horrific abuse. The court impassively declined to grant her custody.

All morning, the image of that scarred child remained etched in my mind. Something must be done, I felt, but what? A couple of hours later, the phone rang. A photographer friend had also seen Arian's photo in the newspaper. "Shirin, we must do something," she said. "I know, let me think," I replied. That afternoon, we convened a meeting with a few friends from a children's rights society and conferred over little cups of Turkish coffee. In the end, we devised a stealthy plan: we would arrange a ceremony ostensibly to mourn her death, but we would also use it as an occasion to protest the civil code that was its cause. We reserved space at a large mosque in central Tehran, Al-Ghadir, and took out ads in the newspaper announcing the death of Arian Golshani and the funeral ceremony in her honor. I asked Javad's uncle, a cleric, to speak about child abuse and to tell the story of her short, brutal life.

The Islamic Revolution had anointed the Muslim family the centerpiece of its ideology of nation. The revolutionaries envisioned the domesticated Muslim mother, confined to the house and caring for her multiplying brood, as key to the restoration of traditional and authentic values. Yet it seemed in no way contradictory to them to then institute a family law that automatically tore children away from mothers in the event of divorce, or made polygamy as convenient as a second mortgage. The question of child custody had weighed heavy on my own mind for years, for my older sister had long felt bound to her failing marriage partly out of fear of losing her children. It numbered among the most destructive of the system's legal codes, and articles and public outcry against the custody law had grown louder with each passing year.

On the day of the ceremony, in the fall of 1997, we lined the funeral hall with flowers and set a small table with plump dates at the entrance. Shortly before the ceremony started, several women walked through the mosque with dazed expressions, their tears flowing. They were Arian's mother and aunts. "I didn't know my daughter had so many friends," her mother said in a strangled voice, searching my face in confusion. "If so, why did she die alone?" I swallowed hard and gently led her to a seat in the front.

Javad's uncle was a gifted orator, and his speech moved the audience from the beginning. Toward the middle, a man named Alavi walked up to him holding the hand of a small child. "Here is another Arian," he said, and he recounted the child's story, his custody granted to his father but the boy desperately wishing to live with his mother. Mr. Alavi lifted the child high into the air and declared to the audience, "People, do something for these children!"

Suddenly the atmosphere grew very charged, and everyone began crying. I strode up to the microphone in the women's section and said, "Today we are here to defend the rights of other Arians. We must reform the law that led to this death." People began shouting slogans, and we asked them to disperse the flowers on the streets on their way out. The whole hall moved toward the doors at once, chanting, "The law must be reformed!" and plucking the petals from their stems.

Within half an hour, the busy streets surrounding the mosque were strewn with white petals, and the taxi drivers and commuters crawling through traffic paused to look at the mosque. Newspapers covered the story, and universities began holding seminars on child abuse. Suddenly, women's custody rights were at the center of a self-generated campaign of public awareness. My office phone, which had begun ringing more frequently ever since Leila's case, now pretty much rang incessantly. And not simply with potential clients but with journalists and international human rights monitors who needed an Iranian interlocutor on the ground to explain how the system worked and how women—not yet organized in those days—were working to change its ways.

When the trial began, I represented Arian's mother and charged the girl's father and stepbrother with torture and murder, respectively. Reporters, including broadcast journalists, crowded the courtroom, and as soon as the trial started the second row whipped out a banner reading, THE PRICE OF ARIAN'S DEATH IS A CHANGE IN THE LAWS IN FAVOR OF IRANIAN CHILDREN. Because the case had become so sensitive, the head of the branch court, a cleric, presided.

My opening statement didn't require much embellishment; the tragedy of Arian's case spoke for itself. I told the court of how she grew weak, malnourished, and disoriented after weeks of torture, how she had started to touch herself, and when her stepbrother found her with her hands between her legs, he kicked her violently, sending her tiny body flying across the floor. I described how her head cracked against the wall, sustaining the concussion that within hours killed her. I made sure to linger on the laws themselves, not simply Arian's case. I paced back and forth, my low heels clicking against the floor of the courtroom, essentially putting the law—rather than these particular defendants—on trial.

When I finished, the head of the branch court took the microphone from me. "Islam," he began ponderously, "is a religion of equality, but the Koran stipulates that a woman's inheritance is half that of a man."

How irrelevant! We were not even discussing inheritance. It was a pretext to accuse me of defaming religion.

I asked the judge permission to speak. "I am not criticizing Islam," I declared flatly. "May the tongue of anyone who does be cut. I am criticizing a law that has been passed by the Iranian parliament. Is it fair," I asked, turning toward the court, "for a child to be abused by her father so cruelly, and for the court to deny her mother custody? Is it fair to expect a mother whose child has just been killed to pay for the execution of justice?"

"Don't worry," said the judge, assuring me that the blood money would be taken from the public treasury.

"But we don't want our taxes to go to murderers!" I said, exasperated.

The judge sentenced Arian's stepbrother to death, and her father and stepmother to one year in prison. Arian's mother eventually consented to stay the stepbrother's execution. I admired her for her compassion, as the stepbrother had been a child of the father's second marriage, and he himself had been taken from his mother after their divorce. His abuse was monstrous, but he was also a victim of the same system.

The trial's end attracted worldwide attention. CNN correspondent Christiane Amanpour interviewed me with Arian's mother, and as I watched her distraught face at home on the television, I felt heartened for a moment: though Arian's death had been senseless, at least her legacy served enormous purpose. Perhaps the Islamic Republic resisted accountability to its citizens, but it wished with each passing year to shed its pariah status in the global community. Slowly, it grew more aware that a nation on uneven footing with the West could not afford to trample its citizens' rights.

When I watched that broadcast, aware that it was being beamed around the world, I also realized for the first time that I had become what you might call famous. Prominence is something that accrues gradually. You work and speak, write articles and lecture, meet with clients and defend them, day after day, night after night, and then you wake up one day and notice that there is a long trial behind you that constitutes a reputation. That's how it happened for me, anyway. How unimportant it was to me as a person, but how useful it became to my work. It meant journalists would listen if I approached them with a case and would help publicize it both inside the country and abroad. It meant that human rights observers around the world knew and trusted me, and launched swift appeals for urgent cases I brought to their attention. It meant there was now a face and a name attached to the abstract term "human rights" in Iran, and that finally millions of women who could not articulate their frustrations and desires had someone to speak on their behalf. I would never assume such a role for myself, but in the Islamic Republic, we have a problem with representation. Our diplomats around the world are, naturally, loyal to the regime, and the regime's credibility is not such that it reflects the true opinions of the people. The responsibility falls, then, on unofficial ambassadors to relate Iranians' perceptions and hopes to the world.

Between my ever-growing reputation and the world's curiosity about how women fared in a society like Iran's, it seemed more possible each year to make the system pay an international price for its refusal to reform its laws at home.

▪ READING AND WRITING

1. How does the story of Leila Fathi and her family function in this piece, rhetorically and thematically?
2. What gender issues does Ebadi raise in her piece? What is her central argument? How does she support her claims?
3. What does Edabi reveal about herself in her text? How does this information affect your view of her argument?

▪ USING RESEARCH

4. Find Ebadi's Nobel Peace Prize lecture online, read the text, and write a 150- to 200-word summary of Ebadi's main points. How are these themes reflected in "From the Living Room to the Courtroom"? Which text do you think presents the more effective argument? Why?

> *Shannon Hayes—the author of* Radical Homemakers, The Farmer and the Grill, *and* The Grassfed Gourmet Cookbook—*wrote this article in February 2010 for* YES! Magazine, *a national, nonprofit media organization that, according to its website, "fuses powerful ideas with practical actions."*

MEET THE RADICAL HOMEMAKERS
Shannon Hayes

Long before we could pronounce Betty Friedan's last name, Americans from my generation felt her impact. Many of us born in the mid-1970s learned from our parents and our teachers that women no longer needed to stay home, that there were professional opportunities awaiting us. In my own school experience, homemaking, like farming, gained a reputation as a vocation for the scholastically impaired. Those of us with academic promise learned that we could do whatever we put our minds to, whether it was conquering the world or saving the world. I was personally interested in saving the world. That path eventually led me to conclude that homemaking would play a major role toward achieving that goal.

My own farming background led me to pursue advanced degrees in the field of sustainable agriculture, with a powerful interest in the local food movement. By the time my Ph.D. was conferred, I was married, and I was in a state of confusion. The more I understood about the importance of small farms and the nutritional, ecological, and social value of local food, the more I questioned the value of a 9-to-5 job. If my husband and I both worked and had children, it appeared that our family's ecological impact would be considerable. We'd require two cars, professional wardrobes, convenience foods to make up for lost time in the kitchen … and we'd have to buy, rather than produce, harvest, and store, our own food.

The economics didn't work out, either. When we crunched the numbers, our gross incomes from two careers would have been high, but the cost of living was also considerable, especially when daycare was figured into the calculation. Abandoning the job market, we re-joined my parents on our small grass-fed livestock farm and became homemakers. For almost ten years now, we've been able to eat locally and organically, support local businesses, avoid big box stores, save money, and support a family of four on less than $45,000 per year.

Wondering if my family was a freaky aberration to the conventional American culture, I decided to post a notice on my webpage, looking to connect with other ecologically minded homemakers. My fingers trembled on the keyboard as I typed the notice. What, exactly, would be the repercussions for taking a pro-homemaker stand and seeking out others? Was encouraging a Radical Homemaking movement going to unravel all the social advancements that have been made in the last 40-plus years? Women, after all, have been the homemakers since the beginning of time. Or so I thought.

■ The origins of homemaking: A vocation for both sexes

Upon further investigation, I learned that the household did not become the "woman's sphere" until the Industrial Revolution. A search for the origin of the word *housewife* traces it back to the thirteenth century, as the feudal period was coming to an end in Europe and the first signs of a middle class were popping up. Historian Ruth Schwartz Cowan explains that housewives were wedded to husbands, whose name came from *hus*, an old spelling of *house*, and *bonded*. Husbands were bonded to houses, rather than to lords. Housewives and husbands were free people, who owned their own homes and lived off their land. While there was a division of labor among the sexes in these early households, there was also an equal distribution of domestic work. Once the Industrial Revolution happened, however, things changed. Men left the household to work for wages, which were then used to purchase goods and services that they were no longer home to provide. Indeed, the men were the first to lose their domestic skills as successive generations forgot how to butcher the family hog, how to sew leather, how to chop firewood.

As the Industrial Revolution forged on and crossed the ocean to America, men and women eventually stopped working together to provide for their household sustenance. They developed their separate spheres—man in the factory, woman in the home. The more a man worked outside the home, the more the household would have to buy in order to have needs met. Soon the factories were able to fabricate products to supplant the housewives' duties as well. The housewife's primary function ultimately became chauffeur and consumer. The household was no longer a unit of production. It was a unit of consumption.

■ Housewife's Syndrome

The effect on the American housewife was devastating. In 1963, Betty Friedan published *The Feminine Mystique*, documenting for the first time "the problem that has no name," Housewife's Syndrome, where American girls grew up fantasizing about finding their husbands, buying their dream homes and appliances, popping out babies, and living happily ever after. In truth, pointed out Friedan, happily-ever-after never came. Countless women suffered from depression and nervous breakdowns as they faced the endless meaningless tasks of shopping and driving children hither and yon. They never had opportunities to fulfill their highest potential, to challenge themselves, to feel as though they were truly contributing to society beyond wielding the credit card to keep the consumer culture humming. Friedan's book sent women to work in droves. And corporate America seized upon a golden opportunity to secure a cheaper workforce and offer countless products to use up their paychecks.

> Before long, the second family income was no longer an option. In the minds of many, it was a necessity. Homemaking, like eating organic foods, seemed a luxury to be enjoyed only by those wives whose husbands garnered substantial

earnings, enabling them to drive their children to school rather than put them on a bus, enroll them in endless enrichment activities, oversee their educational careers, and prepare them for entry into elite colleges in order to win a leg-up in a competitive workforce. At the other extreme, homemaking was seen as the realm of the ultra-religious, where women accepted the role of Biblical "Help Meets" to their husbands. They cooked, cleaned, toiled, served and remained silent and powerless. My husband and I fell into neither category, and I suspected there were more like us.

■ Meet the Radical Homemakers

I was right. I received hundreds of letters from rural, suburban, and city folks alike. Some ascribed to specific religious faiths, others did not. As long as the home showed no signs of domination or oppression, I was interested in learning more about them. I selected twenty households from my pile, plotted them on a map across the United States, and set about visiting each of them to see what homemaking could look like when men and women shared both power and responsibility. Curious to see if Radical Homemaking was a venture suited to more than just women in married couples, I visited with single parents, stay-at-home dads, widows, and divorcées. I spent time in families with and without children.

A glance into America's past suggests that homemaking could play a big part in addressing the ecological, economic and social crises of our present time. Homemakers have played a powerful role during several critical periods in our nation's history. By making use of locally available resources, they made the boycotts leading up to the American Revolution possible. They played a critical role in the foundational civic education required to launch a young democratic nation. They were driving forces behind both the abolition and suffrage movements.

Homemakers today could have a similar influence. The Radical Homemakers I interviewed had chosen to make family, community, social justice, and the health of the planet the governing principles of their lives. They rejected any form of labor or the expenditure of any resource that did not honor these tenets. For about 5,000 years, our culture has been hostage to a form of organization by domination that fails to honor our living systems, under which "he who holds the gold makes the rules." By contrast, the Radical Homemakers are using life skills and relationships as replacements for gold, on the premise that he or she who doesn't need the gold can change the rules. The greater one's domestic skills, be they to plant a garden, grow tomatoes on an apartment balcony, mend a shirt, repair an appliance, provide one's own entertainment, cook and preserve a local harvest, or care for children and loved ones, the less dependent one is on the gold.

By virtue of these skills, the Radical Homemakers I interviewed were building a great bridge from our existing extractive economy—where corporate wealth has been regarded as the foundation of economic health, where mining our Earth's resources and exploiting our international neighbors have been acceptable costs of doing business—to a life serving economy, where the goal is, in the words of David Korten, to generate a living for all, rather than a killing for a few; where our resources are sustained, our waters are kept clean, our air pure, and families and can lead meaningful lives. In situations where one person was still required to work out of the home in the conventional extractive economy, homemakers were able to redirect the family's financial, social and temporal resources toward building the life-serving economy. In most cases, however, the homemakers' skills were so considerable that, while members of the household might hold jobs (more often than not they ran their own businesses), the financial needs of the family were so small that no one in the family was forced to accept any employment that did not honor the four tenets of family, community, social justice and ecological sustainability.

While all the families had some form of income that entered their lives, they were not a privileged set by any means. Most of the families I interviewed were living with a sense of abundance at about 200 percent of the federal poverty level. That's a little over $40,000 for a family of four, about 37 percent below the national median family income, and 45 percent below the median income for married couple families. Some lived on considerably less, few had appreciably more. Not surprisingly, those with the lowest incomes had mastered the most domestic skills and had developed the most innovative approaches to living.

■ Rethinking the impossible

The Radical Homemakers were skilled at the mental exercise of rethinking the "givens" of our society and coming to the following conclusions: nobody (who matters) cares what (or if) you drive; housing does not have to cost more than a single moderate income can afford (and can even cost less); it is okay to accept help from family and friends, to let go of the perceived ideal of independence and strive instead for interdependence; health can be achieved without making monthly payments to an insurance company; child care is not a fixed cost; education can be acquired for free; and retirement is possible, regardless of income.

> As for domestic skills, the range of talents held by these households was as varied as the day is long. Many kept gardens, but not all. Some gardened on city rooftops, some on country acres, some in suburban yards. Some were wizards at car and appliance repairs. Others could sew. Some could build and fix houses; some kept livestock. Others crafted furniture, played music, or wrote. All could cook. (Really well, as my waistline will attest.) None of them could do everything. No one was completely self-sufficient, an independent island separate from the rest of the world. Thus the universal skills that they all possessed were far more complex than simply knowing how to can green beans or build a root cellar. In order to make it as homemakers, these people had to be wizards at nurturing relationships and working with family and community. They needed an intimate understanding of the life-serving economy, where a paycheck is not always exchanged for all services rendered. They needed to be their own teachers—to

pursue their educations throughout life, forever learning new ways to do more, create more, give more.

In addition, the happiest among them were successful at setting realistic expectations for themselves. They did not live in impeccably clean houses on manicured estates. They saw their homes as living systems and accepted the flux, flow, dirt, and chaos that are a natural part of that. They were masters at redefining pleasure not as something that should be bought in the consumer marketplace, but as something that could be created, no matter how much or how little money they had in their pockets. And above all, they were fearless. They did not let themselves be bullied by the conventional ideals regarding money, status, or material possessions. These families did not see their homes as a refuge from the world. Rather, each home was the center for social change, the starting point from which a better life would ripple out for everyone.

Home is where the great change will begin. It is not where it ends. Once we feel sufficiently proficient with our domestic skills, few of us will be content to simply practice them to the end of our days. Many of us will strive for more, to bring more beauty to the world, to bring about greater social change, to make life better for our neighbors, to contribute our creative powers to the building of a new, brighter, more sustainable, and happier future. That is precisely the great work we should all be tackling. If we start by focusing our energies on our domestic lives, we will do more than reduce our ecological impact and help create a living for all. We will craft a safe, nurturing place from which this great creative work can happen.

READING AND WRITING

1. How does Hayes define "homemaking"? Does this definition include any gender-based criteria? How does it compare with Catharine E. Beecher's definition of a "housekeeper" in "On the Preservation of a Good Temper in a Housekeeper"?
2. According to Hayes, radical homemakers subvert the housewife syndrome described by Betty Friedan in 1963. How do they accomplish this? How are the radical homemakers Hayes encounters different than the homemakers Freidan describes?
3. Compare the "radical homemaker" identity that Hayes explores in her article with the domestic portraits that emerge from Marge Piercy's poem "What's that smell in the kitchen?" and the Jody Miller/Mary Taylor song "Queen of the House" (in Chapter 5). What do these texts have in common? Which do you find to be the most compelling? Why?

USING RESEARCH

4. Hayes is the host of two websites, grassfedcooking.com and radicalhomemakers.com. Choose one of these sites, take some time to explore its contents, and write a brief rhetorical analysis of the site. Who do you think Hayes identifies as her audience? How does she appeal to her readers? What do you see as her purpose? How does Hayes come across as the "author" of the site?

■ RESEARCH AND WRITING PROJECTS

1. The readings in the chapter are split almost evenly between those that examine expectations of and roles available to women in the United States and those that deal with similar issues affecting women elsewhere in the world. Use the library's resources and the internet to explore more thoroughly how gender roles and expectations differ in four countries or regions outside the United States. From this research, compile an annotated bibliography of the useful and interesting sources you have found. Finally, compose a 300-word introduction in which you contextualize your annotated bibliography and characterize your sources.

2. Based on the reading you have done in this chapter, craft a formal definition of "feminism." Then, research the library's databases and the internet to find other definitions of the term as it is used in academia, politics, and public discourse. What do these definitions have in common? How are they different? What does this tell you about the complexity of the term?

3. Many of the texts in this chapter present implicit arguments. Choose one of these texts and write an essay in which you make the implicit argument explicit. Because you are not writing a memoir essay, you will have to identify the argument in the original text and then develop an explicit claim of your own. You will also have to conduct research to find sources to support your position.

4. In "The Women's Crusade," Nicholas D. Kristof and Sheryl WuDunn allude to Nobel Prize-winning economist Amartya Sen's 1990 essay "More Than 100 Million Women Are Missing" as they make their case that "the paramount moral challenge" of the 21st century "is the brutality inflicted on so many women and girls around the globe." Find Sen's piece online and use it to write an essay in which you compare and analyze his argument with Kristof and WuDunn's. You should note that this is not a traditional compare-and-contrast assignment. While you should recognize the surface similarities and differences between the

two texts, your focus should be on analyzing the rhetorical choices the authors make as they try to move and persuade their audiences. Think about each text's purpose and the rhetorical moves each author makes to try to achieve that purpose. Then, compare those moves and each text's effectiveness as an argument.

5. Many of the readings in this chapter, while they may focus on other persuasive or creative purposes, deal with definitions: What is a woman? A housekeeper, a homemaker, a mother, a feminist? Who can be a doctor or a lawyer? And most of the authors are interested in complicating, challenging, or rewriting traditional definitions. Using your work on these texts as a starting point, choose a traditionally defined gender role that is changing—as Shannon Hayes does with "homemaker"—and research the origins and evolution of that role. Then, compose an essay in which you argue for a redefinition of the role, based on your findings.

5

What's So Funny?

IMAGE 5.1

The readings collected here grapple with many of the same themes as those in previous chapters, but don't be surprised if they seem a bit different. They are, after all, meant to be funny. As you read these selections, reflect on the purpose and power of humor. Does encountering these issues through humor force you to think about them in a different way? It may seem risky to tackle serious subjects with humor, but the success of *The Onion* and humor writers like David Sedaris and Jill Conner Browne suggests that there is something to be gained from laughter. Put down the rubber chicken. There is a subtext in this silliness.

> The Onion *is a satirical news source that began as a print newspaper in Madison, Wisconsin, but that is now available online at TheOnion.com. The following article was published March 9, 2010.*

NATION SHUDDERS AT LARGE BLOCK OF UNINTERRUPTED TEXT *The Onion*

WASHINGTON—Unable to rest their eyes on a colorful photograph or boldface heading that could be easily skimmed and forgotten about, Americans collectively recoiled Monday when confronted with a solid block of uninterrupted text.

Dumbfounded citizens from Maine to California gazed helplessly at the frightening chunk of print, unsure of what to do next. Without an illustration, chart, or embedded YouTube video to ease them in, millions were frozen in place, terrified by the sight of one long, unbroken string of English words.

"Why won't it just tell me what it's about?" said Boston resident Charlyne Thomson, who was bombarded with the overwhelming mass of black text late Monday afternoon. "There are no bullet points, no highlighted parts. I've looked everywhere—there's nothing here but words."

"Ow," Thomson added after reading the first and last lines in an attempt to get the gist of whatever the article, review, or possibly recipe was about.

At 3:16 p.m., a deafening sigh was heard across the country as the nation grappled with the daunting cascade of syllables, whose unfamiliar letter-upon-letter structure stretched on for an endless 500 words. Children wailed for the attention of their bewildered parents, businesses were shuttered, and local governments ground to a halt as Americans scanned the text in vain for a web link to click on.

Sources also reported a 450 percent rise in temple rubbing and under-the-breath cursing around this time.

"It demands so much of my time and concentration," said Chicago resident Dale Huza, who was confronted by the confusing mound of words early Monday afternoon. "This large block of text, it expects me to figure everything out on my own, and I hate it."

"I've never seen anything like it," said Mark Shelton, a high school teacher from St. Paul, MN who stared blankly at the page in front of him for several minutes before finally holding it up to his ear. "What does it want from us?"

As the public grows more desperate, scholars are working to randomly italicize different sections of the text, hoping the italics will land on the important parts and allow everyone to go on with their day. For now, though, millions of panicked and exhausted Americans continue to repetitively search the single column of print from top to bottom and right to left, looking for even the slightest semblance of meaning or perhaps a blurb.

Some have speculated that the never-ending flood of sentences may be a news article, medical study, urgent product recall notice, letter, user agreement, or even a binding contract of some kind. But until the news does a segment in which they take sections of the text and read them aloud in a slow, calm voice while highlighting those same words on the screen, no one can say for sure.

There are some, however, who remain unfazed by the virtual hailstorm of alternating consonants and vowels, and are determined to ignore it.

"I'm sure if it's important enough, they'll let us know some other way," Detroit local Janet Landsman said. "After all, it can't be that serious. If there were anything worthwhile buried deep in that block of impenetrable English, it would at least have an accompanying photo of a celebrity or a large humorous title containing a pop culture reference."

Added Landsman, "Whatever it is, I'm pretty sure it doesn't even have a point."

■ READING AND WRITING

1. What is being argued here? How can you tell?
2. How does this article use hyperbole? How does this technique help the author advance the argument?
3. What do you learn about the block of text in this article? What do you learn about the people who have encountered the text?
4. The large block of text is described as a "virtual hailstorm of alternating consonants and vowels." What does this mean? Do you think this accurately describes an encounter with an unfamiliar text?

■ DEVELOPING LONGER RESPONSES

5. *The Onion* quotes one person as saying: "Why won't it just tell me what it's about? … There are no bullet points, no highlighted parts. I've looked everywhere—there's nothing here but words." Compare this piece with "Is Google Making Us Stupid?" by Nicholas Carr and "Hooked on Technology" by Matt Richtel, both in Chapter 1. How does *The Onion* use humor to illustrate some of the same points that Carr and Richtel make? Which approach do you find more persuasive? Why?

> *Author, journalist, and master satirist Jonathan Swift (1667-1745) is best known for his novel* Gulliver's Travels. *An Irishman himself, Swift first published "A Modest Proposal" in 1729.*

A MODEST PROPOSAL Jonathan Swift

For preventing the children of poor people in Ireland, from being a burden on their parents or country, and for making them beneficial to the publick

It is a melancholy object to those who walk through this great town or travel in the country, when they see the streets, the roads, and cabin doors, crowded with beggars of the female-sex, followed by three, four, or six children, all in rags and importuning every passenger for an alms. These mothers, instead of being able to work for their honest livelihood, are forced to employ all their time in strolling to beg sustenance for their helpless infants, who, as they grow up, either turn thieves for want of work, or leave their dear native country to fight for the Pretender in Spain, or sell themselves to the Barbadoes.

I think it is agreed by all parties that this prodigious number of children in the arms, or on the backs, or at the heels of their mothers, and frequently of their fathers, is in the present deplorable state of the kingdom a very great additional grievance; and therefore whoever could find out a fair, cheap, and easy method of making these children sound, useful members of the commonwealth would deserve so well of the public as to have his statue set up for a preserver of the nation.

But my intention is very far from being confined to provide only for the children of professed beggars; it is of a much greater extent, and shall take in the whole number of infants at a certain age who are born of parents in effect as little able to support them as those who demand our charity in the streets.

As to my own part, having turned my thoughts for many years upon this important subject, and maturely weighed the several schemes of other projectors, I have always found them grossly mistaken in their computation. It is true, a child just dropped from its dam may be supported by her milk for a solar year, with little other nourishment; at most not above the value of two shillings, which the mother may certainly get, or the value in scraps, by her lawful occupation of begging; and it is exactly at one year old that I propose to provide for them in such a manner as instead of being a charge upon their parents or the parish, or wanting food and raiment for the rest of their lives, they shall on the contrary contribute to the feeding, and partly to the clothing, of many thousands.

There is likewise another great advantage in my scheme, that it will prevent those voluntary abortions, and that horrid practice of women murdering their bastard children, alas, too frequent among us, sacrificing the poor innocent babes, I doubt, more to avoid the expense than the shame, which would move tears and pity in the most savage and inhuman breast. The number of souls in this kingdom being usually reckoned one million and a half, of these I calculate there may be about two hundred thousand couple whose wives are breeders; from which number I subtract thirty thousand couples who are able to maintain their own children, although I apprehend there cannot be so many under the present distresses of the kingdom; but this being granted, there will remain an hundred and seventy thousand breeders. I again subtract fifty thousand for those women who miscarry, or whose children die by accident or disease within the year. There only remain an hundred and twenty thousand children of poor parents annually born. The question therefore is, how this number shall be reared and provided for, which, as I have already said, under the present situation of affairs, is utterly impossible by all the methods hitherto proposed. For we can neither employ them in handicraft or agriculture; we neither build houses (I mean in the country) nor cultivate land. They can very seldom pick up a livelihood by stealing till they arrive at six years old, except where they are of towardly parts; although I confess they learn the rudiments much earlier, during which time they can however be looked upon only as probationers, as I have been informed by a principal gentleman in the county of Cavan, who protested to me that he never knew above one or two instances under the age of six, even in a part of the kingdom so renowned for the quickest proficiency in that art.

I am assured by our merchants that a boy or a girl before twelve years old is no salable commodity; and even when they come to this age they will not yield above three pounds, or three pounds and half a crown at most on the Exchange; which cannot turn to account either to the parents or the kingdom, the charge of nutriment and rags having been at least four times that value.

I shall now therefore humbly propose my own thoughts, which I hope will not be liable to the least objection.

I have been assured by a very knowing American of my acquaintance in London, that a young healthy child well nursed is at a year old a most delicious, nourishing, and wholesome food, whether stewed, roasted, baked, or boiled; and I make no doubt that it will equally serve in a fricassee or a ragout.

I do therefore humbly offer it to public consideration that of the hundred and twenty thousand children, already computed, twenty thousand may be reserved for breed, whereof only one fourth part to be males, which is more than we allow to sheep, black cattle, or swine; and my reason is that these children are seldom the fruits of marriage, a circumstance not much regarded by our savages, therefore one male will be sufficient to serve four females. That the remaining hundred thousand may at a year old be offered in sale to the persons of quality and fortune through the kingdom, always advising the mother to let them suck plentifully in the last month, so as to render them plump and fat for a good table. A child will make two dishes at an entertainment for friends; and when the family dines alone, the fore or hind quarter will make a reasonable dish, and seasoned with a little pepper or salt will be very good boiled on the fourth day, especially in winter.

I have reckoned upon a medium that a child just born will weigh twelve pounds, and in a solar year if tolerably nursed increaseth to twenty-eight pounds.

I grant this food will be somewhat dear, and therefore very proper for landlords, who, as they have already devoured most of the parents, seem to have the best title to the children.

Infant's flesh will be in season throughout the year, but more plentiful in March, and a little before and after. For we are told by a grave author, an eminent French physician, that fish being a prolific diet, there are more children born in Roman Catholic countries about nine months after Lent than at any other season; therefore, reckoning a year after Lent, the markets will be more glutted than usual, because the number of popish infants is at least three to one in this kingdom; and therefore it will have one other collateral advantage, by lessening the number of Papists among us.

I have already computed the charge of nursing a beggar's child (in which list I reckon all cottagers, laborers, and four fifths of the farmers) to be about two shillings per annum, rags included; and I believe no gentleman would repine to give ten shillings for the carcass of a good fat child, which, as I have said, will make four dishes of excellent nutritive meat, when he hath only some particular friend or his own family to dine with him. Thus the squire will learn to be a good landlord, and grow popular among the tenants; the mother will have eight shillings net profit, and be fit for work till she produces another child.

Those who are more thrifty (as I must confess the times require) may flay the carcass; the skin of which artificially dressed will make admirable gloves for ladies, and summer boots for fine gentlemen.

As to our city of Dublin, shambles may be appointed for this purpose in the most convenient parts of it, and butchers we may be assured will not be wanting; although I rather recommend buying the children alive, and dressing them hot from the knife as we do roasting pigs.

A very worthy person, a true lover of his country, and whose virtues I highly esteem, was lately pleased in discoursing on this matter to offer a refinement upon my scheme. He said that many gentlemen of this kingdom, having of late destroyed their deer, he conceived that the want of venison might be well supplied by the bodies of young lads and maidens, not exceeding fourteen years of age nor under twelve, so great a number of both sexes in every county being now ready to starve for want of work and service; and these to be disposed of by their parents, if alive, or otherwise by their nearest relations. But with due deference to so excellent a friend and so deserving a patriot, I cannot be altogether in his sentiments; for as to the males, my American acquaintance assured me from frequent experience that their flesh was generally tough and lean, like that of our schoolboys, by continual exercise, and their taste disagreeable; and to fatten them would not answer the charge. Then as to the females, it would, I think with humble submission, be a loss to the public, because they soon would become breeders themselves: and besides, it is not improbable that some scrupulous people might be apt to censure such a practice (although indeed very unjustly) as a little bordering upon cruelty; which, I confess, hath always been with me the strongest objection against any project, how well soever intended.

But in order to justify my friend, he confessed that this expedient was put into his head by the famous Psalmanazar, a native of the island Formosa, who came from thence to London above twenty years ago, and in conversation told my friend that in his country when any young person happened to be put to death, the executioner sold the carcass to persons of quality as a prime dainty; and that in his time the body of a plump girl of fifteen, who was crucified for an attempt to poison the emperor, was sold to his Imperial Majesty's prime minister of state, and other great mandarins of the court, in joints from the gibbet, at four hundred crowns. Neither indeed can I deny that if the same use were made of several plump young girls in this town, who without one single groat to their fortunes cannot stir abroad without a chair, and appear at the playhouse and assemblies in foreign fineries which they never will pay for, the kingdom would not be the worse.

Some persons of a desponding spirit are in great concern about that vast number of poor people who are aged, diseased, or maimed, and I have been desired to employ my thoughts what course may be taken to ease the nation of so grievous an encumbrance. But I am not in the least pain upon that matter, because it is very well known that they are every day dying and rotting by cold and famine, and filth and vermin, as fast as can be reasonably expected. And as to the younger laborers, they are now in almost as hopeful a condition. They cannot get work, and consequently pine away for want of nourishment to a degree that if at any time they are accidentally hired to common labor, they have not strength to perform it; and thus the country and themselves are happily delivered from the evils to come.

I have too long digressed, and therefore shall return to my subject. I think the advantages by the proposal which I have made are obvious and many, as well as of the highest importance.

For first, as I have already observed, it would greatly lessen the number of Papists, with whom we are yearly overrun, being the principal breeders of the nation as well as our most dangerous enemies; and who stay at home on purpose to deliver the kingdom to the Pretender, hoping to take their advantage by the absence of so many good Protestants, who have chosen rather to leave their country than to stay at home and pay tithes against their conscience to an Episcopal curate.

Secondly, the poorer tenants will have something valuable of their own, which by law may be made liable to distress, and help to pay their landlord's rent, their corn and cattle being already seized and money a thing unknown.

Thirdly, whereas the maintenance of an hundred thousand children, from two years old and upwards, cannot be computed at less than ten shillings a piece per annum, the nation's stock will be thereby increased fifty thousand pounds per annum, besides the profit of a new dish introduced to the tables of all gentlemen of fortune in the kingdom who have any refinement in taste. Arid the money will circulate among ourselves, the goods being entirely of our own growth and manufacture.

Fourthly, the constant breeders, besides the gain of eight shillings sterling per annum by the sale of their children, will be rid of the charge of maintaining them after the first year.

Fifthly, this food would likewise bring great custom to taverns, where the vintners will certainly be so prudent as to procure the best receipts for dressing it to perfection, and consequently have their houses frequented by all the fine gentlemen, who justly value themselves upon their knowledge in good eating; and a skillful cook, who understands how to oblige his guests, will contrive to make it as expensive as they please.

Sixthly, this would be a great inducement to marriage, which all wise nations have either encouraged by rewards or enforced by laws and penalties. It would increase the care and tenderness of mothers toward their children, when they were sure of a settlement for life to the poor babes, provided in some sort by the public, to their annual profit instead of expense. We should see an honest emulation among the married women, which of them could bring the fattest child to the market. Men would become as fond of their wives during the time of their pregnancy as they. are now of their mares in foal, their cows in calf, or sows when they are ready to farrow; nor offer to beat or kick them (as is too frequent a practice) for fear of a miscarriage.

Many other advantages might be enumerated. For instance, the addition of some thousand carcasses in our exportation of barreled beef, the propagation of swine's flesh, and improvement in the art of making good bacon, so much wanted among us by the great destruction of pigs, too frequent at our tables, which are no way comparable in taste or magnificence to a well-grown, fat, yearling child, which roasted whole will make a considerable figure at a lord mayor's feast – or any other public entertainment. But this and many others I omit, being studious of brevity.

Supposing that one thousand families in this city would be constant customers for infants' flesh, besides others who might have it at merry meetings, particularly weddings and christenings, I compute that Dublin would take off annually about twenty thousand carcasses, and the rest of the kingdom (where probably they will be sold somewhat cheaper) the remaining eighty thousand.

I can think of no one objection that will possibly be raised against this proposal, unless it should be urged that the number of people will be thereby much lessened in the kingdom. This I freely own, and it was in deed one principal design in offering it to the world. I desire the reader will observe, that I calculate my remedy for this one individual kingdom of Ireland and for no other that ever was, is, or I think ever can be upon earth. Therefore let no man talk to me of other expedients: of taxing our absentees at five shillings a pound: of using neither clothes nor household furniture except what is of our own growth and manufacture: of utterly rejecting the materials and instruments that promote foreign luxury: of curing the expensiveness of pride, vanity, idleness, and gaming in our women: of introducing a vein of parsimony, prudence, and Temperance: of learning to love our country, in the want of which we differ even from Laplanders and the inhabitants of Topinamboo: of quitting our animosities and factions, nor acting any longer like the Jews, who were murdering one another at the very moment their city was taken: of being a little cautious not to sell our country and conscience for nothing: of teaching landlords to have at least one degree of mercy toward their tenants: lastly, of putting a spirit of honesty, industry, and skill into our shopkeepers; who, if a resolution could now be taken to buy only our native goods, would immediately unite to cheat and exact upon us in the price, the measure, and the goodness, nor could ever yet be brought to make one fair proposal of just dealing, though often and earnestly invited to it.

Therefore I repeat, let no man talk to me of these and the like expedients, till he hath at least some glimpse of hope that there will ever be some hearty and sincere attempt to put them in practice.

But as to myself, having been wearied out for many years with offering vain, idle, visionary thoughts, and at length utterly despairing of success, I fortunately fell upon this proposal, which, as it is wholly new, so it hath something solid and real, of no expense and little trouble, full in our own power, and whereby we can incur no danger in disobliging England. For this kind of commodity will not bear exportation, the flesh being of too tender a consistence to admit a long continuance in salt, although perhaps I could name a country which would be glad to eat up our whole nation without it.

After all, I am not so violently bent upon my own opinion as to reject any offer proposed by wise men, which shall be found equally innocent, cheap, easy, and effectual. But before something of that kind shall be advanced in contradiction to my scheme, and offering a better, I desire the author or authors will be pleased maturely to consider two points. First, as things now stand, how they will be able to find food and raiment for an hundred thousand useless mouths and backs. And secondly, there being a round million of creatures in human figure throughout this kingdom, whose sole subsistence put into a common stock would leave them in debt two millions of pounds sterling, adding those who are beggars by profession to the bulk of farmers, cottagers, and laborers, with their wives and children who are beggars in effect; I desire those politicians who dislike my overture, and may perhaps be so bold to attempt an answer, that they will first ask the parents of these mortals whether they would not at this day think it a great happiness to have been sold for food at a year old in the manner I prescribe, and thereby have avoided such a perpetual scene of misfortunes as they have since gone through by the oppression of landlords, the impossibility of paying rent without money or trade, the want of common sustenance, with neither house nor clothes to cover them from the inclemencies of the weather, and the most inevitable prospect of entailing the like or greater miseries upon their breed forever.

I profess, in the sincerity of my heart, that I have not the least personal interest in endeavoring to promote this necessary work, having no other motive than the public good of my country, by advancing our trade, providing for infants, relieving the poor, and giving some pleasure to the rich. I have no children by which I can propose to get a single penny; the youngest being nine years old, and my wife past childbearing.

■ READING AND WRITING

1. What is the problem that Swift's "proposal" seeks to solve? What other potential solutions does he dismiss? How does he argue against them? What, ultimately, is Swift's point?
2. Is "A Modest Proposal" a successful argument? Why or why not? What sort of "evidence" does Swift use to support his position?
3. How would you classify this type of humor? Does Swift use irony, parody, or something else?

■ USING RESEARCH

4. Humor theory identifies two types of satire: Juvenalian and Horatian. Research these two categories and briefly explain each. Then, classify "A Modest Proposal" as either Juvenalian or Horatian, citing examples from the text to support your position.
5. To fully understand historical uses of humor, it often helps to research the context in which particular humorous texts were produced and received. Use the resources available though the library and online to learn more about Ireland at the time of Swift's writing and about the initial reception history of Swift's essay (did its first readers understand the joke?). Based on this research, provide some historical context for "A Modest Proposal," its purpose, and its intended audience. How does your research illuminate your reading of the text?

Barbara Kingsolver is the author of many books, including The Poisonwood Bible. *The following piece is from her* New York Times *bestseller* Animal, Vegetable, Miracle: A Year of Food Life, *written with her husband, Steven L. Hopp, and her daughter, Camille. In this memoir,* Kingsolver *charts her family's efforts to live completely off the land for one year, forsaking prepared foods and anything unavailable in their own garden or small neighborhood. This excerpt deals with her youngest daughter Lily's desire for a rooster in her chicken coop.*

excerpt from
ZUCCHINI LARCENY   Barbara Kingsolver

In summer a young rooster's fancy turns to . . . how can I say this delicately? The most ham-fisted attempts at courtship I've ever had to watch. (And yes, I'm including high school.) As predicted, half of Lily's chick crop was growing up to be male. This was dawning on everyone as the boys began to venture into mating experiments, climbing aboard the ladies sometimes backwards or perfectly sideways. The young hens shrugged them off and went on looking for bugs in the grass. But the three older hens, mature birds we'd had around awhile, did not suffer fools gladly. Emmy, an elderly Jersey Giant, behaved as any sensible grandmother would if a teenager approached her looking for action: she bit him on the head and chased him into a boxwood bush.

These boys had much to learn, and not just the art of love. A mature, skillful rooster takes his job seriously as protector of the flock, using different vocal calls to alert his hens to food, aerial predators, or dangers on the ground. He leads his wives into the coop every evening at dusk. Lacking a proper coop, he'll coax them up onto a tree branch or other safe nighttime roost (hence, his name). The feminist in me balks to admit it, but a flock of free-range hens behaves very differently without a rooster: scattered, vulnerable, a witless wondering of lost souls. Of course, they're chickens. They have bird brains, evolved in polygamous flocks, and have lived for millennia with humans who reward docility and egg production. Modern hens of the sturdiest breeds can crank out an egg a day for months at a stretch (until winter days grow too short), and *that* they can do with no need for a fella. Large-scale egg operations keep artificial lights on their hens to extend the laying period, and they don't keep roosters at all. The standard white grocery-store egg is sterile. But in a barnyard where chickens forage and risk predation, flock behavior is more interesting when a guy is ruling the roost.

So Lily wanted one rooster, for flock protection and the chance to watch her hens hatch chicks next year. The position was open for a *good* rooster, not a bad one. Over the years we'd had both. Our historic favorite was Mr. Doodle. If a professional circuit had been open to him, as dogs have their sheepherding trials and such, we could have retired Mr. Doodle for stud. He had a keen eye for hen safety and a heart for justice. I saved caterpillars

I pulled off my garden so I could throw them into the chicken yard and watch Mr. Doodle run to snatch up each one, cock his head in judgment, and dole one out to each of six hens in turn before he started the next round. Any number of caterpillars not evenly divisible by six would set him into angst; he hated to play favorites.

But that was the ideal husband. The guys we had now were No-Second-Date. They're still young, we allowed. Even a dreamboat has to start somewhere, getting chased into the boxwood a time or two before finding his inner gentleman. We'd be watching our boys closely now as they played a real game of Survivor. All but one would end up on our table, and we couldn't get soft-hearted. Keeping multiple roosters is no kindness. They inevitably engage in a well-known sport that's illegal in forty-eight states.

Who would get to stay? The criteria are strict and varied: good alarm calls, unselfish instincts for foraging and roasting, and a decent demeanor toward humans. Sometimes an otherwise fine rooster will start attacking kids, a capital crime in our barnyard. And finally our winner would need a good singing voice. We'd be hearing his particular cock-a-doodle for more than a thousand mornings. Chanticleers, as the storybooks call them, are as diversely skilled as opera singers. We wanted a Pavarotti. Crowing skills are mostly genetic, arriving with developing male hormones. So far we'd heard nothing resembling a crow.

And then, one morning, we did. It was in July, soon after my summer-time ritual of moving our bedroom outside onto the screened sleeping porch. The summer nights are balmy and marvelous, though it's hard to sleep with so much going on after dark: crickets, katydids, and fireflies fill every visible and aural space. Screech owls send out their love calls. Deer sometimes startle us at close range with the strange nasal whiffle of their alarm call. And in the early hours of one morning, as I watched the forested hillside color itself in slow motion from gray to green, I heard what I thought must be a new Virginian species of frog: "Cro-oak!"

I woke Steven, as wives wake husbands everywhere, to ask: "What's that sound?"

I knew he wouldn't be annoyed, because this was no tedious burglary suspect — it was wildlife. He sat up, attentive. His research interest is bioacoustics: birdsong and other animal communication. He can identify any bird native to the eastern United States by ear, and can nail most insects, mammals, and amphibians at least to category. (Like most mortals, I cannot. I can mistake mammal calls for birds, and certain insects for power tools.) He offered a professional opinion on this pre-dawn croak: "Idunno."

As we listened, it became clear that two of them were having some kind of contest: "Cro-oa-oak!"

(A pause, for formulation of the response.)

"Cri-iggle-ick!"

Steven figured it out way ahead of me. These were our boys of summer. Yikes.

More rooster voices joined the choir as dawn crept over the ridge. Eventually one emerged as something of a leader, to which the other responded together in the call-and-response style of an old-time religious revival.

"Rrrr-arrr-orrrk!"

"Crii-iggle-ick!" "Cro-oak!" "Crr-rdle-rrr!"

We had on our hands what sounded like a newly opened Berlitz School for Rooster, which a teacher hired on a tight budget.

The girls heard us from downstairs, and came up to the sleeping porch to see what was so funny. Soon we were all flopped across the bed laughing after every chorus. Welcome to our funny farm. Did I say we were hoping for a Pavarotti? We had a gang of tone-deaf idol wannabes. For how many weeks would this harrowing audition go on before we could narrow the field of applicants? One outstanding contestant punctuated the end of his croak, every time, with a sort of burp: "Crr-rr-arrrr . . . *bluup!*"

This guy had a future in the culinary arts. Mine.

■ READING AND WRITING

1. How is the humor in this piece different from that in most of the other texts in this chapter? (Compare, for example, Kingsolver's humor with the satire of *The Onion* or Swift.) How, specifically, does Kingsolver use humor? What is its rhetorical effect? (Think, in particular, about her purpose and audience.)
2. Why does Kingsolver personify the male chicks? How does she describe them? What reasons does Kingsolver cite for wanting a rooster? Why would these reasons trouble her, as a feminist?
3. The food memoir is quickly becoming a recognizable genre in its own right, and some of these books, like Kingsolver's, use humor in their storytelling. Why might writers find a useful link between food and humor? What does humor do, rhetorically, for writers?

■ USING RESEARCH

4. Use the internet to learn more about Kingsolver's yearlong experiment in green living and local eating and about the locavore movement in general. Are all locavore adherents members of rural communities like Kingsolver and her family? Has Kingsolver's family maintained the lifestyle they worked so hard to create? What are the limitations and unique advantages of being a city-dweller and a locavore?

> P.J. O'Rourke is a journalist, humorist, and political commentator. His sixteenth
> book, Don't Vote: It Just Encourages the Bastards, *came out in September of
> 2010. He wrote this essay for the June 28, 1990, edition of* Rolling Stone.

THE GREENHOUSE AFFECT P. J. O'Rourke

If the great outdoors is so swell, how come the homeless aren't more fond of it?

There. ... I wanted to be the one person to say a discouraging word about Earth Day—a lone voice not crying in the wilderness, thank you, but hollering in the rec room.

On April 22nd—while everybody else was engaged in a great, smarmy fit of agreeing with himself about chlorofluorocarbons, while *tout le* rapidly-losing-plant-and-animal-species *monde* traded hugs of unanimity over plastic-milk-bottle recycling, while all of you praised one another to the ozone-depleted skies for your brave opposition to coastal flooding, and every man Jack and woman Jill told child Jason how bad it is to put crude oil on baby seals—I was home in front of the VCR snacking high on the food chain.

But can any decent, caring resident of this planet possibly disagree with the goals and aspirations embodied in the celebration of Earth Day? No.

That's what bothers me. Mass movements are always a worry. There's a whiff of the lynch mob or the lemming migration about any overlarge gathering of like-thinking individuals, no matter how virtuous their cause. Even a band of angels can turn ugly and start looting if enough angels are hanging around unemployed and convinced that the succubi own all the liquor stores in heaven.

Whenever I'm in the middle of conformity, surrounded by oneness of mind, with people oozing concurrence on every side, I get scared. And when I find myself agreeing with everybody, I get really scared.

Sometimes it's worse when everybody's right than when everybody's wrong. Everybody in fifteenth-century Spain was wrong about where China is, and, as a result, Columbus discovered Caribbean Vacations. On the other hand, everybody in fifteenth-century Spain was right about heresies: they're heretical. But that didn't make the Spanish inquisition more fun for the people who were burned at the stake.

A mass movement that's correct is especially dangerous when it's right about a problem that needs fixing. Then all those masses in the mass movement have to be called into action, and that call to action better be exciting, or the masses will lose interest and wander off to play arcade games. What's exciting? Monitoring the release into the atmosphere of glycol ethers used in the manufacture of brake-fluid and anti-icing additives? No. But what about some violence, an enemy, someone to hate?

Mass movements need what Eric Hoffer—in *The True Believer,* his book about the creepy misfits who join mass movements—calls a unifying agent.

"Hatred is the most accessible and comprehensive of all unifying agents," writes Hoffer. "Mass movements can rise and spread without belief in a God, but never without belief in a devil." Hoffer goes on to cite historian F.A. Voigt's accounts of a Japanese mission sent to Berlin in 1932 to study the National Socialist movement. Voigt asked a member of the mission what he thought. He replied, "It is magnificent. I wish we could have something like it in Japan, only we can't, because we haven't got any Jews."

The environmental movement has, I'm afraid, discovered a unifying agent. I almost said "scapegoat," but scapegoats are probably an endangered species. Besides, all animals are innocent, noble, upright, honest, and fair in their dealings, and have a great sense of humor. Anyway, the environmentalist movement has found its necessary enemy in the form of that ubiquitous evil—already so familiar to Hollywood scriptwriters, pulp-paperback authors, minority spokespersons, feminists, members of ACT UP, the Christic Institute, and Democratic candidates for president: Big Business.

Now, you might think Big Business would be hard to define in this day of leveraged finances and interlocking technologies. Not so. Big Business is every kind of business except the kind from which the person who's complaining draws his pay. Thus the Rock Around the Rain Forest crowd imagines that record companies are a cottage industry. The Sheen family considers movie conglomerates to be a part of the arts and crafts movement. And Ralph Nader thinks the wholesale lobbying of Congress by huge tax-exempt, public-interest advocacy groups is akin to working the family farm.

This is why it's rarely an identifiable person (and, of course, never you or me) who pollutes. It's a vague, sinister, faceless thing called "industry." The National Wildlife Federation's booklet on toxic-chemical releases says, "industry dumped more than 2.3 billion pounds of toxic chemicals into or onto the land." What will "industry" do next? Visit us with a plague of boils? Make off with our firstborn? Or maybe it will wreck the Barcalounger. "Once durable products like furniture are made to fall apart quickly, requiring more frequent replacement," claims the press kit of Inform, a New York-based environmental group that seems to be missing a few sunflower seeds from its mix. But even a respectable old establishmentarian organization like the Sierra Club is not above giving a villainous and conspiratorial cast to those who disagree with its legislative agenda. "For the past eight years, this country's major polluters and their friends in the Reagan administration and Congress have impeded the progress of bills introduced by congressional Clean Air advocates," says the Sierra Club's 1989-90 conservation-campaign press package. And here at *Rolling Stone*—where we are so opposed to the profit motive that we work for free, refuse to accept advertising, and give the magazine away at newsstands—writer Trip Gabriel, in his RS 571 article "Coming Back to Earth: A Look at Earth Day 1990" avers, "The yuppie belief in the sanctity of material possessions, no matter what the cost in resource depletion, squared perfectly with the philosophy of the Reaganites—to exploit the nation's natural resources for the sake of business."

Sure, "business" and "industry" and "their friends in the Reagan administration and Congress" make swell targets. Nobody squirts sulfur dioxide into the air as a hobby or tosses PCBs into rivers as an act of charity. Pollution occurs in the course of human enterprise. It is a byproduct of people making things like a living, including yours. If we desire, for ourselves and our progeny, a world that's not too stinky and carcinogenic, we're going to need the technical expertise, entrepreneurial vigor, and marketing genius of every business and industry. And if you think pollution is the fault only of Reaganite yuppies wallowing in capitalist greed, then go take a deep breath in Smolensk or a long drink from the river Volga.

Sorry, but business and industry—trade and manufacture—are inherent to civilization. Every human society, no matter how wholesomely primitive, practices as much trade and manufacturing as it can figure out. It is the fruits of trade and manufacturing that raise us from the wearying muck of subsistence and give us the health, wealth, education, leisure, and warm, dry rooms with Xerox machines—all of which allow us to be the ecology-conscious, selfless, splendid individuals we are.

Our ancestors were too busy wresting a living from nature to go on any nature hikes. The first European ever known to have climbed a mountain for the view was the poet Petrarch. That wasn't until the fourteenth century. And when Petrarch got to the top of Mont Ventoux, be opened a copy of Saint Augustine's *Confessions* and was shamed by the passage about men "who go to admire the high mountains and the immensity of the oceans and the course of the heaven ... and neglect themselves." Worship of nature may be ancient, but seeing nature as cuddlesome, hug-a-bear, and too cute for words is strictly a modern fashion.

The Luddite side of the environmental movement would have us destroy or eschew technology—throw down the ladder by which we climbed. Well, nuts (and berries and fiber) to you, you shrub huggers. It's time we in the industrialized nations admitted what safe, comfortable and fun-filled lives we lead. If we don't, we will cause irreparable harm to the disadvantaged peoples of the world. They're going to laugh themselves to death listening to us whine.

Contempt for material progress is not only funny but unfair. The average Juan, Chang, or Mobutu out there in the parts of the world where every day is Earth Day—or Dirt and Squalor Day anyhow—would like to have a color television too. He'd also like some comfy Reeboks, a Nintendo Power Glove, and a Jeep Cherokee. And he means to get them. I wouldn't care to be the skinny health-food nut waving a copy of *50 Simple Things You Can Do to Save the Earth* who tries to stand in his way.

There was something else keeping me indoors on April 22nd. Certain eco-doomsters are not only unreasonable in their attitude toward business, they're unreasonable in their attitude toward reason. I can understand harboring a mistrust of technology. I myself wouldn't be inclined to wash my dog in toluene or picnic in the nude at Bhopal. But to deny the validity of the scientific method is to resign your position as a sentient being. You'd better go look for work as a lungwort plant or an Eastern-European Communist-party chairman.

For example, here we have the environmental movement screeching like New Kids on the Block fans because President Bush asked for a bit more scientific research on global warming before we cork everybody's Honda, ban the use of underarm deodorants, and replace all the coal fuel in our electrical generating plants with windmills. The greenhouse effect is a complex hypothesis. You can hate George Bush as much as you like and the thing won't get simpler. "The most dire predictions about global warming are being toned down by many experts," said a *Washington Post* story last January. And that same month the *New York Times* told me a new ice age was only a couple of thousand years away.

On the original Earth Day, in 1970—when the world was going to end from overcrowding instead of overheating—the best-selling author of *The Population Bomb*,

Dr. Paul Ehrlich predicted that America would have water rationing by 1974 and food rationing by 1980; that hepatitis and dysentery rates in the United States would increase by 500 percent due to population density; that the oceans could be as dead as Lake Erie by 1979. Today Lake Erie is doing better than Perrier, and Dr. Ehrlich is still pounding sand down a rat hole.

Now, don't get me wrong: Even registered Republicans believe ecological problems are real. Real solutions will not be found through pop hysteria or the merchandising of panic. Genuine hard-got knowledge is required. The collegiate idealists who stuff the ranks of the environmental movement seem willing to do absolutely anything except take science courses and learn something about it. In 1971, American universities awarded 4390 doctorates in the physical sciences. After fifteen years of youthful fretting over the planet's future, the number was 3551.

It wouldn't even be all that expensive to make the world clean and prosperous. According to the September 1989 issue of *Scientific American*, which was devoted to scholarly articles about ecological issues, the cost of achieving sustainable and environmentally healthy worldwide economic development by the year 2000 would be about $729 billion. That's roughly fourteen dollars per person per year for ten years. To translate that into sandal-and-candle terms, $729 billion is less than the world spends annually on armaments.

The Earth can be saved, but not by legislative fiat. Expecting President Bush to cure global warming by sending a bill to Congress is to subscribe to that eternal fantasy of totalitarians and Democrats from Massachusetts: a law against bad weather.

Sometimes I wonder if the fans of Eco-Armageddon even want the world's problems to get better. Improved methods of toxic chemical incineration, stack-scrubbers for fossil-fuel powered plants, and sensible solid-waste management schemes lack melodramatic appeal. There's nothing apocalyptic about gasahol. And it's hard to picture a Byronic hero sorting his beer bottles by color at the recycling center. The beliefs of some environmentalists seem to have little to do with the welfare of the globe or its inhabitants and a lot to do with the parlor primitivism of the Romantic Movement.

There is this horrible idea, beginning with Jean Jacques Rousseau and still going strong in college classrooms, that natural man is naturally good. All we have to is strip away the neuroses, repressions, and Dial soap of modern society, and mankind will return to an Edenic state. Anybody who's ever met a toddler knows this is soy-protein baloney. Neolithic man was not a guy who always left his campsite cleaner than he found it. Ancient humans trashed half the map with indiscriminate use of fire for slash-and-burn agriculture and hunting drives. They caused desertification through overgrazing and firewood cutting in North Africa, the Middle East, and China. And they were responsible for the extinction of mammoths, mastodons, cave bears, giant sloths, New World camels and horses, and thousands of other species. Their record on women's issues and minority rights wasn't so hot either. You can return to nature, go back to leading the simple, fulfilling life of the hunter-gatherer if you want, but don't let me catch you poking around in my garbage cans for food.

Then there are the Beasts-Are-Our-Buddies types. I've got a brochure from the International Fund for Animal Welfare containing a section called "Highlights of IFAW's History," and I quote: "1978—Campaign to save iguanas from cruelty in Nicaraguan marketplaces—people sew animals' mouths shut."

Nineteen-seventy-eight was the middle of the Nicaraguan civil war. This means that while the evil dirtsack Somoza was shooting it out with the idiot Marxist Sandinistas, the International Fund for Animal Welfare was flying somebody to besieged Managua to check on lizard lips.

The neo-hippie-dips, the sentimentality-crazed iguana anthropomorphizers, the Chicken Littles, the three-bong-hit William Blakes—thank God these people don't actually go outdoors much, or the environment would be even worse than it is already.

But ecology's fools don't upset me. It's the wise guys I'm leery of. Tyranny is implicit in the environmental movement. Although Earth Day participants are going to be surprised to hear themselves accused of fascist tendencies, dictatorship is the unspoken agenda of every morality-based political campaign. Check out Moslem fundamentalists or the right-to-lifers. Like abortion opponents and Iranian imams, the environmentalists have the right to tell the rest of us what to do because they are morally correct and we are not. Plus the tree squeezers care more, which makes them an elite—an aristocracy of mushiness. They know what's good for us even when we're too lazy or shortsighted to snip plastic six-pack collars so sea turtles won't strangle.

READING AND WRITING

1. Explain the significance of the title of this essay.
2. According to O'Rourke, who are "ecology's fools"? Why are they of less concern to him than "the wise guys" and others he points to in his essay?
3. What do you think would be O'Rourke's ideal Earth Day? Provide textual evidence to support your response.

DEVELOPING LONGER RESPONSES

4. Write a rebuttal to this essay, taking care to articulate your claims in a stylistic mode that matches O'Rourke's.

USING RESEARCH

5. O'Rourke mentions many other texts, political groups, and events in his essay. Extensively research one such reference. How does your new knowledge of this item influence your reading of O'Rourke's article? What purpose does O'Rourke's references serve?

Despite their inauspicious debut in a St. Patrick's Day parade, the Sweet Potato Queens of Jackson, Mississippi, have developed a worldwide following. "Boss Queen" Jill Conner Browne is the author of eight books detailing the lives and loves of the Queens (each of whom goes by the moniker "Tammy"). What follows is the first chapter from the "wedding" side of Browne's reversible book, The Sweet Potato Queens' Wedding Planner/Divorce Guide.

PRE-WED   Jill Conner Browne

One of the Queens, TammyPippa, owns an architectural salvage company, Backroads Architecturals. This delicate flower of womanhood goes out and tears down old houses and buildings with her own hands and hauls off the good parts to sell to home-building folks with good taste. (Her husband, Charles, does help out.) In one of the fine old houses she was deconstructing, TammyPippa discovered a little paperback book that no doubt had been hidden away because of the shocking nature of its contents. Called *The Book of Nature*, this thin tract was written and sold in the early 1920s for a dollar. The cover notes proclaim it to be for "the married and those intending to marry—a complete explanation of all." TammyPippa called me immediately.

I raced over to pick up the book and found *plenty* of explanations I've been wanting for quite some time. I was expecting to sleep much sounder in the future after getting all my troubling questions answered and all. I also expected to acquire the knowledge to settle a number of unduly vexing issues for you, my readers.

I knew in the opening pages of the book that I had come to the right place. The author, *a guy,* stated that some *other guy* had possibly exaggerated when he said that the reproduction of the species is the only duty a woman has to fulfill in human society. Hmmmm? That *other* guy gave me pause, I gotta tell you. I'm thinking, okay, fine, have it your way, buckwheat. We'll reproduce 'em, and then we will be punching out. Everything else— *everything else*—is now your problem. Since you're so fucking smart, here's a bunch of babies for you. We're going out for margaritas and then we'll be napping. We've fulfilled our duty to society. Good luck with them kids!

To smooth things over, the author wrote that he personally thinks that there are women who have brains as well as ovaries. He was not making a rash, blanket statement of generalization, of course, but simply conceding that it might've happened sometime, somewhere. There are whole piles of women who never have children, he opined, but care for the children of others and thereby may be performing an even greater service than the actual production of children.

What makes me even crazier than reading this kinda crap from some *guy*--even if it was written eighty years ago—is seeing women still buying into it *today*! Young girls are still going off to college with not a thought in their heads about getting an education that will lead to an actual *job* so they can go out into the world as self-actualized, self-supporting people. There are far too many enrolled in Pre-Wed, only to survey the crop of prospective husbands who might be manipulated, cajoled, or otherwise convinced to support them for the rest of their lives—men who'll simply take up where Daddy left off.

I know a little about this kind of thinking. Remember, my own personal financial plan for the future was that my daddy would live forever. I never considered interviewing other potential candidates for the position, and I certainly never thought about taking care of my ownself. As far as I was concerned, Daddy had a lifetime appointment, and his lifetime would naturally coincide with my own. When all of a sudden *his* life was over, there I was with a whole bunch of my life left and no Daddy to finance or direct it. Huh? Now, there's a quandary for you, right there.

So what did I do? The only thing I thought I *could* do—I looked for another man to take his place! Let me just tell you, if you find yourself in a similar situation now or ever, *this ain't the answer*. In fact, it is the very antithesis of the answer.

Now, don't misunderstand me. There's a cosmic difference between having someone who supports you and fixes things and handles all the pesky details of the financial side of life and *believing* that you *need* someone to support you and fix things and handle all the pesky details. Hunny, I am all for sitting on your ass and being waited on hand and foot—it's great work if you can get it—as long as you know, firsthand, that you could do it for your ownself, should the need or desire ever arise.

Because, lemme tell you something else I learned the very hard way: Every potential husband is a potential ex-husband or even a potential *dead* husband, and you need a plan just in case either scenario develops down the road. And sometimes (make that *usually*), whether he leaves your life upright or feet first, he leaves behind a big ole mess, and who do you think gets to clean it up all by herself? Don't be looking around. It's you, sweetie.

Remember how you felt as a teenager, chafing against your parents but having to do what they said because of the "my house, my rules" deal? And how as a young adult, you still had to please them some to hang on to their support because you just couldn't make it on your own yet? Remember how that felt? Well, imagine that you're forty and have no education. You quit school to get married, and you haven't had a paying job in twenty years. You've got one or two children and a fair amount of debt, and your husband is a screaming asshole. Yet the thought of leaving is more terrifying than the thought of staying—because you're totally dependent on him.

If you're gonna go to college for Pre-Wed, I insist that you also take a full course in Pre-Death/Pre-Divorce and get yourself an education that will prepare you for the "unthinkable situation"   taking care of yourself and possibly a bunch of children by yourself for a large part of your life. You'll sleep a whole lot better, I promise. Parents will sleep better, too, if they help their children learn this.

■ Groom Selection Process

Once you're living in the world of reality, you're ready to think about the Groom Selection Process. Our precious Queen Loni had a fascinating screening process, which she used with felicitous results for quite some time. Loni had the great good fortune to live near a very gifted psychic named Bonnie, who could "read" photographs of people and was never known to err. Bob was the guy du jour in Loni's life, and she wanted Bonnie's stamp of approval on him—or *not*, as it were. So the next time Bob came over, Loni told him her daughter, Jackie, had just gotten a new camera and would Bob mind too much, you know, humoring the ten-year-old and posing for a picture? He was only too happy to oblige; it was, after all, a photo of *him*.

Loni then took several pictures over to Bonnie for a "reading," slipping Bob's into the mix. Bonnie spread them all out on a table and gazed at them thoughtfully and mystically for a brief moment, and then, with no hesitation, she snatched up the photo of Bob and in tones dripping vitriol, said, "Who's this prick?" Loni said hesitantly that, well, it was Bob, who was kinda her new boyfriend. Bonnie put the *ole ix-nay* to him quick, declaring Bob unfit for human consumption—a foul-tempered, lyin'-ass drunk. (Don't you love her quaint economy of words, cutting right to the heart of the matter?)

Then Bonnie conjured up another revelation from the images, which Loni had selected randomly, somewhat as a test for the psychic. Bob was the only one Loni had wanted the scoop on, and he had been promptly culled, but in the mix was a photo of a friend of Loni's, a young man, a very young man, a man twenty years younger than Loni to be exact. When Bonnie came upon this photo, she picked it up and said, "Your ship has finally come in." She pronounced to thirty-nine-year-old Loni that nineteen-year-old Jim was her perfect match. Loni laughed nervously and left. She had *a lot* to think about now, for sure. She hadn't expected anything like what Bonnie had just laid on her—not about Bob and certainly not about Jim.

In a very short time, Bob revealed himself to be the very same foul-tempered, lyin'-ass drunk Bonnie had described, and Loni ran him right on out the door. And, by and by, young Jim commenced to coming around pretty regular, and he finally convinced Loni that she needed to pay attention. And, well—you guessed it—Loni and Jim have been very happy together ever since. Who'da thunk it? Well, Bonnie, for one.

It's a crying shame that the very gifted Bonnie has since departed this life. She was a wonderful human being and she's greatly missed by all her family and friends, I'm sure. But hey! She would have been a service to womankind had she lived long enough to provide this excellent screening service to us *all*. She could have had a website, and all we'd have to do was e-mail her a guy's picture for new divinations, saving us untold hours of heartache and tears, not to mention pain, money, and wear and tear on our friends. I'd a whole lot rather pay an anonymous psychic a buttload of money to tell me some guy's a lyin', cheatin' sackashit than listen to it for *free* from my girlfriends—or worse, open my own personal eyeballs to what's smack in front of 'em. But no, Bonnie's dead and gone, and we are just all on our own, winging it here. It behooves us one and all to Be Particular.

That sweet Seattle Queen Natalie wrote me with a question about a vitally important issue. She's only about thirty and therefore *larva*, as we know (women under forty are larvae in SPQueendom), but she was doing the right thing and seeking counsel from me and dipping into the vast storehouse of knowledge and experience held in trust by my Queendom. Natalie had had, it seems, the great good fortune of a Southern birth and childhood in North Carolina, but along about her mid-twenties, her parents divorced and her mama decided she needed to move to the other side of the country for a breather. Our Natalie decided that sounded good to her too, so she loaded up and moved off to Seattle with Mama. For a few years she was liking it out there just fine. She and Mama both have good jobs and share a home they love, *but* . . . (You knew there would be a *but* in there, didn't you? Me, too.)

Everything is fine, Queen Natalie said, but she is 100 percent *not* attracted to the men out there. It took her a little while to figure out why the local guys were off-putting in such a big way, but it finally dawned on her: They don't *smell* right to her. She had grown up around—and learned to love—men who smelled like pit barbecue and the occasional oil change. The men out *there* smell like decidedly unmanly things like cologne and mocha lattes. I see her problem. I feel her pain.

Natalie was shocked to learn her olfactory sense played such a big part in her love life. I was not at all surprised. I've known firsthand for years that most of us humans really and truly cannot get past the end of our own noses. Smell matters. A lot, they say. ("They" are famous scientists in France, I suppose. I worked with a guy once who was always claiming to have read about major breakthroughs in whatever bullshit he was peddling that day. When questioned, he always attributed the breakthroughs to "famous scientists in France.") Anyway, they say that blindfolded mothers can identify their own newborn babies by smell. I haven't tried to do that, but I do know that the smell of a baby's head—and yes, in particular, my own baby's head—is just about the most highly addictive, thrilling, and yet soporific fragrance I have ever personally encountered.

When my own precious daughter, Bailey, was a wee babe, I would lie down with her for a nap and curl her tiny body into the curve of my own and fall asleep breathing her scent. I'd drink in the smell of her the way a recovering drunk sucks on a cigarette. If I could've stuffed her entire *body* up my nose, I would have. I can still close my eyes and remember the feeling I'd get from that fragrance—but maddeningly, I can't conjure up the actual smell. (Now, *there's* a great thing for somebody to figure out how to bottle. Forget "new car." If you could offer a mother a tub of something that smelled exactly like her own baby's head, well, there's a fortune waiting to be made right there, is all I'm saying.)

The smell of a man has always been of paramount importance to me, too. Natalie was blindsided by her nose—but not me. I've always trusted mine. There've been men I liked just fine at first meeting, but upon the first close contact—HUP! YOU'RE OUTTA HERE! Not that they smelled bad—who would even go out with a stinky guy? No, they just didn't smell "right" to me. The right triggers just weren't firing, and that was that. And we're not talking about cologne here—we're talking about skin. The particular hot spot for me is the skin in the area where their jaw meets their neck, and drifting on down to where their neck joins their shoulders. I'll hug a guy and give him a good neck snort and see what registers. The right smell will give me a definite "twitch."

Your nose—or at least *my* nose—will sometimes know when a relationship has ended before your brain does. I remember one relationship in particular that was going from bad to worse, but I was still hanging on in that inexplicable way we too frequently do. After an exceptionally bad boyfriend day, he hauled off and *hugged* me, and I stuck my nose in that neck spot and sniffed, and boy hidee, I'll tell you, I *just knew*. We had hugged—and everything else—our last time. He no longer smelled right to me. He *weren't* mine—and more important, I *weren't* his no mo'.

But back to Queen Natalie's question for me. What she wanted to know was did I think that she should suck it up and stick it out in Seattle and hope to (a) happen on the only barbecue chef in the Great Northwest, (b) change her taste in smells, or (c) just become a none (like a nun, only without the religious theme)? Or should she (d) go into debt to finance a move back to the South to sniff out her Mr. Right? I think you *know* what I advised.

So, what we're saying here is this: However many ways you need to Be Particular in this whole Groom Selection Process, you make sure you don't skip any of them. You pay close attention, hunny chili, because if there's anything you don't like about his *now*, I can assure you you're gonna *not* like it a whole lot more postnup than you ever *thought* about doing prenup.

■ Snag-A-Bride

Okay, I've said much here pertaining to brides, but let's take a little testosterone break and talk about what it's like to be a Groom—or a Wannabe Groom. Where to find a bride and how to go about the wooing and winning process? I imagine this seems a daunting process to all of them—which is as it should be—lest we appear "easy." Rest assured, if we were "easy," it is only an appearance. We may be readily available and at least initially inexpensive, but there ain't nothin' ever been *easy* about any of us, ever.

Anyway, I think we're all pretty well versed in the cat-and-mouse, dog-and-pony, bird-and-bee world of matrimony in this part of the world. But how do some of those other folks do it?

My good friend the excellent writer Edward Cohen sent me an illuminating article from the gold ole *Noo York Times*. Craig Smith wrote the article, but he didn't have the courtesy and forethought to send it to me personally, so Edward gets all the credit for alerting me to this quaint custom of courtship. The article focuses on one of those countries that used to be part of the Soviet Union; now they're on their own but not really much better off, still lacking such basic necessities of life that we in America take for granted, such as running water, dentists, and *vowels*. I swear, the whole name of the country contains *not one single vowel*. This would make for some big cash awards if they happened to have *Wheel of Fortune* over there.

What guys do over yonder is they *select* their desired "brides." Sometimes the man may have actually met her face-to-face and even shared coffee or sheep's eyes or something, but very often, he just spies her waiting for a bus or passing by when he's suddenly convinced beyond any shadow of a doubt that "There she is—the woman of my dreams." Then, enlisting the help of his friends and even his parents, he simply snags her. Sometimes the intended puts up a reeeeally good fight and the elopement committee is forced to concede defeat, at which point the guy simply settles for the next unmarried woman over the age of sixteen who passes by, and snags her instead—possibly as a face-saving maneuver or perhaps just to avoid it being an altogether wasted trip. (The bride-snagging ritual is called *ala kachoo*—sounds a lot like "I'm'on catchyoo" and is the equivalent of "Gotcha!")

Then they just throw her in the car and haul her off to their mommer'n'em's house and keep her there inside until the sun goes clown, after which time she is forevermore "tainted"—as in "used goods" or "no longer a girl" or "crumpled rose" or "former virgin"—and no other man will want her; so she might as well go on and marry the guy on the spot. During this holding period (otherwise known as the "engagement" or "betrothal") the whole gang—friends, Mom and Dad, all the relatives—work in concert to try to throw a white shawl over the head of the fiancée, which, if they're successful, represents her "submission." Some of the potential brides are anything *but* submissive. Some of 'em are downright unruly and manage to thrash the groom and a good many of his kinfolk in the fray.

This business has been going on for *centuries* over there, and somehow we are just now hearing about it. A big selling point, as far as the guys over there are concerned, is the economy of the whole deal. I mean, think of how much money they save! In this part of the world, dating is just a *huge* financial drain. Suppose you date somebody for a year before marriage and you have two dates a week; by the time you add up the entertainment costs and gasoline, and throw in mandatory gifts for Christmas, birthday, and Valentine's, it's easily a ten-thousand-dollar proposition—not counting haircuts and dry-cleaning or even thinking about the mental wear and tear.

In this particular vowel-poor country a basic bride will cost you about eight hundred dollars plus a cow. I know about a million guys—grooms and dads alike—who'd take that deal all day *long*. That right there sounds like the bargain of the century in dollars alone. When you add in the time and the *bullshit* savings, well, it becomes downright irresistible.

I do love analogies from the animal kingdom, and our In-House Frog Genius Queen, Carol—sister of one of the preeminent SPQ Wannabes, Cecilia—shared with me some pertinent facts about frog fucking, which may be beneficial to us all. (Let us hasten to clarify that we are referring to an act done *by* frogs, not *with* frogs, an activity deemed most UnQueenly.)

In late winter a whole bunch of boy frogs will gang up at a water hole and start bellowing to attract girl frogs. (Queen Carol questions the potential effectiveness of this tactic for the human race. What if a bunch of guys got together and just started hollering at the top of their lungs that there was a really great sexual opportunity *right here* for any interested females? Sounds like any bar I've ever been in, actually.) Apparently, female frogs think this is a swell way to choose a mate. Good as any, I suppose, love being the crapshoot that it often is.

So anyway, the girl frogs hear the Big Croak, and they all come a-lookin', and then it all turns into your basic cluster-fuck. As soon as the females arrive on the scene, the males just go completely nuts and start grabbin' and humpin' anybody that comes by. Sometimes they even grab *each other*. (Oh, and I guess then they say it was an "accident." "Sorry, buddy, thought you were a girl." I am *so sure*.) Anyway; the poor girl frogs get in over their heads, figuratively and literally, and sometimes end up severely injured, if not actually fucked slap to death.

Now, apparently wood frogs are a tad more discerning. The boy wood frogs space themselves in neat little rows around a pool of water and start making these quacking noises. The girl wood frogs come up one by one and look and listen and then decide whose croak is most appealing to them personally, usually based on the frequency and pitch. And they also make their decision based on the frog's size. Bigger is better—seems even frogs know this. This mating game is usually a fairly mannerly proceeding, but we *are* dealing with *guys* here, so every once in a while mistakes do happen. Like, for instance, if this guy frog is sitting there singing his heart out and he's so into his song and all that he kinda tunes out his surroundings but then detects that someone has moved in close to him, well, without so much as an introductory "Hidee!" he just *assumes* it's a willing female and grabs her up in the "mating clasp" (known to frog people as the "amplexus"). But—get this—if it's another guy frog, he will know at once from the feel. A desirable female is round and plump, because she's full of eggs. So if he grabs a *skinny* frog, he lets go pretty dang quick, because he knows he's either got hold of a *guy* or a girl that's already mated and released her eggs and is therefore just too skinny to fool with. Now, I like that part right there—don't nobody wanna fool around with no skinny-ass frog girl. "Fat is Fine" if you're a frog, and I'm hopeful that one day, in my lifetime, big asses will be back in demand for us human folk as well.

Sometimes, Carol tells me, a girl frog will have picked out just the Very One she's after and begin her approach, only to be waylaid (that pun is irresistible!) by "satellite males." These little wimp-bag frogs hang around the big frog's area, hoping to snag the girls as they come in. Some researchers call these guys "gauntlet males" on account of the female may have to fool around with a whole bunch of them before she can get to the Real Prince. Now, isn't *that* just The Truth? She'll persevere until she gets to Mr. Right, though. As usual, we can learn a lot from the animal kingdom.

■ READING AND WRITING

1. Browne states that finding a man to replace her father was "the antithesis of the answer." What does she mean?
2. Browne occasionally uses obscenities and other vulgar language. How are these words used? What is their rhetorical effect? (Think especially about her intended audience.) In addition to foul language, she also plays with grammatical conventions. Does this stylistic choice work in the same way as her colorful diction?
3. What gender stereotypes and cultural assumptions does Browne rely on in her writing? Does her use of these undercut the humor of the chapter or Browne's ultimate message?

■ DEVELOPING LONGER RESPONSES

4. Browne writes in a conversational style, often using a Southern dialect. Using Browne's chapter as a model, try composing a short, personal story in your own regional dialect. Then, think about what the dialect adds to the piece.

■ USING RESEARCH

5. Research the Sweet Potato Queens or another similar women's organization, like the Red Hat Society or the Blue Thong Society. What sort of services or events do they offer? Do you think these groups empower women? Compare your findings with research on the history of women's clubs and sororities. Do more recent "sisterhoods" like the Queens share the same purpose as these older (and often secretive) organizations? Why are their differences important?
6. Look up images of the Sweet Potato Queens in their parade regalia. Perform a visual analysis, paying close attention to the details of their dress and postures. How does their appearance subvert or conform to traditional standards of feminine beauty? How do these performances by the Sweet Potato Queen compare with those that Nancy Bauer analyzes in her essay on Lady Gaga (in Chapter 4)?

> *"Queen of the House" was a Billboard hit written by Mary Taylor for Jody Miller, reaching number 12 on the charts when it was released by Capitol Records in 1965. The song is a response to Roger Miller's "King of the Road," and shares the same tune. Miller won a Grammy for Best Female Country Vocal Performance for this song and was inducted into the Country Gospel Music Association Hall of Fame in 1998. Miller continues to perform, most often for church groups.*

QUEEN OF THE HOUSE Lyrics by Mary Taylor

Up every day at six
Bacon and eggs to fix
Four kids from one to four
Pretty soon there'll be one more

I got old floors to wax and scrub
And there's a dirty old ring in the tub
I'll get a maid someday
But till then I'm
Queen of the house

No time to fix my hair
Need a new dress to wear
Old clothes will have to do
'Cause the kids all need new shoes

I got bridge club each Tuesday night
He goes out with the boys and gets tight
But when the evening's through
He comes a home to the
Queen of the house

I know the milkman, the iceman
They come every day
They give me tips on the horses to play
And when I got the time to spare
I sit and wish that I had picked a rich millionaire

I sing up every day at six
Bacon and eggs to fix
Four kids from one to four
Pretty soon there'll be one more

Oh by Sundays I'm mighty glad
We send the kids to his Mom and Dad
It's the day that makes me glad I'm
Queen of the house

Up every day at six
Bacon and eggs to fix
Four kids from one to four
Pretty soon there'll be one more

Oh, but Sundays I'm mighty glad
We send the kids to his Mom and Dad
It's the day that makes me glad I'm
Queen of the house

■ READING AND WRITING

1. What is the tone of these song lyrics? Is the song sincere, sarcastic, or tongue-in-cheek? How can you tell?
2. Analyze the chorus. What is the message the song is trying to convey? How does the chorus represent this message?
3. The song shows the daily routine of a housewife. What, if anything, about this routine surprises you? What insights does the song divulge about the speaker's attitude? How does this song compare with Marge Piercy's poem "What's that smell in the kitchen?" in Chapter 4?

■ DEVELOPING LONGER RESPONSES

4. Find a video online of Jody Miller performing "Queen of the House." How does her delivery change your perception of the song? Next, listen to Roger Miller's "King of the Road." What ideas about masculinity does that song present? How does "Queen of the House" respond to or revise the male gender stereotype presented by "King of the Road"? Is Jody Miller's song a critique, or does it function in another way?

Using sarcasm and wit to deliver cutting social critiques, David Sedaris has become one of America's most popular humor writers. "Chicken in the Henhouse," from the 2004 collection, Dress Your Family in Corduroy and Denim, showcases Sedaris's ability to use seemingly ordinary details from daily life to slice through the "cultural euphemisms and political correctness," as his online biography puts it, that so many of us tend to accept or ignore.

CHICKEN IN THE HENHOUSE   David Sedaris

It was one of those hotels without room service, the type you wouldn't mind if you were paying your own bill but would complain about if someone else was paying. I was not paying my own bill, and so the deficiencies stuck out and were taken as evidence of my host's indifference. There was no tub, just a plastic shower stall, and the soap was brittle and smelled like dishwashing detergent. The bedside lamp was missing a bulb, but that could have been remedied easily enough. I could have asked for one at the front desk, but I didn't want a light bulb. I just wanted to feel put-upon.

It started when the airline lost my luggage. Time was lost filling out forms, and I'd had to go directly from the airport to a college an hour north of Manchester, where I gave a talk to a group of students. Then there was a reception and a forty-five-minute drive to the hotel, which was out in the middle of nowhere. I arrived at one A.M. and found they had booked me into a basement room. Late at night it didn't much matter, but in the morning it did. To open the curtains was to invite scrutiny, and the people of New Hampshire stared in without a hint of shame. There wasn't much to look at, just me, sitting on the edge of the bed with a phone to my ear. The airline had sworn my suitcase would arrive overnight, and when it didn't, I called the 800 number printed on the inside of my ticket jacket. My choices were either to speak to a machine or to wait for an available human. I chose the human, and after eight minutes on hold I hung up and started looking for someone to blame.

"I don't care if it's my son, my congressman, what have you. I just don't approve of that lifestyle." The speaker was a woman named Audrey who'd called the local talk-radio station to offer her opinion. The Catholic Church scandal had been front-page news for over a week, and when the priest angle had been exhausted, the discussion filtered down to pedophilia in general and then, homosexual pedophilia, which was commonly agreed to be the worst kind. It was for talk radio, one of those easy topics, like tax hikes or mass murder. "What do you think of full-grown men practicing sodomy on children?"

"Well, I'm *against* it!" This was always said as if it was somehow startling, a minority position no one had yet dared lay claim to.

I'd been traveling around the country for the past ten days, and everywhere I went I heard the same thing. The host would congratulate the caller on his or her moral fortitude, and wanting to feel that approval again, the person would rephrase the original statement, freshening it up with an adverb or qualifier. "Call me old-fashioned, but I just hugely think it's wrong." Then, little by little, they'd begin interchanging the words *homosexual* and *pedophile*, speaking as if they were one and the same. "Now they've even got them on TV," Audrey said. "And in the schools! Talk about the proverbial chicken in the henhouse."

"Fox," the host said.

"Oh, they're the worst," Audrey said. "*The Simpsons* and such—I never watch that station."

I meant in the henhouse," the host said. "I believe the saying is 'the fox in the henhouse,' not 'the chicken in the henhouse.'"

Audrey regrouped. "Did I say chicken? Well, you get my point. These homosexuals can't reproduce themselves, and so they go into the schools and try to recruit our young people."

It was nothing I hadn't heard before, but I was crankier than usual and found myself in the middle of the room, one sock on and one sock off, shouting at the clock radio. "Nobody recruited *me*, Audrey. And I *begged* for it."

It was *her* fault I was stuck in a basement room with no luggage, her and all the people just like her: the satisfied families trotting from the parking lot to the first-floor restaurant, the hotel guests with whirlpool baths and rooms overlooking the surrounding forest. *Why waste the view on a homosexual? He only looks at schoolboys' rectums. And a suitcase? Please! We all know what they do with those.* They might not have come out and said it, but they are sure thinking it. I could tell.

It stood to reason that if the world was conspiring against me, my Mr. Coffee machine was broken. It sat on the bathroom counter, dribbling cold water, and after a brief, completely unsatisfying cry, I finished getting dressed and left the room. There was a staircase at the end of the hall, and beside it a little cleared area where a dozen or so elderly women knelt upon the carpet, piecing together a patchwork quilt. They looked up as I passed, one of them turning to ask me a question. "Yoin' shurch?" Her mouth was full of pins and it took me a moment to realize what she was saying—You going to church? It was an odd question, but then I remembered that it was a Sunday, and I was wearing a tie. Someone at the college had loaned it to me the night before, and I'd put it on in hopes it might distract from my shirt, which was wrinkled and discolored beneath the arms. "No," I told her, "I'm *not* going to church." Oh, I was in a horrible mood. Midway up the stairs I stopped and turned back around. "I *never* go to church," I said. "Never. And I'm not about to start now."

"Shute shelf," she said.

Past the restaurant and gift shop, in the center of the lobby, was a complimentary beverage stand. I thought I'd get a coffee and take it outdoors, but just as I approached, a boy swooped in and began mixing himself a cup of hot chocolate. He looked like all of the kids I'd been seeing lately, in airports, in parking lots: the oversize sweatshirts stamped with team emblems, the baggy jeans and jazzy sneakers. His watch was fat and plastic, like a yo-yo strapped to his wrist, and his hair looked as if it had been cut with the lid of a can, the irregular hanks stiffened with gel and coaxed to stand at peculiar angles.

It was a complicated business, mixing a cup of hot chocolate. You had to spread the powdered cocoa from one end of the table to the other and use as many stirrers as possible, making sure to thoroughly chew the wetted ends before tossing them upon the stack of unused napkins. This is what I like about children: complete attention to one detail and complete disregard of another. When finally finished, he scooted over to the coffee urn, filling two cups, black, and fitting them with lids. The drinks were stacked into a tower, then tentatively lifted off the table. "Whoa," he whispered. Hot chocolate seeped from beneath the lid of the bottom cup and ran down his hand.

"Do you need some help with those?" I asked.

The boy looked at me for a moment. "Yeah," he said. "Carry these upstairs." There was no *please* or *thank you*, just "I'll take the hot chocolate myself."

He set the coffees back on the table, and as I reached for them it occurred to me that maybe this was not such a good idea. I was a stranger, an admitted homosexual traveling through a small town, and he was, like, ten. And alone. The voice of reason whispered in my ear. *Don't do it, buster. You're playing with fire.*

I withdrew my hands, then stopped, thinking, *Wait a minute. That's not reason. It's Audrey, that crackpot from the radio.* The real voice of reason sounds like Bea Arthur, and when it failed to pipe up, I lifted the coffees off the table and carried them toward the elevator, where the boy stood mashing the call button with his chocolate-coated fingers.

A maid passed and rolled her eyes at the desk clerk. "Cute kid."

Before the church scandal I might have said the same thing, only without the sarcasm. Now, though, any such observation seemed suspect. Though Audrey would never believe it, I am not physically attracted to children. They're like animals to me, fun to watch but beyond the bounds of my sexual imagination. That said, I am a person who feels guilty for crimes I have not committed, or have not committed in years. The police search the train station for a serial rapist and I cover my face with a newspaper, wondering if maybe I did it in my sleep. The last thing I stole was an eight-track tape, but to this day I'm unable to enter a store without feeling like a shoplifter. It's all the anxiety with none of the free stuff. To make things just that much worse, I seem to have developed a remarkable perspiration problem. My conscience is cross-wired with my sweat glands, but there's a short in the system and I break out over things I didn't do, which only makes me look more suspect. Innocently helping to lighten a child's burden was a *good* thing—I knew this—yet moments after lifting the coffees off the table I was soaking wet. As usual, the sweat was fiercest on my forehead, under my arms, and, cruelly, on my ass, which is a great mystery to me. If the stress is prolonged, I'll feel the droplets inching down the back of my legs, trapped, finally, by my socks, which are cotton and bought expressly for their absorbent powers.

If there was a security camera in the lobby, this is what it would have shown: A four-and-a-half-foot-tall boy stands mashing and then pounding the elevator call button. Beside him is a man, maybe a foot taller, dressed in a shirt and tie and holding a lidded cup in each hand. Is it raining outside? If not, perhaps he just stepped from the shower and threw on his clothes without drying himself. His eyes shift this way and that, giving the impression that he is searching for somebody. Could it be this silver-haired gentleman? He's just walked up, looking very dapper in his tweed jacket and matching cap. He talks to the boy and lays a hand on the back of his head, scolding him probably, which is good, as somebody needed to. The other man, the wet one, is just standing there, holding the cups and trying to wipe his forehead with his sleeve at the same time. A lid pops off and something—it looks like coffee—spills down the front of his shirt. He leaps about, prancing almost, and pulls the fabric away from his skin. The boy seems angry now and says something. The older gentleman offers a handkerchief, and the man sets down one of his cups and runs—literally runs, panting—off camera, returning thirty seconds later with another lidded cup, a replacement. By this time the elevator has arrived. The gentleman holds open the door, and he and the boy wait as the man picks the other cup off the floor and joins them. Then the door closes, and they are gone.

"So, who have we got here?" the gentleman asked. His voice was jovial and enthusiastic. "What do you call yourself, big fella?"

"Michael," the boy said.

"Well, that's a grown-up name, isn't it."

Michael guessed that it was, and the man caught my eye and winked, the way people do when they're establishing a partnership. *We'll just put on the small fry, what do you say?* "I bet a big guy like you must have a lot of girlfriends," he said. "Is that true?"

"No."

"You *don't*? Well, what's the problem?"

"I don't know. I just don't have one. That's all," Michael said.

I had always hated it when men asked the girlfriend question. Not only was it corny, but it set you in their imaginations in a way that seemed private to me. Answer yes and they'd picture your wee courtship: the candlelit dinner of hot dogs and potato chips, the rumpled Snoopy sheets. Answer no and you were blue-balled, the frustrated bachelor of the second grade. It was an idea of children as miniature adults, which was about as funny to me as the dog in sunglasses.

"Well, there must be *someone* you have your eye on."

The boy did not answer, but the man persisted in trying to draw him out. "Is Mommy sleeping in this morning?"

Again, nothing.

The man gave up and turned to me. Your wife," he said. "I take it she's still in bed?"

He thought I was Michael's father, and I did not correct him. "Yes," I said. "She's upstairs … passed out." I don't know why I said this, or then again, maybe I do. The man had constructed a little family portrait, and there was a pleasure in defacing it. Here was Michael, here was Michael's dad, and now, here was Mom, lying face down on the bathroom floor.

The elevator stopped on three, and the man tipped his hat. "All right, then," he said. "You two enjoy the rest of the morning." Michael had pressed the button for the fifth floor no less than twenty times, and now he gave it an extra few jabs just for good measure. We were alone now, and something unpleasant entered my mind.

Sometimes when I'm in a tight situation, I'll feel a need to touch somebody's head. It happens a lot on airplanes. I'll look at the person seated in front of me, and within a moment the idea will have grown from a possibility to a compulsion. There is no option—I simply have to do it. The easiest method is to make like I'm getting up, to grab the forward seat for support and just sort of pat the person's hair with my fingers. "Oh, I'm sorry," I say.

"No problem."

Most often I'll continue getting out of my seat, then walk to the back of the plane or go to the bathroom and stand there for a few minutes, trying to fight off what I know is inevitable: I need to touch the person's head again. Experience has taught me that you can do this three times before the head's owner either yells at you or rings for the flight attendant. "Is something wrong?" she'll ask.

"I don't think so, no."

"What do you mean 'no,'" the passenger will say. "This freak keeps touching my head."

"Is that true, sir?"

It's not always a head. Sometimes I need to touch a particular purse or briefcase. When I was a child this sort of compulsive behavior was my life, but now I practice it only if I'm in a situation where I can't smoke: planes—as I mentioned—and elevators.

Just touch the boy's head, I thought. *The old man did it, so why can't you?*

To remind myself that this is inappropriate only makes the voice more insistent. The thing must be done *because* it is inappropriate. If it weren't, there'd be no point in bothering with it.

He won't even notice it. Touch him now, quick.

Were we traveling a long distance, I would have lost the battle, but fortunately we weren't going far. The elevator arrived on the fifth floor and I scrambled out the door, set the coffees on the carpet, and lit a cigarette. "You're going to have to give me a minute here," I said.

"But my room's just down the hall. And this is non-smoking."

"I know, I know."

"It's not good for you," he said.

"That's true for a lot of people," I told him. "But it *really is* good for me. Take my word for it."

He leaned against a door and removed the DO NOT DISTURB sign, studying it for a moment before sticking it in his back pocket.

I only needed to smoke for a minute, but realized when I was finished that there was no ashtray. Beside the elevator was a window, but of course it was sealed shut. Hotels. They do everything in their power to make you want to jump to your death, and then they make certain that you can't do it. "Are you finished with your cocoa?" I asked.

"No."

"Well, are you finished with the lid?"

"I guess so."

He handed it to me and I spit into the center—no easy task, as my mouth was completely dry. Fifty percent of my body water was seeping out my ass, and the other half was in transit.

"That's gross," he said. "Yeah, well, you're just going to have to forgive me." I stubbed the cigarette into the spit, set the lid on the carpet, and picked up the coffees. "Okay. Where to?"

He pointed out a long corridor and I followed him, gnawing on a question that's been troubling me for years. What if you had a baby and you just … you just needed to touch it where you knew you shouldn't. I don't mean that you'd want to. You wouldn't *desire* the baby any more than you desire a person whose head you've just touched. The act would be compulsive rather than sexual, and while to you there'd be a big difference, you couldn't expect a prosecutor, much less an infant, to recognize it. You'd be a bad parent, and once the child could talk and you told it not to tell anyone, you would become a manipulator—a monster, basically—and the reason behind your actions would no longer matter.

The closer we got to the end of the hall, the more anxious I became. I had not laid a finger on the boy's head. I have never poked or prodded either a baby or a child, so why did I feel so dirty? Part of it was just my makeup, the deep-seated belief that I deserve a basement room, but a larger, uglier part had to do with the voices I hear on talk radio, and my tendency, in spite of myself, to pay them heed. The man in the elevator had not thought twice about asking Michael personal questions or about laying a hand on the back of his head. Because he was neither a priest nor a homosexual, he hadn't felt the need to watch himself, worrying that every word or gesture might be misinterpreted. He could unthinkingly wander the halls with a strange boy, while for me it amounted to a political act—an insistence that I was as good as the next guy. Yes, I am a homosexual; yes, I am soaking wet; yes, I sometimes feel an urge to touch people's heads, but still I can safely see a ten-year-old back to his room. It bothered me that I needed to prove something this elementary. And prove it to people whom I could never hope to convince.

"This is it," Michael said. From the other side of the door I heard the sound of a television. It was one of those Sunday-morning magazine programs, a weekly hour where all news is good news. Blind Jimmy Henderson coaches a volley ball team. An ailing groundhog is fitted for a back brace. That type of thing. The boy inserted his card key into the slot, and the door opened onto a bright, well-furnished room. It was twice the size of mine, with higher ceilings and a sitting area. One window framed a view of the lake, and the other a stand of scarlet maples.

"Oh, you're back," a woman said. She was clearly the boy's mother, as their profiles were identical, the foreheads easing almost imperceptibly into blunt freckled noses. Both too had spiky blond hair, though for her I imagined the style was accidental, the result of the pillows piled behind her head. She was lying beneath the covers of a canopy bed, examining one of the many brochures scattered across the comforter. A man slept beside her, and when she spoke, he shifted slightly and covered his face with the crook of his arm. "What took you so long?" She looked toward the open door, and her eyes widened as they met mine. "What the …"

There was a yellow robe at the foot of the bed, and the woman turned her back to me as she got up and stepped into it. Her son reached for the coffees, and I tightened my grip, unwilling to surrender what I'd come to think of as my props. They turned me from a stranger to a kindly stranger, and I'd seen myself holding them as his parents rounded on me, demanding to know what was going on.

"Give them to me," he said, and rather than making a scene, I relaxed my grip. The coffees were taken, and I felt my resolve starting to crumble. Empty-handed, I was just a creep, the spooky wet guy who'd crawled up from the basement. The woman crossed to the dresser, and as the door started to close she called out to me. "Hey," she said. "Wait a minute." I turned, ready to begin the fight of my life, and she stepped forward and pressed a dollar into my hand. "You people run a very nice hotel," she told me. "I just wish we could stay longer."

The door closed and I stood alone in the empty corridor, examining my tip and thinking, *Is that all?*

READING AND WRITING

1. What arguments does Sedaris make about sexuality, stereotypes, and intolerance? How does he use himself as his primary "evidence"?
2. How does Sedaris use humor to convey his feelings about Audrey and her homophobic comments? Why is humor a more effective rhetorical tool in this case than anger or indignation?

DEVELOPING LONGER RESPONSES

3. How would you describe the ethos that Sedaris presents in his text? What does he do to convey this ethos to his audience? Compare Sedaris's ethos with that of Jill Connor Browne or P.J. O'Rourke. What do the three have in common? How are they different? What role does ethos play in the success (or failure) of a humorous composition?

George Saunders, who teaches creative writing at Syracuse University, has published two collections of stories, Pastoralia *and* CivilWarLand in Bad Decline, *and a children's story,* The Very Persistent Gappers of Frip. *This essay appeared in the March 8, 2004, edition of* The New Yorker.

MY AMENDMENT George Saunders

As an obscure, middle-aged, heterosexual short-story writer, I am often asked, George, do you have any feelings about Same-Sex Marriage?

To which I answer, Actually, yes, I do.

Like any sane person, I am against Same-Sex Marriage, and in favor of a constitutional amendment to ban it.

To tell the truth, I feel that, in the interest of moral rigor, it is necessary for us to go a step further, which is why I would like to propose a supplementary constitutional amendment.

In the town where I live, I have frequently observed a phenomenon I have come to think of as Samish-Sex Marriage. Take, for example, K, a male friend of mine, of slight build, with a ponytail. K is married to S, a tall, stocky female with extremely short hair, almost a crewcut. Often, while watching K play with his own ponytail as S towers over him, I have wondered, Isn't it odd that this somewhat effeminate man should be married to this somewhat masculine woman? Is K not, on some level, imperfectly expressing a slight latent desire to be married to a man? And is not S, on some level, imperfectly expressing a slight latent desire to be married to a woman?

Then I ask myself, Is this truly what God had in mind?

Take the case of L, a female friend with a deep, booming voice. I have often found myself looking askance at her husband, H. Though H is basically pretty masculine, having neither a ponytail nor a tight feminine derriere like K, still I wonder: H, when you are having marital relations with L, and she calls out your name in that deep, booming, nearly male voice, and you continue having marital relations with her (i.e., you are not "turned off"), does this not imply that you, H, are, in fact, still "turned on"? And doesn't this indicate that, on some level, you, H, have a slight latent desire to make love to a man?

Or consider the case of T, a male friend with an extremely small penis. (We attend the same gym.) He is married to O, an average-looking woman who knows how to fix cars. I wonder about O. How does she know so much about cars? Is she not, by tolerating this non-car-fixing, short-penised friend of mine, indicating that, on some level, she wouldn't mind being married to a woman, and is therefore, perhaps, a tiny bit functionally gay?

And what about T? Doesn't the fact that T can stand there in the shower room at our gym, confidently towelling off his tiny unit, while O is at home changing their sparkplugs with alacrity, indicate that it is only a short stroll down a slippery slope before he is completely happy being the "girl" in their relationship, from which it is only a small fey hop down the same slope before T is happily married to another man, perhaps my car mechanic, a handsome Portuguese fellow I shall refer to as J?

Because my feeling is, when God made man and woman He had something very specific in mind. It goes without saying that He did not want men marrying men, or women marrying women, but also what He did not want, in my view, was feminine men marrying masculine women.

Which is why I developed my Manly Scale of Absolute Gender.

Using my Scale, which assigns numerical values according to a set of masculine and feminine characteristics, it is now easy to determine how Manly a man is and how Fem a woman is, and therefore how close to a Samish-Sex Marriage a given marriage is.

Here's how it works. Say we determine that a man is an 8 on the Manly Scale, with 10 being the most Manly of all and 0 basically a Neuter. And say we determine that his fiancee is a -6 on the Manly Scale, with a -10 being the most Fem of all. Calculating the difference between the man's rating and the woman's rating—the Gender Differential—we see that this proposed union is not, in fact, a Samish-Sex Marriage, which I have defined as "any marriage for which the Gender Differential is less than or equal to 10 points."

Friends whom I have identified as being in Samish-Sex Marriages often ask me, George, given that we have scored poorly, what exactly would you have us do about it?

Well, one solution I have proposed is divorce—divorce followed by remarriage to a more suitable partner. K, for example, could marry a voluptuous high-voiced N.F.L. cheerleader, who would more than offset his tight feminine derriere, while his ex-wife, S, might choose to become involved with a lumberjack with very large arms, thereby neutralizing her thick calves and faint mustache.

Another, and of course preferable, solution would be to repair the existing marriage, converting it from a Samish-Sex Marriage to a healthy Normal Marriage, by having the feminine man become more masculine and/or the masculine woman become more feminine.

Often, when I propose this, my friends become surly. How dare I, they ask. What business is it of mine? Do I think it is easy to change in such a profound way?

To which I say, It is not easy to change, but it is possible.

I know, because I have done it.

When young, I had a tendency to speak too quickly, while gesturing too much with my hands. Also, my opinions were unfirm. I was constantly contradicting myself in that fast voice, while gesturing like a girl. Also, I cried often. Things seemed so sad. I had long blond hair, and liked it. My hair was layered and fell down across my shoulders, and, I admit it, I would sometimes slow down when passing a shop window to look at it, to look at my hair! I had a strange constant feeling of being happy to be alive. This feeling of infinite possibility sometimes caused me to laugh when alone, or even, on occasion, to literally skip down the street, before pausing in front of a shop window and giving my beautiful hair a cavalier toss.

To tell the truth, I do not think I would have scored very high on my Manly Scale, if the Scale had been invented at that time, by me. I suspect I would have scored so Fem on the test that I would have been prohibited from marrying my wife, P, the love of my life. And I think, somewhere in my heart, I knew that.

I knew I was too Fem.

So what did I do about it? Did I complain? Did I whine? Did I expect activist judges to step in on my behalf, manipulating the system to accommodate my peculiarity?

No, I did not.

What I did was I changed. I undertook what I like to think of as a classic American project of self-improvement. I made videos of myself talking, and studied these, and in time succeeded in training myself to speak more slowly, while almost never moving my hands. Now, if you ever meet me, you will observe that I always speak in an extremely slow and manly and almost painfully deliberate way, with my hands either driven deep into my pockets or held stock-still at the ends of my arms, which are bent slightly at the elbows, as if I were ready to respond to the slightest provocation by punching you in the face. As for my opinions, they are very firm. I rarely change them. When I feel like skipping, I absolutely do not skip. As for my long beautiful hair—well, I am lucky, in that I am rapidly going bald. Every month, when I recalculate my ranking on the Manly Scale, I find myself becoming more and more Manly, as my hair gets thinner and my girth increases, thickening my once lithe, almost girlish physique, thus insuring the continuing morality and legality of my marriage to P.

My point is simply this: If I was able to effect these tremendous positive changes in my life, to avoid finding myself in the moral/legal quagmire of a Samish-Sex Marriage, why can't K, S, L, H, T, and O do the same?

I implore any of my readers who find themselves in a Samish-Sex Marriage: Change. If you are a feminine man, become more manly. If you are a masculine woman, become more feminine. If you are a woman and are thick-necked or lumbering, or have ever had the slightest feeling of attraction to a man who is somewhat pale and fey, deny these feelings and, in a spirit of self-correction, try to become more thin-necked and light-footed, while, if you find it helpful, watching videos of naked masculine men, to sort of retrain yourself in the proper mode of attraction. If you are a man and, upon seeing a thick-waisted, athletic young woman walking with a quasi-mannish gait through your local grocery, you imagine yourself in a passionate embrace with her, in your car, a car that is parked just outside, and which is suddenly, in your imagination, full of the smell of her fresh young breath—well, stop thinking that! Are you a man or not?

I, for one, am sick and tired of this creeping national tendency to let certain types of people take advantage of our national good nature by marrying individuals who are essentially of their own gender. If this trend continues, before long our towns and cities will be full of people like K, S, L, H, T, and O, people "asserting their rights" by dating, falling in love with, marrying, and spending the rest of their lives with whomever they please.

I, for one, am not about to stand by and let that happen.

Because then what will we have? A nation ruled by the anarchy of unconstrained desire. A nation of willful human hearts, each lurching this way and that and reaching out for whatever it spontaneously desires, trying desperately to find some comforting temporary shred of warmth in a mostly cold world, totally unconcerned about the external form in which that other, long-desired heart is embodied.

That is not the kind of world in which I wish to live.

I, for one, intend to become ever more firmly male, enjoying my golden years, while watching P become ever more female, each of us vigilant for any hint of ambiguity in the other.

And as our children grow, should they begin to show the slightest hint of some lingering residue of the opposite gender, P and I will lovingly pull them aside and list all the particulars by which we were able to identify their unintentional deficiency.

Then, together, we will devise a suitable correction.

And, in this way, the race will go on.

■ READING AND WRITING

1. How does Saunders define "Samish-Sex Marriage"? How does he use the term in his argument?
2. Many satirists rely on tone, among other literary elements, to help convey their purpose. How would you characterize Saunders' tone? Point to some examples in the essay to show how he establishes his tone.
3. In the third paragraph of his essay, Saunders writes, "Like any sane person, I am against Same-Sex Marriage, and in favor of a constitutional amendment to ban it." Do you believe him? In explaining your answer, point to specific passages in his text to support your position.

■ DEVELOPING LONGER RESPONSES

4. Like Jonathan Swift, whose infamous satire appears earlier in this chapter, Saunders offers a modest proposal to solve a pressing social problem—in this case, to the same-sex marriage debate. Compare the two essays and write a brief analysis of their similarities and differences. Which piece do you find more interesting? Why?

■ RESEARCH AND WRITING PROJECTS

1. Using all of the texts in this chapter and outside research, create a glossary of terms relating to humor in literature. For each term, identify an example and describe how that type of humor functions in context. After assembling your glossary, write a brief essay analyzing how humor works as a rhetorical device within one or two of the readings in this chapter. What types of humor are represented in the reading(s) you've selected? Does the type of humor being used intensify, obscure, or clarify the argument?

2. What makes humor a useful tool for getting people to think and talk about difficult or uncomfortable subjects? Are there issues that we should never use humor to discuss? Explain, using at least two of the essays from this chapter and two humorous texts that you have found online or through the library in your response.

3. Choose one text from this chapter to pair with a reading in another chapter that deals with the same issue (you might, for example, read "Nation Shudders at Large Block of Uninterrupted Text" alongside "Is Google Making Us Stupid" or "The Greenhouse Affect" with "For the Love of Life"). How are these texts similar? Does the humorous text alter the argument being made or approach the topic in a different way? After thoroughly analyzing these two texts, compose an evaluative essay in which you make an argument about which text is more successful as an argument.

4. The internet is a fertile resource for visual humor, especially in the form of memes, gifs, and inventive Tumblr accounts and web comics. Choose your favorite humorous online phenomenon that makes some kind of larger argument and research its origins and usage. Use your research to prepare a rhetorical analysis of the subject you have chosen. Your instructor will provide details about this assignment.

5. Compose a four- to five-page humorous or satirical essay for either the online publication *The Onion* or for *The Atlantic Monthly,* a magazine known for its commitment to good writing and its incisive examination

of pressing social issues. Your essay should use humor to address—either directly or indirectly—an issue of social import. As you think about your essay, look back over the texts in this chapter that use humor to make arguments about relevant social issues. As these examples suggest, there are nearly no restrictions on the issue you choose. From politics to entertainment to commonly held beliefs, your essay can address any subject matter that people care about. Don't be timid as you write this essay. Few people write as well as Sedaris or Kingsolver, and your paper won't be judged solely on how funny it is. Rather, a successful response to this assignment will use humor strategically to explore and comment on an issue of interest to the public and will demonstrate your careful and unique consideration of how this issue impacts your readers.

Index of Authors and Titles

Credits

Chapter One

Plato. "The Allegory of the Cave." *The Dialogues of Plato.* Trans. Benjamin Jowett. New York: Random House. 773-780. Print. (Copyright © 2001 Random House.)

Dillard, Annie. "The Wreck of Time: Taking Our Century's Measure." *Harper's Magazine* 296.1772 (Jan. 1998): 51-56. Print.

Richtel, Matt. "Hooked on Technology, and Paying a Price." *The New York Times* 7 June 2010: n pag. Web. 10 Oct. 2010.

Carr, Nicholas. "Is Google Making Us Stupid." *The Atlantic Monthly* 302.1 (July/August 2008): 56-63. Print. (Copyright © 2008 by Nicholas Carr. Reprinted with permission of the author.)

Cascio, Jamie. "Get Smarter." *The Atlantic Monthly* 304.1 (July/August 2009): 94-100. Print.

Wiesel, Elie, and Richard D. Heffner. "Am I My Brother's Keeper." *Conservations with Elie Wiesel.* New York: Random House, 2001. 3-15. Print. (Copyright © 2001 by Random House.)

Lichtenberg, Judith. "Is Pure Altruism Possible?" *The New York Times* 9 Oct. 2010: n. pag. Web. 10 Oct. 2010.

Kahn, Jeremy. "The Story of a Snitch." *The Atlantic Monthly* 299.3 (Apr. 2007): 80-92. Print. (Reprinted with permission.)

Chapter Two

Townsend, Elisabeth. "The Cooking Ape: An Interview with Richard Wrangham." *Gastronomica: The Journal of Food and Culture* 5.1 (Winter 2005): 29-37. Web. 11 Oct. 2010.

Berry, Wendell. "The Pleasures of Eating." *What Are People For?* New York: North Point Press, 2000. 145-152. Print.

Harris, Jessica B. "The Culinary Seasons of My Childhood." *Gastropolis: Food and New York City.* Ed. Annie Hauck-Lawson and Jonathan Deutsch. New York: Columbia UP, 2009. 108-115. Print. (Copyright © 2009 Columbia University Press. Reprinted with permission.)

Waters, Alice. "A Healthy Constitution." *The Nation* 289.8 (Sept. 21, 2009): 11-15. Print.

Paarlberg, Robert. "Attention Whole Food Shoppers." *Foreign Policy* May/June 2010: n. pag. Web. 10 Oct. 2010.

Scully, Matthew. "Fear Factories: The Case for Compassionate Conservatism—for Animals." *The American Conservative* May 23, 2005: n pag. Web. 10 Oct. 2010. (Copyright © 2005 *The American Conservative*. Reprinted with permission.)

Dahm, Molly J., Aurelia V. Samonte, and Amy R. Shows. "Organic Foods: Do Eco-Friendly Attitudes Predict Eco-Friendly Behaviors?" *Journal of American College Health* 58.3 (2009): 195-202. Print.

Salatin, Joel. "Declare Your Independence." *Food, Inc.* Ed. Karl Weber. New York: Perseus Books, 2009. 183-196. Print. (Copyright © 2009 Perseus Books Group.)

Chapter Three

Wilson, Edward O. "For the Love of Life." *The Future of Life*. New York: Knopf Doubleday, 2002. 129-140. Print.

Montenegro, Maywa, and Terry Glavin. "In Defense of Difference." *Seed* magazine 9 July 2010: n pag. Web. 20 Oct. 2010.

Muir, John. "The American Forests." *The Atlantic Monthly* 80 (Aug. 1897): n. pag. Web. 10 Oct. 2010. (*The Atlantic Monthly Group,* www.theatlantic.com.)

Ray, Janisse. *Ecology of a Cracker Childhood*. Minneapolis: Milkweed Editions, 1999. 5-12 and 123-127. Print.

Jensen, Derrick and McMillan, Stephanie. *As the World Burns: 50 Simple Things You Can Do to Stay in Denial*. New York: Seven Stories Press, 2007. 1-10. Print.

Todd, Anne Marie. "Prime-Time Subversion: The Environmental Rhetoric of *The Simpsons*" *Enviropop: Studies in Environmental Rhetoric and Popular Culture*. Ed. Mark Meister and Phyllis M. Japp. Westport, CT: Praeger Publishers, 2002. 63-80. Print.

Bullis, Kevin. "The Geoengineering Gambit." *Technology Review* 113.1 (Jan./Feb. 2010): 50-56. Print. (MIT Technology Review Press).

Brand, Stewart. "Reframing the Problems." *The Clock of the Long Now: Time and Responsibility*. New York: Basic Books, 2000. 131-136. Print.

Chapter Four

Kristof, Nicholas D., and Sheryl WuDunn. "The Women's Crusade." *The New York Times Magazine* Aug. 23 2009: n. pag. Web. 7 June 2010. (Reprinted with permission.)

Beecher, Catharine Esther. "Chapter XIII: On the Preservation of a Good Temper in a Housekeeper." *A Treatise on Domestic Economy, For the Use of Young Ladies at Home, and At School*. Boston: T.H. Webb, 1842. N. pag. Web. 10 Oct. 2010.

Piercy, Marge. "What's That Smell in the Kitchen?" *Circles on the Water: Selected Poems of Marge Piercy*. New York: Knopf Doubleday, 1982. 288. Print.

Bauer, Nancy. "Lady Power." *The New York Times* 20 June 2010: n. pag. Web. 21 June 2010.

Blakely, Mary Kay. "A Wrestling Mom." *American Mom: Motherhood, Politics, and Humble Pie*. Chapel Hill, NC: Algonquin Books, 1994. 252-263. Print. (Copyright © 1994 Algonquin Books.)

Hirshberg, Charles. "My Mother, the Scientist." *Popular Science* 260.5 (May 2002): 66. Print.

el-Saadawi, Nawal. *Memoirs of a Woman Doctor*. London: Saqi Books, 1988. 9-22. Print. (Copyright © 1988 Saqi Books.)

Ebadi, Shirin, with Azadeh Moaveni. "From the Living Room to the Courtroom." *Iran Awakening: One Woman's Journey to Reclaim Her Life and Country.* New York: Random House, 2006. 112-127. Print. (Copyright © 2006 Random House.)

Hayes, Shannon. "Meet the Radical Homemakers." *Yes!* magazine 10 Feb. 2010: n. pag. Web. 10 Oct. 2010.

Chapter Five

The Onion. "Nation Shudders at Large Block of Uninterrupted Text." *The Onion* 9 March 2010: n. pag. Web. 10 Oct. 2010.

Swift, Jonathan. "A Modest Proposal." *Project Guttenberg.* Web. 10 Oct. 2010.

Kingsolver, Barbara. Excerpt from "Zucchini Larceny." *Animal, Vegetable, Miracle: A Year of Food Life.* New York: Harper Perennial, 2007. 180-183. Print.

O'Rourke, P.J. "The Greenhouse Affect." *Rolling Stone* 581 (June 28, 1990): 38+. Print.

Browne, Jill Conner. "Pre-Wed." *The Sweet Potato Queens' Wedding Planner/Divorce Guide.* New York: Crown Publishers, 2005. 1-15. Print.

Taylor, Mary. "Queen of the House" lyrics. *Queen of the House.* Capitol Records, 1965. Web. 10 Oct. 2010.

Sedaris, David. "Chicken in the Henhouse." *Dress Your Family in Corduroy and Denim.* New York: Little Brown, 2004. 211-224. Print. (Copyright © 2004 by David Sedaris. By Permission of Little Brown and Company.)

Saunders, George. "My Amendment." *The New Yorker* 8 March 8, 2004: n. pag. Web. 10. Oct. 2010.

NOTES

NOTES

NOTES

NOTES

NOTES

NOTES

NOTES

NOTES